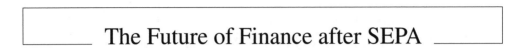

The Future of Finance after SEPA

**For other titles in the Wiley Finance series
please see www.wiley.com/finance**

The Future of Finance after SEPA

Edited by

Chris Skinner

John Wiley & Sons, Ltd

Other Wiley Editorial Offices

John Wiley & Sons Inc., 111 River Street, Hoboken, NJ 07030, USA

Jossey-Bass, 989 Market Street, San Francisco, CA 94103-1741, USA

Wiley-VCH Verlag GmbH, Boschstr. 12, D-69469 Weinheim, Germany

John Wiley & Sons Australia Ltd, 42 McDougall Street, Milton, Queensland 4064, Australia

John Wiley & Sons (Asia) Pte Ltd, 2 Clementi Loop #02-01, Jin Xing Distripark, Singapore 129809

John Wiley & Sons Canada Ltd, 6045 Freemont Blvd, Mississauga, ONT, L5R 4J3, Canada

Wiley also publishes its books in a variety of electronic formats. Some content that appears in print may not be
available in electronic books.

Library of Congress Cataloging-in-Publication Data

The future of finance after SEPA / [edited by] Chris Skinner.
        p. cm. – (Wiley finance series)
    Includes bibliographical references and index.
    ISBN 978-0-470-98782-7 (cloth)
    1. Finance–European Union countries.   2. Payment–European Union
countries.   3. Euro area.   I. Skinner, Chris.
    HG186.A2F88 2008
    332.094–dc22

                                                        2008007636

British Library Cataloguing in Publication Data

A catalogue record for this book is available from the British Library

ISBN 978-0-470-98782-7 (H/B)

Typeset in 10/12pt Times by Aptara Inc., New Delhi, India
Printed and bound in Great Britain by Antony Rowe Ltd, Chippenham, Wiltshire

Contents

About the Editor

Chris Skinner

CHRIS SKINNER is known worldwide as a leading commentator and strategist on the financial markets. He works full-time as the Chief Executive of the think tank Balatro, as well as being the Chairman of the Financial Services Club and a co-founder of the website Shaping Tomorrow. He writes a regular column in the Banker magazine, and blogs on the FinanSer and Finextra. Chris is a regular key note speaker at the world's largest financial services conferences including SWIFT's SIBOS, BAI, IIR and the Financial Times and the author of several other books published by John Wiley, including *The Future of Banking in a Globalised World* and The *Future of Investing in Europe's Markets after MiFID*.

About the Contributors

James Barclay

James Barclay is Vice President for Industry Issues in the Treasury and Security Services team at JPMorgan Chase, joining in June 2007. In this role, he is jointly responsible for managing strategic regulatory issues across Europe, the Middle East and Africa. The position also involves relationship management with industry bodies and market infrastructures. James actively works with the European Commission's informal e-invoicing Task Force and the Payment Systems Market Group and the EPC's Programme Management Forum.

James has had extensive experience in both the payments and securities industries from operational delivery to strategic positioning and is regarded as an industry expert in the payments and infrastructure arena. His experience at the EBA has given him a clear insight into the workings of industry bodies and the development of solutions requiring international agreement. Based in Paris for the past 25 years, James brings the combination of his experience in the financial sector in Europe to the Global Industry Issues team at JPMorgan Chase.

Sharon Bowles

After training for professional qualification with leading London firms, Sharon established a professional practice in 1981, which is now the Bowles Horton partnership. Sharon became a Liberal Democrat Parliamentary Candidate in 1992 and became a Member of the European Parliament in May 2005, replacing Chris Huhne. She is a full member of the Economic and Monetary Affairs committee and, as shadow rapporteur for ALDE, has been a key player in the Payment Services Directive (PSD) negotiations. As rapporteur she is also leading for the Parliament on fiscal fraud and has recently been appointed shadow rapporteur on Solvency II.

Robert Bradfield

Robert Bradfield is a Senior Manager with Ernst & Young, where he combines his extensive Financial Services knowledge and experience with Ernst & Young's core capability around performance improvement to bring about business process transformations.

Prior to joining Ernst & Young, Robert was with LogicaCMG as deputy head of their UK Payments Practice, where he was engaged with both UK and European banks in the development and enhancement of their payments processing capabilities.

Robert's career in Financial Services began in Eurobond sales and trading with Société Générale Strauss Turnbull. After a decade with Société Générale, Robert moved to the supply side of the Financial Markets and joined Unisys as a Solutions Director for their International Banking Services Centre.

John Bullard

John is Gobal Ambassador for Iden Trust, having joined the company at its foundation in 1999 as Manging Director (Participant Relations), from Barclays who were one of the Founding Banking of Iden Trust. At Barclays he enjoyed a career spanning some 20 years primarily focused around corporate and institutional relationship management during periods of change such as the 'Big Bang' opening up of Londons financial markets in the 1980's.

He was worked on two separate occasions in the USA, once in San Francisco, and 10 years later in Barclays corporate banking operations on Wall Street. In the latter part of his time at the bank, he held senior positions in the Services Business Division, and in Group Operational Risk with specific responsibilities around European banking legislation and eCommerce.

Neil Burton

Neil Burton is a Solutions Executive in IBM's Global Banking Solutions team, with responsibility for Payments. His role is to identify matket opportunity, provide solution content and guidance to customers and colleagues. He is an active participant in conferences and industry forums. Neil holds a BA in Physics, an MBA and is Member of the Chartered Institute of Marketing.

Tom Buschman

Tom Buschman is founder, chairman & CEO of the Transaction Workflow Innovation Standards Team (TWIST), a not-for-profit industry group of corporate treasures, fund managers, banks, system suppliers, electronic trading platform, market infrastructures and professional services firms.

Tom left Shell to dedicate his time to TWIST in May 2006, and the application of its standards. Over a period of 15 years, Tom held various managerial finance positions for the Shell Group. He was industry liaison and development manager for Shell's corporate treasury after having been responsible for Shell's central foreign exchange and money market activities. Before coming to London in 1999, he worked for Shell's Dutch Pension Fund and held several positions for Shell in Brazil. Tom was also a fellow at the London School of Economics for innovation in financial markets.

The primary aim of TWIST is to develop new and rationalise existing XML standards that connect the financial and physical supply chains, releasing the enormous value locked up in disjointed paper-based processes.

TWIST has developed standards covering payments and cash management; financial supply chain areas including ordering, e-invoicing and financing; billing of bank services; opening and administration of bank accounts; and wholesale financial market transaction processing; all with in-built identity management and security.

John Chaplin

John Chaplin is European Payments Adviser for First Data and liaises closely with the European Commission, European Central Bank and other regulatory authorities around SEPA's issues as they relate to the cards industry. John also leads First Data's activities in support of banks as they seek to address the challenges and opportunities that SEPA will bring.

He has extensive experience of the European payments business having held senior executive roles at Visa Europe over 17 years, including assignments as Head of Strategy and Chief Information Officer. Latterly, he was Executive Vice President of Visa's processing business in Europe, providing services to 6000 banks and also serving as a member of the executive management board.

Prior to joining Visa, John held a number of executive positions at Honeywell, in the information systems and electronics businesses. John is also Chairman of the Glasshouse Partnership, a London based marketing communications company.

Daniele Danese

Daniele Danese is the Manager for International Payments Systems and Cash Management at Banca Popolare di Verona, where he has always held posts related to international business on both the technical and business areas. Recent projects include implementation of the SEPA commercial project, international products on the corporate remote banking platform and products for electronic collections both in Italy and Europe.

At present he is responsible for overall group strategy, internal marketing and new implementations for international payments systems and international cash management. Since 2006 he has been a Board member of EBA Clearing.

Married since 1979, Italian by passport but European by choice, fluent in Italian and English, he likes music and photography, as well as performing with a musical theatrical company.

Geoffroy de Schrevel

After completing his PhD Programme, Geoffroy de Schrevel taught economics in various universities in Europe and Africa. From Prague then Istanbul, he developed domestic card payment infrastructures in several emerging markets for Europay International. He then moved as an executive member of the founding team of Maestro International and held senior positions with KPMG Management Consulting.

Geoffroy joined SWIFT in September 2005 in charge of driving the development of SWIFT strategy and Solutions in the payments space. He is currently heading the SWIFT Banking, Corporate and Trade Initiatives group in Europe, Middle East and Africa.

As SWIFT SEPA programme director, he is responsible for strategy definition and execution of this key initiative for the SWIFT community.

Ashley Dowson

Ashley Dowson is Chairman of The SEPA Consultancy, a specialist company that aims to provide strategic advice to banks, corporates, public authorities and suppliers to the European payments industry. He previously occupied senior positions in Barclays for over 30 years, latterly as Chief Operating Officer and Managing Director of Barclays Group Treasury. Ashley was an EBA Board Member during the period of the introduction of the Euro and was highly instrumental in the creation of the EBA's EURO1 Clearing System.

David Doyle

Dr David P. Doyle is known across Europe as a leading expert on EU financial market regulation and has an in-depth understanding and knowledge of the critical aspects associated with issues such as MiFID, UCITS and SEPA.

David is a former diplomat with over 25 years of service on mainland Europe and now acts as an EU Policy Advisor between Brussels, London and Paris, specialising in EU Financial

Services. He is a member of the Executive Board of the joint MEP-EU industry association, 'The Kangaroo Group', based at the European Parliament, the Board of Directors of the Genesis Initiative at Westminster, and sits on the Transatlantic Business Dialogue Taskforce on Capital Markets and the Corporation of London EU Regulatory Working Group.

He is a graduate in marketing and statistics from the Dublin Institute of Technology and Trinity College, University of Dublin. In 2004, David was awarded a Doctorate of Business Administration honoris causa from Kingston University (UK) in recognition of his contribution to European policy development for the growth and sustainability of small businesses.

David's career spans a number of public sector assignments commencing with the Irish Board of Trade (now Enterprise Ireland) in 1975, where he served with the Irish trade mission in Paris, followed by an appointment to a multi-governmental, economic development agency in Paris in various financial roles. His Authored books include 'Cost Control: A Strategic Guide' (Elsevier), which has appeared in 12 foreign editions.

Sean Fitzgerald

Sean Fitzgerald is the Chief Executive Officer of Sentenial, a company focused exclusively on the direct debit payment instrument, supplies total direct debit process solutions to the Financial Institution, Bureau, Corporate and SME markets internationally.

Sean is responsible for corporate strategy and every aspect of the business operations to support of clients and fuelling Sentenial's business growth. In addition, Sean has been strongly involved with the EC during the creation of the SEPA legal framework, helping to advise on direct debit considerations for SEPA.

Sean has a 20-year track record in the industry. Before founding Sentenial in 2003, Sean held senior management roles in the global microelectronics and speciality chemicals industries driving the introduction of new technologies. He is a science graduate of Trinity College, Dublin, Ireland.

Mark Hale

Mark Hale was Director of Payments and Settlements at Barclays Bank PLC, where he led many of the bank's Euro related change programmes starting with the introduction of the Euro and culminating in the creation of SEPA. He recently left Barclays to join PricewaterhouseCoopers LLP, where he is responsible for the development of their financial services transactions banking practice.

Mark has served on the Boards of all of the main UK payment clearing companies and has also represented the UK financial services industry at the European level. He has been at the heart of the decision making processes, and therefore the changes that are now shaping the future of banking. In particular, Mark has been a leading member of the European Payments Council and was the Chairperson of the SEPA Credit Transfer scheme, which launched on the 28th of January 2008.

Bo Harald

Bo Harald is head of Executive Advisors at TietoEnator and a former Group Executive with Nordea in charge of their Electronic Banking operations. His specialist interest is in demonstrating that the e-habit created in banking can be transferred to other services and will take off faster as the end-user uses the banking e-habit in other services. This is demonstrtated in his regular blogspot at http://boharald.blogspot.com.

He began his banking career in 1975 when he joined Union Bank of Finland. After the merger of Union Bank of Finland and Kansallis-Osake-Pankki to form Merita Bank in Bo 1995, was appointed Deputy Member of the Board with responsibility for Western Finland and Payments and Network Banking within the Retail Banking division. In 1998 Merita Bank and Nordbanken (Sweden) formed MeritaNordbanken and Mr.Harald was appointed Executive Vice President, Payments and Network Banking. In 1999 he also became member of the Group Management. After the integration with Unibank and Christiania Bank the bank changed its name to Nordea in December 2000.

Bo also acted as Chairman of Mobey (Mobile Financial Services Forum) and has held and holds directorships in various companies and associations. He is a frequent lecturer of Internet and E-commerce topics and was named by Institutional Investor in April 2000 as one of the most influential technologists of the 20th century. He was granted the first award by the Finnish Ministry of Transport and Communications for promoting the information society in 2004.

Gerard Hartsink

Gerard Hartsink is Senior Executive Vice President of Market Infrastructures of the ABN AMRO Bank and Chairman of the European Payments Council. During his career he has had managerial roles in sales, product development and operations in several business units within the ABN AMRO Group. Today he holds responsibility for the relationships ABN AMRO has with the market infrastructures in the payments and cards industry and the forex and securities industry and with public authorities involved. Gerard Hartsink represents ABN AMRO Bank in the following organisations: EPC, EBA, CLS, LCH.Clearnet, Euroclear MAC, CESAME, ISO20022 RMG and SWIFT NMG.

Eva King

Eva King is a senior economist and principal policy advisor with the European Commission. In 2003 Eva was seconded to the European Commission by the Austrian Central Bank to lead the policy development for a common EU legal framework for payment services and help develop new supervisory standards for payment service providers. In this role she has taken main responsibility for drafting the Payment Service Directive adopted in 2007. Also she has been the main interlocutor for industry and the European Payments Council, monitoring the self-regulatory process of banks for SEPA.

Before 2003 Eva has worked in different roles in the banking sector, in particular the Austrian and European payments market and was responsible for several projects in the area of cards and payments clearing infrastructure. She also held positions with the World Bank and acted as a consultant to leading financial institutions.

Anthony Kirby

Dr Anthony W. Kirby was appointed Director, FS Regulatory & Risk, at Emst & Young as of the start of 2008. he was formerly head of Regulation and Compliance within the FS Division at Accenture for three years. He was responsible there for driving transformational change and strategic programmes in the Regulation space, including AML, KYC, MiFID, Basel II, PSD/SEPA and Solvency II.

Anthony is an active and well-known member of the financial community with twenty years' experience. He has a standards backgrounds havings founded the Securities market Practice Group in 1998, the Reference Data User Group (RDUG) in June 2002 and helped co-found the MiFID Joind Working Group in April 2005. He is also a member of the British Standards Institute Technical Standards Committee since 2004.

Anthony gained vital knowledge and experience from working within the industry in senior roles for Merrill Lynch, SWIFT, Deutsche Börse, Reuters and Instinet. He has chosen to specialise in the field of Risk & Regulatory Convergence, to help financial institutions comply with regulatory measures such as MiFID, AML and KYC risk management measures such as credit, operational and liquidity risk management and while helping them achive strategic transformation.

Anthony has also been a member of FIX and ISSA, is an Executive Committee member of ISITC and a participant within the FSA's Market Advisory Committee on MiFID since 2003. He also liaises regularly with the European Central Bank and other bodies such as CESR. Anthony is also a visiting Fellow of the Promethee Think Tank in France, A Freeman of the City of London, and a member of both the Worshipful Companies of Information Technologists and the Bowyers. Anthony received his Mphil., M.A. and his Phd from the University of Cambridge, England in 1986.

Harry Leinonen

Harry Leinonen is Advisor to the Board of the Bank of Finland, and is in charge of payment system policy issues in the central bank. He is the Finnish representative on the payment and settlement system committee (PSSC) within the Eurosystem and a participant the Government Expert Group and Payment System Market Group of the European Commission Internal Markets.

He joined the Bank of Finland in 1996 as head of the payment system division and was appointed adviser to the Board in 1999. Before that he worked in the banking industry for about 20 years in managerial positions connected to payment system activities within both the savings banks' and cooperative banks' groups in Finland.

For most of the past 30 years he has been active in developing interbank payment systems and standards within the Finnish banking community. Harry has also been active on international payment system forums throughout his career and has published several articles and books on payment system issues.

He was born in Helsinki in 1951 and holds a Master's degree in economics and a Bachelor's degree in Business Administration.

Bodil Nelsson

Bodil Nelsson has spent 20 years in the Swedish financial services industry with Swedbank, SEB and now Bankgirocentralen BGC AB. Her areas of specialisation include direct debit and EBPP, and she was responsible as the sponsor of the direct debit project for Sweden in 2005.

Brenda O'Connell

Brenda O'Connell is currently the SEPA Programme Manager for Bank of Ireland Group, and is responsible for defining and implementing the bank's strategic business response to SEPA; coordinating responses to corporate, legal and regulatory developments; and managing material payments and settlements issues.

Brenda has managed a broad range of business, programme and project functions spanning twenty years. Her first placement was within the Branch and Area Networks before moving to Business Process Design and Delivery. She has subsequently been appointed as Project

Manager for various projects from the transition to euro, to the rollout of domestic, US and UK business and compliance programmes. Brenda also represents the bank on a number of industry bodies and working groups in Ireland and the UK.

Henrik Parl

Henrik Parl joined Eurogiro as Managing Director in 1997. His responsibilities include running the Eurogiro Network and co-ordinating the co-operation between 63 members of the Eurogiro payment club. During his time with Eurogiro, the firm has demonstrated strong growth as volumes in 2007 are six times higher than in 1997.

Henrik Parl is also active in international work and advisory groups such as member of the UN Advisory Group for Inclusive Financial Services, on the Steering Committee of Global Payment Forum (NACHA) and on the Advisory Council of International Association of Money Transfer Networks (IAMTN).

Before joining Eurogiro, Henrik worked in Fund Management and Investment Banking in Copenhagen and in London as Deputy General Manager of the Danish Savings bank: Bikuben/BG Bank. He holds a degree in International Economics and Finance from Copenhagen Business School.

Eurogiro Network A/S has a vision of acting as a gateway provider for its members and partners, thereby providing cost efficient links between different products, geographical regions or technologies. Eurogiro has alliance agreements with Federal Reserve of US, Western Union, WSBI (savings Banks), Visa, Universal Postal Union, Citibank, Deutsche Bank and SWIFT.

René Pelegero

René Pelegero is senior director of industry relations, strategy, and compliance for the financial services department at PayPal, an eBay company. He is responsible for managing PayPal's relations with the financial services industry, and defining the strategies that will maximise the benefits provided by these financial networks.

Prior to joining PayPal, Pelegero was president and managing director at RPGC Group LLC, an e-commerce consultancy practice. Previously, René served as director of global payments at Amazon.com. He was responsible for all aspects of payments processing for more than 30 million customers and managed relationships with banks, processors, credit card companies and associations.

Rene Pelegero has also held senior management positions at Electronic Payment Services, Inc., a leading electronic funds transfer (EFT) processor; GE Capital, an international consumer lending group; and Tandem Computers, an information technology company which is now part of Hewlett Packard.

He has also served as board member of the Direct Response Forum (DRF) and as co-chair of the e-commerce purchasing council of the Electronic Funds Transfer Association (EFTA). He received his bachelor's degree in business administration and his masters of business administration from San Francisco State University.

PayPal was founded in 1998 and acquired by eBay in July 2002. It was best known at that time as the preferred way to complete an eBay transaction and has grown into a user-friendly, secure and efficient payment technology that handles over 1.9 million global transactions daily. It handles payment processing for online vendors, auction sites and other corporate users. Consumers pay by their preferred method such as credit card, debit card, bank account through their PayPal account or account balances, all without sharing financial information.

Payments can be made in Euros as well as Pounds Sterling and the Czech, Danish, Hungarian, Norwegian, Polish, Swedish and Swiss currencies. As of September 2007, PayPal had over 35 million European customer accounts, up 150 % from 2006 and over 100000 active European website merchants. Total European payment volume in 2006 was $ 8.4bn and a recent Forrester survey confirmed that 23 % of European internet shoppers prefer PayPal to other methods of online payment.

Chris Pickles

Chris Pickles is Manager, Industry Relations for BT Radianz, and chair of the MiFID Joint Working Group. Chris is also Co-Chair of the Global Education & Marketing Committee of FIX Protocol Ltd and a member of the Executive Committee of SIIA/FISD.

He has been involved in the financial technology industry as an international marketing manager for over 30 years. His previous jobs have included being secretary-general of the European Association of Securities Dealers in Brussels; Head of Exchange Products at Deutsche Börse in Frankfurt; and marketing with Reuters in London, Paris and Frankfurt.

Hervé Postic

Hervé Postic is the Managing Partner of French treasury consultancy UTSIT, and a recognised expert of SWIFT connectivity for corporations. Hervé became an independent consultant and, in 2002, he created the UTSIT Consultancy Company to promote a vision of e-banking freed of bank's proprietary or national channels.

Hervé is tutor in AFTE (French Treasurers Association) where he is responsible for Payments and connectivity training. He also teaches in a 'Practical Treasury Master', within AFTE team, at Paris La Sorbonne and Dauphine Universities.

Hervé is a graduate from Saint-Cyr, French Army Officer's School and, after a short career in the Armoured, he joined in Axe-DCI, a software company specialised in e-banking software for both banks and corporations 1992, where he held all the customer service responsibilities for implementation, education, support and consulting.

Erkki Poutiainen

Erkki Poutiainen is Head of Infrastructure, Nordea Cash Management. Previously, he has served Nordea Bank and its predecessors in different positions, countries and business areas from 1980 ranging from branch office duties, consultancy to e-business and strategy. For the last few years he has worked with payments and cash management.

He is a Member of the European Payments Council Plenary, a former chair of an EPC group working for e, a&m-payment solutions board member of the EBA Association. Chairman of the EBA E-Invoice Working Group, and a board member of the IBOS Cash Management club 2001–2004.

John Ryan

Professor Dr John Ryan is the MSc Course Leader in Global Banking and Finance at the European Business School. Dr. Ryan is a graduate of Oxford University, Cambridge University, the London School of Economics and the Kiel Institute of World Economics, Germany.

Dr Ryan has been an external expert with the European Commission, United Nations and the OECD. From 1996–2002 he was a Euro adviser/consultant to four national governments and various multinational corporations. Since 2002 Dr Ryan has been working on Corporate Governance and Financial Regulation for Industry.

Dr Ryan was visiting Senior Fellow at the Center of European Studies, Bonn, Germany between 2002 and 2003. He teaches International Economics, Strategy and Corporate Governance and Financial Regulation at the EDHEC Grande Ecole School of Management, Lille, France and New York University.

Dr Ryan has attended British Foreign Office conferences, and has been a fellow of the Salzburg Seminar on three occasions. He was Fellow of the 21st Century Trust and observer at the Trilateral Commission in 2001. He was also a member of the Aspen Institute Berlin Transatlantic Study Group on 'A New transatlantic Agenda for the Next Century' from 1997–98. Dr. Ryan has undertaken four lecture tours for the Deutsch-Britische Gesellschaft on the Euro and German Economy, and is the Editor of Zeitgeist, the quarterly magazine of the British-German Association.

Heiko Schmiedel

Dr Heiko Schmiedel is a policy expert in the Directorate General Payment Systems and Market Infrastructure at the European Central Bank. He conducts economic research and policy analysis in the field of securities trading, clearing and settlement systems, as well as payment systems. Before he joined the ECB in 2003, he served as an economist at the Hamburg Institute of International Economics. He was visiting research scholar at the Research Department at Central Bank of Finland, the Dutch Central Bank, and Stern School of Business at the New York University. Heiko received a PhD in international finance from the University of Hamburg. He has many published articles in econometrics and finance including monographs, book chapters, academic journals and reviews.

Nick Senechal

Nick Senechal heads new product development within VocaLink, and has been influential in the development of the company's business strategy as it has developed from BACS to Voca and on to VocaLink. His major focus is on the further development of its real-time payments services, the next generation of value-added services for banks and their corporate customers and the future convergence of payments systems.

Nick joined VocaLink when it was part of BACS, following a career in business analysis with major American corporations. With BACS he worked at the intersection between business and IT contributing to many major initiatives including the introduction of tokenised security for BACSTEL, Inter-Bank Data Exchange, (IBDE) and the automation of the UK Direct Debit scheme.

In 2000, Nick served on the APACS Future Payments System Development (FPSD) task force, and then as one of a small team developing the future vision for BACS. Nickplayed a leading role in both the NewBACS technology renewal programme and the Governance programme which separated BACS into scheme and Infrastructure company - later to become Voca. In 2005, Nick lead the Voca team which in conjunction with LINK (prior to the two firms merger in July 2007) successfully won the bid for the UK Faster Payments service.

Richard Spong

Richard Spong is Solutions Marketing Manager, Financial Services, Europe, Middle East and Africa (EMEA) for Sterling Commerce, a subsidiary of SBC Communications and a global provider of business integration solutions.

Richard is responsible for the strategic marketing efforts for Sterling Commerce solutions into finance sector business processes across EMEA. Richard joined Sterling Commerce in

2003, and most recently was responsible for the product management, sales and marketing of financial risk applications and transaction processing products for Reuters.

Prior to that Richard was responsible for the specification and implementation of system of system solutions for the NatWest (now RBS) Bank Group.

Daniel Szmukler

Since 2003, Daniel Szmukler is Head of Communications and Corporate Governance of EBA CLEARING. He completed a first term of office as Company Secretary of EBA CLEARING from 1998 till 2000. From 2001 to 2002, Daniel Szmukler was a Payment Systems Advisor to the European Banking Federation (FBE) in Brussels. He began his professional career in 1994 with SWIFT in Brussels. Daniel Szmukler holds graduate degrees in business administration and management from Boston University, Mass. and the University of Brussels.

EBA CLEARING was created in 1998 to be the operator of the EURO1 payment system and thereafter the STEP1 and STEP2 systems. The EURO1/STEP1 payments platform processes an average 200 000 payments per day for a total value in excess of 220 billion euros at the end of 2007. The EURO1/STEP1 payments platform comprises over 190 direct bank participants and 52 indirect participants. The STEP2 platform accounts today for over 1.25 million payments per day. As of November 2007, 108 direct participants and over 1600 indirect participants are registered with STEP2.

Gianfranco Tabasso

Gianfranco Tabasso is Co-ordinator of The European Association of Corporate Treasurers (EACT) and founding partner and managing director of the FMS Group, an Italian-based financial software and consulting company. Gianfranco is a consultant to corporates and banks and a frequent lecturer on international treasury, financial risk management, payment systems and electronic banking. As vice-president of the AITI (the Italian association of corporate treasurers) and co-ordinator of the EACT Payment Commission, he participates in bank-industry working groups on payment standardisation and SEPA.

Gianfranco Tabasso graduated in Economics & Business from Bocconi University in Milan and gained an MBA from Columbia University, NY in 1968. He then worked for McKinsey & Co. Management Consulting from 1971–78 where he specialised in banking and insurance.

The EACT is a non-profit organisation covering the National Treasurers Associations in 16 European countries, representing almost 7000 members in 4000 corporations.

Mats Wallén

Mats Wallen has been working in the financial industry for 30 years in a number of different positions. As a commercial banker he spent 20 years with Swedish banks, mainly focusing on payments and electronic banking, as well as four years with SWIFT in Brussels. For the past 14 years, Mats has been working for the Bankgirocentralen BGC AB in Sweden with domestic retail payments.

Ruth Wandhöfer

Ruth Wandhöfer is a Vice President and the International Payments Market Manager with Citi Global Transaction Services. Prior to that, she worked for the European Banking Federation in Brussels as Policy Advisor since 2003. In this role she has had unparalleled exposure to the ongoing market developments in the Payments and Securities arenas. She was closely involved in the work of the European Payments Council in co-authoring the SEPA Credit Transfer scheme rulebook and active lobbyist in the successful negotiation of the EU Payment Services Directive. Ms Wandhöfer is highly regarded across the payment industry as a subject matter expert and one of the key drivers in the evolution of SEPA through her in-depth knowledge of the regulatory, market and competitive landscape in the European payments space.

Prior to 2003 Ms Wandhöfer worked in financial management in the banking sector as well as in the European Commission DG Economic & Financial Affairs. She has completed studies in various countries, including an MA Financial Economics in the UK and France and an MA International Politics in Belgium. She is currently completing an LLM in International Economic Law.

Juergen Weiss

Juergen Weiss is Research Analyst at Gartner, the the world's leading information technology research and advisory company. He is part of the Industry Advisory Service focusing on Financial Services and especially the insurance software market in EMEA. Before joing Gartner, Juergen was Consulting Manager at SAP Germany, directing an international team of consultants and being responsible for successfully positioning various SAP applications within the European SAP subsidiaries. In addition he developed and coordinated SAP consulting services for the Single Euro Payments Area (SEPA).

Before his current position, Juergen was Director of Solution Management in the Application Solution Management ERP Financials (Enterprise Resource Planning). He was globally responsible for the Financial Supply Chain Management applications including Electronic Bill Presentment and Payment, Dispute Management, Collections Management, Credit Management, Treasury and Risk Management, Bank Relationship Management and In-House Cash as well as Accounts Payable and Receivable. In 2006 he was listed as one of the 100 Most Influential People in Finance by the Treasury & Risk Management Magazine.

His career at SAP began in 1997 after a previous position as PR Manager in a large German bank. Juergen has degrees in Economics and Business Administration from the Universities of Heidelberg and Hagen. Juergen is author of various articles and published in 2008 a book on the SEPA implementation with SAP.

Jonathan Williams

Jonathan is Director of Communications and Product Strategy in the payments group at Experian and isresponsible for identifying and developing new product ideas, managing media, industry and public relations and customer communications.

Before joining Eiger Systems in 2000, Jonathan promoted strategies for growth as European Business Development Manager for Fujitsu Telecom. He has held engineering and IT roles at British Aerospace, University of Cambridge and Advanced Telecommunications Modules Ltd as well as senior marketing roles at Virata Corporation and Content Technologies (now Clearswift).

Supported by his capable team spanning both technical and marketing, Jonathan is focussed on the commercial opportunities created by market change, partnership or technological developments.

Jonathan holds an MA in Theoretical Physics and a postgraduate qualification in Computer Science from the University of Cambridge and is the Eiger Systems representative to the Euro Banking Association (EBA), the Payments Council, APACS Affiliates and Australian Payments Clearing Association (APCA) and monitors Bacs' Affiliates Interest.

Originally from a technical background, Jonathan joined Eiger Systems in 2002 from a position as European Business Development Manager for Fujitsu Telecom. He has held engineering and IT roles at British Aerospace, Cambridge University and Advanced Telecommunications Modules Ltd as well as senior marketing roles at Virata and Baltimore Technologies.

In addition to strong commercial and customer-handling skills (including sales and support experience), he brings his extensive systems and networking expertise to bear to create solutions for the benefit of customers and partners.

Jonathan holds an MA in Theoretical Physics and a postgraduate qualification in Computer Science from the University of Cambridge and is the Eiger Systems representative to the Euro Banking Association (EBA), APACS Affiliates, Australian Payments Clearing Association (APCA) and BACS Affiliates Interest Group.

Preface

In the early part of this decade, I became involved in two major change initiatives: The Single Euro Payments Area (SEPA) and the Markets in Financial Instruments Directive (MiFID). MiFID came into force in 2007, and I produced a book called *The Future of Investing in Europe after MiFID* with a wide range of chapters written by all the relevant market constituents.

With the introduction of SEPA in January 2008, Wiley and I decided it warranted similar treatment and hence this book.

I became involved with SEPA early in its lifecycle about a year after the European Payments Council (EPC) launched it in 2002. As a result, I've written a lengthy opening that I do not want to repeat here. However, there are some things that need to be stressed for the sake of clarity.

First, SEPA is a bank initiative. It is not a regulation. The regulation is the Payment Services Directive (PSD).

Second, SEPA is just for the Eurozone whilst the PSD covers all of Europe. SEPA itself does not incorporate non-euro countries, although it will dramatically alter their ability to compete in the future banking markets of Europe. This is because SEPA enables new forms of cross-border competitiveness through new, more efficient infrastructures enjoying much greater economies of scale and lower costs. This is not just for the infrastructures, but also for the banks and processors who operate these systems.

Third, and leading on from this point, SEPA and the PSD combined create a revolution in the landscape of European banking. This is because payments, money transmissions, credit and debit cards, direct debits, cash, cheques, credit transfers, infrastructures, clearing and settlement and so on and so forth, are all fundamental to retail and commercial bank services. This is the arena that is being revolutionised and so all aspects of finance will be revolutionised across Europe as a result. This is why banks are shifting their focus towards corporate needs with a major investment in positioning for their future role in the supply chain of commerce.

For all of these reasons, this is why this book is titled *The Future of Finance after SEPA*, rather than the future of payments.

The contributors are many. This is because I have tried to include all perspectives from the shapers of this future: the European Parliament, the European Commission, the European Central Bank and the European Payments Council; through to the implementers of SEPA who are the banks, corporates, infrastructures, consultancies and solutions providers.

The result I think is a strong and balanced view, a 360-degree view, of the future of banking, payments and commerce after SEPA. In other words, the future of finance after SEPA.

I hope you agree and would welcome your views on this dynamic area going forward.

Chris Skinner
Contact: info@balatroltd.com

Acknowledgements

There are far too many acknowledgements for me to list here as it would include everyone in the markets involved in payments.

Even so, I do obviously have to extend a big vote of thanks to those who have contributed to this book. These folks are building a new Europe and, for that, I thank them.

For those of you who were asked to contribute to this book but could not make the time, it would have been nice to include you. I wish you success and trust that 2008 onwards will keep you healthy and possibly wealthy too.

For those of you I asked to contribute but you didn't . . . I know where you live.

For all of the rest, may the force be with you and may you enjoy a little fortune. . . and a lot of luck, patience and tolerance.

SEPA'S MILESTONES

1992, February	Maastricht Treaty signed by European Union's Member States to create a Economic and Monetary Union (EMU)
1993, November	The Maastricht Treaty changes the European Economic Community (EEC) into the European Union.
1994, January	EU expanded to cover Iceland, Norway and Liechtenstein through the European Economic Area (EEA)
1999, January	11 countries have successfully joined the EMU – Austria, Belgium, Finland, France, Germany, Ireland, Italy, Luxembourg, the Netherlands, Portugal, and Spain – and adopt the Euro as a trading currency
2000, March	The Lisbon meeting of the European Council creates the Financial Services Action Plan (FSAP) and the Single Payments Area
2001, January	Greece becomes the 12th country to join the EMU
2001, December	The release of Regulation (EC) No 2560/2001 on cross-border payments in euro, which eliminated the difference of price between cross-border and national payments
2002, January	The Euro-12 countries replace national currencies with Euro notes and coins
2002, April	Creation of the EPC in Brussels by the major European banks and banking associations to respond to the call for a Single Payments Area
2002, May	Announcement of SEPA, the Single Euro Payments Area, with the release of the EPC White Paper: 'Euroland: our Single Payment Area'
2002, July	Regulation 2560/2001 came into force ensuring that cash withdrawals and card payments in euro were charged at the same rate for both domestic and cross-border payments
2003, July	EC Regulation 2560/2001 extends to credit transfers valued under € 12500
2004, May	Ten new countries join the EU: Latvia, Lithuania, Estonia, Poland, the Czech Republic, Slovakia, Hungary, Slovenia, Malta and Cyprus, increasing the EU to 25 countries
2004, December	The EPC agrees the Roadmap 2004–2010 to implement SEPA
2005, December	The Payment Services Directive released by the European Commission for consultation
2005, May	UK Office of Fair Trading announces the Payment Systems Taskforce's decision to mandate a UK Faster Payments Service
2006, January	Bulgaria and Romania join the EU, bringing its ranks to 27 members
2006, March	EPC publishes the SEPA Cards Framework (SCF)
2007, January	Slovenia becomes the 13th member of the euro currency group
2007, March	Adoption of the Payment Services Directive by the European Parliament
2007, June	EPC publishes the SEPA Credit Transfer (SCT) and SEPA Direct Debit (SDD) rulebooks
2008, January	The official launch of SEPA with the SCT live whilst Malta and Cyprus join the Eurozone
2008, Summer	The delayed UK Faster Payments Project launches
2009, January	Slovakia aims to join the Eurozone
2009, November	The Payment Services Directive is transposed into national law and SDD is live
2010, January	Hungary, the Czech Republic and Estonia aim to join the Eurozone
2010, December	SEPA to be 'irreversible' although not mandatory
2012, January	Movement towards D+1 as a standard, with most credit transfers made at the latest by the end of the next business day

An Introduction to SEPA

Chris Skinner, Chairman the Financial Services Club
and Chief Executive, Balatro

EXECUTIVE SUMMARY

Europe's financial markets are entering a transition phase that is greater than any seen before. This transition includes major changes to risk management practices, investment banking operations, insurance structures and retail financial services. One of the greatest of these transition is the creation a Single Payments Area for Europe.[1]

The aim is to create an integrated European commercial zone, where it is as easy to do business in any European country across-borders as it is domestically. The objective of a Single Payments Area is to dismantle the payments barriers to trading across Europe's borders by harmonising all products, of which payments is a major component.

The implications of this are far wider than just creating a harmonised payments zone however, in that it means that banks will be competing on a level playing field for both retail and commercial business. For retail and commercial banks therefore, they will have lost any national protections for their business and business practices, and will be competing against banks across the who European territory of 27 countries, plus the Extended Economic Area (EEA) of Norway, Iceland and Liechtenstein, as well as with the Swiss banks who play a strong role in European commerce.

Nevertheless, Europe's politicians and leaders agreed to this path when they created the Economic and Monetary Union (EMU) in 1992 and paved the way for the new European currency, the euro.

The result is that a strong drive to create new European bank operations has been created, particularly as the banks have created the technical infrastructures for this new harmonised Eurozone through the introduction of the Single Euro Payments Area (SEPA) in January 2008. In support of SEPA, the European Commission has removed the legal barriers to cross-border European payments integration through the implementation of the Payment Services Directive

---

[1] Throughout this chapter, we refer to the 'Single Payments Area' which some people refer to as the 'Single Payments Market'. We use this as the term because it was the phrase that was at the core of the announcement of SEPA by the ECP in 2002. However, we see the use of 'Area' or 'Market' as being interchangeable.

(PSD) in November 2009. The result is that, by the end of 2010, a Single Payments Area will be realised as the process will be irreversible.

This does not mean that all European countries have embraced the Single Payments Markets, SEPA and the PSD that easily. Only the Netherlands appears to have whole-heartedly embraced the opportunities here, by mandating that all existing national direct debit, credit transfer and debit card products must migrate to SEPA-compliance as soon as possible. Other counties within the Eurozone are in some denial of moving to these new SEPA-products, with Italy stating that for their national direct debit product, which is very different to others, they will try to influence the powers that be to change the European direct debits to their national scheme.

Equally, only 13 countries are within Eurozone in summer 2007, and yet 31 countries are affected: the 27 countries of the European Union, the EEA and Switzerland. For the eighteen countries outside the Eurozone, some are comfortable with the demands of the Single Payments Market because they are planning to join the Eurozone whilst others, such as the UK, Sweden, Norway and others are facing the challenge of running a dual-currency scheme where the euro runs alongside their existing national domestic currencies.

This does mean that banks will be severely challenged by the new markets.

These challenges include:

- commercial challenges to re-engineer existing card, cash, credit transfer and direct debit products to be compliant with the new legal and technical market structures;
- technical challenges to adapt existing national infrastructures for low and high value clearing of and settlement of payments;
- efficiency challenges to compete with non-domestic European banks who are now able to run and offer products and services across-borders; and
- effectiveness challenges in identifying whether or not it is worthwhile to compete anyway.

These are not just banking challenges though, as many of Europe's nations have invested heavily in domestic bank operations both from a central bank real-time gross settlement capability, as well as retail payments clearing structures. The idea of abandoning these infrastructures is causing many member states to wonder what this new Single Payments Market means.

The end result is that most of Europe's nations will have to either obsolete or evolve their national central and retail clearing infrastructures to work on a pan-European basis. This is the path that appears to be followed by the UK, Netherlands and France.

Meanwhile, banks will have to consider whether they have the capability to become either a pan-European payments processor, which implies reachability across all European nations as well as significant existing payments capabilities across the Eurozone, or view payments as a commodity and focus upon other value-add customer capabilities. The former will only be tenable for large banks or those that can find suitable partnerships and most will opt for the latter strategy.

If the bank chooses the latter course, then they will outsource their payments processing to a pan-European bank or other specialist agency. These agencies may be new payments processors, who specialise in parts of the cross-border payments process, including First Data and PayPal, or existing processors who are now offering pan-European commercial service including existing ACHs such as Vocalink and Equens, as well as banks who may feel this is a service they can offer commercially, including BNP Paribas and Citi.

For those banks who outsource their payments operations to these providers, they will be left with a critical focus upon retail and corporate customer services. For these banks, the ability to provide information services to their clients that differentiate their business capability are paramount, and has led to an in-depth discussion of 'supply-chain management'. This is a discussion that looks at the requirements of businesses in terms of their purchase and sales operations, accounts payable and receivable, purchase orders and invoices, and tries to make that whole operation as efficient and effective as possible through the bank's support and integration of standards and technologies with their corporate clients.

The real challenge however, lies with the banks that fall between these two extremes. The banks that cannot face the ignominy of giving up their payments specialisations, technologies and investments, only to find that they are not large enough to offer or be able to maintain pan-European capabilities. For these banks, they may try to compete in the new pan-European space, but will fail to have the reachability, breadth, depth or investments to compete. As a result, these banks will be acquired by larger banks who seek to become pan-European processors and competitors.

The end game therefore is a new European financial marketplace where the thousands of existing banks are rationalised into localised specialists and pan-European behemoths and, for the latter, there will only be room for a few.

The question is: who are they?

This chapter concludes with a view that it will be those who already have reachability, namely ABN AMRO, BNP Paribas, Citigroup, Deutsche Bank, HSBC, ING, JPMorgan Chase, Société Générale, UBS and Unicredito. A few others may play, such as Banco Santander, but the space for the new pan-European goliaths is limited and being rapidly filled by those who see the opportunity. The rest will just follow these leaders and the new European landscape is going to be one where you are either a leader, value-adder or lost. It will be interesting to see which banks fall into which camp as head towards 2010 and beyond.

In conclusion, Europe if facing fundamental restructuring of bank operations through the requirements of MiFID, Basel II and a multitude of other European Directives. SEPA and the PSD are just a part of this change process, but a fundamental part. These two initiatives are creating a newly integrated European commercial zone and for those banks who seize the initiative, the opportunities for new commercial banking capabilities are tremendous.

This chapter is split into three sections.

The first section describes the background to the Single Payments Area, the introduction of the euro and the activities that led up to the announcements of SEPA and the PSD.

The second section looks at the options presented to a bank as a result of the introduction of SEPA and the PSD, and the likely implications on clearing and settlement.

The third section reviews the way in which the key nations of Europe and the Eurozone have approached SEPA and the PSD, and their individual country migration plans.

SECTION 1: EUROPE'S SINGLE PAYMENTS AREA

Since the Treaty of Rome in 1957, which created a European Union, there has been a gradual movement towards the creation of a United States of Europe that can compete with the other leading nation of United States, America.

During the past 50 years therefore, European politicians and lobbyists have been working hard to overcome the technical, commercial and legal barriers to an integrated Europe. These barriers include tax and fiscal policies, company laws, technological capabilities and standards, social policies, and many more.

One of the greatest barriers has also been the financial services markets. This barrier has come to a head over the past decade as a result of the implications Economic and Monetary Union (EMU), which was agreed in 1992 with the Maastricht Treaty.

Since the EMU agreement, there has been an ongoing challenge across Europe's member states to conform with and meet the requirements of EMU. In particular, the constraints over unemployment and inflation rates has meant that many countries outside the union are either finding it too difficult to meet these challenges or, as in the case of the United Kingdom, have determined to stay out of the EMU. Some of those inside the EMU wish they were out too as Italy and Germany suffered heavy unemployment issues and poor growth prospects during the period of the bedding in of the Union.

Over a decade and a half later though, we have moved to a position where being inside or outside the EMU does not matter as just being inside the European Union means that countries need to manage the infrastructural challenges of the EMU.

This is because the EMU has created a new financial and commercial market through the agreements made by the European Commission at the turn of the century to create 'The Lisbon Agenda'. This agenda came out of the meeting of politicians in Lisbon in March 2000 which ratified the Financial Services Action Plan (FSAP).

The FSAP represents the European agenda to create an integrated financial marketplace by 2010, and has produced a range of European Directives including Solvency II for insurance firms, the Capital Requirements Directive for Basel II, the Market Abuse Directive, the Markets in Financial Instruments Directive (MiFID) and many more.

One of the key components of the FSAP and the Lisbon Agenda is also the Single Payments Area. The Single Payments Area aims to create a level playing field for payments in the retail and commercial banking markets of Europe, with single infrastructures, charging and fee rates across the Eurozone.

This will be good for Europe and Europe's corporations and consumers, as citizens, retailers, manufacturers and service corporations have to maintain multiple bank accounts in each country of Europe due to the charging and movement of monies across-borders being so challenging.[2] The objective therefore is to reduce bank costs, increase bank and corporate efficiency, and eradicate wasteful country practices.

Here's a summary of the benefits the European Commission anticipates from a Single Payments Area:

- **Banks:** payments processing represents around 40 % of a banks costs but only 20 % of their revenues, and so most banks are running payments at a loss. With a Single Payments Area, banks will deal with pan-European infrastructures for the clearing and settlement of

---

[2] At Sibos 2004, Heidi Miller of JPMorgan Chase asked some tough questions. This excerpt shows why SEPA is so important to European Markets: 'Let me tell you a story about a friend who lives in Europe and bought a boat in the United Kingdom. This gentleman is a very well-known former executive of a large global financial services company. He is eminently creditworthy. He had enough money sitting in his US bank account to buy many boats. He had patiently waited months for the boat to be built to his precise specifications . . . When the boat was ready, he called his bank to arrange payment. And his bank told him it would take about six weeks to transfer the funds. Six weeks? Think about it: My friend could have sailed to New York, withdrawn the cash from his bank account, had a leisurely dinner, sailed back to the United Kingdom, paid for the boat, and still had time left over for a Mediterranean cruise before that funds transfer would have been completed'.

payments. This will enable Europe's banks to reap over € 10 billion in savings through the rationalisation, consolidation and sharing of infrastructures. A further € 5 billion will be saved through reduced cash usage as Europe's citizens' move towards increasing usage of cards, prepaid and other electronic payment transactions. Banks can also generate new revenue streams by moving towards new products and services, such as the automation of the financial supply chain, rather than provide pure vanilla payments processing.[3]

- **Corporations:** as it is today, most corporations have to maintain multiple bank accounts, often one for each country of operation, due to the expense and complexity of cross-border payments operations. After the introduction of the Single Payments Area, any business should theoretically be able to run one treasury operation with one bank for the whole of Europe. Eradicating the need for multiple resources, currencies, languages, banks and financial managers will generate significant savings. It is also anticipated that billions of euro's can be saved through improvements to treasury operations through the automation of accounts payables and receivables. This will focus corporations and their banks on releasing much greater efficiencies through 'supply chain automation'.

- **Merchants:** the European Commission believes that merchants are penalised through credit and debit card fees, with a 9:1 range across Europe for merchant acquisition charges rising to a 20:1 disparity for debit cards. An example is a PIN-based debit card payment in Belgium costs merchants 5 eurocents (€ 0.05), compared to a € 1 cost in Spain. The levelling of these charges will be good for merchants, as a single charging structure for acquisition fees will ensure more predictability and consistency for stores and operations.

- **Citizens:** payment costs will be reduced to a standard fee structure across Europe, benefitting citizens in countries with high cost. For example, Italian banks charge € 252 a year for consumer payments whilst Dutch banks charge only € 34 a year.[4] This 8:1 disparity will disappear, with the expectation that the average cost for payment services for citizens will be around € 100 a year as choice and competition amongst financial providers increases. In addition, those citizens who travel or own properties in other EU Member States can now manage their financial requirements through a single bank account with standard charging and fee structures, encouraging more business and commerce across Europe.

- **Society:** the European Commission estimates the costs of inefficiencies in the current payment systems costs Europe 2 %–3 % of GDP. This equates to around € 100 billion of costs per annum that could be saved, with half of these costs wrapped up in payments infrastructures, whilst the other half is tied up in poor working capital and corporate payments processing for accounts payables and receivables.

As can be seen, this is why the Single Payments Area is a critical foundation for EMU, EU and the future competitiveness of Europe.

1.1 The euro

At the core of the Single Payments Area is the new currency for Europe, the euro. The euro, introduced as a trading instrument in 1999 and a full currency in 2002, has fundamentally changed the nature of the European Union as the twelve original countries within the Eurozone are now harmonised, in terms of cross-border trade and operations.

---

[3] All figures based upon presentations from the European Commission at various conferences in 2007.
[4] EFMA, ING and Cap Gemini, *World Retail Banking* Report, 2005.

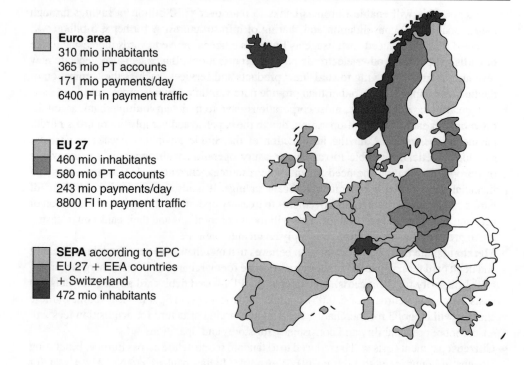

Euro area
310 mio inhabitants
365 mio PT accounts
171 mio payments/day
6400 FI in payment traffic

EU 27
460 mio inhabitants
580 mio PT accounts
243 mio payments/day
8800 FI in payment traffic

SEPA according to EPC
EU 27 + EEA countries
+ Switzerland
472 mio inhabitants

Or are they?

From a banking perspective they are not, because each country has its own clearing and settlement operations. They all have Automated Clearing Houses (ACHs) for low-value processing of credit transfers and direct debits. Most countries also have their own infrastructures for credit and debit card processing, and cash management processes differ between countries too.

Equally, most European member states operate their own real-time gross settlement systems for the National Central Banks. All of these systems are incompatible, separated and segregated. As a result, Europe comprises 27 countries and four associated countries: Norway, Iceland, Liechtenstein and Switzerland, is suffering from 31 separate payments infrastructures which inhibits the region's competitiveness.

The European Commission and the European Payments Council (EPC), which represents the banks of Europe, have been working hard to rectify this situation by introducing a harmonised infrastructure for the Eurozone called the Single Euro Payments Area, or SEPA for short.

SEPA is incredibly important to Europe as the challenges of running separate infrastructures makes Europe uncompetitive when compared with America, where integrated structures are in place. Effectively, Europe's position today if you translated it to the USA, would be one where each American state would have its own banking infrastructure.

So this is Europe's and SEPA's challenge and objective: to create a single payment operation and infrastructure for the euro currency that enables all euro payments to be treated as though they are domestic payments.

In this opening section we shall clarify what SEPA and what it is not. In Section 2, we shall outline the impact SEPA will have upon Europe's banks and banking systems.

1.2 The Single Euro Payments Area (SEPA)

Some people believe SEPA is a law or a European Directive. It is not. SEPA is a bank programme designed to create an integrated and harmonised pan-European payments infrastructure.

The European Directive is the Payments Services Directive (PSD) which created the legal framework for a harmonized and integrated European payments marketplace. The two go hand in hand as SEPA creates the technical environment and the PSD the legal environment, to enable a Eurozone where all cross-border payments within that zone are treated in the same way as domestic payments.

Another misperception is that some people refer to SEPA as the Single European Payments Area. This is also incorrect, as SEPA only applies to the euro currency within the Eurozone. The PSD and the European Commission however does cover all of Europe, as a Single Payments Area.

For these reasons, we must be clear from the start that although SEPA does relate to Europe and all of the European financial markets, it is a programme primarily focused upon the euro and the Eurozone, and the implementation of the banking infrastructures for clearing and settlement in that zone.

SEPA began in Brussels in 2002 when representatives of the major European banks and banking associations met to identify how to respond to an EU Regulation, introduced in late 2001, forcing cash withdrawal, card payments and credit transfers to be charged the same for cross-border as domestic payments within the Eurozone. This Regulation, known as EC Regulation 2560/2001, came into force over a period of time, with euro cash withdrawals and card payments priced the same for cross-border as domestic charges from July 2002, followed by low-value credit transfers in 2003.[5]

The Regulation also introduced major changes to bank systems, as it mandated that banks change from national sort codes and account numbers to new standards using International Bank Account Numbers (IBANs) and Bank Identification Codes (BICs).

This is one of the biggest challenges for banks within the SEPA and the Single Payments Area, as IBAN and BIC requires major changes to current bank operations.

Although the IBAN is purely a method of recognising individual bank account numbers across-borders, and the BIC is purely an international sort code for a bank, the fact that these codes are radically different to the existing codes used by most banks (see Figure 1) means that most banks will have to radically reprogramme their systems and operations to handle these new code structures.

For example, in the UK a typical account code is 8-digits (although for Lloyds TSB, it is 7-digits) and sort code is 6-digits, the combined code is not 14-digits under SEPA and Regulation 2560/2001, but 22-digits. This is such a radical change to payment systems that it equates to a Y2K for European banks.

Nevertheless, from 1 January 2006 European banks mandated that corporate customers cross-border euro transactions must conform to BIC and IBAN data formats or they may punitive charging fees. This was followed by the instruction that, from 1 January 2007, banks would reject cross-border euro transactions and charge for the return of the transaction if the IBAN and BIC were missing.

This bank response came out of the Brussels meeting in April 2002 when 42 major European banks, along with other key banking associations, came together to discuss how to implement

---

[5] EU Regulation 2560 mandated this for credit transfers valued under € 12,500 from 2003, increasing to € 50,000 from 2006.

country check			
code	number bank		sort code & account number
GB	**19**	**LOYD**	**3096 1700 7099 43**

Examples of European IBANs:

Austria	AT611904300234573201	Italy	IT40S0542811101000000123456
Belgium	BE62510007547061	Luxembourg	LU280019400644750000
Denmark	DK5000400440116243	Netherlands	NL39RABO0300065264
Finland	FI2112345600000785	Norway	NO9386011117947
France	FR1420041010050500013M02606	Poland	PL60102010260000042270201111
Germany	DE89370400440532013000	Portugal	PT50000201231234567890154
Gibraltar	GI75NWBK000000007099453	Spain	ES0700120345030000067890
Greece	GR1601101250000000012300695	Sweden	SE3550000000054910000003
Iceland	IS140159260076545510730339	Switzerland	CH9300762011623852957
Ireland	IE29AIBK93115212345678	UK	GB19LOYD30961700709943

Figure 1   International Bank Identification Code Structures *Source:* APACS

the demands for IBAN, BIC and Regulation 2560. The outcome was the creation of the Credeuro scheme and the European Payments Council (EPC).

Credeuro is the bank-to-bank transfer service created to manage the requirements of low-value credit transfer payments. The EPC is the council of bankers who act as the governing body to guide the creation of the payments infrastructures to support a Single Payments Area. This council is managed by influential banker Gerard Hartsink, who has been Chairman of the EPC since its inception in 2002.

The importance of the EPC is that they have created the critical frameworks and rulebooks for SEPA to become a reality. This has taken a lot of hard work, which crystallised in 2007 with the release of the rulebooks for the SEPA Credit Transfer (SCT) and SEPA Direct Debit (SDD) schemes.

The SCT Scheme replaces the Credeuro Convention of 2002, and enables payment providers to offer a core credit transfer service for single, bulk and repetitive payments from 1 January 2008. The scheme aims to have no value limits or deductions from the payment principal, and delivers a maximum execution time of three days between any two points in the SEPA geography.

The SDD Scheme aims to replace existing domestic direct debit schemes by 2010, and enables payment providers to offer a pan-European direct debit euro service.

The EPC has also created schemes that address cards and cash entitled the SEPA Cards Framework (SCF) and the SEPA Euro Cash Area Framework (SECA). However, to be clear, the SEPA SCT and SDD Schemes create *infrastructures* for pan-European clearing and settlement of credit transfers and direct debits, whilst the Cards and Cash areas are *framework* for banks to adhere to in their cards and cash payments processing. This difference is noteworthy as the former requires new technologies to be established, whilst the latter involves policies, procedures and processes.

The complete details of the EPC's work can be found at http://www.europeanpayments council.eu. This website also publishes guidance for the critical milestones for SEPA

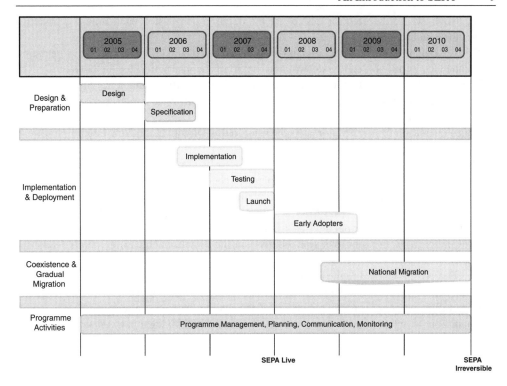

Figure 2 The Critical SEPA Milestones *Source:* European Payments Council

(Figure 2) which shows that SEPA becomes a reality from January 2008. January 2008 however is just the start however, as the process of moving to SEPA will actually transpire over a 36 month period as national infrastructures for clearing and settlement are dismantled. This means that the national ACH's become obsolete or evolve to compliance with the SEPA schemes.

Originally, any non-SEPA compliant national schemes were then meant to have been closed down at the end of 2010, although this has been modified to being the date by which SEPA is 'irreversible'. This means that it has reached critical mass and that, within the Eurozone, it is mandatory for SEPA-compliant SCT and SDD instruments to be used for any euro payments, as well as compliance with the SCF and SECA principles.

1.3   The Payment Services Directive (PSD)

As part of developing a Single Payments Area for Europe, there also needs to be a legal framework in place that harmonises the products and services around SEPA. This is because the traditional structure of retail and corporate banking allowed different products to operate in different ways.

By way of example, Italy has two versions of a direct debit called RID (Rapporti Interbancari Diretti) and RiBa (Ricevuta Bancaria Elettronica). RIDs are pre-authorised direct debits which operate in the same way as direct debits in many other European states where the creditor's bank draws monies from their debtors automatically on a regular basis. RiBa's are for unauthorised direct debits, where the creditor has to ask the debtor's permission each time they want to collect their receivables.

This is a unique service in Italy and has a raft of unique characteristics, such as value dating where the date of transfer can be determined as part of the instruction for the payment.

These are features you do not find in other direct debit operations and hence there needed to be a consolidated ruleset for the legal structures across the Eurozone or one country's payments would not be legally recognised by another.

Hence the reason for the PSD or, as some refer to this Directive, the New Legal Framework for Payment Services Directive.

The PSD is 'a legal framework designed to make cashless payments – such as card transactions, bank transfers and direct debits – simpler and cheaper, paving the way for the creation a single Euro payments area'.[6] It was adopted by the European Parliament in April 2007 after a wide-ranging consultation period from its first publication in December 2005. The Directive is to be transposed into national laws by 1 November 2009, although it was originally targeted for November 2007, in order to enable the dismantling of national clearing operations during 2010.

This Directive is critical to the achievement of SEPA as, without it, there would be no legal capability to enable cross-border payments across the Eurozone. For example, identifying who is at fault if the payment is not made on time – the sending bank or the received bank – would be impossible to legislate if the two countries concerned had no legal harmonisation.

However, the final Directive text agreed in 2007 was a compromise between Europe's member states, because there were major arguments over the details of the text.

One example was a North:South divide over the nature of competition in the newly opened European payments market. Northern Europe believes in free market economics, and were happy to have non-bank payment providers competing with the banks. These non-bank payment providers would include traditional firms such as First Data and Vocalink, but also new entrants such as PayPal and Google. Southern European Member States felt that this could be damaging to their national competitiveness, and wanted some form of protection left in place.

There was also a major divide over what was feasible by when, especially in relation to payment cycles and whether they should be one-day (T+1 or D+1), two-day (T+2 or D+2), or longer.

This debate focused upon the ability for some countries to evolve infrastructures from processing cycles of up to five days for certain products and instruments, particularly in the short timeframes given for 2010. For example, the original 2005 PSD stated that payment execution had to occur by the end of the next business day as a rule ('the D+1 Rule'). This was argued by the banks as being far too difficult to achieve by 2010.

For these reasons, the PSD's adoption slipped back from the original target dates of November 2007 implementation, to implement ion by 1 November 2009. This is also why, even after the Economic and Monetary Affairs Committee adopted the PSD in September 2006, it took until March 2007 for the Member States to reach agreement on a text and send it forward for Parliamentary approval in April 2007.

So the final text is known as a compromise text. One example of this compromise is the D+1 Rule itself. Originally slated to be processing of all payments in any currency by end of

---

[6] From the European Parliament announcement of 24 April 2007, http://www.europarl.europa.eu/news/expert/infopress_page/042-5721-113-04-17-907-20070420IPR05537-23-04-2007-2007-false/default_en.htm.

business the following day by 2010, the final text was watered down to:

From 1st January 2012 the following credit transfers must be made at the latest by the end of the next business day:

- euro currency payment transactions, both national and cross-border within the EU;
- national payment transactions in the currency of the Member State concerned;
- certain payment transactions involving currency conversion between the euro and the currency of a non-euro Member State.

Before 1 January 2012, a payer and his/her payment service provider may agree on a maximum period of 3 business days.

Whilst, for other payments, different rules apply:

- 'for intra community credit transfers not covered above (e.g. cross-border transfers in a non-euro, EU currency), the maximum period to make a payment shall not exceed four days'.
- 'for paper initiated payments, the period may be extended by an extra business day'.
- 'for direct debits, settlement should take place on the agreed date'.
- 'for cards, the parties enjoy contractual freedom[7].'

On the other key debating point, regarding non-bank payment providers, the compromise text also created specific rules for their capital and supervision. These payment providers are now defined as 'payment institutions', and have specific capital requirements for € 20,000 to € 125,000 of Initial Capital, compared to € 5 million for a bank, plus ongoing capital that covers 10 %, rising to up to 25 % of fixed overhead costs, or 0.5 % to 0.8 % of payments volumes for money remitters and mobile payments providers respectively.

It should also be noted that, from a legal framework, this Directive applies to all European Member States, and the Extended Economic Area (EEA)[8] and Switzerland, not just the euro area. This means that the banks in the non-euro countries must be able to provide SEPA instruments for euro payments, even though their national currency payments will continue as they are today.

SECTION 2: SEPA'S IMPLICATIONS

As a result of the introduction of SEPA and the PSD, major changes are occurring across the European payments landscape. Some of these changes impact central banks, such as the introduction of TARGET2 from the European Central Bank, whilst other changes cause major restructuring in the nature of competition in Europe, such as the European Commission's announcement when the PSD was released that it was unfair for charges in some countries to be eight times the cost of those in other countries.

In this section we shall review the key implications for wholesale and retail banks, bank infrastructures, payment providers, corporations, merchants and consumers.

From the banking markets' perspective, there are two major areas of impact:

- high and low value clearing and settlement operations and infrastructures;
- cross-border competition and banking market structures.

Let's look at each of these in turn.

---

[7] From the Payment Services Directive's Frequently Asked Questions section on Payment Execution Times http://europa.eu/rapid/pressReleasesAction.do?reference=MEMO/07/152&format=HTML&aged=0&language=EN&guiLanguage=en.

[8] Iceland, Norway and Liechtenstein.

2.1 Implications for Bank Infrastructures

In this section we review the implications for high value and low value clearing and settlement. Before we do this, it should be noted that the terminology of 'high value' versus 'low value' clearing and settlement is actually a legacy classification of the banking markets based upon two factors:

- the separation of high and low value due to the difference between wholesale and retail payment operations; and
- the manual, human and paper-based requirements of processing high-value payments in terms of gathering authentication, identification and verification documentation, especially for cross-border payments.

This separation may continue in the minds of banks and bankers, but is eroding as many now discuss urgent versus non-urgent payments. Urgent payments are also referred to as priority payments, faster payments, real-time payments and D+0. For urgent payments users will pay a premium and, therefore, the future focus of payments providers is upon urgent versus non-urgent payments.

In this classification of immediate versus delayed payment, there is no separation between low and high value infrastructures, as technologies are capable of processing in real-time any payment. In fact, the historical reasons for separating such payments were due to the documentation requirements of central banks, as mentioned, which has gone away in today's digitised society.

Today, with the correct authentication, a high value or low value payments costs the same within the banking system to process. It is just a transport of a file with validation, authentication and identification. This file transport is the same, whether the payment is high or low value. The future dialogue around clearing and settlement will be around fast payments in real-time versus mass payments in D+1, rather than high value and low value payments. However, the current structure continues to be high value and low value clearing and settlement systems and it makes sense to review the European landscape in this structure therefore.

Implications for High Value Clearing and Settlement

Since SEPA was announced, the European Central Bank (ECB) based in Frankfurt, Germany, has been working on a major change programme for Europe's Real Time Gross Settlement (RTGS) systems to link the National Central Banks (NCBs) of each of Europe's Member States. The programme is focused upon high-value payments, defined as those over € 50,000 by EU Regulation 2560/2001, and is meant to focus primarily upon wholesale payments.

Initially, the NCBs linked through a system launched in 1999 to support the euro called TARGET: the Trans-European Automated Real-time Gross settlement Express Transfer system. TARGET was a base platform architected via point-to-point connectivity enabling the NCBs to continue with their traditional clearing platforms.

Shortly after SEPA was announced, the ECB stated its intention to build the next generation RTGS system, TARGET2, in October 2002. TARGET2 will provide a Single Shared Platform (SSP) for connecting all the national central banks of Europe and is hosted and operated by three banks: the Banca d'Italia, the Banque de France and the Deutsche Bundesbank. The single technical platform replaces the original NCBs decentralised systems, and delivers a high value clearing and settlement operation with pan-European liquidity management.

The key objectives for TARGET2 are threefold, namely to:

- harmonise Europe's RTGS systems through an integrated and common technical platform and IT architecture;
- deliver cost efficiency through a single price structure for both intra-national and cross-border payments; and
- provide flexibility to meet the demands of users and new entrants as the Eurosystem enlarges to embrace new Member States in the EU.

In particular, the over-arching requirement is to deliver enhanced liquidity management and liquidity-efficient RTGS systems through features such as payments prioritisation, pooling of intraday liquidity and cash settlement services in central bank money for all kinds of ancillary systems (ASs), including retail payment systems, large-value payment systems, foreign exchange settlement systems, money market systems, clearing houses and securities settlement systems (SSSs).

The AS interfaces have been the area of most controversy, as this potentially implies that TARGET2 could provide low-value payment processing as well as displacement of securities clearing operations in Europe's capital markets. In other words, TARGET2 could become the panacea for all pan-European payments clearing and settlement.

Certainly, there is a possibility for TARGET2 to clear low-value payments as, in 2006, 63 % of TARGET payments were for values less than € 50,000 whilst payments above € 1 million only accounted for 11 % of the traffic.[9] Therefore, TARGET2 could be a low-value payments mechanism, a statement embedded in the ECB's SIBOS Presentation of 2005 but never repeated since.[10]

Equally, the Securities markets were extremely concerned about the announcements of TARGET2 for Securities. The announcements were made in July 2006 with four national central banks – Deutsche Bundesbank, Banco de España, Banque de France and Banca d'Italia – ready to develop and operate the settlement system.

The controversy of this announcement is that it implies the ECB will be competing against the businesses of Clearstream, LCH.Clearnet and Euroclear, the Clearing and Settlement Mechanisms (CSM) of Deutsche Bourse, London Stock Exchange and Euronext respectively.

Therefore, there is a compromise with the ECB stating that TARGET2-Securities (T2S) would only provide overnight or intraday processing and not real-time settlement. The fact that the ECB could do this is still concerning the markets however, with a final decision to be made on T2S in 2008.

Generally though, in the context of SEPA, TARGET2 is the gorilla of euro payments processing. After considerable planning, the new TARGET2 system becomes operational on 19 November 2007, with migration dates in 2008 on 18 February and 19 May, such that all national central banks and TARGET users will have migrated to the new SSP by May 2008 (Figure 3). The final implementation will therefore see a single shared platform across Europe processing over € 2 trillion a day and connecting over 1000 financial institutions. In other words, it will be one of the two largest wholesale RTGS systems in the world, alongside Fedwire in the USA. Although there are alternatives to the ECB's TARGET2, such as the EBA's EURO1 system., most of them are not of the same magnitude. For example, EURO1 in summer

---

[9] TARGET Annual Report 2006 published May 2007.
[10] Presentation at SIBOS 2005: Slides of the special interest session on TARGET2, September 2005.

Group 1 19 November 2007	Group 2 18 February 2008	Group 3 18 May 2008	Group 4
Austria	Belgium	Denmark	
Cyprus	Finland	Estonia	
Germany	France	ECB	
Latvia	Ireland	Greece	Reserved for contingency
Lithuania	Netherlands	Italy	
Luxembourg	Portugal	Poland	
Malta	Spain		
Slovenia			

Figure 3   Migration to TARGET2

2007, only has 71 participating banks processing an average € 195 billion a day through 185 000 transactions.

Implications for low value clearing and settlement

The other key initiative launched when SEPA was announced was the creation of a PE-ACH, a Pan-European Automated Clearing House, for low-value, cross-border euro payments. 'Low value' is classified as under € 50,000, as defined in EU Regulation 2560/2001, and is meant to focus primarily upon retail payments. In order to develop a PE-ACH, the EPC determined to use the EBA Clearing's STEP system.

The EBA was established in 1985 by 18 commercial banks and the European Investment Bank in order to promote the European Currency Unit (ECU), the unit of account which preceded the euro. This association led to the formation of the company EBA Clearing in June 1998 to operate and manage EURO1, the private-sector owned high value RTGS system.

This was followed in November 2000 by the launch of STEP – 'Straight Through Euro Processing' – as a stop-gap solution for single transaction cross-border euro payments, followed by STEP2 in April 2003 as a total solution for the bulk processing of low-value cross-border euro payments.

The EPC were keen to rationalise and endorse the EBA's STEP2 as a single PE-ACH for SEPA, especially as most bank payments are domestic rather than cross-border, with most banks estimating that only 2 % of Europe's transactions are cross-border. Therefore, what

Reachability
Number of Banking Institutions in the European Union, 2003

Austria	899	Italy	745
Belgium	114	Latvia	23
Cyprus	376	Lithuania	69
Czech Republic	41	Luxembourg	171
Denmark	183	Malta	18
Estonia	19	Netherlands	97
Finland	344	Poland	650
France	1491	Portugal	198
Germany	2311	Slovakia	22
Greece	55	Slovenia	32
Hungary	233	Spain	291
Ireland	83	Sweden	31
		United Kingdom	427

Figure 4   Reachability – over 9000 banks across Europe *Source:* ECB

would be the point of creating major, functionality-rich infrastructures? Instead, go for a base service that functions well, which is what is delivered by STEP2.

The EBA began operation of STEP2 in April 2003 selecting SIA,[11] the Italian provider of banking and payment solutions, to development the system in collaboration with Microsoft and SWIFT. Since its launch in 2003, there have also been continual improvements and upgrades to support further SEPA functionality. For example, the service is being enhanced through 2007 with SEPA Credit Transfer and Direct Debit Services using the SCT and SDD rulebooks.

For these reasons, the EBA has delivered the first fully SEPA compliant service for cross-border euro payments with the 'reachability'[12] to cover all Eurozone, EU and EEA bank clearing and settlement needs. This is why Spain, Luxembourg and Italy are standardising on STEP2 for retail payments clearing and settlement, as well as the EBA's STEP2 system having success by incorporating cross-border payments with the EEA and the newer EU Member States. This makes the EBA's STEP2 the only system with true pan-European reach (see Figure 4).

The reason for its success is that STEP2 is a highly automated, simple to use service, based on broadly accepted industry standards, enabling a bank to send and receive large batches of payments. STEP2 processing includes the validation of payment instructions, their routing to the beneficiary banks as well as an automated settlement in EURO1/STEP1 at the beginning of the day.

---

[11] Set up in 1977, SIA automated the Italian banking and financial system and then embarked on a strategy of internationalisation with the developments of the bond trading platform of the MTS Group and STEP2 for the EBA.

[12] Reachability is a key term for the banking community in relationship with SEPA, and relates to the fact that all financial Institutions must be able to provide credit transfer and direct debit payment services from any domestic account to any receiving account within the participating countries.

However, there was a little controversy during this period as the EPC had effectively blessed the EBA as their selection for a PE-ACH, potentially at the expense of other key retail clearing operations, such as the UK's BACS and the Netherlands Interpay.

As a result, a period of debate took place during the mid-2000's, with the UK bank-owned BACS operation being spun-off into a commercial payments provider, Voca, which later merged in 2007 with the ATM operator Link to become Vocalink. In the same way, Interpay merged with German processor Transaktionsinstitut in September 2006 to become Equens and further expanded their reachability in 2007 through a friendly merger with Seceti in Italy.

Effectively, all of Europe's national ACH's are fighting for survival and only a few will remain in the post-SEPA European operations. For these reasons, some countries are investing in new ACH operations, such as France, where the current ACH, System Interbancaire de Telecompensation (SIT), has created a new company STET (Systèmes Technologiques d'Echange et de Traitement) in 2004. The creation of STET is in order to build a new retail payment system to replace SIT in 2007 that supports Single Euro Payment Area (SEPA), as well as some of the unique requirements within France for storing and transmitting digitised cheque images, *les images-chèques*, and other payment types.

In this regard, you cannot overstate the importance of *les images-chèques* for the French banking markets, as most other markets have eradicated or minimised cheque usage.

France has the highest usage of cheques of any European constituency, with this form of payments representing just under a third of all payments. This is very high when compared with other countries, where Austria, Germany, Netherlands, Poland and Sweden processing less than 1 % of payments in the form of cheques.

There are other PE-ACH considerations as well. For example, there's the possibility of TARGET2 entering into low-value payments, as already mentioned. Some also believe that SIA could offer a PE-ACH service as an independent commercial payments processor.

The culmination of these pressures created an agreement in October 2007 where the major players – Vocalink, Equens, Iberpay, Seceti and STET – established bilateral interoperability for the exchange of SEPA payments from January 2008. The combined group handled over 18 billion direct debit and credit transfer payments in 2006.

Meanwhile, others believe that the largest European banks could form a bilateral pan-European clearing operation for retail payments. For example, a small group of leading payments processors – such as ABN AMRO, BNP Paribas, Citigroup, Deutsche Bank, HSBC, ING, JPMorgan Chase, Société Générale, UBS and Unicredito – could form a payments processing entity in the same way as the investments banks responded to MiFID.[13] If this were the case, then the battles between Equens, Vocalink, STET and the EBA for value and volume would become inconsequential.

Finally, other thoughts for pan-European processing of retail payments include the fact that the PE-ACH is primarily concerned with the new regime for credit transfers and direct debits. These are new cross-border euro products and adhere with the SCT and SDD rulebooks. These are the areas that demand new infrastructures as discussed. We should not forget though that SEPA requires other frameworks, the SCF and SECA, and there are several independent payment processors who are offering services in this space, including First Data and PayPal.

---

[13] MiFID is the Markets in Financial Instruments Directive. It is similar to the Payment Services Directive in impact, and creates a single European investment market. The reaction of the banks was to create their own market data service and equities exchange, named Project Boat and Project Turquoise respectively. The banks involved include ABN Amro, Citigroup, Credit Suisse, Deutsche Bank, Goldman Sachs, HSBC, Merrill Lynch, Morgan Stanley and UBS.

First Data has been aggressively creating a pan-European independent card processing presence with acquisitions from Austria's Payment Systems Services GmbH in November 2005, to Germany's Gesellschaft fur Zahlungssysteme mbH in June 2006, to Poland's POLCARD in August 2007, amongst several others.

Meanwhile, PayPal recently relocated its European Headquarters from Ireland to Luxembourg to take advantage of the opportunities of SEPA as well as the fact that the banking authorities there granted them a full bank status. With 35 million accounts in Europe in 2006, combined with 100 000 European merchant sites and coverage across most countries, PayPal believes it can really leverage its status as a low-cost and competitive retail payments provider in the post-SEPA world.

So the end game in the low-value clearing and settlement space is still unclear. What we can be certain of is that there will be more than one PE-ACH providing new SCT and SDD instruments. These PE-ACHs are likely to be represented by the most aggressive providers in this space with delineation and differences between each.

In this space, the major discussion is around a thin or thick PE-ACH. What's the difference? Well, similar to the idea of a thin and thick client in the computer world, a thin PE-ACH purely settles and clears cross-border euro payments whilst a thick PE-ACH is information and functionality rich. The thick PE-ACH not only settles and clears, but also captures and received the payments, with reporting and information services overlaid, alongside store and forward services to provide more comprehensives services. The last description fits the major systems investments made by Vocalink and Equens whilst the 'thin ACH' description could be more appropriately applied the EBA's STEP2.

Therefore, the likelihood is that we will see a longer-term clearing operation for low-value retail credit transfers and direct debits provided by four SEPA compliant ACH operations, rather than just the one originally envisaged.

First, the EBA's STEP2 service will be used as an underlying cross-border euro service by all banks, countries and clearing services, because it offers full SEPA compliance and reachability across all EU and EEA countries at low cost.

Vocalink and Equens will then seek to offer high functionality payments integrated with the EBA service, in order to enable euro payments that are information-rich with far more data around the sending and receiving banks details. These providers will support some country-wide ACH operations, as demonstrated in Figure 5, as well as a number of bilateral arrangements with key banks who desire to offer higher value services to their clients.

STET will also provide a functionally rich ACH capability on a Pan-European basis with an additional difference and advantage: cheque image processing. As a result, STET will continue to provide ACH operations for France and some other countries, such as Ireland and Italy, where cheque usage is high and digitised cheque processing makes sense.

The Importance of SWIFT and ISO20022

One area we also need to consider, before we move away from the infrastructures discussion, is the importance of SWIFT and ISO20022. SWIFT, the Society for Worldwide Interbank Financial Telecommunication, provides a critical service for the global banking community through the provision of secure infrastructure and standards for payments. The organisation funded by the banking community as a not-for-profit organisation that aims to enable and facilitate simple and secure payments transactions.

Country	2001 (Domestic ACHs)	2011+ (SEPA PEACHs)
Austria	Not applicable	STEP2 and Equens
Belgium	Centre for Exchange and Clearing (CEC)	STEP2
Belgium	Brussels Clearing House (CHS)	STET
Denmark	Retail Clearing	STEP2
Finland	Banks Payment System (PMJ)	STEP2
France	Systeme Interbancaire de Telecompensation (SIT)	STEP2 and STET
Germany	Retail Payment System (RPS)	STEP2 and Equens
Greece	Athens Clearing Office (ACO)	STEP2
Greece	Interbanking System (DIAS)	STEP2
Ireland	The Irish Retail Electronic Payments Clearing Company Limited (IRECC)	STEP2 and Vocalink
Ireland	The Irish Paper Clearing Company Limited (IPCC)	STET
Italy	Clearing system for interbank payments (BI-COMP)	STEP2
Luxembourg	Luxembourg Interbank Payment System on a Net basis (LIPS-Net)	STEP2
Netherlands	Clearing and Settlement System (Interpay's CSS)	STEP2 and Equens
Portugal	Interbank Clearing System (SICOI)	STEP2
Spain	National Electronic Clearing System (SNCE)	STEP2
Sweden	Bank Giro Centrale(BGC)	STEP2 and Vocalink
UK	BACS (Vocalink)	STEP2 and Vocalink

Figure 5   The Migration to SEPA for Europe's National ACH's

SWIFT's SEPA value proposition is to provide the common denominator between the competing clearing and settlement mechanisms across Europe, and enable them to seamlessly interoperate. In this context, SWIFT has focused upon developing standards based around the International Standard, ISO20022.

ISO20022, known as the UNIFI or UNIversal Financial Industry message scheme standard, aims to standardize the full end-to-end life-cycle of payments, clearing and settlement for the financial markets. These standards include the coverage of credit transfers and direct debits; rejected, returned and refunded payments, known as r-transactions; alongside exceptions, investigations and cash management. Equally, ISO20022 covers both corporate to bank and interbank cycles, and hence is very comprehensive.

The standard provides the financial industry with a common platform for the development of messages using a modelling methodology to capture syntax-independent financial transactions and associated message flows, as well as a set of design rules to convert the messages.

SWIFT has invested heavily in driving the UNIFI standard and incorporating the standard into their services and network, SWIFTNet, in order to provide a secure and resilient transport solution common to all clearing and settlement mechanisms and providers in the financial supply chain. They have also enhanced this with an identification code database, containing BIC and local clearing codes to ensure coherence of BIC and IBANs, and a SEPA reachability directory to identify which clearing solution to use to reach a specific bank.

In summer 2007 SWIFT also launched the SWIFT SEPA Testing Programme, a testing platform that allows banks to test and declare their SEPA compliance to the EPC.

The Impact on the Card Community

Although most of the focus of SEPA is upon the direct debit and credit transfer products, we must not forget the cards community are equally impacted, particularly the debit card community as these are primarily run by national schemes. The credit card community is also impacted, but the positioning and dominance of the major Visa and MasterCard schemes means that these are not as radically changed as the debit card schemes.

The fact is that SEPA's impact on debit card schemes is that, in effect, national schemes and network are obsolete for Eurozone countries from 2011. Many of these schemes date back to pre-ATM operations of the 1960's, such as the German card scheme which was introduced to guarantee cheques. The result is that each nation has evolved an infrastructure scheme, or multiple schemes, for card payments that are different. Germany has the ec-Karte and GeldKarte, whilst the UK has LINK. Spain has Euro 6000, ServiRed and 4B whilst Portugal has Multibanco. Then there's Dankort in Denmark and PIN in the Netherlands. The list goes on with perhaps France being the most dramatics where the Groupement des Cartes Bancaires (CB) consortia has controlled the payment card business since the 1980's with BNP Paribas, Crédit Agricole and Société Générale as members and major influences.

The actual total landscape is represented below:

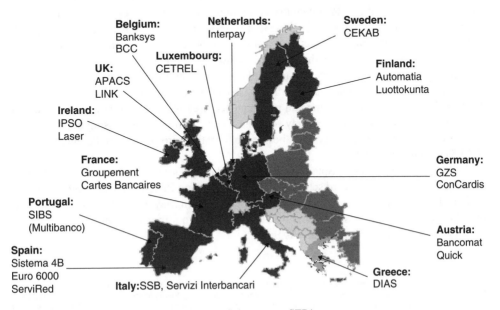

Domestic Payment Schemes in the "Original" EU (Card Processing Infrastructures)

Belgium:
Banksys
BCC

Netherlands:
Interpay

Sweden:
CEKAB

Luxembourg:
CETREL

UK:
APACS
LINK

Finland:
Automatia
Luottokunta

Ireland:
IPSO
Laser

France:
Groupement
Cartes Bancaires

Germany:
GZS
ConCardis

Portugal:
SIBS
(Multibanco)

Austria:
Bancomat
Quick

Spain:
Sistema 4B
Euro 6000
ServiRed

Italy:SSB, Servizi Interbancari

Greece:
DIAS

Figure 6   National Card Processing Payment Schemes pre SEPA

The result is a complex range of card spaghetti processing systems which are straining under the pressures of modern payment scheme requirements as well as the requirement for a Single Payment Area.

This was the issue that was tackled by the European Payments Council as an early priority, and the SEPA Cards Framework (SCF) was released in late 2005 and finalised in March 2006.

This Framework aims to rationalise the infrastructures for cash withdrawals, debit card transactions and credit card processes, and harmonise these across Europe. The SCF rules apply to all banks that are members of the EPC, and cover all aspects of transactions at POS and ATM.[14] Furthermore, the SCF makes it clear that EMV chip cards with PIN are the recommended methods of cards payments, with no support for magnetic stripe based payments from 2010.

This is good news for some, as the creation of a true pan-European cross-border debit and credit card payments and settlement process pretty well plays into the hands of MasterCard and Visa. For example, current cross-border debit card payments are currently managed almost completely by the MasterCard and Visa debit schemes Maestro and Visa Electron. As a result, European politicians have been very concerned that such changes to the national schemes could play into a duopoly of MasterCard and Visa, and have launched considerable investigation into their fees and practices, with major pressure on both card processors to lower interchange fees and merchant service charges.

In addition, a concern with such political lobbyists is that the opening of the Eurozone to cross-border competition may open the flood gates to a European credit card market which has been traditionally confined to the UK. Most UK citizens have 2.33 credit cards and use credit actively compared with their Italian counterparts who average only 0.37 credit cards per person (see Figure 7). This is because it has been promoted heavily by UK banks due to revolving credit being a high margin revenue generator, whereas debit does not make money.

The concern around a massive upsurge of credit card usage in Europe may be a false one however, as the lack of credit card products in most European countries is potentially an advantage to building the SEPA integrated community. After all, the lack of credit card take-up presents an incentive for banks to become more pan-European in focus, product and markets, as lucrative new credit card markets may just be the motivator to make this happen.

Mainland European banks are therefore in a positive position to both capitalise on the newly opening opportunities for launching card products across the Eurozone, as well as expanding credit card levers to new markets. This is why Royal Bank of Scotland, Citi and others have been aggressive in building issuing and merchant acquirer networks across Europe, as well as why First Data have been aggressively building a pan-#European processing capability. It is also why the major debit networks collaborated to form the Euro Alliance of Payment Schemes (EAPS) in September 2006.

EAPS is a collaboration of Spain's EURO 6000, Portugal's Multibanco, the UK's LINK Interchange Network, Italian card schemes PagoBancomat and Bancomat, Germany's electronic cash, and European card payment processor EUFISERV. In May 2007, this group announced their intention is to link these schemes by 1 January 2008 to form a pan-European network for debit cards and ATM processing across Europe.

---

[14] The SCF does not apply to transactions without a guarantee of payment, such as Germany's 'Elektronisches Lastschriftverfahren', ELV. ELV is an electronic debit procedure where customers identify themselves by PIN rather than signature and is viewed by the German credit services sector as being unguaranteed as it is in direct competition with their electronic cash and POZ (point of sale without guarantee of payment) systems. Equally, the SCF does not address electronic purses such as Germany's GeldKarte.

European Cards Headline Data
(2004)

Country	Population (millions)	GDP ($bn)	Total Cards per Person	Credit as % disposable income	Total cards with cash function (m)	Card accepting merchants	Fraud as % of payments
UK	59.5	1470	2.33	107	111.9	599 000	0.128
France	59	1460	0.7	49.5	37.5	586 000	0.026
Germany	82	2021	0.88	88	98.6	307 000	0.1
Italy	57.6	1402	0.37	15	21.3	N/A	'average'
Spain	40	828	1.15	54	39.4	666 000	0.025

Figure 7   National Card Processing Payment Schemes pre SEPA

Between them, these seven providers represent over 2 million POS terminals, 228 million payment cards and 200 000 ATMs around Europe, and are supported actively by the Dutch ACH Equens and the UK's Voca, who merged with LINK in 2007 to form Vocalink.

The Importance of Prepaid Cards

A factor in the cards space that is under-emphasised is the importance of prepaid cards. By the mid-2000's hardly any prepaid card programmes were operational in Europe, but the changes necessary to deliver SEPA, the PSD and specifically SECA – the Single European Cash Area – also mandates finding new ways to eradicate cash. Prepay offers a cash substitute as prepaid cards, unlike chip-based credit and debit cards, can be as anonymous as cash for online and offline payments. Banks across Europe are therefore likely to support delivery of prepaid cards as a market to overcome the costs of cash management and the reduced margins of cross-border payment schemes.

Alongside this trend, retailers are recognising the marketing opportunities, whilst corporate and governments are beginning to identify the cost savings prepaid could deliver. For example, corporates have long recognised that there are significant inefficiencies in cash usage and cash movements which impacts working capital and liquidity. How to overcome such inefficiencies has historically been a challenge when there is no viable alternative to cash.

Equally, banks recognise that cash management and treasury operations need an overhaul if they are to deliver the efficiencies required of SEPA and still make margin. Yet again, even though card usage is being encouraged, there has still been no viable alternative to cash.

MasterCard International performed a study of European opportunities for prepaid during the first half of 2006. The report found that Europe's prepaid cards market is on the cusp of rapid expansion, with an estimated total market opportunity worth over € 700 billion

($ 870 billion) per annum by 2010. This is based upon a wide range of prepaid card target markets, including:

- consumer use of pre-purchased foreign currency for use on holiday/abroad;
- the donation of funds as a gift, either be on a peer to peer basis or as part of a loyalty/rewards programme;
- the regular or ad-hoc transfer of value by migrant workers to family members in their town/ country of origin;
- the provision of products to segments of the population who either by choice, or exclusion, do not regularly use mainstream financial products such as credit cards or current accounts;
- products targeted at users who are unwilling, unable, or uncomfortable in using other forms of payments on-line;
- products targeted at consumers wishing to spend within a gaming environment. This includes both peer to peer gaming and adult gambling;
- products used by firms to distribute pay to their employees either on a regular monthly basis or for work completed;
- the provision of financial benefits to employees, suppliers or customers in recognition of performance or as part an employment contract. This also includes remuneration for travel/ expenses;
- the distribution of benefits to citizens – this could include tax rebates, child, unemployment benefits and student grants;
- the bundling of transit applications with a payment application designed to purchase low value goods such as coffees or newspapers;

and more. However, not all of this potential will be realized due to a number of inhibiting factors which include:

- banks do not see the business case;
- corporate antipathy;
- lack of consumer markets;
- europe is different;
- infrastructures are not built for prepaid solutions.

Many European bankers believe the business case for prepaid cards is not proven and that consumers have enough cards in their wallet already. As a result, European bankers cannot see the revenue and profitability of such cards, particularly in an area where debit systems dominate and are largely free. Even if there were a business case, many European banks are allocating all spend towards regulatory changes implied by SEPA and the PSD, rather than thinking around introducing new products and programs, such as prepaid.

From the corporate perspective, why would European corporates want to switch to prepaid benefits programme when they are happy with existing credit transfer systems that are in place? These Credit Transfer systems are already subject to considerable change under the new EPC SEPA Credit Transfer Rulebooks and Scheme changes. This will mean changes to clearing house operations, and corporates will be focusing upon their bank supporting the transfer with minimal disruption. Therefore, the idea of suddenly switching the payment instrument from electronic transfers to prepaid cards may be too radical for some banks, who will be loathe to upset their corporate clients further during the period of change that SEPA introduces.

With regards to both of these points, an alternative view could be that as corporates and banks have to change anyway, due to the PSD regulations on credit transfers, why not release the potential and introduce these new prepaid cards as part of that overhaul?

This point is somewhat substantiated here is, however, optimism that as successful products emerge over the next 12 to 18 months, that demonstrate a viable business case, there is likely to be a growing momentum behind prepaid, particularly in the business to business sales environment. The majority of banks are currently 'dipping their toes in the water' with prepaid, and many will to be piloting their propositions in the coming months. One expert stated 'banks are relatively small scale at the moment, principally because closed loop is not as interesting to the banks, and open loop hasn't taken off yet'.

A third inhibitor would be due to consumers continuing to make larger payments with existing solutions, such as credit and debit cards, or being too wedded to traditional cash and check usage. Although check has declined significantly across Europe, cash is till dominant in most countries. By way of example, Royal Bank of Scotland announced the launch of a massive rollout of 'tap-and-go' contactless payment credit cards in June 2006. The reaction sparked an online survey of London commuters by the free magazine *Metro* that has over 2 million readers. The survey result showed the 74 % of Londoners still provider cold, hard cash as opposed to 26 % who preferred plastic cards.

Consumer resistance can be overcome through punitive costs for cash and check usage, or incentives to use cards through discount and loyalty card programs. This is already happening in some countries as a result of EC Regulation 2560/2001, as mentioned earlier, but will be fuelled further as banks see the opportunity for prepaid to displace cash and checks. Equally, prepaid card benefits to consumers should be highlighted, such as their convenience and fitness-for-purpose.

The convenience factor may come from contactless payment systems and the ease and speed of using such systems, whilst the fit-for-purpose can be delivered through giftcards being purchased by parents to allow children to pay for services online without using mum or dad's credit card.

In fact, within the European analysis performed by MasterCard, the major growth area will be in gift cards for this reason. However, these may not be gift cards provided by banks but may be closed loop systems offered by retailers with an online presence such as Virgin. A great way to hook tomorrow's youth into the brand early.

A fourth barrier to prepay is the nature of the European markets. Whilst the US has succeeded in introducing prepaid through targeting specific sections such as the unbanked or underbanked, Europe does not offer the same opportunities. For example, the US model for prepaid cards for the under- and un-banked is based upon a system where checks involve the individual paying $ 50 or more per month in check cashing bill payments and remittances or $ 200 per annum on a deposit account. Europe does not levy these fees in the same way due to the dominance of ACH (Automated Clearing House) for credit transfer payments, such as payroll. Europe has also offered free banking for its basic products such as deposit accounts, due to government policies of financial inclusion. The result is that the business case for banking the unbanked as a profitable new market is much less realistic in the European context.

Finally, although SEPA is changing the base infrastructures across Europe, the current structures supported by the banks are not necessarily as suited to prepay as other credit and debit payments. This means that the distribution systems needed to support offering unbanked or youth prepays would mandate additional costs in terms of merchant and issuer incentive models, training and marketing. Such cost during the SEPA change period may not be realistic.

Therefore, for some areas of prepaid, banks will need to provide strong support and education to their customer base in order to make these services successful and change behaviors, in other areas customers, corporates and consumers will naturally transition regardless.

As a result of these factors, I do not expect that banks will address the total € 700 billion market opportunity for prepaid cards but will target specific areas, such as giftcards for the youth markets and corporate benefits programs, because of their value and volume of payments. This market is still substantial, valued at over € 75 billion – a 600 % increase over 2005 – and with 375 million cards in circulation, up over 1000 %, this is a market that cannot be overlooked.

2.2   Implications for Banking Markets

As mentioned in the opening section regarding, the European Commission believe that the Single Payments Area will have significant benefits for banks, corporates, merchants, citizens and society. Not only will SEPA and the PSD create a harmonised and integrated financial marketplace, but it also means that Europe's banks will be open to competition across-borders from existing players, as well as new payments providers.

For the banking community, this has meant significant soul-searching to work out where to allocate focus with the first question asked as to whether to be a payments processor at all.

In the future, as a bank, you have to have economies of scale and reachability to be a payments provider. Otherwise there is no point in managing payments internally.

This has resulted in many banks arguing about whether to continue to deal with payments, with comments ranging from *'money transmissions is the heart and core of banking'* to *'a payment is a payment is a payment, it's a commodity'* to *'if we don't do payments, what do we do?'*.

In reality, all of these comments are correct. It just depends which bank you are as to which statement works for you.

'Money transmissions is the heart and core of banking'

'Money transmissions is the heart and core of banking' applies to the major pan-European banks that currently have the infrastructure investments and see payments as their major competence.

Who are these banks?

There are a few, and are categorized on the basis that they have pan-European footprints. A pan-European footprint means that you have reachability today, and can cover payments across at least ten of Europe's Member States. There are only a few banks that have that scale and reachability, namely: ABN AMRO, BNP Paribas, Crédit Agricole and Deutsche Bank; as well as the major US banks: Citigroup and JPMorgan Chase.[15]

These are the banks who are consolidating and rationalising infrastructures to leverage their position as pan-European payment providers. Many are opening shared service centres in Poland, Romania and other low-cost European centres. Several have consolidated global platforms to create a single payments platform for their operations, including a few who are not in this original group such as UBS and HSBC, who also perceive they have a role to play in a post-SEPA Europe.

---

[15] Source: 'To what extent will the banking industry be globalized?' A study of bank nationality and reach in 20 European nations by A. Berger, Q. Dai, S. Ongena and D. Smith, *Journal of Banking and Finance, 27,* 383–415.

All of these banks will be major low-cost, high-scale payments providers, and they will move towards offering white label services to smaller banks, which leads us to our second group: *'a payment is a payment is a payment, it's a commodity'*.

'A payment is a payment is a payment, it's a commodity'.

'A payment is a payment is a payment, it's a commodity' applies to many of the domestic banks of Europe, especially those within the Eurozone, who do not process a significant volume of cross-border payments and must now use SEPA-compliant instruments in order to process payments.

For many of these banks, they may have to remove or refresh current payments systems to cope with new PE-ACH interfaces; they will need to change information structures and systems to comply with the SCT and SDD rulebooks for credit transfers and direct debits, as well as IBAN and BIC codes; and they will be having to implement these changes within a payments market subject to new fee structures with diminished margins for both domestic and cross-border payments.

For these banks, and many others, they have woken up to the fact that they need to move on and move out. This means they will look towards our first group of banks – the pan-European payments providers – as outsourcing firms who could take over their infrastructures and run their payment services on a cost-per-transaction or similar basis. Equally, they could be using one of the commercial PE-ACHs to do this, such as EBA Clearing, Vocalink, STET or Equens; or even general outsourcing providers focused upon the payments space.

The good news is that these banks, as well as the pan-European payments processors mentioned in the previous section, have moved on to focus upon delivering value-added services for their customers. In particular, they are seeking to deliver more value to their corporate customers and this has resulted in a major shift towards a dialogue around supply chains, rather than payments. This is exactly what the European Commission has hoped for, and it means that banks of all sizes are considering how to help their clients and how to retain them in this pan-European competitive market.

One example of this focus on the client is a major shift towards the automation of invoices. 85 % of European invoices are paper-based, with a cost to process of around € 5 per invoice when it is correct, and € 60 per invoice when it's incorrect due to the reprocessing and human intervention costs involved. That produces around € 60 billion of cost per annum in processing paper invoices.

If this process could be automated, the estimates are that it would save anything between 75 % and 95 % of those costs, in other words at least € 45 billion a year. This makes it worthwhile and is the reason why the European Commission has been trying hard to include e-invoicing – the automation of invoices using corporate-to-bank and interbank technology standards – in the SEPA programme.[16]

Another example of focus upon the supply chain is the interest European banks are now showing in real-time nostro. Originally developed in the early 2000's due to many banks requesting such a service, there are a number of real-time nostro services in the markets

---

[16] It could have been achieved but was viewed as too much too soon in the context of all the other changes the EPC and the Eurozone banks have to handle, but e-invoicing and supply chain is still very much on the European Commission's agenda with a Directive being drafted by the European Committee for Standardisation. This Committee has already made proposals to incorporate e-invoicing through an update to Commission Recommendation 1994/820/EC October 1994 with the requirements of Directive 2001/115/EC, present day e-Commerce practices and revised definition of EDI Electronic Data Interchange. This will become an e-invoicing Directive therefore. See http://www.cen.eu/isss/eINV for more information.

although few have been particularly successful. The reason they were unsuccessful is that, even though they requested the service, many banks could not see why they should buy such services.

The original reasons banks requested real-time nostro was to avoid risk exposures due to corporate clients' cash positions exceeding risk limits. However, internal risk management of the odd client exceeding their cash limits did not really cut the ice when it came to asking senior bank executives for these investments.

With SEPA's impact upon client relationships, and the possible loss of those relationships, banks are now beginning to buy into real-time nostro as a corporate information services, as in providing banks' corporate customers with a real-time view of their own cash positions and exposures. In this sense, real-time nostro is a customer value-add and therefore is starting to gain traction.

A third example is the change in attitudes towards corporates within the SWIFT community. Bearing in mind that SWIFT represents a largely European audience, the move towards corporate inclusion in SWIFTNet has been quite dramatic over the past few years. In fact, it has been a u-turn.

For example, in 2005 and before, SWIFT's members voted overwhelmingly against allowing direct corporate access to SWIFTNet. As a result, the only way for a corporate to send secure payments through the SWIFT network was by connecting one by one with their SWIFT networked banks using the SWIFT Member Administered Closed User Groups (MA-CUGs), and paying each bank a large fee for the privilege.

In 2006, two things happened which changed all this. The first was a major re-pricing of MA-CUG connectivity such that corporates only had to pay one fee to link to as many banks as they wanted through the MA-CUG connection; and the second was the launch of SCORE – Standardised Corporate Environment – for larger public companies to connect to SWIFTNet direct, rather than through a MA-CUG managed by a bank.

This was quite an amazing turn-around, as only two years before the bank members of the SWIFT community voted unanimously against this action. Again, it is a reflection of the changing focus within Europe to recognise the importance of their corporate clients, to deliver more service and value to them, and to focus upon retention of the customer before the customers consolidates all their banking activities to other providers within and across Europe.[17]

In other words, the bank to corporate space has become a major area of focus because the banks have finally woken up to the fact that their competitors are now pan-European seeking to manage pan-European bank account services for pan-European corporate clients. This is very different to the pre-SEPA world where most corporate were forced to maintain bank services in every European Member State.

'If we don't do payments, what do we do?'

With the banks that are operating major cross-border, pan-European payments factories moving into our first group and those who have little cross-border internal capabilities moving into our second, there is a third group of bankers left in Europe. These banks are the 'devil and deep

---

[17] It is worth noting that many banks have communicated little of the advantages and opportunities SEPA offers for exactly this reason. Therefore, few corporates even know what SEPA is in 2007.

blue sea' brigade, as in they don't think or cannot throw away their investment in payments but are also far away from having a fully SEPA-compliant infrastructure.

For these banks, they are asking the fundamental question: *'if we don't do payments, what do we do?'* and are coming up with problematical answers.

An illustration is Nordea in Scandinavia and the Baltic's, who have stated that SEPA has added significant costs to their payments operations for a negative return.[18] These banks would like to close down their payments operations, but cannot. In the case of Nordea for example, they are running a complex multi-currency operation with non-euro countries Sweden, Norway, Denmark and Iceland, combined with euro operations in Finland and a burgeoning euro-nation in Estonia and the Baltic states. It may be for these reasons that the Baltic nations will migrate to SEPA compliant domestic payments infrastructures sooner rather than later, even though they are not within the Eurozone.

For these geographic players who fall half-way in and half-way out of the Eurozone, there is a dilemma in that they need to remain in payments to keep their customers, operations, products and services operating, even though it may be undesirable to do so. Their only other strategic move would be to sell their payments operations to an outsourcing firm to do it for them. Some will no doubt take this direction although they will wonder whether and how an outsourcing firm could do this cheaper or better than they could themselves.

For the banks in this third category therefore, they have to make the tough choice of either dumping their payments investment and losing revenue and profitability, or investing in their payments infrastructure to be SEPA-compliant creating cost with potentially no long-term gain.

Tough choices, but it may be resolved by the final impact of SEPA on these banks: Bank M&A.

Bank Mergers and Acquisitions

As a result of SEPA, the European markets will face significant upheaval in all areas, as Italian banks compete head-to-head with German banks, who compete with French banks, who compete with Spanish banks and others. In effect, the United States of Europe will see a similar transition for the next 20 years that the American bank markets have been through over the last twenty years.

The US markets has seen significant consolidation towards national universal banking operations as a result of law changes from the Supreme Court ruling on Bank Holding Companies in 1987, through to the Gramm-Leach-Bliley ending of the Glass-Steagall Act in 1999. The result has been major bank mergers and acquisitions leading to a consolidation of US banking into a few large players: the Bank of America, Citigroup, JPMorgan Chase, Wells Fargo and Wachovia. Each of these banks has acquired significant numbers of other bank networks and operations over the past 20 years, although their combined operations still only represent a quarter of the total bank business in America. SEPA will start a similar process.

In fact, it may already have started with the Spanish Banco Santander's spending $ 15 billion on the UK's Abbey in 2004, and Italy's UniCredit buying Germany's HVB for $ 18 billion in 2005. This was eclipsed by the $ 30 billion domestic acquisition of Capitalia by UniCredit in

---

[18] Comments made by Per-Eric Skotthag, Deputy Head of Global Operations Services for Nordea, at the Financial Times payments conference, April 2006.

	Number of Institutions	Number of branches	Number of accounts (thousands)	Value of accounts (EUR billion)
Credit institutions	2295	46 693	84 265	631.5
Of which:				
Commercial banks*	397	16 254	16 765	265.8
Savings banks	502	15 830	40 900	241.0
Cooperative and rural banks	1396	14 609	26 600	124.7
Branches of foreign banks	121	144	N.A.	7.9

* Includes big banks, regional banks and other commercial banks, branches of foreign banks, mortgage banks and banks with a special function

Figure 8 German's Fragmented Banking Market *Source:* Bank for International Settlements (2004)

May 2007, to become Europe's second largest bank, combined with the $ 100 billion battle for ABN AMRO between the UK's Barclays and Royal Bank of Scotland.

There are also other opportunities presented by SEPA, especially for a bank that wants to be in the pan-European payments space. In this case, they may take their euro payments processing investments into non-euro countries selected on the basis that those countries require cross-border euro services and is likely to move towards SEPA-compliance and the euro currency over time.

An example is the strategy taken by the cooperative Raiffeisen Bank of Austria. Raiffeisen has taken an aggressive growth path around Eastern Europe over the past few years and now has operations in Albania, Belarus, Bosnia and Herzegovina, Bulgaria, Croatia, the Czech Republic, Hungary, Moldova, Poland, Romania, Russia, Serbia, Kosovo, Slovakia, Slovenia and Ukraine. Without building new infrastructures, Raiffeisen is able to buy up bank operations in non-Eurozone countries knowing that many of them will convert over time and that they have the infrastructure to consolidate, rationalise and become a major pan-Eastern European payments processor.

In the greater scheme of things, Bank M&A will heat up rapidly as more banks take this path and see the opportunities of consolidation, volume and economies of scale. This is particularly true because Europe is over-banked right now.

A strong example of the over-banked nature of Europe is the fragmented German markets as illustrated in Figure 8.

As can be seen, Germany has a large multi-tiered banking market, with under 20 % of credit institutions classed as commercial banks, whilst cooperative and rural banks are the largest contributors to the overall number of credit institutions. The influence of public sector policies is clear, as demonstrated by the fact that the German savings banks are market leaders in retail banking by number of accounts.

Germany has also had very restrictive laws for foreign bank entry, which is why there are so few foreign bank institutions represented, and M&A activity amongst private sector institutions is virtually non-existent.

For these reasons, Germany is also one of the poorest performers in the payments space and was bitterly opposed to the imposition of D+1 which was not surprising, as their direct debit instruments typically operate to D+5 cycles.

With SEPA, the PSD and the FSAP, this is all about to change and Germany, at the heart of the Eurozone, we will see a significant wave of consolidation as inefficient public sector savings banks become exposed to French, Dutch, Italian, British and other bank entry and acquisitions. Across Europe we shall see the same and, by around 2025, only a fifth of today's banks will still exist, with many acquired into major universal, pan-European bank operators led by the likes of BNP Paribas Crédit Agricole, Deutsche Bank, HSBC and UBS, alongside Citigroup and JPMorgan Chase.

Bank Pricing

One of the biggest impacts SEPA introduces is a dramatic reduction in bank margins and pricing for cross-border payment transactions. Historically, financial institutions have used cross-border payments within the EU to generate healthy profits. For example, a payment from the UK to a Eurozone country currently will incur a typical minimum charge of £25 to £40 (€37.50 – €60) dependent upon the transaction. These charges relate to CHAPS, the central bank clearing system, and the administrative processes involved. Equally, a payment of more than £1,000 (€1400) would usually require the payee to visit a branch to complete forms and provide identification.

SEPA should change this process such that a credit transfer of the nature above will be charged at the same price as a domestic transfer. This style of payment would usually be made over the internet, through branch or via call centre, and would not require additional identification. In other words, a radical change from the current process.

In addition, the fees incurred for the current process are high due to the administrative burden of making a cross-border payment for the bank's internal systems. These overheads should be removed and so the fees charged will be lower anyway.

According to presentations from the European Commission,[19] it is anticipated that typical bank fees for a cross-border euro transaction will be reduced by 85% or more, from an average of almost €25 per transaction to €3.75 or less. This will be a significant gain for Europeans making cross-border payments, but it will cause issues for the banks who see up to €29 billion per annum in fees disappearing.[20]

For some banks, this means a focus upon economy of scale by building pan-European processing centres. These may be internal shared service centres and are also, increasingly, being offered as outsourcing payments centres to other banks who may not have the internal capabilities to achieve such scale. Other specialists are also building scale in this arena, such as payments processors First Data, PayPal, Vocalink and Equens, all of whom seek to build high volume, low cost capabilities.

Bank Technologies

Finally, SEPA does have major implications on bank technologies covering:

- the changes to accommodate IBAN and BIC;
- changes to interfaces with all bank infrastructures as they move from national to pan-European schemes;
- the implementation of new standards, such as ISO20022; and
- the rethinking of products as they move from national operations with national legal processes, to European operations and processes.

---

[19] Jean Allix, DG Internal Market, European Commission Presentation to Eurogiro Strategy Forum, April 2004.
[20] ABN AMRO, EFMA, Cap Gemini Annual 'World Payments Report', 2007.

The first and last of these challenges are probably the greatest. For example, adhering to new IBAN and BIC code structures has been irksome to say the least. The IBAN and BIC codes are 22 digits, whilst each country's coding structures for account numbers and bank identifications are all different, as shown earlier in Exhibit 1. In some ways, this challenge can best be understood by thinking about the challenges we all faced in the late 1990's with Y2K.

Y2K was all about changing systems that had been written over the past four decades with the use of MM/YY or DD/MM/YY as the date field. All of these programmes had to be rewritten to reflect the fact that we had moved from one century to a new one, and hence all fields needed to be MM/YYYY or DD/MM/YYYY. The IBAN and BIC changes are similar, with banks moving from short codes to the full international standards. As a result, they have had to rewrite many systems to manage this transition. However, by 2007, most banks were able to do this. It had only taken six years.[21]

The last challenge is even greater, as this means not only changing the programs, systems and software for core products – cards, debits and credits – but also changing all aspects of current operations to accommodate new products. After all, many of the detailed requirements of SDD and SCT are new direct debit and credit transfer operations which, for the corporate and retail customer, means education and dialogue for them to understand the new product workings whilst, for the systems and software, will often require new date, value, timing and field structures.

For example, in Italy, banks offer a direct debit product that allows authorisation for each payment from the payee. This scheme is totally different to most other national direct debit schemes and, as a result, is in conflict with the SDD scheme. Italian banks' choice is either adhere to the new scheme or offer a non-SEPA compliant solution.

The choice they have actually taken is to continue with the current system and try to convince the EPC to incorporate this direct debit scheme into the SDD. The reasons for this is that to move from a current scheme to one where payments are taken without the payee's authorisation, involves both a major customer education challenge and systems need to be rewritten. Although the costs of such a redesign may be prohibitive for many, Eurozone banks have no choice but to implement the new SEPA SDD, SCT, SCF and SECA schemes. Eurozone banks have to redesign all current systems and software to operate in this new way, or breach the SEPA scheme rules.

As a result, SEPA is the greatest reinvention of bank payment systems since these systems were originally implemented, and is a fantastic opportunity for banks to re-engineer systems and processes to suit 21st century technologies, consumer requirements and operational capabilities.

SECTION 3: SEPA NATIONAL MIGRATION PLANS

SEPA means different things for each European nation and, in this final section, we take a brief European tour of the SEPA migration plans covering:

- France;
- Germany;
- Italy;

---

[21] IBAN and BIC were part of Regulation 2560/2001 released in September 2001.

- Spain;
- Netherlands;
- UK;
- Nordics;
- Eastern Europe.

3.1 France

End of 2005:

- 234 commercial banks, with over 10 000 branches between them;
- around 139 savings, co-operative and rural banks;
- French postal services also provide a wide range of retail services;
- 160 foreign banks, including all the international cash management banks.

Payment Systems:

- RTGS: Transferts Banque de France (TBF);
- RTNI[22]: Paris Net Settlement (PNS);
- ACH: Système Interbancaire de Télécompensation (SIT).

	Millions of transactions		% change	Traffic (EUR billion)		% change
	2004	2005	05/04	2004	2005	05/04
Cheques	4133.8	3916.3	−5.3	2084.2	2175.7	4.4
Card payments	4650.0	5243.8	12.8	219.6	260.2	18.5
Credit transfers	2599.2	2408.4*	−7.3	107 554.3	13 462.3*	−87.4
Direct debits	2542.7	2512.8	−1.2	782.5	906.7	15.9
Card-based e-money	16.1	17.0	6.4	0.05	0.04	−20.0
Total	**14 071.0**	**14 279.6**	**1.5**	**111 150.4**	**17 280.1**	**−84.5**

*Bank clients' transactions only.

Payment statistics *Source:* ECB Blue Book statistical update, December 2006

To prepare the French migration plan for SEPA, the Banque de France and the French Banking Federation formed the National SEPA Committee. This committee has representatives of all of the key stakeholders in the French payment system, including banks, public administrations, companies, merchants and consumers, as well as members of Parliament and a representative of the Economic and Social Council.

This meant that France were one of the first countries to publish their National Migration Plan in October 2006, and the Committee has based its definition of future payment instruments on the basis that current service levels must be maintained. It has considered the fact that many of the existing French payment instruments will need to be replaced with European payment instruments, although it did leave cheques and e-money outside the scope of the French SEPA project. For these payment instruments, their use would continue to run in France as per today.

The Committee separated the migration to SEPA between simple products and complex ones. This is because France has its own unique range of credit transfer products which are

---

[22] Real-Time Net Settlement.

the most popular method of payment for wages, pensions and social security benefits, and are increasingly used to pay suppliers and taxes.

France's electronic credit transfer types include:

- *virement de gros montant* (VGM): high-value and / or urgent payments which are made through TBF (an RTGS system) and PNS (a real-time net settlement system);
- *virement d'origine extérieure* (VOE): a credit transfer issued by a bank located outside France to a bank located in France with the French bank being responsible for transmitting all information in its possession, particularly on the currency conversion effected and charges, to the beneficiary's bank via SIT;
- *virement échange de données informatiques* (VEDI): electronic credit transfer using the EDIFACT format;
- *virement référencé* (VR): credit transfer for which the payer's banker guarantees the details contained in the labelled zones are correct and transmitted only to creditors registered as being concerned with the service being rendered;
- *virement spécifique orienté trésorerie* (VSOT): a special inter-bank transfer for treasury management operations; and
- *virement commercial* (VCOM): an irrevocable deferred electronic payment order accompanied with invoice details which the remitters bank forwards to the beneficiary when issued; there are two types of VCOM and these are called *finançable* and *non finançable* (discountable and non-discountable); in the former case, creditors can obtain immediate value (less interest charges) by discounting the payment with the bank on which the transfer is issued.

Several other payment types exist in France that are not generally found in other European countries, including:

- *titre électronique de paiement* (TEP): an electronic payment order that allows remote payment for goods and services via data links or telephone designed as an alternative for customers reluctant to use direct debits;
- *titre interbancaire de paiement* (TIP): a pre-formatted interbank payment order that allows remote payments and is used for regular payments such as utility payments and tax instalments;
- *lettre de change relevé* (LCR): an electronic commercial trade bill that represents an order from one party to another to pay a specified sum on demand, or on a specified date, which is widely used to finance trade and to obtain credit;
- *billet à ordre relevé* (BOR): an electronically processed promissory note; and

The last two are meant to work such that LCRs are issued by the creditor for acceptance by the debtor, while BORs are debtor-initiated instruments. In practice, the majority of LCRs are issued by the debtor, who accepts and sends the LCR to the creditor, with both instruments truncated when cleared. Customers are notified about the value of the payment four days in advance through the use of an electronic or paper-based advice (*relevé*).

Due to the complexity of the range of credit transfers and other instruments, the National SEPA Committee made the decision to move simple products to SEPA SCT and SDD schemes, but to keep the more complex credit transfers, as well as interbank payment orders (*TIP*), electronic payment orders (*télérèglement*), promissory notes and bills of exchange until a later date. The date will be announced before the end of 2007 further to work with the EPC.

3.2 Germany

End of 2004 (see Figure 6):

- 2295 credit institutions, including 397 commercial banks;
- almost 1900 savings, co-operative and rural banks;
- Deutsche Postbank is one of the largest providers of retail services;
- 121 foreign banks, including all the international cash management banks.

Payment Systems:

- RTGS: RTGSplus;
- ACH: RPS (also known as Elektronischer Massenzahlungsverkehr or EMZ.).

	Millions of transactions		% change	Traffic (EUR billion)		% change
	2003	2004	03/04	2003	2004	03/04
Cheques	133.3	112.7	−15.4	674.6	567.8	−15.8
Credit transfers	5839.0	6241.7	6.9	28 893.6	29 289.7	1.4
Direct debits	5541.7	6156.6	11.1	3346.0	3443.3	2.9
Debit cards	1670.3	1869.0	11.9	109.3	115.7	5.8
Credit cards	346.2	367.4	6.1	31.1	34.4	10.6
Card-based e-money	37.4	38.3	2.5	0.08	0.08	ø
Total	**13 567.9**	**14 785.7**	**9.0**	**33 054.6**	**33 450.9**	**1.2**

Payment statistics *Source:* ECB Blue Book statistical update, March 2006

As the home of the European Central Bank in Frankfurt, Germany's main centralised payment systems should be highly geared towards SEPA from the start, with the Bundesbank describing their role as being the link between the German banking industry and the political decision-making process in the Eurosystem. Therefore, it is surprising that Germany are one of the last to issue a National SEPA Migration Plan.

On the one hand, it is true that the TARGET2 connected RTGSplus high value clearing systems of the Bundesbank, combined with their retail payments ACH operations of RPS, which has been linked to STEP2 for cross-border euro payments since 2003, is a good start. In fact, a specific advantage that comes out of this is that all German banks can be directly accessed via RPS since they hold accounts at the Bundesbank.

In addition, the Bundesbank has had very active involvement in the EPC working groups, and established equivalent groups within Germany to interpret and outline implementation plans for SCT, SDD, SCF and SECA at the national level. They also cooperate with the German Banking Industry through the Central Credit Committee (CCC) that comprises the five central associations of the German banking industry. The CCC, Bundesbank and the banking industry are all working hard to outline the strategy for implementing SEPA in Germany as a result.

All of this is fine in principle but, in reality, Germany has no central payment structures as the banking industry's strongly decentralised three-pillar structure of private, public and co-operative banks, means that no central settlement structures emerged in Germany, unlike in other countries. In fact, it is one of the most fragmented banking markets in Europe with the public sector Sparkassen savings banks and the regional state-owned Landesbanks dominating the retail market, while the large private banks – Deutsche Bank, Commerzbank and Dresdner Bank – rule investment banking.

For these reasons, there is no central Automated Clearing House (ACH) specifically for Germany itself. In this sense Germany has developed in a different system to many other European countries inside the euro area, apart from Austria, Finland and Ireland that also have no national ACH.

The result is that German savings banks and co-operatives are so fragmented that they will not be able to adapt to domestic clearing through a SEPA-compliant Bundesbank by 2008, nor will they be able to implement SEPA-compliant SDD and SCT instruments themselves.

This lack of a national SEPA migration strategy with transparency for planned developments for all parties involved – banks, business companies and consumers – is Germany's current major challenge and weakness. Until the Bundesbank and the CCC come up with a published approach to SEPA, which was still lacking in summer 2007, there is a distinct concern around Germany's future fitness for SEPA.

Based upon traditional experiences within the German domestic payment markets, separation of the domestic procedures and their evolution to SEPA instruments will only take place in the medium to long term, and certainly will not be before 2010.

3.3   Italy

March 2006:

- the Italian banking market has been fragmented and localised, as laws prevented bank mergers until the reform of the markets in the 1990's;
- the reforms led to the number of banks falling from 1 156 in 1990 to 788 in 2006;
- there are now 246 commercial banks, 38 co-operative banks, 439 mutual banks and 68 foreign banks.

Payment Systems:

- RTGS: BI-REL, recently upgraded for SWIFTNet;
- ACH: BI-COMP which uses SIA's Rete Dettaglio for electronic payments and Banca Italia's Recapiti Locali for paper payments;
- RPS (also known as Elektronischer Massenzahlungsverkehr or EMZ).

	Millions of transactions		% change	Traffic (EUR billion)		% change
	2003	2004	03/04	2003	2004	03/04
Cheques	505.8	487.2	−3.7	1180.1	1186.8	0.6
Debit cards	610.7	672.0	10.0	50.9	58.0	14.1
Credit cards	374.0	433.6	15.9	35.1	42.0	19.8
Credit transfers	1018.4	1048.8	3.0	3998.1	4203.0	5.1
Direct debits	414.4	453.2	9.4	234.6	274.3	16.9
E-money	2.7	14.8	439.1	0.18	0.95	427.8
Other instruments	306.8	319.2	4.1	616.4	658.9	6.9
Total	**3232.8**	**3428.8**	**6.1**	**7053.3**	**7536.5**	**6.9**

Payment statistics *Source:* ECB Blue Book statistical update, March 2006

Italy has created an ad-hoc organisation to guide and monitor the implementation of SEPA with the National SEPA Migration Committee co-chaired by the Italian Bankers' Association

(ABI) and Banca d'Italia, and attended by representatives of the main payments stakeholders including corporates, public administration, merchants and consumers.

The National Migration Plan was published in May 2007. Similar to the French experience, Italy has a range of products that are non-standard, such as the Riba mentioned earlier.

If it should prove difficult to serve the needs of Italian users through the instruments envisaged in the EPC's Rulebooks then 'every possible effort' will be made to close the gap between the basic instruments and those currently provided by the Italian banking system by means of Additional Optional Services (AOS).

For example, Italy has gradually moved away from paper-based credit transfers but these still exist in volume in two forms:

- *Mediante Avviso* (MAV) is a paper-based giro system where the creditor's bank sends a payment form to the debtor, which the debtor can pay in at any bank or post office branch in Italy with settlement through BI-COMP's 'Rete Dettaglio'; and
- *Bollettino Bancario* is a new paper-based system which is similar to MAV but can be printed and mailed by the creditor, rather than the creditor's bank.

Italy's greater challenge is in the areas of direct debits where there are a range of non-standard products with pre-authorised direct debits commonly used for regular low-value payments, such as utility bills, insurance and instalment payments, as well as non pre-authorised direct debit products used to collect trade credits and bills of exchange.

The two main products are:

- *Rapporti Interbancari Diretti* (RID): a fully automated pre-authorised direct debit system where debtors sign a mandate for their creditor allowing the creidtor's bank to draw payments at reulgatr intervals; and
- *Ricevuta Bancaria Elettronica* (RiBa) is an electronic collection instrument that is gradually replacing paper-based collection methods where the creditor requires the debtor's agreement to collect receivables each time a payment is required; in effect, RiBa's are used by firms to collect trade and other credits, as well as using bank receipts as a form of bill of exchange.

As a result, although adoption of SEPA frameworks will start in 2008 for simple credit transfers and direct debits, AOS is likely to be made available for credit transfers and direct debits in the following areas:

Credit Transfers

- fixed value-dates for beneficiaries allowing the payment originator to determine the value date for the beneficiary customer;
- credit transfer at beneficiary's initiative allowing the originator to specify the banking details for the debit but not to alter the amount with the time required to execution dependent upon how long the executing banks take; and
- execution report to originator and beneficiary and credit reports to the originator.

Direct Debits

- The existing interbank service in support of the RID procedure, permitting central electronic management of the various types of RID mandates.

- 'Fast' direct debit allowing a SEPA Direct Debit to be enhanced with the specific function of Italy's fast RID procedure.
- Development of a SEPA-DD initiation and reporting messages for the customer-to-bank and bank-to-customer domain.

These AOS will be agreed between the banking system and the other stakeholders, and then promoted as appropriate for usage in other regions of the EU. In other words, Italy wants to maintain the existing MAV, RID and RiBa functionality through their AOS and persuade the EPC that these are good enhancements for the EPC Rulebooks.

This approach is unlikely to succeed – if they were appropriate, they would have been included in the published Rulebooks – and so Italy is likely to have both a SEPA-compliant service and domestic non-SEPA compliant set of products that will be converged over time.

3.4   Spain

2006:

- 73 commercial banks, 47 savings banks and 85 credit co-operatives;
- 55 representative offices and 68 branches of foreign banks;
- foreign bank presence is fairly limited however and most banks operate small branch footprints serving remote communities.

Payment Systems:

- RTGS: Servicio de Liquidación de Banco de España (SLBE);
- ACH: Sistema Nacional de Compensación (SNCE).

	Millions of transactions		% change	Traffic (EUR billion)		% change
	2003	2004	03/04	2003	2004	03/04
Cheques	277.0	214.4	21.2	1053.7	910.3	−13.6
Credit transfers	622.1	731.6	17.6	2536.6	7057.7	178.2
Direct debits	1383.0	2118.2	53.2	459.9	770.9	67.6
Debit cards	630.9	692.8	9.8	27.5	30.6	11.2
Credit cards	465.4	578.1	24.2	28.5	35.4	24.3
Card-based e-money	1.3	0.6	−54.7	0.00	0.00	0
Other instruments	–	130.8	–	448.6	–	
Total	**3279.6**	**4466.4**	**36.2**	**4106.1**	**9253.4**	**125.4**

Payment statistics *Source:* ECB Blue Book statistical update, March 2006

Spain published its national migration plan for SEPA in May 2007 and has a similar approach and challenge to that of France and Italy, namely a number of non-SEPA standard direct debit and credit transfer products. For example, direct debits are commonly used for low-value recurring payments, such as utility bills and insurance premia, but they can be given a maturity date, such as *anticipos de credito* and *efectos comerciales*. As a result, these products are increasingly being used as bills of exchange for short-term financing purposes. Therefore, it is interesting to see that the Spanish Migration Plan clearly states that bills of exchange are not within the migration plan!

According to the published document, there are two forms of payments instrument: those that are susceptible to migrate and those that are not. The chart in the plan is shown below:

Susceptible to Migrate	Not Susceptible to Migrate
Utility bills and other direct debits	Cheques and petrol cheques
Card purchases and cash withdrawals	Bills of exchange
Credit transfers	Others (fund transfers, diverse operations, etc.)

Payment Operations Supported by Banking Instruments (Broad Classification) *Source:* Spain's SEPA Migration Plan, May 2007

Therefore, credit transfers, yes. Low-value recurring payments via direct debit, yes. Other forms of direct debit payment, no. That is why the Spanish banking community is committed to meet the 2008 and 2010 milestones for credit transfers and for cards, but not for direct debits.

The Spanish plan also notes that the new SEPA instruments have some peculiarities in operation which may affect the roll-out. For example, where the Spanish practice in relation to customer's fees is based upon whoever initiates a payments transaction bears the costs. This is different from the way SEPA payments will work, which promotes the sharing of costs between the issuer and the beneficiary.

Spanish payments have other peculiarities including differentiated processing of certain operations such as credit transfers for payroll and pension payments and for those exceeding € 50,000.

For all of the reasons above, it will be surprising if Spain has fully implemented SEPA-compliant payment instruments by the end of 2010.

3.5 Netherlands

2006:

- 95 commercial banks including the co-operative Rabobank;
- 7 securities credit institutions, 4 savings banks and 4 mortgage banks;
- 31 foreign bank branches.

Payment Systems:

- RTGS: TOP (managed by DNB);
- ACH: Interpay Nederland BV (rebranded Equens in September 2006).

	Millions of transactions		% change	Traffic (EUR billion)		% change
	2003	2004	03/04	2003	2004	03/04
Debit cards	1157.1	1247.1	7.8	53.9	56.7	5.3
Credit and delayed debit cards	44.1	48.5	10.0	4.9	5.3	6.5
Credit transfers	1271.4	1264.2	−0.6	3715.9	4340.0	16.8
– *Paper-based*	*315.8*	*291.6*	*−7.7*	*497.1*	*380.1*	*−23.5*
– *Electronic*	*955.6*	*972.6*	*1.8*	*3218.8*	*3960.0*	*23.0*
Direct debits	1000.8	1051.3	5.1	211.5	219.2	3.7
Card-based e-money	109.2	127.3	16.6	0.30	0.35	16.7
Total	**3582.5**	**3738.4**	**4.4**	**3986.5**	**4621.6**	**15.9**

Payment statistics *Source:* ECB Blue Book statistical update, March 2006

Being the home of the EPC's Chairman, Gerard Hartsink, and next door to Brussels, the Netherlands National Migration Plan is probably the most comprehensive of the published national plans, and was released in June 2007.

The Dutch SEPA plans started when the banks formed a SEPA Migration Steering Group in early 2007 together with DNB, the RTGS system, and Currence. Currence operate many of the Dutch payment schemes, including the direct debit and acceptgiro system for bill payments, PIN for point of sale payments, and the e-purse Chipknip.

As can be seen from the list of Currence's products and the payment statistics shown, the Netherlands is quite different to most other countries in their use of payments instruments as they are heavily oriented towards electronic payments already via direct debits and credit transfers, as well as being one of the few European countries that has successfully eradicated the use of cheques. This is because the Netherlands has many innovative payment instruments including:

- domestic one-off and recurrent fast payments for credit transfers;
- direct debits for payments to both consumers, companies and for special purposes like lotteries;
- a Dutch application of e-invoicing in the business to consumer market called *digitale nota* from Rabobank; and
- iDEAL is provided as a secure customer/bank interface for online payments to internet shops.

Figure 9 shows the relative volumes of payments made with these instruments.

In terms of cross-border payments, similar to most other Eurozone countries, the Netherlands has a low volume of cross-border payments representing around 2 % of total payment volumes, or 70 million transactions. Of these, 15 % are credit transfers and 85 % are debit card or credit

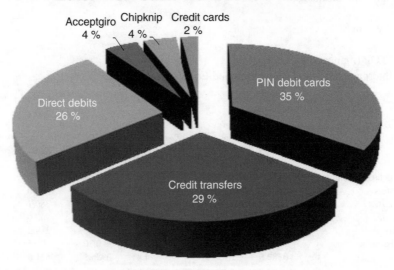

Dutch Non-Cash Transaction Volumes

Figure 9   Dutch Payments by Transaction Volumes, 2006

card payments, with 17 out of 20 transactions being made to another account within the European Union. Pre-SEPA, cross-border direct debits do not exist.

As a result of looking at SEPA's implications however, the Dutch banks are scrapping most of their existing credit transfer, direct debit and debit card products and replacing them with three new payment products from 2008: SEPA credit transfers, SEPA direct debits and SEPA debit card payments. In other words, the Dutch products that existed pre-2008 are non-SEPA compliant and will be phased out.

The fact that these products represented 92 % of total domestic non-cash has not stopped the banking industry classifying these as legacy products. The result is that the Dutch will maintain them in coexistence with the new SEPA products until migration is completed[23] whilst, for the other 8 % of products, a decision as to whether or not to migrate these products to a SEPA version will be made on a product by product basis.

3.6   United Kingdom

2006:

- 161 UK banks dominated by the Big 5: RBOS, HBOS, HSBC, Barclays and Lloyds TSB;
- 176 branches of foreign banks, although most of these are purely present in the City of London.

Payment Systems:

- RTGS: NewCHAPS (Clearing House Automated Payment System);
- ACH: NewBACS (BACSTEL-IP, operated by Vocalink).

	Millions of transactions		% change	Traffic (EUR billion)		% change
	2003	2004	03/04	2003	2004	03/04
Cheques	2251	2089	−7.2	1843.3	1779.6	−3.5
Credit Transfers	2211.5	2600.7	17.6	74 859.8	76 514.2	2.2
– Paper-based	370.5	364.7	−1.6	195.7	187.3	−4.3
– Electronic	1841	2236	21.5	74 664.1	76 326.9	2.2
Direct debits	2429.9	2589.9	6.6	662.2	750.4	13.3
Card payments	5185	5639	8.8	243.9	273.0	11.9
Total	12 077.4	12 918.6	7.0	77 609.2	79 317.2	2.2

Payment statistics *Source:* ECB Blue Book statistical update, March 2006

The UK is not part of the Eurozone and therefore has no SEPA Migration Plan as it does not apply to the country, only to euro payments made into and out of the UK. Therefore, whilst Eurozone banks have been frantically running around trying to sort out the implications of SEPA for their infrastructure and operations, most UK banks have been more focused upon other matters, such as the Office of Fair Trading's rules for Faster Payments.

Faster Payments was launched in May 2005 as a result of the Office of Fair Trading Payments Task Force concluding that banks were using the clearing and settlement cycle to generate unwarranted fee income at the expense of their customers. This was because a typically payment would require three days to clear, and hence a bank could use that time to generate interest income on what is called their 'float' of funds.

---

[23] No date was set for the end-point of migration at the time of writing.

Fast Payments is therefore a government-mandated requirement for UK banks to offer their customers near real-time payments rather than the traditional three-day clearing cycles.

The target is for payments of values up to £ 10,000 (€ 15,000) that are made over the Internet or via the telephone must be guaranteed to reach the beneficiary's bank account within two hours. This service must also be available 24 hours a day, seven days a week.

The result will be lower payments volumes processed through the national RTGS, CHAPS, at far lower cost, and will be implemented in May 2008. This is six months later than originally planned – the OFT had demanded implementation for 1 November 2007 – but is due to systems development challenges for the clearing system being developed by Vocalink, the UK's ACH.

A significant factor within the Faster Payments process is that it also expands the offerings available to corporates by allowing them to gain direct access to clearing and settlement through Vocalink. This is because over 25 000 corporates have been using direct access to Vocalink in the past for credit transfers and direct debits. This is different to most European ACHs, apart from Equens and some Nordic ACHs, where corporates typically send their payment files to the bank to store and forward onwards to the ACH.

In fact, it is for these reasons that Vocalink and Equens have both been very active in their focus upon winning PE-ACH capabilities longer-term, and supports the discussions outlined in the earlier Section on SEPA's implications for low-value clearing and settlement as shown in Figure 5.

Nevertheless, although the UK's Faster Payments challenge is a key priority and underpins the objectives of the PSD's D+1 payments cycles, there is a greater question for the UK: *Is SEPA relevant?*

The UK is outside the Eurozone but is affected by SEPA as the PSD applies to all European Union countries. Therefore, the D+1 payment cycles, legal framework and related matters within the PSD will apply to the UK, Sweden, the EEA, Switzerland and other non-euro countries from November 2009, when the PSD is transposed into national law in all European Union nations.

For most of these nations, the view is to treat euro as just another foreign currency, and this certainly appears to be true for most UK domestic banks and bankers.

This view is wrong however, as there are considerable changes required in the UK to be SEPA-compliant, not the least of which are the IBAN and BIC requirements which the UK banks have successfully managed to force through.

This view of SEPA being irrelevant however is not surprising, as the assumption for most banks is that SEPA just requires euro-to-euro cross-border payments being treated as domestic payments. Today, to make a euro payment is pretty much impossible as a simple transaction in any UK bank. You cannot process euro payments online, nor can you write a euro cheque or get euro notes from a UK bank's ATM.

This is all about to change.

It is obvious that with the introduction of the PSD and SEPA, we will have all of Europe's Eurozone banks able to process cross-border payments at the same price and costs as domestic payments from 1 January 2008. Having harmonised their infrastructures and reduced costs, the banks that are most aggressive in the SEPA community will then target expansion across that geography, as discussed in Section 2.2 in relation to Bank M&A.

Once this is in play, the euro geography is not just within the Eurozone as much trade takes place outside the thirteen countries which are now euro-based. So what would stop a bank from

Holland or France or Spain considering opportunities within the UK, Sweden and Denmark for euro services ... or even domestic to euro services.

UK banks will then need to consider carefully their attitudes towards the opportunities and threats created by SEPA and the newly harmonized Eurozone of banks. If the European Commission really do create a single European financial marketplace, which is the aim, then UK banks ignoring these changes will surely be likened to the proverbial ostrich with its head stuck in the sand.

What UK banks should really be doing about SEPA and the Eurozone is looking to build a dual-currency strategy towards UK operations. For example, fly through many European airports these days and, if you insert a UK bank card, you will be presented with making the payment in euro or UK pounds sterling. That is a dual currency payment point.

As a result, the truly innovative banks will begin to create more and more dual currency payment points. Dual-currency ATMs, dual currency internet sites and dual currency cheque books.

UK citizens will be able to use bank services in sterling and euro's seamlessly, and will be charged the same price and costs for sterling and euro transactions. If UK banks do not do this, then European banks operating in the UK will definitely see this as an opportunity with Allied Irish Bank, Bank of Ireland, ING Direct and Santander all eagerly anticipating market growth opportunities.

The implications of a dual-currency UK may sound simple as relatively few transactions are cross-border transactions between sterling and euro, and those that fall into such categories are likely to be handled through Vocalink as a euro Clearing and Settlement Mechanism (€ CSM).

Vocalink signed up a range of bank partners including ABN Amro, Bank of America, Citi, Dexia Bank, Fortis, Lloyds TSB, RBS and Santander, and launched the VocaLink € CSM partnership in July 2007. This service will provide banks and their clients with services for the SEPA from January 2008 by using the infrastructure of the member banks, who are both partners and clients.

Simple.

Well, things are never as simple as that. For example, what happens when a euro cheque payment is made from a UK account? How could a UK bank handle a European organisation's payroll if that credit transfer needed to be made using euro denominated payments? Could a UK bank easily handle direct debits from consumers to Spanish water and electricity firms?

The answer today is that none of these requirements are addressed. The UK's BACS and APACS operations do not conform to SEPA rulebooks and infrastructures for credit transfers (SCT), direct debits, cards and cash. There has been and is no intention publicly for this to be the case for UK banks in the near-term future.

That is why the latest 'World Payments Report' produced by EFMA states that 57 % of UK payments products fall significantly short of SEPA-compliance, with only credit and debit card services coming close. For cheques, credit transfers and direct debits, the UK's infrastructure falls significantly short of SEPA-compliance.

To be SEPA-compliant, UK banks need to take a number of actions. They particularly need to find a cheap way to process euro credit transfers and direct debits to and from other EU banks. This may be achieved through SWIFT or Vocalink services, although that will still leave a heavy internal overhead for processing payments to and from euro's.

The net:net is that Vocalink are playing a critical role in making the UK SEPA-compliant, but the domestic bank's attitudes of the euro just being a foreign currency is far too simplistic and misses the point. It will be interesting to see how the UK's competitive position lays out into the future.

3.7   Nordics

Similar to the Baltic and Eastern Europe countries, the Nordic countries of Sweden, Norway, Denmark, Iceland and Finland face SEPA challenges. However, the region has a few fundamental differences. In particular, there are a small number of regional banks in existence who recognise that the pan-European passport for payments offered by SEPA is both a threat and an opportunity, as outlined in the comments from Nordea in Section 2.2. These regional banks have considerable legacy payments infrastructures and now have to incorporate SEPA to service clients in Finland as part of their regional presence.

Therefore, it is expected that Nordea, as well as DNB Nor, Sampo, Danske, Hansa and others, will provide a two-tier payments operation incorporating both the existing and future SEPA instruments.

The aim is to allow Nordic banks to run a dual-currency operation, where non-SEPA countries continue to use non-SEPA instruments but are able to exploit SEPA-style credit transfers and direct debits. After all, SEPA-compliant instruments have to be offered within Finland so why not offer those instruments in the other Nordic countries for both cross-border and, if desired, domestic payments. For example, Nordea state that outside Finland for 'the other Nordic countries, in the Baltics and in Poland the new SEPA services will be adopted in euro-denominated payments only, i.e. mainly in cross-border payments'.[24]

This is why the banks have been working closely with Microsoft and other technology firms to develop SEPA-compliant services for corporate-to-bank connectivity using ISO20022 standards, alongside XML, SOAP and other services linked to SWIFTNet.

Therefore, to understand the Nordic strategy for SEPA, the best idea is to look at the Finnish strategy for SEPA with the expectation that when these services are in place, most Nordic banks will be able to offer such services for cross-border euro payments in Sweden, Norway, Denmark and Iceland.

	Millions of transactions		% change	Traffic (EUR billion)		% change
	2003	2004	03/04	2003	2004	03/04
Cheques	1	1	ø	62	50	−19.4
Credittransfers	569	573	0.7	3754.9	3725.2	−0.8
– paper-based	*58*	*52*	*−10.3*	*357.5*	*377.9*	*5.7*
– electronic	*511*	*521*	*2.0*	*3397.4*	*3347.3*	*−1.5*
Direct debits	64	85	32.8	25.9	35.7	37.8
Card payments	518	585	12.9	19.7	21.8	10.7
Card-based e-money	1	1	ø	0.00	0.00	–
Total	**1153**	**1244**	**7.9**	**3862.47**	**3832.62**	**−0.8**

Finland's statistics *Source:* ECB Blue Book statistical update, March 2006

In Finland, the SEPA Migration Plan was first published in March 2006 and hence is one of the first nations to issue a national plan. This plan states that Finland believes the SCT is a

---

[24] Nordea Finland SEPA Fact Sheet.

'well-founded basic model for payments'[25] which should maintain the high quality of Finnish credit transfer services; the SCF is seen as credible as well, with each bank at its own discretion to introduce SEPA-compliant card products in the euro area no later than 1 January 2008; but that the SDD has too many issues related to 'customer demand, profitability and risks' for the Finnish banks to commit to implementation.

This response is not surprising as Finland's payments profile is very different to other European countries. Almost 100 % of payments made electronically via cards and credit transfers as in the chart of Finland's statistics. Nevertheless, direct debit usage is increasing rapidly with a particular focus upon direct invoicing.

Finland is fairly unique in this respect, in that they have created a new e-invoicing standard called Finvoice.[26] Finvoice is an electronic standard designed to replace paper invoices with electronic invoices using XML standards with rapid take-up amongst the corporate community. This standard is a critical focus for the European Commission where, as already mentioned in Section 2.2, e-invoicing is seen as a critical platform for the Single Payments Area in the future. With a potential € 50 billion of savings this is not surprising.

Therefore, the Nordic example is actually a leading example of payments at the electronic edge. The core resistance to the current SDD model is therefore of some concern, but more in the context of how Nordic customers view the direct debit product itself, rather than the SDD scheme. As a result, this should cause less concern than perhaps it would at first sight. Of more concern is the usage and success of Finland's e-invoicing standards and their applicability to the rest of Europe.

3.8 Eastern Europe

Eastern Europe has undergone a transformation to enable these countries to join the European Union. In financial services and payments, this has been a major challenge for some of the countries but not for others.

Those who will find adapting to the euro world easier include the Czech Republic and Hungary, where companies can use strong liquidity management practices, such as zero balancing and cash pooling, without restriction. Similarly, the Czech Republic, Hungary, Slovakia and Slovenia allow inter-company loans and pooling which has made them more attractive to foreign investors. These countries also had the benefit of easily moving into the age of electronic payments and paperless clearing.

This is not the case in Poland, where local tax and company laws not only restrict money movements across-borders but also domestically, as intercompany loans are managed through tight regulations that effectively mean corporations are unable to use common liquidity practices, such as cash pooling and zero balancing. Poland's legal framework also prevented legal entities from sharing cash in a common account, even if those entities belong to the same parent company, and all payments over € 10,000 had to be accompanied by documentation for the central bank.

Nevertheless, the Baltic states of Latvia, Lithuania, Estonia, and Poland have very modern information technology (IT) systems for national clearings and payments, with the other states having far less restrictive regulatory frameworks for cash pooling. The fact that all of these nations had no ACH to speak of means that the access to and use of the EBA Clearing

---

[25] http://www.pankkiyhdistys.fi/sisalto/upload/pdf/SEPAimplementation2006.pdf.
[26] See http://www.pankkiyhdistys.fi/finvoice/

mechanism is a major bonus. In addition, the fact that these countries were left behind, in terms of electronic banking during the Soviet era, means that they have now leapfrogged a generation of IT systems since the opening of their borders. This means they do not have the ties of legacy systems that other European banks are running and trying to phase out, and have easily transitioned to modern payment infrastructures that are easily able to support and transition towards SEPA compliant instruments.

Moreover, in all four countries there are clear trends that will rely on further investment in modern IT, most notably the growing use of electronic banking solutions, whether PC-based or internet-based. This is why Slovenia achieved euro conversion in January 2006, only two years after joining the EU, whilst Poland's legal framework will make them the last of the ten Eastern European countries to adopt the euro sometime in 2010 or shortly thereafter.[27]

All of this does not mean that every country can simply adapt to SEPA compliant markets though, as there are more challenges than having new systems and legal structures.

For example, in the case of the two countries that used to be one, Slovakia and the Czech Republic, domestic clearing is through non-SWIFT utilities. As a result, Slovakia has decided that domestic euro processing will continue through the local Slovak Inter-bank Payment System, SIPS. This is to allow local banks to continue clearing without having ot adapt their transaction systems. This will be for processing only however, over time, as the settlement and liquidity processes will be managed by banks becoming direct participants in TARGET2. In other words, the major SEPA instruments of D+1 payments and improved corporate liquidity services will only be available through TARGET2 clearing and settlement of payments. This is another reason why TARGET2's two-thirds proportions of payments under € 50,000 will increase.

Generally, however, Eastern Europe is much more SEPA-ready than the rest of Europe.

---

[27] It should be noted that these timeframes are not only related to domestic payment structures and company law challenges, but also related to issues of meeting the EMU requirements of interest rates and unemployment.

Part 1
The Views of the Architects

- the European Payments Council
- the European Central Bank
- the European Commission
- the European Parliamentarian

1

The EPC and the Single Euro Payments Area (SEPA): It's now up to the banks and their customers!

Gerard Hartsink, the EPC

How were all of these frameworks, rulebooks and guidelines developed and what is their current state? A brief review of the core SEPA instruments and tools is outlined with background to how they were developed.

The SEPA project has entered into a critical phase with the official launch of SEPA on 28 January 2008. The realisation of SEPA is seen as essential to enable the vision of the European Community. That vision was committed to in the Lisbon Agenda of 2000 by the Heads of State and Governments to make the EU 'the most competitive and knowledge driven economy by 2010'.

The European authorities expect that the self regulatory initiative from the payment industry will lead to SEPA. The vision of the payments industry was released in a White Paper in 2002 and was subsequently incorporated into the preamble of the charter of the European Payments Council (EPC), being that the members 'share the common vision that Euroland payments are domestic payments; join forces to implement this vision for the benefit of customers, industry and banks; and accordingly launch our Single Payments Area'.

The EPC has continuously met its commitments and delivery, as worded in the Roadmap 2004–2010, delivering to the industry the frameworks, business rules and standards for SEPA. It is now time for the individual banks to honour that commitment and to make that commitment a reality for their customers.

1.1 EPC ROADMAP 2004–2010

In December 2004, the EPC Plenary approved its Roadmap 2004–2010 for SEPA. In the Roadmap it was agreed that: 'SEPA will be the area where citizens, companies and other economic actors will be able to make and receive payments in euro within Europe, whether between, or within national boundaries, under the same basic conditions, rights and obligations, regardless of their location'.

The content of the Roadmap was reviewed in the first quarter of 2005 by all EPC members and by all banking communities, in particular in the euro area. The aim was to ensure that the objectives, scope, deliverables, timelines and roles for SEPA, were also supported by non-members and the national banking communities.

Based on the feedback of the members and national banking communities, the EPC Plenary concluded that the EPC Roadmap was indeed supported and approved as stated in the EPC Crown Plaza Declaration of 17 March 2005 with the focus on the primary EPC deliverables:

> We will deliver the two new Pan-Euro Payment Schemes for electronic credit transfer and for direct debits. We will also design a Cards Framework to define a single market for cards. The scheme rulebooks and the cards framework definition will be delivered by end 2005, and the services will become operational from January 2008.
>
> We know from feedback from the community in the Eurozone that by the beginning of 2008 the vast majority of banks will offer these new Pan-Euro services to their customers. We are also convinced that a critical mass of transactions will naturally migrate to these payment instruments by 2010 such that SEPA will be irreversible through the operation of market forces and network effects.
>
> SEPA will be delivered by the banking industry in close conjunction with all stakeholder communities (consumers, SME's, merchants, corporates and government bodies) and supportive public authorities. The community of European banks is strongly committed to this ambitious programme of action, based on self-regulation and a full recognition of the role of market forces and competition.

The EPC Plenary did meet the expectations of the regulators for the January 2008 deliverables for credit transfers, direct debits and for cards. The deliverables of the value added service, such as priority payments and e-invoicing, are being handled by the Euro Banking Association.

Next to the primary deliverables of the EPC Roadmap, complementary deliverables such as for cash, e-payments for web retailers, and mobile payments, have been or will be approved.

It is however worth stressing that the EPC is a decision making body and has primarily a design, support and monitoring role. It is now up to the banks and their national communities to take the lead for the implementation and migration plans. These implementation plans of the euro countries are available on http://www.sepa.eu.

1.2   PUBLICATIONS AVAILABLE ON HTTP://WWW.EUROPEANPAYMENTSCOUNCIL.EU

- EPC Roadmap 2004–2010 – December 2004
- EPC Crown Plaza Declaration – March 2005
- SEPA Cards Framework – March 2006
- SECA (Cash) Framework – March 2006
- UNIFI (ISO20022) XML standards approved by ISO see http://www.ISO20022.org – July 2006
- EPC CSM/PE-ACH Framework – July 2006
- SEPA Communication document 'Making SEPA a Reality' – August 2006
- SEPA Credit Transfer Scheme Rulebook and the Implementation Guidelines Version 2.3 – June 2007
- SEPA Direct Debit Scheme Rulebook and the Implementation Guidelines Version 2.3 – June 2007

1.3   PROGRESS FOR CREDIT TRANSFERS AND DIRECT DEBITS

The EPC pursued a strategy to replace the current Euro credit transfer and direct debit instruments with SEPA instruments. The business rules and standards are set out in the Scheme

Rulebooks for the new SEPA Credit Transfers and SEPA Direct Debit payment instruments and are complemented by the Implementation Guidelines.

The legal model for the SEPA credit transfer and SEPA direct debits are based on "adherence agreements' of Banks and of Payments Institutions participating in the two schemes, with the EPC as the Scheme Management Entity (SME).

In June 2007 the EPC approved the structure for both a SEPA Credit Transfer Scheme and a SEPA Direct Debit Scheme. The two Scheme Rulebooks mainly cover the mandatory business rules and standards (ISO20022 XML) for the bank-to-bank space and the recommended standards for the bank-to-customer space.

The EPC decided recently for the principle to take care that the same Implementation guidelines will be used for the bank-to-corporates space in SEPA. These are the basis for the value propositions of banks for their customers. Banks compete with their value propositions for core and for added value payments services. The Rulebooks will allow the banks and payment institutions to offer SEPA credit transfers and direct debits to their customers throughout SEPA.

The ECB has accepted the EPC's Plenary decision that those banks, whose payment volumes represent the critical mass of payments, should be capable of both sending and receiving SEPA credit transfers from 28 January 2008. The remaining smaller banks are all expected to receive SEPA credit transfers from 28 January 2008, and should be able to send them in the course of 2008. On 28 January about 4,100 had signed the adherence agreement.[1]

The initial launch of SEPA direct debit products was scheduled for January 2008, and it was expected that a critical mass of transactions would have migrated to the new scheme by the end of 2010. On account of delays in the adoption of the Payments Services Directive (PSD), the EPC has stated that because of legal uncertainty banks cannot launch the scheme in January 2008. A new launch date is expected to be agreed for availability by November 2009.

1.4 PROGRESS FOR CARDS

The EPC strategy for cards is an adaptation strategy approved by the EPC Plenary in March 2006. This strategy decided to develop the SEPA Cards Framework (SCF) with high level principles and rules for banks, card schemes and card processors. This will enable European customers to use general purpose cards to make and receive payments and cash withdrawals in euro throughout the SEPA area, with the same ease and convenience as they do in their home country.

Banks are expected to start delivering SEPA Cards Framework (SCF) compliant services from January 2008 to their customers – both consumers and merchants – and to ensure that payments scheme(s) in which they participate become SCF compliant.

The Eurosystem (ECB) made it clear in their SEPA for Cards Report of November 2006 that more standardisation is expected for the different parts of the card payments process. The EPC has responded positively by taken a coordinating role in the definition of card standards, bringing together existing standardisation initiation and developing business requirements in conjunction with these initiatives.

The EPC has set up a specific taskforce to review and formulate the four domains of the card transaction process where there is no industry-wide standardisation initiative. These domains are card-to-terminal, terminal-to-acquiring-host, acquiring-not-issuing-host and the certification process. Also non-bank stakeholders, merchants, card schemes processors and others participate in the work of the taskforce.

---

[1] See www.europeanpaymentscouncil.org

While banks, card schemes and processors are reviewing their options, the Eurosystem (ECB) decided to review the current status of these strategic dialogues. Jointly with the European Commission, they expressed their concerns that there might not be sufficient scheme competition left in the end game.

The ECB then strongly recommended in their Fifth Progress Report on SEPA, published in July 2007, that they expect that at least one additional European debit card scheme will be created. This will mainly be used in the euro area countries to enhance further competition. The ECB therefore encourages the EPC to review the option of creating a SEPA debit card scheme, in addition to the SEPA credit transfer and SEPA direct debit schemes.

The DG Competition of the European Commission also organised an inquiry into the competition of the current cards payments market in the European Union. Their findings were presented for consultation with a position paper from the Commission published early in 2007, mainly focused upon interchange fees and arrangements.

The EPC also received a questionnaire of DG Competition, with questions of the members of the European competition network on the SEPA Card Framework. The EPC responded to this questionnaire in September 2007 and the outcomes published will no doubt add further change to the cards markets. The EPC agreed with the DG Competition of the European Commission at the end of 2007, that they should give more clarification on the SEPA Cards Framework, which were published during 2008 on the EPC's website.

1.5   CLEARING AND SETTLEMENT MECHANISMS

The SEPA credit transfers, SEPA direct debits and the SEPA cards transactions, need to be cleared and settled in an efficient way. The settlements will be executed in central bank money via TARGET. The new Eurosystem's TARGET2 platform was also implemented in all Euro markets from November 2007 through the beginning of 2008.

The EPC developed a Clearing and Settlement PE-ACH Framework, allowing for five clearing venues for banks. Some banks prefer to continue with their bilateral clearing, whereas others are strong defenders of the PE-ACH model. A PE-ACH offers pan European reachability for euro clearing services to all banks.

EACHA, the European Automated Clearing House Association, has also worked on the development of an interoperability framework for retail payments, clearing and settlement infrastructure, and defined criteria that support a technical interoperability for information and settlement streams.

Finally, in their Fifth Progress Report of July 2007, the ECB published four criteria for the compliance of SEPA infrastructures. These criteria were submitted to the ECB and the EPC for consultation in May 2007.

1.6   PROGRESS FOR CASH

The EPC strategy regarding cash is focused on a two pillar strategy: reducing the costs of cash processing and repositioning cash as a payments instrument.

The Single Euro Cash Area (SECA) Framework was approved by the EPC Plenary in March 2006, and is focussed on reducing the processing costs of cash. In addition, a study by McKinsey published in 2005 made it clear that banks are losing at least € 21 billion on cash in nine of the EU27 markets. For this reason the EPC decided to formulate a document on the positioning of cash based on the lessons learned in several markets in Europe.

In February 2007, the ECB adopted a roadmap which made clear a number of medium term measures to increase convergence of cash services offered by euro area NCB's.

1.7   PROGRESS FOR M- AND E- PAYMENT CHANNELS

Progress has been made regarding the next steps for m- and e- payments. These emerging markets are still fragmented with many proprietary solutions and an increasing number of non-banking companies offering payments services dedicated to these payment channels. It therefore makes sense that banks agree on the business rules and standards for these payment channels.

The number of users and the services delivered by mobiles and by e-commerce is growing fast, and borderless solutions are required to meet the need of consumers and merchants.

The EPC will develop a framework with the business rules and standards for initiating payments for online merchants in the outline SEPA online payments. The EPC proposals will take into account the functionalities of the current national solutions. The SEPA on-line payments proposal is based upon the usage of the SEPA credit transfer. With respect to m-payment channels, the EPC decided to develop a framework with business rules and standards for the use of a mobile to initiate a SEPA payment.

1.8   COMMUNICATION

Communicating the benefits of SEPA for all the stakeholders, and for society, is essential for a successful migration to SEPA. The SEPA communication policy is coordinated by the ECB, the European Commission and the EPC.

The EPC developed a communication document *'Making SEPA a Reality'* for two audiences. Firstly for banks, for their marketing communications, training and so forth; and secondly for national banking associations, for their dialogues with all stakeholders in their communities.

The European Commission and the Eurosystem (ECB) intensified this communication with the launch of SEPA on 28 January 2008, in close cooperation with the EPC.

1.9   INVOLVEMENT OF END-USERS IN THE DESIGN PROCESS

End-users have been involved in the design process of the EPC's deliverables. Both the SEPA Credit Transfer Rulebook and the SEPA Direct Debit Rulebook were reviewed, approved and supported by corporates, and their national and European associations, such as the EACT. A Customer Stakeholder Forum also had the task to give input and feedback on further developments of the functionalities and standards for the two Rulebooks. The Customer Stakeholder Forum with representatives of European associations of corporates, SME's and consumers, evaluates the further developments of the standards of the two Rulebooks.

The EPC also gave the European Commission and the Eurosystem (ECB) several opportunities to provide their feedback for public administrations on these rulebooks.

1.10   IMPLEMENTATION OF JANUARY 2008 DELIVERABLES

The EPC Plenary made it clear in its Declaration of 17 March 2005 that banks are committed to deliver SEPA payments services from January 2008, and banks have designed these value propositions for their customers.

Banks and national communities are in the lead for realising the implementation. Banks have made substantial efforts to be ready for the launch of SEPA Credit Transfers on 28 January 2008. The SEPA Direct Debit services of banks will be launched by November 2009. The EPC will supply the support and tools to monitor this implementation, as stated in its mandate.

Several initiatives have been taken by the EPC to reduce the coordination risks of the implementation in the euro countries, such as the creation of the SEPA Testing Framework. Support is also given to a National Implementation Managers Forum.

Communication is a key element of the national implementation and migration plans. All national communities of the Euro area and other countries have published comprehensive national implementation plans. All these plans must be finalised and published by the end of 2007.[2] The EPC and the ECB, as well as national implementation committees with representations of the banks and of the users, are monitoring the implementation of SEPA.

1.11   SEPA AND OUR CUSTOMERS

Several bankers and banking associations have expressed their concern at the speed of customer acceptance for SEPA. This is due to the fact that, whilst European Associations of corporates and merchants have confirmed that they see the economic benefits of SEPA, the commitment of Public Administrations is not yet clear.

Both the Governing Council of the ECB and the European Commission stated in their joint statement of 4 May 2006 that Public Administrations should become launching customers for the new SEPA payments services.

The public procurement rules in the European Union are based on the principle that responses to a tender of public administrations for payments services should include more than just the national providers. This approach may lead to a better deal for the benefit of the tax payers.

In its Fifth Progress Report on SEPA, published in June 2007, the ECB expressed some concern regarding the readiness of public administrations. The ECB has urged them to take concrete actions by becoming operationally ready to send and receive SEPA payments by the start of SEPA in early 2008.

Several consumer organisations have expressed that they support the SEPA payment instruments, provided these instruments are as easy to use, safe and efficient as those they are currently using. This change for consumers is therefore limited.

The new euro SEPA payment instruments are in the majority of the cases an upgrade of the current payment instruments, with the additional feature of reachability to all bank accounts in the Euro area. The introduction of mobile telephones, internet and the euro was of a far greater significance for consumers than the replacement of the current payment instruments by SEPA payment instruments.

1.12   PAYMENT SERVICES DIRECTIVE

The realisation of SEPA requires harmonisation of the legislation by public authorities and harmonisation of business rules and standards by the industry.

In December 2005 the European Commission published its first proposal of the Payment Services Directive (PSD). Since then a lot of market participants, including the EPC, have given their comments on this proposal. The European Parliament and the Council of the European

---

[2] See: http://www.sepa.eu.

Union passed the final proposal for a Payment Services Directive of the European Commission in April 2007. All 27 EU Member States are transposing the PSD into their national law before November 2009.

This Directive provides the legal foundation to make SEPA possible. By harmonising the underlying legal framework for payment services, it will facilitate the operational implementation of SEPA payment instruments by the banking industry as well as their adoption by end-users.

The PSD also underpins consumer protection and enhances competition and innovation by establishing an appropriate prudential framework for new entrants to the market for retail payments.

Bankers however should not underestimate the impact of the PSD. Not all banks realise that the PSD will also apply to their current payments services and not only to the new SEPA payments services.

The PSD will not only apply to the euro, but to all currencies of the EU27.

1.13 ECONOMIC BENEFITS OF SEPA

Over time all customers, corporates, public administrations and consumers, are expected to benefit from SEPA. In the mean time various studies have been conducted to assess the cost and benefits of SEPA.

McKinsey clarified in their study 'European Payment Profit Pool Analysis' of June 2005 the importance of payments for the suppliers' side. In this study, they found that at least 24 % of banking revenues and 34 % of the banking cost and 9 % of the profits are related to payments. McKinsey also clarified that there are structural differences in the revenue models and for the instrument mix in the euro area. In some markets in the euro area customers pay more than others. Some countries and markets in the Eurozone have markets where the consumers are paying relatively more than corporates and vice versa.

The EPC will not take any position on the revenue models of banks, because this is beyond its mandate and in conflict with the correct behaviour required by the competition rules.

Nevertheless, in August 2007 the ECB published its Occasional Paper No. 61 'The Economic Impact of the Single Euro Payments Area'.[3] This paper concludes that the interest revenues and interchange commission for banks will be put under more and more pressure. Cost savings are expected to be possible by restructuring the processing functions, and several regulators have said they are in favour of such a development, because it gives more transparency to the customers and reduces the volatility of the profits, and so the risks, of banks.

The European Commission issued the conclusions of a study, "SEPA: potential benefits at stake", on 28 January 2008. This study was produced by CAP Gemini.[4] This study explains the potential impact on banks (supply side) and their customers (buy side) in four scenarios. It was concluded that the market as a whole could gain the most if banks and customers together moved forward to SEPA as early and complete as possible. In this scenario, € 123 billion of net accumulated benefits over six years for 16 of the EU27 countries is anticipated.

Banks gave their full commitment to the Single Euro Payments Area and empowered the EPC to make it happen. Now, in union, we must turn our SEPA vision into reality for the benefit of banks' customers.

---

[3] Heiko Schmeidel of the ECB provides a more in-depth review and analysis which summarises this paper in his chapter.
[4] http://ec.europa.eu/internal_market/payments/docs/sepa/sepa-capgemini_study-final_report-en.pdf

2

The economic impact of SEPA on Europe's banks

Heiko Schmiedel, the European Central Bank

In the short-term, SEPA will cost banks as it requires an investment alongside a parallel scheme where current national infrastructures run alongside new SEPA infrastructures. Long-term however, the business case is compelling and proven.

Despite the introduction of the euro banknotes and coins in 2002, a true 'domestic' and internal market for non-cash retail payments has so far not been achieved within the euro area. With the realisation of the Single Euro Payments Area (SEPA), this will be achieved as SEPA delivers a market where there will be no difference in the euro area between national and cross-border retail payments.

With its harmonisation and restructuring efforts, SEPA is an important driver in opening up the different national retail payment markets, allowing euro area-wide competition and fostering innovation in the euro area. Within SEPA, customers should be able to make and receive payments in euro throughout the Eurozone from and through a single bank account, using a single set of payment instruments, as easily and safely as in the national context today. This means that all payments within the euro area and in the common currency become domestic, without any difference in user experience between national or intra-euro area payment transactions.

The establishment of SEPA may also permit the different stakeholders to take opportunities and to benefit from potential economies of scale and scope, thereby increasing the overall economic efficiency of the payments industry. SEPA also entails shifts in service levels and the development of new, added value products for customers. This requires concerted efforts from various stakeholders, especially the banking industry, to align national practices.

The Eurosystem strongly supports the SEPA project and, in its catalyst role, the European Central Bank (ECB) closely monitors and assesses the overall development of SEPA.

So far only a limited number of industry and consultancy studies have been published addressing the potential impact of SEPA for different SEPA stakeholders. Based on different approaches, underlying methodologies, and assumptions, the existing literature does not provide a clear and balanced picture of SEPA-related investments for the banking industry.

Against this background, the ECB has carried out, in close cooperation with the banking industry, a SEPA impact study with the aim of enriching its understanding of the potential economic consequences of SEPA for different future scenarios. This article highlights the main findings of the economic impact study of SEPA on Europe's banks.[1]

---

[1] For the full study, see Schmiedel (2007) 'The economic impact of the single euro payments area', European Central Bank Occasional Paper Series, No. 71, August 2007.

2.1 SEPA'S ECONOMIC IMPACT ON EUROPE'S BANKS

The SEPA economic impact assessment was drawn up with the aim of obtaining a view of the potential cost and revenue impact of SEPA under four different scenarios: the baseline, coexistence, ideal SEPA world, and e-SEPA scenario.[2] According to the four identified SEPA scenarios, the participating banks were invited to report on their individual calculation and estimation of the SEPA impact on payment-related costs and revenues.

From the survey, it emerges that the average impact on an average European bank is expected to be limited, but vary according to the different stages and scenarios of SEPA. Over time, two opposing effects – a competition effect and an improved cost efficiency effect – are expected to determine the overall SEPA economic impact.

At the beginning of SEPA, banks will have to offer the 'old' payment instruments, as well as the 'new' SEPA payment instruments. In the short run, this will lead to higher costs mainly due to the setting-up of the new schemes and their coexistence with the old schemes.

During this dual phase, the impact on the revenue side of the total payments business seems to be relatively limited as cross-border competition is not expected to materialise in the short run whereas, in the longer term, it is likely that banks' revenues and costs will be affected in different ways. On the one hand, although some banks expect new business opportunities, revenues might decrease because of growing cross-border competition which would squeeze margins. On the other hand, banks reported that there are substantial potential cost savings due to economies of scope and scale, and a possible reduction of manual processes.

The findings confirm that in the medium to long run, SEPA will allow banks to benefit from economies of scale and from new business opportunities in an integrated euro area market. Banks reported that they are undertaking the necessary changes in their internal systems and their services so that they, and their customers, will benefit from SEPA. Payment processing costs are expected to come down due to the economies of scale and higher competition that common standards and procedures will bring.

In concrete terms, banks expect their revenues to decline by between 3 % and 10 %, depending on the SEPA scenario under consideration.

On the cost side, banks are likely to face high initial investments resulting in extra costs of about 5 % in the SEPA coexistence scenario. Later however, when total migration has been completed, these initial investments are likely to pay off as full advantage is taken of SEPA harmonised and standardised schemes and products.

The improved cost efficiency is estimated to result in cost savings of 1 % in the ideal SEPA and 7 % in the e-SEPA world. In sum, the net effect compared with the baseline scenario, which reflects the aggregate effect on banks' revenues and costs, ranges from -9 % in the dual phase to between −1.5 % and −3 % in the long-term e-SEPA scenario.

With respect to payment-related revenues by instruments, *cash* payment revenues would not be directly affected by SEPA. However, the banks reported that cash is the 'bleeder' in all markets. The cost related to the use of cash seems to outweigh the revenue arising from cash. Within SEPA, the banks would welcome a repositioning of cash, where there would be an increased use of other more electronic payment means and better pricing models. In particular,

---

[2] The *'baseline'* scenario reflects an extrapolation of the current status quo. The *'coexistence'* scenario reflects a situation where the SEPA schemes and frameworks are being implemented. This phase is based on the assumption that the current rules and payment schemes will prevail and exist in parallel to the new SEPA schemes and products. In addition, it is assumed that no consolidation of IT platforms or infrastructure has been achieved. The *'ideal SEPA world'* scenario reflects a situation when taking full advantage of SEPA schemes and products and with the migration to SEPA having been completed. The *'e-SEPA'* aims to go beyond SEPA and describes the future payments world which is fully electronic, paperless and with less cash (but not cashless).

the expectation is that a change in the mix of POS payment instruments will lead to increased volumes and revenues of direct debits and cards.

Furthermore, banks anticipate significant growth in the volume of ***direct debits*** for all SEPA scenarios, which would largely compensate for the downward pressure on prices due to increasing cross-border competition. The increase in the volume of direct debits would mainly be attributable to three factors:

- The volume of direct debits is expected to increase because of the opening-up of the euro payments market across-borders.
- Banks might also be able to expand their market share for direct debits due to market consolidation and concentration, as well as overall organic growth in the payments business.
- The use of direct debits is likely to increase because of a volume transfer from other payment mechanisms, for example, from cheques.

Revenues from ***credit transfers*** would remain stable in the coexistence scenario. Like direct debits, credit transfers would partly benefit from a volume transfer from other payment means. However, this positive effect is likely to be offset by downward pressure on prices due to increased competition. This latter effect is expected to be stronger in the longer term.

In the ***cards*** business, the overall impact is not expected to be material. However, banks expressed their strong interest within SEPA to encourage customers to change their payment behaviour and to switch to less costly and more efficient payment means.

Revenues on ***cheque payments*** would only be marginally impaired in the short run. However, banks expect a substantial decrease in commissions and fees in some markets in the ideal SEPA and e-SEPA scenarios. It is anticipated that in some markets cheque payments will be phased out in the long run.

Once SEPA has been fully implemented, country- and market-specific additional revenues and new business opportunities are expected from ***value-added services*** such as e-invoicing, e- and m- payments, e-identification, reporting and reconciliation. In the bilateral interviews, some bank representatives indicated that the scope and application of additional and value-added services tend to be currently underestimated and not yet fully reflected in the reported figures.

Banks' ***balance-related revenues*** are also likely to face downward pressure as cross-border competition will increase within SEPA. One key reason mentioned during the interviews is that consumers are likely to adopt more active cash management themselves. Companies and private individuals will more easily be able to transfer funds across-borders to accounts with higher interest rates. This trend is expected to continue in the near future as consumers will have better access to the internet and, for example, will make more use of internet banking. In addition, more easy and active cash management by customers may also have the result that balance-related income becomes more volatile and can therefore only be invested for shorter periods. As a side result, it is interesting to observe that balance-related income is clearly an important revenue stream for the banks.

2.2 CONCLUSION

The SEPA project represents a major step towards closer European integration. SEPA will become a reality when all euro payments in the euro area are treated as domestic payments, and when the current differentiation between national and cross-border payments disappears. SEPA will bring substantial economic benefits and opportunities, as it will foster competition and innovation, and improve conditions for customers. However, substantial efforts are required to align national banking industry practices and to change the habits of economic actors in all euro area countries.

The overall impact for the banking industry varies across the SEPA scenarios and, over time, two opposing effects will determine the benefits and challenges of SEPA.

First, SEPA will increase competition in the banking industry as it removes the barriers that formerly protected national markets. Second, the SEPA project will ensure cost savings in payment processing and give rise to business opportunities.

From the study it emerges that in the short run – during the coexistence of 'old' schemes and SEPA schemes – the banking industry expects SEPA to lead to initial investment costs and a relatively limited impact on the revenue side. In the long term, when national schemes have been fully replaced by SEPA schemes, the costs for banks are expected to decrease because of economies of scale and scope, and innovations such as electronic invoicing. The revenue side will also be affected by increased cross-border competition and by new market entrants.

The findings of this study support the view that a dual SEPA implementation phase should be as short as possible. In fact, a longer migration period will create more costs than a shorter period.

It seems that the impact on costs and revenues will be determined by the approach chosen by the banks. New and innovative products, new markets and new relationships could bring new sources of revenue for banks. Banks that take a forward-looking view, and opt for additional services which will automate the payment process, will create new business opportunities. The changes which are required in the initial phase of SEPA are substantial and benefits can be reaped especially by those institutions that embrace new technological developments and provide innovative services. A positive approach towards innovation will increase the benefits of SEPA for the involved stakeholders and, finally, a key factor for these developments is open and fair pan-European competition.

3

The vision of a Single European Payments Market

Eva King, the European Commission

SEPA and the Single Payments Area make absolute sense when you realise that Europe spends around Ä160 billion a year on payments, and inefficiencies in the process costs anything up to 2 % of our GDP.

In the not so distant past, Europeans were faced with an array of obstacles to managing and investing their money throughout the European Union (EU). Most people had little option but to use the services offered by banks and other financial institutions that were available in their home market, irrespective of price or the quality of service on offer. This was not supposed to be the case, given the EU's rules on the free movement of capital along with the much-trumpeted single market announcements of 1993. These should have made a difference here, as should the later arrival of the single currency in 11 (now 13) Member States of the EU.

Despite the undeniable benefits of the single market in many areas of the economy and everyday life, transferring money and effecting payments across the EU have remained cumbersome and expensive, even today. Together, business and consumers spend approximately € 160 billion every year just to make payments. This acts as a drag on the economy – some estimate payments cost the EU 1.5–2 % of GDP – hurting investment and growth in the EU.

Part of the reason for this inefficiency resides in the fact that EU single market rules have not so far touched directly on the payments market. Payments between banks, businesses and consumers are therefore still largely governed by national rules. This has meant that payment markets have grown along national lines, and the technology allowing millions of payments to be made in a single day has been developed separately in each Member State. Processing payments across-borders is therefore time-consuming and expensive, as it involves working with different payments systems that operate on different technological platforms. The fact that payment systems in the EU have grown along national lines has also limited the ability of payments providers and banks to compete across-borders. This means that there has been little chance for real cross-border competition, and consumers and businesses have not had the opportunity to shop around for the best prices. This status quo lack of change has also meant that banks and other payments providers have had little incentive to construct a pan-European infrastructure that could handle payments efficiently between Member States.

Faced with this situation, a number of institutions, including the European Commission, the European Central Bank and a group of commercial banks, set to work to consider whether it would be possible to stimulate the development of an EU payments market.

This consideration covered a range of questions: what would the benefits be? What would the milestones be to develop a pan-EU payments system? And, not least, how long would it be before ordinary consumers and business started to see some benefits from a new payments system?

3.1   THE BENEFITS OF SEPA

The SEPA project aims to ensure that all payment transactions are based on the same standards or interoperable technological standards, thereby easing cross-border payment services in the EU and creating a true single market for payments. Ultimately, there should be no distinction, from a technology point of view, between payments made domestically or payments made between EU Member States.

As the distinction between cross-border and national payments disappears, it will become possible to effect money transfers across Europe in an instant. High prices for cross-border payments, uncertainty of execution and lengthy delays should become things of the past. Consumers, SME's and other corporates will be able to use just one account for receiving and transferring money across the euro zone.

The SEPA project should also lead to greater competition between payment service providers for both domestic and cross-border payments. This should lower prices for both citizens and businesses. It has been estimated that this increased competition between service providers could lead to savings on the part of users of around € 30 billion a year.

Along with more efficient payment structures and increased use of electronic payment methods, the net benefits to consumers of SEPA could be in the region of € 100 billion or more a year. Added to these savings should be the benefits that could accrue to businesses from more efficient payment processes, such as e-invoicing, over time. These could flow from interoperable payment standards and a rationalisation of the technologies that businesses currently have to cope with to make their payments through multiple providers.

Competition should also lead to an improvement in the quality of services offered, with new payment products possibly finding their way onto the market. Not least, investment opportunities should increase, as citizens and businesses will no longer face artificial barriers to diversifying their holdings and seeking optimum returns across the EU's integrated financial market.

Indeed, businesses in the EU should be the major beneficiaries from a successful implementation of SEPA. They should be able to benefit from lower payment service costs as a result of greater competition, and will also be able to shop around for the cheapest and most reliable provider. Estimates suggest that they will benefit from a 15 % reduction in operational costs relating to payments. There will also be spill over benefits in their internal business processes reducing paper based processes and manual handling. An integrated EU payment services market means that businesses should be able to use a single service centre for processing payments, and interact with a single payment service provider. They should also be able to centralise their treasury operations which together with the shortened execution time results in greater predictability of and improved cash flow. The legal framework for payments in the EU, PSD, will give businesses the legal certainty that their payments get to their destination and arrive on time.

As for the banks themselves, SEPA will be an opportunity but it will also carry some initial costs that have been well documented by various studies including CapGemini and McKinsey. The costs of investments in new technology and payments infrastructure will, however, be offset by reduced operational cost savings of an estimated 15 % per annum. Within the payment services community itself, the most efficient providers stand to gain enormously, if they are able to successfully penetrate new markets.

It is of course perfectly understandable that there is some residual nervousness on the part of the banking community as to how best to take the project forward, given that large upfront investments are needed on their part and there is no certainty as to which individual banking institutions will emerge in the years ahead as market leaders. This is where the role of government and public agencies is critical in moving the SEPA project forward to a successful conclusion.

National governments, the European Commission, the European Central Bank and National Central Banks have an important role to play in sending appropriate political signals to the banking community so that they remain committed to the project, and that they will be early users of SEPA payment services. This political dialogue is designed to reassure banks that their investments are worthwhile, whilst also making clear that the public sector reserves its rights to legislate for SEPA if the self-regulatory process does not deliver the expected benefits within a reasonable timeframe.

3.2 MILESTONES

The public and private sector both have their roles to play to implement a workable and value-creating single market for payments, and there are three key issues that need to be tackled:

1. Abolish national rules for payment services in 27 countries and replace them by a single set of legally binding rules that are valid throughout the EU;
2. Design new standards for payment services in the areas of credit transfer, direct debit and card payments, that will operate on all technological platforms throughout the EU; and
3. Market these new products successfully to citizens and businesses so that they can use them to make payments on both national and cross-border basis throughout the EU.

The first piece in this jigsaw is a legal instrument tabled by the European Commission known as the EU Directive on Payment Services in the Internal Market or PSD. The PSD aims to remove legal obstacles to the creation of SEPA by introducing common legal rules for payment services, common standards of consumer protection and common supervisory standards for payment service providers. It also introduces a new licence for specialised Payments Institutions which will open commercial opportunities for new market entrants. A common legal instrument that is implemented in all jurisdictions should also promote consumer confidence in modern payment instruments.

There was extensive consultation between all interested parties in the years prior to the tabling of the proposal by the Commission in December 2005. The proposal strictly keeps to minimum regulation while enhancing the role of self-regulation, which forms an important part of the entire project. The European Parliament and the Council of Ministers agreed on the proposal in April 2007, with the aim to have the PSD implemented throughout the EU by national Parliaments in national law by 1 November 2009. As a result of this, the legal foundation for SEPA will be in place, and commercial parties and the banking industry will have a solid legal basis for conducting payment transactions across the EU.

The second element is equally important in the SEPA process as the banking industry will have to craft new standards for payment transactions that can be used by all payment service providers throughout the EU.

The lead in this important work has been taken by an industry body known as the European Payments Council (EPC). The EPC is made up of major financial institutions from a range of EU countries and is the official representative body of the payments industry. Its mandate is to develop a set of interbank arrangements, and the necessary contractual and technical details, to create a number of transnational payment schemes for credit transfers, direct debits and debit cards. The EPC also has a role in overseeing the implementation of these schemes.

The third element, marketing and uptake of SEPA products, will be the responsibility of individual banks and payment institutions. The onus will be on them to reap the rewards from their investments and market new payments products to their existing customer base and potentially to new customers. It is expected that there will be real competition for the first time in the payments industry and there might even be some new entrants and exits from the market.

3.3   HOW LONG WILL IT TAKE

The design phase for SEPA is already complete, with SEPA products for debit cards and credit transfers successfully launched by individual payments providers in January 2008. The scope of these SEPA products should even reach outside the EU as they will be available in all 27 EU countries as well as Switzerland, Lichtenstein, Norway and Iceland. However, SEPA products for direct debits are only deployed on 1 November 2009, when the PSD is implemented in national law in all EU Member States.

It is expected that there will be a transitional phase of co-existence between current payment products and new SEPA products until 2010, as the adoption and take up of SEPA products gathers pace amongst consumers. Indeed, public authorities have stressed their intention to see the SEPA project completed by the end of 2010. After that date, banks will start to phase out their legacy payment systems, as they will be able to deliver all of their payments products on SEPA compliant payment platforms.

Of course, the success of the SEPA Project is not a given, despite the obvious benefits for all parties concerned. A key issue is the migration of all banks to the new SEPA payments products. This is a huge undertaking, and its success rests on the confidence of all concerned that migration will take place by all other players according to an agreed schedule.

This will require central coordination by the EPC, Commission and European Central Bank, and a commitment to a deadline. In addition, banks need to be convinced of the business case for migration because, for them, the benefits of SEPA emerge only in the longer term as their operational costs decrease sufficiently to cover the up-front costs of new investments. The success of the SEPA project therefore depends on all parties moving in step to a new system. Laggards could destabilise the project and undermine confidence, as there needs to be a critical mass in the market place to allow SEPA products to be run at a profit.

A further point of concern that will need to be addressed is the involvement of future SEPA product users in the project. Currently, new standards for payment services are being developed by banks themselves, through the EPC. However, there would be a greater likelihood of large-scale uptake of SEPA products by corporates if they are sufficiently involved in the design of the new products, so that their needs are taken into account. SEPA products that are easy for banks to manage, but do not provide businesses or retail customers with the level of service they require, are unlikely to be a commercial success. The governance of the EPC structure will therefore have to prove, that it is transparent, that it successfully involves users and that it can emulate innovative ideas in the design of SEPA products.

Care should also be taken by regulators in the future that the SEPA framework does not lead to a foreclosing of competition in some market segments. Although greater levels of competition are forecast for the payments market as a whole in the wake of SEPA, it is unlikely to cure all competition issues without continued vigilance from regulators. The cards market, for example, has seen a deterioration of competitive conditions and a reduction in the number of service providers in the run-up to 2008. This will be an issue of concern for regulators going forward.

A further risk factor will be the introduction of additional optional services (AOS) as add-ons to basic SEPA products, such as e-invoicing. Again, regulatory vigilance and continued presence will be required to ensure that standards for new services are developed in a transparent manner. Only through such vigilance will we be able to ensure that the payments market stays open to new entrants and avoids renewed fragmentation.

The European Commission is reviewing these critical issues and the success of SEPA clearly depends on the trust of all players involved, alongside continued regulatory vigilance. It is a difficult project to bring off successfully because there can be no leaders and no laggards. All must move together to implement new standards and invest in new technological plat-forms, whilst simultaneously convincing their customers that the new products will be better, and preparing themselves for competition in a segment of the banking business that has not previously been subject to rigorous competitive conditions.

Nevertheless, the benefits of a successful SEPA are evident which is why all parties, both public and private, have a responsibility to ensure that they fulfil their ends of the bargain and make the necessary preparations for a successful launch of SEPA.

Indeed, the political imperative for success is clear, and the European Commission and European Central Bank have already stated that they will take further action if necessary. To quote from their joint statement issued in 2006, 'given the importance and the size of the social and economic benefits of SEPA, the Commission expressly reserves the right to introduce or propose necessary legislation to achieve it'. That should be incentive enough for the banking industry to move ahead rapidly to implement SEPA.

It should be explicitly noted by the reader that the views expressed in this chapter are those of Eva King personally. These views do not necessarily represent the opinions of the European commission.

4

Creating the Payment Services Directive for SEPA

Sharon Bowles, Member of the European Parliament

The process of drafting the PSD was painful, with arguments between geographic views rather than political views. Although the final result was disappointing, at least it provides a solid foundation as a beginning.

The Payment Services Directive (PSD) is the legal framework that underpins the introduction of SEPA. Whilst other chapters may examine the details, this chapter focuses upon the transit of the PSD through the European Parliament.

SEPA was already set to commence in January 2008, with full implementation by 2010, before the Commission's PSD proposal reached Parliament. Banks and other institutions were already working on their implementation and the detailed rule books, and they had also been following closely the various drafts of the PSD in the Commission.

Well ahead of the final draft, lobbyists were queuing up to talk to MEPs about problems that they saw in the various drafts. How some things had been in and then were taken out, then reappeared. All of this proved to be very confusing to a Parliamentarian who has not been privy to any draft. In retrospect I think there was too much attention paid by lobbyists to technical details, which due to my own experience in international payments I did not need, and not enough attention to likely political or national differences.

Once the PSD arrived in Parliament, key MEPs submitted over 600 amendments to the proposal at the Economic and Monetary Affairs committee (ECON) stage. This is not a record, but certainly not far off.

Broadly speaking there were amendments to technical detail which, once understood, were rarely contentious; amendments relating to consumer protection; amendments relating to the capital requirements of payment institutions; and amendments to the time in which payments had to be completed, such as should that be next day (D+1) or longer.

The initial and ongoing capital requirement for payment institutions was the most important and controversial issue during the whole process, dividing Parliament's political Groups along national lines. British MEPs, who are used to payment institutions other than banks alongside 'principles based' regulation, found themselves in a stand-off against German colleagues, whose preference was for a more regimented 'rules based' approach of defined, staggered levels of capital requirements dependent upon the type of services offered by the payment institution.

At the committee stage, when compromises were being sought, deals were struck around capital, payment time and consumer protection. The European People's Party (the Christian Democratic Party) and Socialist Groups reached agreement although it seemed incomprehensible to me why the Socialists, who are so keen on consumer protection, traded away the D+1 requirement in return for some wording relating to how information was to be made available.

To reach agreement within my own political Group, the Alliance of Liberals and Democrats for Europe (ALDE), I accepted a fixed capital regime in return for staying closer to D+1 by removing all the extra time, for example for currency changes, leaving a tightly defined D+2. I took the view that the tightly defined D+2 was in some ways more difficult to comply with than D+1 with extra time for special requirements, and that at a later stage this might make going back to D+1 possible. Whether I guessed that right or not remains to be seen.

In the end, after informal trilogue meetings of the Parliament, Presidency and Commission, the final agreement reverted to D+1 but allowed for an extension to three days execution time until 2012, and a further extra day for paper-initiated payment transactions. The final capital regimes, though differing from those of the Parliament, still followed the 'tick box' format of fixed amounts.

The exemption waiver provided for nationally based simple money remitters was a position the UK fought hard to maintain, both in the Council and Parliament, although other countries were also interested. A frequent example used was the transfer of monies from London to Krakow, although this example did little to counter the general belief that this was a 'British issue'. Nevertheless, the example does serve a valuable purpose in highlighting the important social function of payments institutions. The simple fact is that while there is the demand for this sort of service, these institutions will exist, whether legally or otherwise. It then seemed impossible to persuade many Parliamentarians that money remitters existed in their own countries and, at one stage, I seriously contemplated going on a photo safari around cities such as Munich in order to gather evidence. The debate on this in the Parliament seemed to be replayed in Council, but eventually a waiver was agreed that was a general derogation applicable to all payments institutions as long as their monthly payment turnover is below € 3 million.

Liability also became contentious, more so at the trilogue stage than in the Parliament. We took the view that consumers could not dictate to banks and payment intuitions which intermediaries they used, and that the institutions should therefore carry end-to-end liability, at least as far as the far end payment institution. This was opposed in Council as unconstitutional in some countries although, eventually, the Parliament prevailed.

There are many aspects on which I remain somewhat disappointed. One is that the scope of this directive was limited to payment services within the European Union made in euro or in any other official currency of the Member States: a so-called two-leg approach. The original global application, as proposed by the Commission, would have set out the framework for all payments with an EU link, even if the payment destination or origin was outside. This would have ensured that there were certain procedures and conditions met for the EU leg of its journey.

This is important because, in much the same way as end-to-end liability, consumers do not choose the reciprocal payment institution at the far end of a link. This is a part of the service they expect from a payment provider. It seems rather ironic that in some ways there is a superior ethos in the unregulated, trust-based system of money remitters, than would be accepted amongst the EU regulated payment providers!

Another disappointment was the loss of the open ended time limit for cross-border credit and revolving credit which, if accepted, would have meant a major triumph towards a fully liberalised payments market. Unfortunately, the ECON position restricted the granting of credit by payment institutions to short term credit directly linked to payments business, suggesting that 'short term' means three months. In the end, in the trilogue, the granting of credit up to 12 months was accepted with a clarification that credit cannot be revolving.

There were more national than political lines in the PSD, both in the Parliament and the Council. Nevertheless the Parliament dealt with the dossier promptly and became rather annoyed that having done so, slow progress was made in Council and we had, in turn, negotiations with three Council Presidencies – Austria, Finland and Germany – before any agreement could be reached. At times it seemed, and indeed we had to threaten, that we would go to a second reading. The reason we did not was that we were conscious that industry had already put into place as much as it could. It was now waiting nervously and impatiently for the detail, especially as the SEPA clock was ticking and preparations had to be made.

We also remained committed to the view that speeding up and integrating the EU payments system would benefit business and the consumer and be useful in the context of external competitiveness.

The PSD does strengthen competition in the payments markets by removing national barriers to market entry, allowing 'passporting' of authorisation in one Member State to others, and setting conditions applicable over the entire EU for new payment service providers such as mobile telephone operators. By laying down a set of rules concerning the information requirements and the rights and obligations linked to the provision and use of payment services, both individual consumers and businesses will find cross-border transactions and moving between Member States easier, which is all of benefit to a fully functioning single market.

One important last minute inclusion was that of a review clause. Indeed, if truth be told without that I do not think the final package would have been good enough for me.

This does give a further opportunity to come back to some major issues, most notably my 'disappointments' of expansion of scope and prudential requirements for payment institutions, by 1 November 2012 at the latest. Maybe there will be more confidence by then in the development of new payment techniques, and we will see if some of the capital has been set so high as to stifle EU wide development, as was the case with the e-money Directive. So I may be looking for that review to bite the bullet at that stage and take some bigger steps.

As I said in my speech to Parliament 'Am I happy with this package? Answer: "not really". Am I supporting it? Yes, because I believe it does make sense to have a European Payments system to improve the single market, and therefore it does make sense to take this step, far from perfect though it is'.

Part 2
The Views of the Payment Processors

- SWIFT
- the Euro Banking Association (EBA)
- Eurogiro
- VocaLink, UK
- Bankgirocentralen BGC AB, Sweden
- First Data, UK
- PayPal, Luxembourg

5

Was SEPA worth the effort after all?

Geoffroy de Schrevel, SWIFT

We are in a world that is sometime after 2010. SEPA Credit Transfer (SCT) and SEPA Direct Debit (SDD) have been implemented. Substantial progress has been achieved on the cards front. Suppose the industry takes a moment to run an introspective investigation on SEPA :

- Was it worth the investment and effort?
- Has SEPA's expected benefits materialised and how?
- Are all of the stakeholders better off?
- Has it created a dynamic market that will provide recurrent improvement over the pre-SEPA situation?

It would be naïve to believe that we will have a single and clear-cut answer to these questions since, from the outset, the various stakeholders engaged on the SEPA route started from different starting points, with various ambitions and sometimes conflicting expectations.

SEPA's impact will largely be determined by how fast and how deep its stakeholders will respond strategically to the market dynamics. These dynamics are influenced by so many predictable and unpredictable factors that nobody can reasonably forecast their lifecycle or their end-state. The assertion of competitive strengths and the definition of strategic progression need to be steady and flexible to cope with these uncertainties, the moving targets and the ambiguities that surrounded SEPA stakeholders since the inception of this sometimes Homeric, sometimes surrealistic undertaking.

This chapter looks at the various challenges that the key SEPA stakeholders had to face during the implementation of the Single Euro Payment Area. In a more prospective way, it also takes a post-2010 view on the key factors against which these stakeholders will declare success or failure of this biggest ever transformation in the European payment landscape.

5.1 REGULATORY AUTHORITIES

The regulatory authorities had a clear vision, set in the Lisbon agenda, to make the European financial market the most efficient one in the world. This meant that the European financial market, which was very much fragmented along national borders, needed to be harmonised. Simply put, the harmonisation would bring more transparency to the market. This would allow participants across the whole region to enjoy the same information and offerings in order to make educated choices on products and services.

Harmonisation would create healthy competition between providers of financial products and services which, in turn, would improve market efficiency, foster innovation and dismantle unjustified lock-in situations. Regulators would declare SEPA a success when consumers and businesses are provided with more efficient, openly accessible and easy-to-use payment instruments, in a more competitive and innovative market.

Nobody can blame regulators to define, communicate and expect execution of this vision for, as part of the Lisbon agenda, SEPA was a political decision and therefore not an option for the European financial industry.

The biggest challenge for the regulatory authorities was time. On the one hand, the momentum created by insisting on the industry providing an ambitious implementation agenda could not be sustained indefinitely, and risked disappearing in the soft consensus that past instruments were not so bad after all. A long cohabitation of legacy and SEPA payment products would be extremely costly to everyone. On the other hand, SEPA implementation needed massive and rapid investment that, in several instances, was clashing with the investment cycles of stakeholders. Finally, rather than a big bang, SEPA roll-out ended up being a succession of stepping stones, starting with credit transfers and followed by direct debits, cards and e-payments, giving the impression of an open-ended regulatory pressure.

5.2   BANKS

Across Europe, payments represent around a quarter of a bank's operating revenues and a third of their operating costs. As a result, payments contribute to less than 12 % of a bank's overall profits but, for many banks, payments are considered a core business if only because it is very close to gaining client intimacy. Although the definition of what is 'core', and thus of what would be the success criteria for the bank, varies geographically and over time, banks usually rate the quality of infrastructure and the sustainability of the business models as their key for payments processing. As a result, these are two conditions to making SEPA a success.

In general, banks expect SEPA will push market infrastructures to be more cost-efficient. Through the EPC, SEPA is defining a single set of standards and market infrastructures are not only expected to adopt them strictly, but also to adhere to a single implementation. This should allow financial institutions to maximise their scale benefits and to choose their infrastructure providers, without the risk of being locked-in by technical constraints. Besides the adoption of common standards and the associated freedom of choice, banks also clearly expect their market infrastructures to be more cost-efficient in their operations. At the end of the day, there cannot be a SEPA success if processing a SEPA payment tomorrow costs more than processing an equivalent national payment yesterday.

Banks also expects market infrastructures to be more flexible and agile. If there is a need for common standards on basic payment functions, then the 'one size fits all' approach cannot continue. Market infrastructures will have to be able to not only segment and diversify their offerings, but also to help their customers better serve their clients and fight off competitors through faster time-to-market and proactive product innovation.

Last but not least, because payments will have to travel faster and more securely across Europe, banks will not be able to compromise any of the resilience and the security of their market infrastructures. In the newly competitive environment created by SEPA, reputational risk is going to be managed even more closely than before.

Banks will measure SEPA success in terms of the function of their market infrastructures' ability to be cheaper and, at the same time, more flexible, more agile, more secure and more resilient. They will pay an equal amount of attention to the economic sustainability of their payments business models. Whether they are niche players or major transaction banks or anything else in between, they do not expect SEPA to become a launch pad for open-ended compliance requirements; nor to inhibit their capacity to differentiate; nor to dry up the income flows of existing payment instruments that are also necessary to fund product innovation.

In 2010, the situation could look rather gloomy. Banks have been forced to make SEPA investments outside their natural investment cycle and the gradual approach of regulators appears to be like an endless quest for compliance. Meanwhile, revenue from existing and more traditional payment products has severely shrunk due to the D+1 requirement, and the regulations on interchange fees. One can hardly expect banks to call it a success.

But the picture is fundamentally different if SEPA, instead, forces banks and the other stakeholders to raise their game. For instance, banks could look at other industries, such as the automotive, and organise their payment businesses like a car assembly line. They could collect and assemble parts from various internal and external sources. They could force themselves to better identify the various components of the payments value chain, and then build a sourcing strategy that supports a wider business strategy. Banks could then combine growth and industrial strategies, could use and develop white label products and could thus far more efficiently utilise innovation and development resources.

Indeed, in recent years, a number of banks have already taken this entrepreneurial route, and they will claim SEPA a success when their strategy bears fruit for the bottom-line.

5.3   END-USERS

Since the Lisbon agenda agreement, consumers and corporations have been at the centre of the regulator's attention. At the end of the day, authorities have based most of their SEPA cost-benefit case on the benefits it will bring to society in general, and to the financial services' end-user in particular. The main benefit the EU authorities usually identify for end-users is a reduction in bank transaction charges for all payments.

This all started in July 2003, with regulation 2560/2001. The regulation reduced the charges for cross-border transactions to the same level of an intra-country transaction, for transactions valued up to € 12 500 originally and to € 50 000 later, and ensured they were properly formatted. This began the construction of a single domestic market in the Eurozone. The regulation mainly benefitted consumers travelling in Europe, as they could use their international debit cards at Point-of-Sale and ATMs across the Eurozone in mostly the same way, and at the same cost, as they would do at home. Corporate organisations did not really benefit from the regulation, because the cost of updating their payment systems to the required format outweighed the cumulative charge reductions they could realise on their cross-border payments.

But the rule has been reversed. With SEPA, all euro transactions within the Eurozone are domestic. The new format and standards applies to all transactions, and extra charges for repairs and rejects can be charged by beneficiaries with no cap on the amount. The benefit anticipated is to reach STP rates from the corporate payment initiator to the corporate payment beneficiary that are far higher than the 40 % STP rates commonly estimated for such processing in 2007.

Clearly large corporations, with significant activities in different countries, will be satisfied by SEPA only if its benefits go beyond the charge reductions on cross-border payments and the avoidance of new charges on intra-border ones. What many have expressed is that they are looking for the harmonisation of technology and the customisation of commercial products, for simplification of operating processes and for more differentiation in business relationships.

The implementation of the new set of XML[1] standards for credit transfers and direct debit across SEPA allows major corporates to consolidate their payment systems to a much reduced number for all payment operations. After 2010, this should improve operational efficiency, facilitate risk management and generate scale benefits but, at the end of the day, this is not sufficient to significantly improve end-to-end STP. Corporates want the major elements of an invoice, together with the payment details, are able to be passed from the payer through to the beneficiary at the very least. Similarly, they want all of the information necessary for reconciliation to be included. In the end, they will expect that SEPA payments standards encompass a minimum set of invoice and remittance data.

Large corporations also want improved visibility of cash and a better ability to centralise treasury and working capital activities globally. This is to allow them to more effectively consolidate cash for investment purposes, and thus to increase interest income and to redirect staff to more strategic activities.

The new, single set of payment standards needs to be taken up by Enterprise Resource Planning (ERP)[2] application vendors, as corporates are looking for maximum integration in their back-office systems to go as deep as possible. But their expectation for technology harmonisation goes beyond this, and includes their interfaces with banks and their messaging channels. They will measure SEPA success in terms of their ability to get rid of proprietary bank channels that lock them in, and replace them by shared industry-defined corporate-to-bank interfaces with a common industry messaging infrastructure. It is very likely that this will happen after SEPA's implementation. It is up to the banks to meet this demand or to leave the field open to non-banks.

The request for an encompassing harmonisation of technology is not shared with the same acuity by small and medium sized corporations, particularly those in a single bank relationship, or those firms that value the workflow tools offered through banks' proprietary channels. Like consumers, SMEs will measure SEPA success in terms of the ease-of-use of the SEPA payment products and services, whether these are traditional or new products. By releasing resources away from basic payment functions and channel support, they become free to use these critical resources to mind their core business, their bottom line or any other activity that brings more value to them.

Like SMEs, consumers want user-friendly payment instruments that are low-risk. Many of these payment instruments such as credit transfers, direct debit and debit cards, deal with the end-users' own money. Therefore, strong security that preserves the confidentiality of private data is critical, as well as authenticating all of the parties involved in a payment transaction. It should not come at the cost of ease-of-use or the ubiquity of transacting however. These customers want their payments instruments to be completely intuitive, recognised across all of the channels they use in their everyday lives, and accepted at virtually all merchants that matter. This requires the innovative implementation of new products that have not fundamentally changed over many years.

---

[1] The Extensible Mark-up Language (XML) is a general-purpose mark-up language. It is classified as an extensible language because it allows its users to define tags and is mainly used to facilitate the sharing of structured data across different information systems, particularly via the Internet. In general, a mark-up language provides a way to combine a text and extra information about it, such as structure, layout or other information. This is expressed using mark-up, which is typically intermingled with the primary text. The best-known mark-up language in modern use is the HyperText Markup Language (HTML), the foundation of the World Wide Web.

[2] ERP covers all core systems including payroll, general ledger, accounting and so forth.

After 2010, end-users will be better off if the payment instruments and services they want to use contribute to the improvement of their business, help in their relationship with their own clients, work on all channels, and provide better security and ease of use.

5.4   MARKET INFRASTRUCTURES

Market infrastructure providers are probably the only SEPA stakeholders for which 2010, and thereafter, is going to be a zero-sum game. Not only will their number reduce substantially, driven by the need to get scale in order to meet the other SEPA stakeholders' pressure for lower payment processing costs, but many will see their own traditional clients compete with them, as large global transaction banks will offer sourcing alternatives to smaller institutions.

The dynamics of the market infrastructure landscape evolution has been difficult to identify because it was blurred by adjournments in the SEPA legislative framework, the PSD, and by unexpected difficulties for many banks in implementing the new SEPA XML formats in time for January 2008. The delay was also due to some late decisions made at the EPC level that has affected banks' preparedness. Indeed, the likelihood of market consolidation around a single PE-ACH gave way to the emergence of a multiple ACHs model, with a PE-ACH of last resort. This was then challenged in the second half of 2007 by a PE-ACH of first resort set-up, used as a fallback to cope with the SEPA implementation delays of some institutions.

As payments products are compliant to the single SCT and SDD product rules and standards, many ACHs find themselves confined to the role of commodity operators. In order to survive, many have re-assessed their role in the payments value chain. In this reassessment, they have considered the minimum size they need to gain reachability and maximise economies of scale, and the governance model they have to adopt in order to better function in an open and commercial environment.

All of this would have been a fairly academic market consolidation phenomena if two major elements had not emerged that largely complicate the matter. First, ACHs started facing competition from some large transactional banks that were their clients, owners or even supervisors at the same time. As value could be created around payment processing, large transactional banks started offering their service to other banks that have become demanding buyers of services. As they were considerably upgrading their own payment engines, many transaction banks insourced a number of services they used to buy from their ACHs, and started approaching banks that were considering their own sourcing strategy.

In an industry largely volume driven and dependent on fixed costs, such a redistribution of roles had forced market infrastructures to fundamentally re-think their growth strategy but also their business model.

Second, the market experienced a major value shift, from a focus upon applications to a focus upon networks. If payment instruments are standardised across SEPA, they can be processed in a fairly standardised way. Financial institutions, particularly the largest ones, focused on cross-border interoperability and on 'switchability'[3] across ACHs. They wanted independence from proprietary standards and channels, which can change as a result of mergers, platform upgrades, compliance requirements and a host of other factors around which they have little control. They wanted to internalise as much value creation as possible, by focusing upon the

---

[3] Switchability is the capacity for an institution to use various clearing and settlement mehanisms (CSMs) and to be ensured they can 'plug and play' from one CSM to another at marginal cost.

major payment routes, without falling back on the more traditional and costlier correspondent banking model.

At the same time SEPA required full reachability across the Single Payments Area so, while they were looking for lean and mean processing services, banks wanted to ensure that they could rely on networks that could carry payments fast and securely, with strong resilience from any end-user to any other end-user across the Eurozone. These networks needed to be agile enough to know and accommodate various routing strategies, and able to copy and drop information about payments where and when banks or their clients wanted to see it processed.

'Switchability' across clearing and settlement mechanisms, together with such a network, and with access to shared routing and reference data, was a necessary condition for SEPA to create an environment where banks, their clients and their providers could benefit from volume and competition.

This large value shift did not happen overnight, as some banks were reluctant to give up their proprietary channels with corporates in favour of a common and open network. By the same token, some ACHs believed that the channel could provide a significant form of differentiation, and that the absence of this differentiation would lead to greater client attrition levels. Therefore, it was not a surprise to see that it is the banks that opted for a common industry infrastructure for their corporate-to-bank interfaces sooner that were also the more adamant to use the same infrastructure in the bank-to-bank space. They clearly wanted to maximise the benefits of using a single window end-to-end, rather than being forced to integrate with multiple standards and channels.

It is clear that it is the banks and market infrastructures that aggressively help stakeholders to opt for a common industry network that will gain a larger share of wallet, and new opportunities to create value and differentiate.

In conclusion, SEPA is an opportunity and it will be up to each participant to find its way through the change to end up on the winning edge. Because it will require structural changes, participants must be ready to engage in a new cooperation/competition model. There is hardly ever a business case for each stakeholder to invest in infrastructure, unless it is done in cooperation and with clear leadership. The purely competitive approach, like the soft and wide consensual method, have both shown their limits when it comes to radically change an industry with heavy legacy systems.

Success will be there after 2010 if financial institutions continue to provide leadership through an effective and neutral governance structure. They could build on the embryonic structure they setup around SEPA standards testing. They could, before 2010, bring it to the next level – a structure to go 'beyond compliance'.

6

Europe's future payments infrastructures

Daniel Szmukler, EBA CLEARING

There are three clear trends in payments infrastructures: concentration of providers, increasing bilateral arrangements, and a move towards a hub-and-spoke clearing system, where STEP2 provides the central hub for Europe.

Europe's payments infrastructures are undergoing a tremendous transformation. From a multiplicity of payments mechanisms dating back to before the introduction of the euro we now face the advance of the Single Euro Payments Area (SEPA). No longer will the European payments industry be structured, and priced, around such distinctions as between domestic and cross-border transactions. No longer will individual cross-border payment instructions have to be passed between national ACH's with differing standards, methodologies and pricing structures. SEPA offers a uniform Europe-wide payments environment for credit transfers, direct debits and card payments alike.

In its purest form, the SEPA vision is of a single set of payments standards that will apply across 31 countries, with payments typically processed by a pan-European ACH (PE-ACH) and priced without regard to the distance between origin and destination.

SEPA payments will travel from one end of Europe to the other as efficiently and at the same price as between one bank and its immediate neighbour. Such a concept sits well with the wider European vision of a single market with a single currency, but how will it translate into reality and how will SEPA evolve over time?

To begin with, SEPA's progress to date, and the impact of that progress, is broadly on schedule. The implementation phase runs from 2008 to 2010 and beyond, with banks required to offer 'SEPA-compliant' payment instruments for credit transfers first, with direct-debit instruments following shortly thereafter.

The European Union's Payment Services Directive, underpinning SEPA, has its transposition into national legislations during 2008 and 2009.

However, there is no mandatory requirement for legacy payment instruments to be abandoned at any point during the implementation phase. This means that full implementation may not effectively be achieved until 2011 or possibly later. Until SEPA is fully in place, some customers may prefer to retain their tried-and-tested, pre-SEPA, possibly idiosyncratic payments arrangements with counterparties.

SEPA will have to win over such customers by its merits, which are already becoming apparent. Indeed, even before its implementation, SEPA has had a significant impact on European payments. Three trends in particular are partly attributable to SEPA, each of which has the potential to influence the longer-term development of the industry.

The first such trend is towards concentration. Against a background of ongoing M&A in the European and wider banking sector, we have seen increased concentration of banking activity into a smaller number of larger institutions, leading into an increased concentration of payments.

In a parallel realignment, the major banks have begun developing commercial SEPA-compliant payment services to offer to smaller banks, whose reach might not extend across the zone that will be SEPA. Although size may not be the only factor in a bank's strategic decision as to whether to develop SEPA-compliant payment-processing as a commercial proposition, it is significant in that Europe-wide reach is a key determinant of SEPA-competitiveness.

The second identifiable trend, which follows on from the first, is towards the development of bilateral payment relationships. In markets such as Finland and the Netherlands, for example, where a small number of banks account for most payments traffic, the argument in favour of using a PE-ACH for all their transfers is less compelling. In such markets, banks have tended to move towards bilateral payments processing, with the PE-ACH used in those cases where a bilateral solution cannot be achieved.

It might have been expected, given the trends described above towards concentration and bilateral payment-processing, that there might have been also a trend towards consolidation among Clearing and Settlement Mechanisms (CSM's). After all, their role has seemed to be destined to change.

However, CSM consolidation is proving to be a long, slow process. This is for a variety of reasons. In the short term, national ACHs will process large volumes of non-SEPA payments traffic still generated by their existing customer base. Legacy traffic is likely to continue for some time yet, and it is hardly surprising that national ACHs have begun to seek new roles that will carry them through into the SEPA payments environment, rather than planning to scale their activities down as their pre-SEPA business dwindles away.

As some of the national ACHs have already discovered, it is possible to find a new role. For an ACH aspiring to be a SEPA-compliant CSM, it is only necessary to be able to handle SEPA instruments; without the need to become a full-scale PE-ACH with SEPA reach. There has been some consolidation among national ACHs, but much of it has been aimed at achieving commercial advantage.

The third trend, therefore, has been for the unexpected to happen. As payments activity concentrates, as the major banks develop bilateral relationships and connect to the PE-ACH, national ACHs begin to find SEPA-compliant roles. Significantly, several ACHs already act as technical facilitators for banks participating in EBA CLEARING's STEP2 PE-ACH.

In the long term, the European payments market is therefore likely to develop a 'hub-and-spoke' structure in which STEP2 acts as the hub and connectivity and reach would be available to any SEPA-compliant CSM who could attract volume at a competitive price and provide high quality, locally-focused customer service.

7

Bilateral clearing likely to be dominant clearing method in SEPA

Henrik Parl, Eurogiro

SEPA was to a high degree motivated by the vision of a common EU payment market, where domestic infrastructures and legacy payment system are migrated into centralised and low cost infrastructures facilitating EU-domestic payment transfers. However, a strong case can be made for a future payment landscape, where bilateral – and not centralised – clearing is the dominant clearing method within SEPA.

7.1 OBJECTIVES AND DRIVERS BEHIND CHANGING THE EUROPEAN PAYMENT INFRASTRUCTURE

SEPA is very much a political project for the EU. In the 1990's, the EU tried to push the banks into providing more low-cost cross-border transfers to their customers, but with limited effect. At the beginning of the new Millennium, the EU lost patience and changed tactics. Now the market should be 'forced' to adapt to Europe through regulation and legislation.

The guiding principle was to secure an EU-internal payment market without any difference between domestic and cross-border payments, such that all payments within the community should be treated as domestic and priced as such. While it is logical that a Euro payment from Frankfurt to Hamburg should not be priced any different than a Euro payment from Frankfurt to Amsterdam, this has resulted in challenges for the banks.

For example, domestic transfers in Europe are generally very low cost, a few eurocents, while cross-border transfers are considerably more expensive to produce, a few euros, because the banks need to create a bridge between the different domestic systems. This is quite costly, although the cross-border volumes only account for about 1 % of the total payment volumes in Europe.

For the EU, a key tool to achieve the vision of a SEPA payment market was therefore to push for a process where legacy domestic systems were phased out and replaced by pan-European solutions. As part of this process, the EU has several times stressed the need to end up with one or two Pan European Automated Clearing Houses (PE-ACH's). The simple logic is that a concentration of this kind will not only remove the costs of bridging different systems, but also that economies of scale would drive down unit costs and eventually secure the objective for payments in Europe to be processed significantly cheaper than today.

The European banks have chosen a self-regulation approach to support the EU objectives, through the creation of the European Payment Council (EPC), EBA STEP2, etc. This means that all seems on track to fulfil the EU vision of the clearing of payments through a few centralised structures.

However, a number of recent events have thrown new light on the EU vision, and have given indications that we may see a much more complex infrastructure landscape than envisioned.

Firstly, a number of Clearing and Settlement Mechanisms (CSM's) have emerged out of former domestic ACH's and international payment systems. These CSM's have developed principles for interoperability through the European ACH Association (EACHA), thereby providing alternatives to PE-ACH solutions. However, the EACHA interoperability is created for ACH-to-ACH interoperability and not for direct exchanges between banks.

Secondly, the big banks have increasingly focused on the opportunities for cost efficiencies through bilateral clearing and thereby their need for a interoperability framework.

The market reality could therefore be that we end up with a market dominated by bilateral exchanges between CSM's and between banks, while central PE-ACH clearing plays a more limited role.

This hypothesis will be investigated in more depth through this chapter.

7.2   THE CASE FOR BILATERAL CLEARING AS THE DOMINANT CLEARING METHOD POST 2010

The main reasons why bilateral clearing could be a dominant clearing method after 2010 are:

- The need for large volume players to achieve the lowest possible cost of processing payments. Seen isolated, bilateral clearing can be done at very low unit costs if the volumes between the organisations are big and relatively balanced.
- The German 'garagen clearing' has demonstrated that a simplified approach to bilateral clearing can result in a high level of cost efficiency through a common clearing agreement and simple bilateral gross settlement (no collateral or net settlement). In Germany about 90 % of the volumes are cleared bilaterally and it should be underlined that this has happened through a market driven approach in spite of a central clearing opportunity (Bundesbank).
- Benefits for the big banks of disassociating themselves from central clearing solutions (ACH's) for costs and competitive reasons. In fact SEPA is an opportunity for big banks to get out of the domestic solutions that have provided smaller banks with a level playing field. By removing the large volumes from existing ACH's the big banks will obtain the cost efficiencies from economies of scale while the smaller banks either have to buy services from the big banks or accept higher unit cost of accessing payment infrastructures.
- Maintaining strategic control of payments through bilateral exchanges but also avoiding risks of concentrating all volumes with one or few central infrastructures. There are few examples of where monopolies have been able to provide lower costs than a well functioning market.

The strategic vision for bilateral exchanges can be seen in Figure 7.1. The exhibit illustrates a hypothesis on the (end-game) segmentation between:

- **Smaller and medium banks,** which will have an advantage by using CSM's or PE-ACH's directly or indirectly via banks outsourcing. Their main need will be to achieve reach.
- **The Top 40 or 50 European banks and CSM's,** which will have the volumes to achieve further reductions in costs through bilateral exchanges. This will mean a loss of volumes for the CSM's especially for domestic corridors

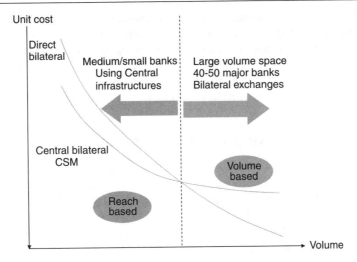

Figure 7.1   End-game segmentation of reach based and volume based SEPA

PE-ACH's will, in this scenario, still play an important role for small and medium sized banks and will also act as a 'clearer of last resort' for large banks.

If the above scenario materialises, the main effects could be:

- the big banks driving the changes and gaining competitive advantages from their volumes;
- CSM's and PE-ACH's lose the business from large volume corridors to bilateral exchange between the large banks domestically; and
- smaller banks will either outsource to the large banks, pay the high costs of joining PE-ACH's or link to domestic and regional CSM's, where they may pay a higher fee due to the volumes taken away by the big banks.

The above argument is built on the assumption that bilateral exchanges can provide services cheaper than central clearers.

Some might ask if this is not just a return to costly and complex correspondent banking and, for bilateral clearing to work cost efficiently, there are therefore a number of requirements:

- That the set-up is as simple as possible. A reason for the success of the German Garagen clearing is exactly that it does the necessary minimum. Too many add-on features such as validation, net settlement, etc. may only complicate matters and increase costs.
- The basic standards must be built upon what exists, such as the SEPA rule books and the rules for the Scheme Management Entity.
- There must be a framework that secures reusability through a:
  - common clearing agreement,
  - common settlement framework, for example TARGET2,
  - simple rules for interoperability, such as cut-off times, exception handling, etc.

If there is not a common framework securing reusability, it will become too costly for banks to expand bilateral clearing beyond a few domestic large volume corridors.

EACHA is the first example of how organisations can define common rules for interoperability, in this case for bilateral exchanges between former ACH's. It will be logical for the big banks to initiate a similar initiative, aimed at a framework for bilateral exchange between the banks, as this will enable the large banks to capitalise on their size.

The above future, dominated by bilateral exchange, is not only substantiated by logical reasoning but also by statements by many of the largest banks. These banks state that they are not only strategically positioned for bilateral exchanges, but also that they are in the process of realising these for their major corridors regionally.

7.3   WHEN MAY BILATERAL CLEARING EMERGE?

Initially SEPA volumes are likely to be very low. Private customers will have little interest in the issue and it will take time for corporates to adjust their systems to SEPA. In spite of the political pressure, it seems that even implementation of SEPA in public institutions will be slow.

The speed of change will depend on the incentives which are given for SEPA for the various customer groups, and it will depend upon the extent to which financial institutions elect to translate traditionally formatted payments into SEPA formats.

It can therefore be questioned as to how fast the process of SEPA will be. However, it is quite certain that bilateral exchanges will initially only be attractive for bilateral transactions within national and regional borders; and only for payments across national borders in the longer term. The latter can only happen if there is a common framework. With the above in mind and if a common approach among big banks is implemented, we could see the evolution of volumes as shown in Figure 7.2.

As SEPA volumes grow, although they are still modest, CSM's will see an initial boost in volumes as it will be too costly to set-up within the bilateral exchanges. However, as SEPA volumes continue to grow, the largest banks will gradually have a business case for transferring volumes towards bilateral exchange. An end-game scenario could be 90 % of payments processed through bilateral exchange and only 10 % through a PE-ACH or SEPA-compliant ACH, with these volumes corresponding to the actual situation in Germany.

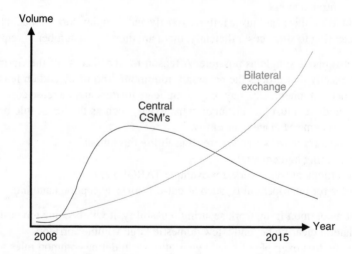

Figure 7.2   Potential evolution of volumes

7.4 CONCLUSIONS AND EFFECTS

This chapter has sought to argue that it is not an unrealistic scenario that bilateral clearing will become the dominant clearing method post-2010. The argument is based upon the interest of the large volume players seeking to obtain a cost and strategic advantage.

How will the EU and the ECB view such a development? On the one hand, some would argue that the process has been market driven and, as such, delivers the best guarantee of low costs. On the other hand, the dominance of bilateral exchange might have a number of effects that contradict the objectives of the legislators:

- The large players will obtain cost advantages, while the smaller players are forced to accept higher cost solutions, removing the present level playing field provided by the present ACH's.
- Existing ACH's, who are the future CSM's, will lose the majority of their present volumes which will negatively affect their unit costs.
- There will not be a simple infrastructure set-up in 2010, with one or two PE-ACH's, but a complex mixture of PE-ACH's, CSM's and bilateral exchanges.
- Although the large banks might have a cost advantage of bilateral exchange, there is an overall risk that the total cost of infrastructures on a pan-European basis will be higher than if there was a single PE-ACH. If the customer has to pay for this, as expected, will the EU accept this?
- The € 5 billion investments in infrastructures have to be recovered and, again, the customer has to pay: will the EU accept this?

SEPA started out with a vision of low cost payments facilitated by a few centralised solutions. What may emerge are complex solutions that could have both less functionality than the existing ACH's, and also carry the risk of higher costs for the customers in the end.

If this happens, what can the EU and the ECB do about it? On the one hand, some would argue that if the regulation in a market economy is too strict, it will not work and the EU should pursue a policy of de-regulation. On the other hand, and much more likely, the regulators and legislators may be tempted to create new regulation, and the ECB may be tempted to provide the market with retail payment clearing through TARGET2.

Then we may have to start the circle once again, where new regulation results in new market initiatives. Something we should surely be trying to avoid?

8

Is listening to the regulator enough?

Nick Senechal, VocaLink

Rather than being forced to change, banks should see SEPA and other changes to payments systems as an opportunity to rethink and re-engineer to meet today's and tomorrow's consumer and business needs.

Payments executives usually struggle to gain buy-in for a major upheaval to the status quo because investment in new systems and processes are high risk and costly. One way of ensuring that a payments business case will pass however, is to claim that it is mandatory. This is certainly the case for anything that is a regulatory requirement. This ensures the funds will be found from somewhere, for an activity that has little glamour and a lot of hard work and slow progress.

The implementation of SEPA has given European banks what must be the ultimate mandatory justification for a re-engineering of their payment systems. As compliance is required from even the most reluctant of banks, it provides the rationale for introducing changes. These changes are not mandatory. SEPA is a self regulatory response to pressure, along with indirect legislation from the European Commission. However, the level of peer pressure is so huge that rejecting SEPA is akin to getting out of the payments business altogether.

There are two ways to view SEPA. For many it is a tiresome compliance issue, and one which will incur compliance costs at a time of reducing revenues. Others have made strong public statements of their ambition to use SEPA as a vehicle to achieve greater dominance in the markets. In private, other banks, some not currently players in the European market, admit they will use the disruption caused by SEPA to gain market-share through low pricing of what are becoming commoditised services.

This reaction is, of course, just what the regulators in the European Commission wanted, as this will generate consolidation and competition to improve the efficiency of the market. In doing so, banks and other payment providers must consider what they seek to achieve from this and how they will make money. With limited revenue attached to a SEPA transaction, enormous scale and high levels of efficiency are a prerequisite for success.

For some banks, SEPA payments may be regarded as a loss leader for other banking services. In other words, the glue that ensures customers stick to their banks.

For others, SEPA can create innovation. SEPA will provide standardisation and a commodity backbone for banks to build new services. As such it is an enormous step forward. As ideas emerge, they are rapidly gathered into an EPC sub-committee. On-line payments, e-invoicing and e-mandates for direct debits, have all spawned working groups. This is good, in that payment-related solutions often need a community approach to ensure reach and promote take-up. However, historically, the consensus approach had a tendency to stifle innovation and can inhibit speed to market.

This is conventional thinking. Traditional payments executives would have no problem with any of this, as it is all a matter of compliance. Indeed they may be rubbing their hands with glee, as the high profile of SEPA allows them to justify the total renovation of the banks payment system.

Nevertheless, creating a profitable payments business which is flexible to the needs of customers, requires one to think differently. Consider another world where SEPA contributes but does not drive the agenda. Customers' needs do.

In this world, the offering the bank puts before a customer is distinctive, even if the components are off the shelf. In this world, the banks will drive the regulators and promote change, not the reverse. In this world we exploit the SEPA and, if it is not sufficient, we do something else.

PayPal is an example of what can be achieved using this model, and they are a non-bank player. There are of course who try to belittle PayPal: 'it's low value only', 'it generates money for the bank through the card fees', 'it stops me having to deal with sub-scale merchants', 'they wouldn't be anywhere without eBay'. Probably all true, but the truth is that banks have lost their most valuable asset – their customer relationship – thanks to PayPal's innovations. And guess what? It's not all about a credit relationship. PayPal is now a bank.

And PayPal isn't alone. Look-alikes from Yahoo and Google are obvious, but we can see other non-bank providers who address payments needs in a distinctive and in some cases dominant way. Western Union, for example, in the workers' remittances domain.

These players are responding to emerging customer needs in key areas, while anticipating and creating them in others, all with the agility that leaves many banks standing. They do so whilst happily using the banks to provide the fundamental building blocks of much of their service, achieving margin at the point of delivery.

By looking at a few key areas, we can contrast the legacy behaviours in the payments world against emerging needs, and perhaps identify factors that should drive new payments products rather than just looking to the regulator.

8.1   THE REACH MYTH

Banks see universal reach as the holy grail of banking. How often does a good idea die in its infancy because, theoretically, it cannot deliver a payment to 100 % of the payees in a given community? This is certainly much of the discussion in SEPA, where a bank has to reach every other bank and be reachable, but elsewhere it is accepted that reach is more about a critical mass.

Cards have proven this model over many years. The near-universal reach of major card schemes today started with a different proposition: 'If I have a card, and I can see the merchant accepts that card, then we can transact'. Incentives for all involved widened the acceptability, furthered by inter-operability until we have the global system we now all use. PayPal and on-line payment mechanisms follow the same trick, but at a much accelerated rate.

8.2   THE SELF-ACTUALISING CONSUMER

Today's mobile, wireless, internet society has created a world where the consumer will not accept restrictions on the way they live their lives. As in Maslow's hierarchy of needs, the hygiene factors around personal communication and meeting day-to-day needs have long been superseded by a 'self actualising' model, where the consumer is defined by the ability to do things when they want, where they want, with extreme convenience.

In payment terms, this self actualising consumer is faced with a disconnect. Traditional payment systems are still emerging from the basic hygiene factors of a welfare state of payments. D+3 for a cross-border SEPA payment is no good if PayPal can deliver the money today. Payment instruments that only work five days a week do not meet the needs of a 24 × 7 society. The consumer, and the merchant, will not accept any restriction on the use of an instrument. Just look at how 'cardholder not present' on-line transactions grew ahead of any effective control or protection.

The cards world has been most responsive to these needs, allowing a 24 × 7 world for some lower value transactions, but only by hiding the crude mechanisms and delays in completing the transaction from the consumer. Even though the payment is authorised and the consumer walks away with the goods, the merchant still has to wait for his money. Effectively, both parties would far rather have a 'Delivery Versus Payment' model where, at the end of the transaction, goods and money have both changed hands.

Equally, the consumer has given up a lot for their convenience with cards and this begins to undermine the self actualisation model as it begins to attack a basic hygiene factor, namely personal security. This is the result of the fact that all card models are debit-based and rely on the consumer exposing their credentials to a third party to take money from him or her.

Although expensive technologies have been deployed to prevent it, currently nearly half a billion pounds is lost in card fraud in the UK alone each year. Cardholder not present (CNP) fraud, including online transactions, currently represent the largest and fastest growing fraudulent area, despite the adoption of 3-D Secure by Visa, MasterCard and JCB International.

The consumer and the merchant, who faces the highly costly element of charge backs, want to dramatically reduce the level of fraud, and future models should look to eliminate the exposure of the customer in this way.

The final thing the self-actualising consumer wants is choice. Choice of channel in particular, be it mobile telephone, card, internet, kiosk or ATM. They want the same instruments available over each and every channel. When they make a payment, they do not want it to be tied to a series of other products – credit, purchase protection – unless they opt to take these at the time of transaction.

8.3   THE DEMANDING CORPORATE CUSTOMER

If the retail customer is becoming more assertive, the corporate world is even more demanding. Whilst the corporate has most to gain from SEPA, it will only serve to whet their appetite for better services. After all, banks have been great at stimulating debate amongst corporates about value added services – think of all those endless presentations on SWIFT MT940 messages or the benefits of e-invoicing – but delivery has often been more problematic.

Many businesses have taken on the pain of transformation and are now realising the benefits of integrating real-time logistics, stock control, delivery and accounting and the maximisation of the utilisation of their resources. But this integration does not extend easily into the payments world. Here, information about available funds may take several hours, if not days, to discover and could well be out of date by the time it is received. Payments need to be sent via diverse channels, dependent on their destination, value, importance, and the number of banks the corporate deals with.

SEPA will solve some of these issues for euro payments but, even with SEPA, problems remain. Once sent, little information may be available to confirm they have reached their destination, with some inexplicably returning days after they were sent. For these businesses, as everything else becomes automated, fully integrating and automating payments and cash management becomes an increasing priority.

For integration to be truly successful, the corporate will look for a single payment mechanism which is capable of successful alignment with the corresponding real-time transactions within the business. For example, an electronic invoice can contain its own embedded payment instruction that is activated automatically on the due date, and notifies the payer and payee of the success of the transaction. A real-time retail transaction can deliver funds conditionally and instantaneously on the release of goods. At the successful close of the transaction all parties can 'close their books' without the need for post-event reconciliation. All can be tightly integrated with logistics, stock control and financial accounting systems.

All this whilst recognising that if working in the retail space, the customer is still that same, self-actualising, wired, 24 × 7 person we discussed earlier.

8.4   TOWARDS NEW PAYMENT SYSTEMS

The world is moving towards standardisation in payment systems. SEPA is a positive step on the way for the Eurozone, and its intrinsic ISO standards are theoretically transferable worldwide. However the world outside payments is moving at a faster pace than can be met by standardisation alone, and payment practitioners must move further to embrace the world our customers already inhabit. For payments to meet the challenge of this new world, they must be capable of meeting a variety of needs, from low to high value, retail to wholesale. This means simplifying the infrastructure required to a single, highly capable backbone.

We must think not of 'adding value' to payments by adding lumps of reference material, but instead look to how the payment integrates seamlessly into the business processes it supports. This will be in real-time, 24 hours a day. The wired world, be it business-to-business or consumer-to-business, can't wait for clearing cycles and doesn't want to reconcile exceptions after the fact. It wants to do business and move on.

To move things on, banks have to start developing products that work in a different way. First they must think collaboratively and not collectively. This means working hand-in-hand with other banks and service providers to launch new products on to the market, whilst not waiting to sign up everyone else and move at the speed of the slowest. When we worked in national communities this was acceptable but, as those national communities get subsumed into regional markets – such as SEPA – or even global markets, this becomes a less credible way of working. In such a world the **only** way to move significantly forwards is for similarly orientated banks and service providers to create 'coalitions of the willing' to move innovative products forward.

If a service is good, it will soon create demand for others to join as it creates competitive advantage for the founders. As mentioned earlier, cards are early examples of successful business growth in this way. Another example is the LINK ATM scheme which, originally started by small UK Building societies, is now embraced by all UK banks.

The 'coalition of the willing' must also include non-banking interests, such as those businesses who will gain from the proposition. It is easy to see how these split into client businesses, retailers for example, and partners such as credit agencies, payment and network providers. Each will have its own business model: for the client probably cost saving or customer service; for the partner, revenue creation.

For a model we can again look to PayPal. Here the client businesses – merchants – and partners' credit and debit card schemes, and banks are all linked by PayPal to offer a seamless presentation to the consumer. More importantly all stakeholders benefit commercially from the service. Merchants have a cheap to implement model, albeit with significant transaction charges, and PayPal can legitimately claim that it pays its way by creating transaction revenue for banks and schemes.[1]

Banks can go further than a provider like PayPal, which relies on existing, legacy payment processes. They can deliver a more efficient backbone that delivers a payment method capable of eliminating the security problems of debit based systems, reducing the cost of slow clearing cycles and batched transactions, and interfacing in real-time with the core transactions of retail or wholesale business. If they are also able to create the right coalitions to go to market themselves, rather than allow others to step in to do this, they will have succeeded.

In the UK, the Faster Payments[2] service is delivering just such a backbone. In doing so, its creators have been mindful to build the kind of service that is capable of meeting the kind of needs outlined above. As a real-time backbone it allows banks, businesses and individuals to participate in both value and information based messaging, and the core capability is there to support any number of propositions. As a channel agnostic service, it also has the potential to be accessed by internet and mobile for individuals and SMEs, as well as via SWIFT and VPN for banks, corporates, government and wholesale customers. This flexibility will enable groups of banks or even individual banks to offer distinctive and customer engaging services.

Far-sighted banks have already started building the 'coalitions' they need to offer these services when Faster Payments comes on-line in 2008 and we would expect this model to soon be replicated elsewhere in the world.

8.5   THE OPPORTUNITY FOR BANKS

The future is one of possibilities where banks can re-intermediate themselves into their customers lives but the banks must change. They must develop the infrastructure and backbone into one that delivers immediate payments that are final, truly secure and capable of being embedded in the larger transactions of daily life, whether these transactions are business to business, consumer to business or even bank to bank. It makes sense to invest in such an infrastructure, so that eventually it becomes the core backbone for all payments, enabling greater flexibility and economies of scale to address the needs of the customer.

To do this, providers will need to approach the world in a new way. We expect payments to continue to operate in a co-operative world, but one where the innovators move quickly – rather than wait for the regulator to pronounce and the laggards to join. Banks are best placed to be those innovators. They possess the attributes such as scale, infrastructure, investment potential and the customer relationship to achieve this transformation. To what extent they will succeed will depend on how much they value the last of these attributes: the customer.

---

[1] PayPal is now one of the largest merchants and direct debit originators in its own right.
[2] Faster Payments is a UK specific regulation implemented in 2008, which allows real-time debit and credit payments when requested or needed.

The implications of SEPA to the Nordics

Bodil Nelsson and Mats Wallén, Bankgirocentralen BGC AB, Sweden

Nordic ACH's and infrastructures face stiff competition from larger European players. Alongside being mainly non-Euro operators, can existing ACH's survive?

9.1   WHAT CHALLENGES ARE THE NORDICS FACING?

Scandinavia commonly refers to Norway and Sweden, which cover the Scandinavian peninsula, as well as Denmark including the archipelagos and Jutland. Many people also include Finland and the Faeroe Islands, which belong to Denmark, in the definition of Scandinavia. These countries are more often called the Nordics however, or the Nordic countries or Nordic region, and have many common cultural, geographical and geological features. This is why they form a relatively homogeneous region in Europe.

The Nordic countries are shaped by their topographical and demographic conditions and, apart from Denmark, they are large, sparsely populated countries. The capacity to communicate at a distance has been vital therefore to their social development, and may also be why the percentage of *early adopters* has been so high in the Nordics with regard to innovations like mobile telephony and the internet.

One might say that companies like Nokia and Ericsson laid the foundations of the high-tech societies that distinguish our countries in so many ways. The banking system was rapidly computerised in the 1960's and almost 100 % of the population in Sweden, Denmark, Norway and Finland have had bank accounts for several decades now. Innovations such as automated cash dispensers, bank cards and electronic giro payments quickly became the stuff of everyday life. The widespread breakthrough of the online banks happened around 1996–1998 with very strong take-up, as evidenced by the fact that Swedish consumers have around 7.2 million online bank accounts in a country whose population is only about 9 million.[1]

A distinctive feature of the payment services market in the Nordics, especially Sweden, Norway and Denmark, is that the banks elected early on to outsource large parts of the payment infrastructure to intermediaries. Bankgirocentralen BGC AB in Sweden, Bankenes Betalingssentral BBS AS in Norway and Payment Business Services PBS AS in Denmark, are prime examples.[2] Traditionally, the banks in these countries have developed thin products, for which a substantial portion of the payment process is managed by one of the giro payment firms. The reasons for this are that the banks understood the advantages of creating open systems in which all players could communicate with each other, and that the transaction volume was relatively

---

[1] Statistics from the Swedish Bankers' Association, 2006. The statistics include both business and household customers. The same player may have several different Internet bank relationships.
[2] Formerly Pengeinstitutternes Betalningssystemer.

limited, which made partnership and developing high-tech products a profitable enterprise. Finland chose to go another route, in part because there were considerably fewer players in the banking market from the outset than is the case with Finland's neighbours to the west.

This is going to be interesting as the market becomes internationalised and subject to new competitive conditions as SEPA becomes a reality around 2010, because the operations of the Nordic giro payment firms and clearinghouses are going to change. The main challenge will be to respond to competition from the considerably larger market players in the rest of Europe.

The Nordics differ from the rest of Europe in several ways. Only Finland is part of the EMU. Possible accession to the EMU is currently a low-priority issue in Sweden and Denmark, and entry into the EMU in the next few years is considered unlikely. Norway is not a member of the EU, although it is a part of the EEA.

Despite the separate status of our countries, we will be affected by the new reality that SEPA is bringing as the Nordic players must adjust their product portfolios to the standards developed within the SEPA framework if firms demand it.

Transaction volume is low by European comparison. For instance, Bankgirocentralen BGC AB in Sweden processed about 600 million transactions in 2006, while the corresponding figure for Equens (Netherlands/Germany) was 7 billion.

As SEPA only applies to payments in euro, the Swedish, Norwegian and Danish banking systems must determine the implications for the product portfolios in each country. Domestic payment products will not actually be affected by SEPA until the countries join the EMU or when laws and regulations are changed. But since the banks and other firms often have operations in more than one country, they may nonetheless be affected. It could mean that domestic firms will have to comply with several different sets of regulations, but no company wants to adjust to several different sets of product regulations. It follows that the products Nordic market players sell should preferably be harmonised with SEPA regulations and the standards adopted by the European Payments Council, EPC. For instance, they must be able to manage the IBAN and BIC structures. Naturally, the products must also meet the requirements imposed by laws related to payment services enacted on the basis of the Payment Services Directive.

But what should Nordic firms do to remain competitive from a future perspective? As we shall see, there are a number of challenges ahead, but they also entail substantial opportunities for Nordic banking systems.

9.2   HOW CAN THE CHALLENGES BE MET? IMPORTANT FACTORS TO CONSIDER

Much of European integration involves exchanging knowledge and services across-borders. In a product development context, the resulting dynamic is of vital importance. When markets are internationalised, as is now happening in the payments market, perspectives are shifted and new demands and approaches arise. The positive experiences gained via the Nordic central payment systems can be brought to the fore in that context. Likewise, the Nordic players have new lessons waiting to be learnt.

Once SEPA is realised, it will not only entail thinner products, but also very low costs. The whole idea behind SEPA is to make the market more competitive: products are supposed to become sharper, simpler and cheaper but, since the products will also become more standardised, competition will be shifted towards a more service-oriented world where focus is on the overall value proposition. This will reshape market conditions, which will change the way the products are sold.

This can be compared to the development of the automobile industry. Many years ago, Volvo could sell cars by emphasising their safety; this was a *unique selling point.* Today, safety is one piece of the value proposition; customers presume the cars they buy are safe. Likewise, customer expectations for payments have changed. Concepts like quality and security are implicit in the value proposition and the focus must be on other values.

Another example that illustrates a new approach is low-price air travel, where the flight itself is very cheap these days. In return, customers pay extra for baggage, in-flight meals and other services. A plane trip used to be an entire package of services, but nowadays it is made up of selectable components.

A changing market demands new methods. New conditions compel innovative thinking in areas like pricing, product development and long-term strategies. In the rest of this chapter, we describe some of the incentives for achieving the lower costs that are one of the key drivers behind SEPA. We will also look at some of the lessons we have learnt so far with regard to product development. Finally, we outline why we believe strategic alliances are going to be formed among various industry players.

9.3   COST REDUCTION

SEPA is being used to create a European payments market with common standards aimed at higher efficiency, a more competitive market and lower prices for the end customer. In order to remain an attractive alternative, the Nordic clearinghouses will probably have to continue lowering their transaction costs. A payment transaction will cost less in the future than it does today. Price may be the most important criterion for the banks after SEPA has been realised.

Several actions may be used to achieve greater cost-effectiveness. The banks currently use several different interfaces, systems and vendors to manage their payment and clearing flows. The more interfaces they have, the higher the costs to the bank. In the ideal world, are moving towards a single interface.

More standardised product portfolios common to the banks should be developed. More distinct economies of scale will be obtained in operations, administration and development through standardising and simplifying the product range.

A more modularised product structure should be created in parallel. In order to meet the banks' wishes for unique solutions, the solutions will have to be created from standardised product components that can be combined as needed and desired. Although products are moving towards standardisation, it must be possible for banks to choose and pay for the use of various functionalities and segments of the products. For that reason, the product portfolio will have a basic structure accompanied by linked optional services and functionalities.

Simpler sign-up is important to keeping costs down. It must be easy for banks and end customers and corporates to sign up for the products. Simple sign-up minimises the threshold for switching from one network to another. Simplicity can thus drive competition, but also help reduce the operational resource requirement.

Dependency on paper must be reduced. Players in the Nordics have been working for several years to reduce paper reporting in favour of electronic reporting. Costs should be cut substantially by reducing, or completely eliminating, the share of paper reporting in the products.

9.4   PRODUCT DEVELOPMENT THAT CREATES ADDED VALUE

In order to avoid competing on the basis of price alone, products must create added value for the banks and their customers, by means including product bundling and support services.

Other ways for the banks to create added value include:

- **Sophisticated information.** This means that end customers can be given options for additional information services so that they can gain direct access to payment information, such as the status of a payment order, history, monitoring, accounting, etc, to a greater extent than currently.
- **Speed.** Payment execution speed is becoming more important. At present, this is often controlled by the central bank's settlement hours, which limits opportunities to make express payments. More frequent settlement must be possible in the future.
- **Straight Through Processing (STP)** into end customers' payables and receivables ledgers and systems will minimise the manual labour involved in payments. A higher degree of STP will be made possible through close partnerships with business system vendors. As a result, the operations of business system vendors will increasingly converge with the operations of clearinghouses.

9.4.1   A changing society is driving development

The payment services business is not an island unto itself. Product development is not necessarily driven only by technical innovations and customer demands. Changes in financial systems accompany wider social changes. Examples of social trends that the Nordic countries must take into account in future years are the large numbers who will be retiring from the labour force and an ageing population, population decline in rural areas, limited resources in the public sector and increased demands for public services. Major efforts towards e-administration are in progress in Sweden, for example. A number of initiatives have been taken in the Nordics to streamline public administrations. High IT maturity among the citizenry is facilitating development.

Major investments in broadband infrastructure have been made in the Nordics to make it easier for all citizens, including those who reside in peripheral areas, to benefit from the solutions enabled by new technology. E-identification is one example of such a new technology, which has been used in Sweden for more than six years. One of the key promoters has been the Swedish Tax Agency, which has worked steadily to encourage electronic processing of tax returns. Taxpayers no longer have to sign their tax returns, but are instead expected to file returns online or via mobile telephone. Another example is the Swedish Social Insurance Agency, whose services to a large extent are available over the Internet and require e-identification.

The development of an effective e-identification solution has required high-level cooperation among clearinghouses, banks and government agencies. Once the infrastructure was in place, the parties could proceed with development of other services for which e-identification serves a vital function.

The most recent example from the Swedish payments system is signing direct debit (autogiro) authorisations online with e-identification. The customer does not have to sign a piece of paper, which saves substantial costs for firms and a great deal of time for payers.

Solutions like this are going to be developed at an increasing rate in the next few years. There will be greater focus on product development because the customers (both the banks and firms) are putting increasingly higher demands on payment-linked services.

9.4.2   E-billing volumes are rising

Services such as being able send a payment from point A to point B at any time around the clock, being able to send all the information in a single file and being able to link electronic services such as e-billing to the payment will probably be expected as a matter of course within a few years.

E-billing has existed in the Nordic market since the late 1990's and is considered a mature product in several Nordic countries, at least in the B2C market. As a result of strong willingness to cooperate among banks in Norway, volume growth for the service has been excellent ever since it was introduced. Development in Finland, especially among business customers, has been facilitated by the Fin-Voice standard. The lack of standards is otherwise impeding the development of e-billing on a European basis; for instance, there is no uniform definition of what an e-bill actually is.

Openness to interoperability – the ability for all players to reach one another – is a key incentive for volume increases. In what started out as a fragmented market, several alliances have been entered into in recent years aimed at creating interoperability in both the B2B and B2C markets. With more uniform solutions in sight, it is becoming easier for customers to understand the value propositions and express their wishes.

The results of the e-billing initiative include a requirement that all Swedish government agencies must fully implement e-billing by 1 July 2008, which is going to be a real volume driver in the Swedish market.

9.4.3   Availability is important

Innovative optional services are going to take on greater importance to the payments business. They must also be associated with a high level of service, if such service is desired. Availability is yet another important requirement for future payment products. This refers not only to business hours for the banking systems, but also the level of service, format and channels that vendors must support. The products offered must be adapted to the world in which the online banks do business. This means they must be available 24 hours a day, seven days a week, 365 days a year. This will involve a major change compared to historical conditions, as the products in the past were often adapted to customary office hours of nine to five.

The products must also be available in the sense of being manageable for all targeted customer categories. This puts high demands on the capacity to communicate electronically. Communication products must be designed so that availability and simplicity are achieved, regardless of whether the firm is large or small or which bank the firm uses.

9.4.4   How can the market be convinced?

It must be easy for the banks to sell the products that are developed. It must be easy for customers to understand their benefits. None of this is actually anything new. The real challenge is that the products developed must be sufficiently interesting to persuade customers to switch – otherwise, the migration phase from legacy products to new ones will be protracted and costly. As in the rest of Europe, there is a challenge entailed in getting Nordic customers to understand the benefits of SEPA. Why else would they abandon systems that work, and which are already perceived as secure, reliable and high-quality?

One way to convince the market of the superiority of new products is to allow the customer to start with simple functionality and add additional features later as their needs and maturity increase. In the old world, customers were forced to replace a product or buy an additional one to gain access to other features. In the new world, a gentler transition must instead be possible, which can be achieved by means of thin, scalable products.

But two characteristics will remain more important than all the rest: quality and security. The Nordic payment systems have historically been associated with quality and security, which will remain the hallmarks in the future as well.

9.5   STRATEGIC ALLIANCES AND THE ROLE OF BUSINESS SYSTEM VENDORS

Payment processing is a volume business. Alliances with large-volume clearinghouses entail distinct advantages for small players, including lower costs accompanied by lower capital expenditures. The banks can also be offered a wider range of products.

In order to make the Nordic banks more competitive and future-proof Nordic payment systems, it is likely that various alliances will be formed. Continued consolidation of the banking market is also in progress and cross-border mergers and acquisitions should be expected. NETS, a merger of the Danish PBS and Norwegian BBS with regard to the respective firms' card operations is a relatively recent example.[3] NETS provides processing of card transactions for the northern European market and has gained distinct economies of scale through the merger.

9.5.1   Industry convergence

In the post-SEPA world, solutions will be standardised, flexible and transparent. For the customer to successfully transition from a legacy system to a new one, another player becomes critical: the business system vendor. The value chain for a payment lengthens and the steps that precede the payment, or ensue after the payment is made, must become more electronic to achieve Straight Through Processing. The products become more sophisticated and must be integrated with each other to provide customer benefit. New functionalities will be built into business systems that enables integration with the value propositions of both the banks and the clearinghouses.

But there are two sides to the coin: business system vendors will enable the realisation of SEPA by means of upgrades, support services, etc. On the flip side, they may become competitors to the banks and clearinghouses. Thus, an industry convergence is occurring wherein the operations of business system vendors and banks are overlapping. For that reason, new alliances and business models are to be expected.

9.5.2   Strategic alliances may yield several advantages

These alliances may involve Nordic clearinghouses maintaining their relationships with local banks and government agencies while developing SEPA-adapted products together with a selected partner. Alliances can provide substantial advantages to the Nordic banks and their customers. Some of the most important, as mentioned above, are economies of scale, access to a wider product range and swifter adjustment to customer demands. But it also means that clearinghouses will be able to take more long-term decisions for their operations, that payment

---

[3] NETS stands for Northern European Transaction Services and was formed in 2007.

flows can be coordinated, and that banks will have the option to buy only selected components of the payment process.

In several cases, the older, national Nordic systems will require extensive development to ensure SEPA compatibility and, possibly, compliance with new European legal requirements. Strategic alliances will make it possible to secure development in the long run and may also make it cheaper and less risky to upgrade existing technology.

9.6   CONCLUSIONS

The following chart summarises the conceivable future structure of the value propositions of Nordic clearinghouses.

The future value proposition in the Nordics will consist of thin products. The core product will be basic functionality with high quality and security. But there will be more sophisticated optional functionalities, to an even higher extent than currently. Since the banks select the options that suit their customers, modularity will be very important, which imposes heavy demands on platform flexibility.

Customer demands will rule to an even higher extent after 2010. After all, one of the main ideas behind SEPA is to make services available to customers regardless of national borders. For that reason, the banks must be able to quickly adapt their value propositions to the customer's wishes, with regard to both price and functionality. For that reason, we believe proprietary solutions have no future. Instead, the solutions will be standardised, flexible and transparent. That is one of the cornerstones of SEPA (and the inner market): freedom of choice for the customer, which is predicated on the opportunity to make correct, rational choices. But the products and services must contain such functionality that their promises can be kept. When persuading bank customers to abandon their old solutions in favour of a SEPA-harmonised product, precisely that will be a cogent argument: not only the freedom to choose – but also the opportunity.

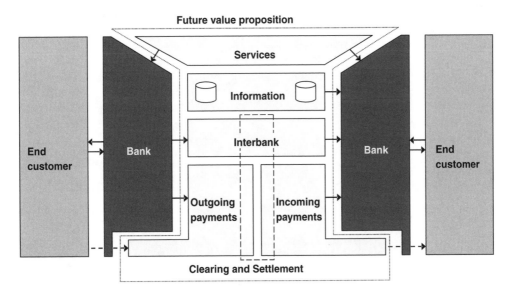

Figure 9.1   Products in a post-SEPA world

In summary, there are many challenges ahead for both the Nordic banks and Nordic clearinghouses from a longer-term perspective. Several things must be done if they are to remain competitive players in an integrated European financial services market after 2010.

Cost-effectiveness is important. This may be achieved through things like large-scale operations and a more standardised product range. Standards must be adopted with regard to products, communication, etc. The SEPA standard will be part of the value proposition along with optional local functionalities.

With the above in mind, the clearinghouses must provide simple, standardised products to banks. But the products must be scalable and upgradable with sophisticated optional services, such as infrastructure and standards for e-billing and e-identification. Generally speaking, there will be intense focus on product development and innovations. IT platforms must enable fast and flexible development.

The Nordic players must proactively follow developments and distribute the necessary development over larger transaction volume. This can be accomplished through partnerships.

Close cooperation with business system vendors towards STP integration with business systems will be highly important. In parallel, this will stimulate industry convergence.

Supplier reputations for reliable delivery and reliable products are critically important now and will remain so. The future hallmarks will still be quality and security. The Nordic clearinghouses must be able to continue delivering competitive advantages to the banks even after SEPA has become a reality.

10
Eight Predictions for SEPA's Impact on Payment Cards

John Chaplin, First Data

Although SEPA will help MasterCard and Visa to achieve greater domination in the battle for share of European consumers wallets, the separation of scheme brands from processing will be a challenge for them, allowing some new, competitive processors to evolve.

10.1   THE NEW RULES FOR PLAYING CARDS

Card payments were not the primary target of the SEPA initiative but when the European Commission and the European Payments Council, representing the banks, agreed that a streamlined business model was needed for electronic payments, the decision was taken to address all low value electronic payments. This proved to be a momentous decision as cards got swept into the SEPA net. Many card industry participants were against this move, on the grounds that Mr. or Mrs. European Citizen could already pay by card in most markets, and that payment schemes like MasterCard and Visa already provided sufficient coverage and efficiency. With over 350 million European consumers already using their payment cards successfully, shouldn't we be saying 'nothing is broken, so why fix it?'

The regulators, in the form of the European Commission and the European Central Bank, did not see it that way. As they looked out across the European payments landscape, they saw:

- Two major supranational card schemes – MasterCard and Visa – exercising great market power and subject to very limited European governance;
- A number of national payment scheme and organisations running their own markets in ways that disadvantaged or excluded other European banks; and
- Vastly differing economic structures and pricing levels, especially in terms of what merchants pay to accept cards.

They believed that these factors were preventing the establishment of an integrated European market which, it was argued, would increase economic efficiency and boost growth. The so called Lisbon Agenda. So, cards were included within SEPA.

Although cards were included, they are treated differently. Unlike direct debits and credit transfers, no new schemes were to be established. Instead, current scheme operations are to be forcibly adjusted to conform to a SEPA Cards Framework (SCF) that sets out the new rules of the game. All significant card schemes are now required to become SEPA-compliant by observing the requirements of the SCF.

Another factor is that cards are subject to the rules of the Payment Services Directive, the initiative of the European Commission's DG Market group to establish a more consistent and competitive legal framework structure across the European market. Just for good measure, the cards industry is also under strong pressure to change from the European Commission's DG Competition group, which identified a number of competition issues as a result of a detailed sector review. The DG Competition has been heavily involved in considering both the principle and level of issuer reimbursement fees, or interchange fees, which so impact the profitability of the industry. Interchange is the fee paid by acquiring banks to card issuers, which is the major factor behind the charges that merchants pay to accept payment by card from MasterCard and Visa.

As if that were not pressure enough, the European Central Bank has been increasingly vocal about how it sees the card industry developing within the euro zone, and has been actively supporting the creation of a new European debit card scheme.

With great pressure for change coming from the regulatory authorities, and the banks being able to influence events but not control them, what is the likely SEPA impact on the card industry?

Forecasting impacts of major regulatory initiatives is a risky business as many lawmakers have found to their cost. The example of the Yellow Pages deregulation in UK is a clear example of the law of unintended consequences.

Yellow Pages was a service operated by British Telecom which allowed UK citizens to call one number, 192, and ask for the telephone number of business or service they were seeking such as the number for a plumber or electrician. It was argued that a single provider with a free, universal service, was preventing new competitors and thus depriving consumers of greater choice. Therefore, the service was deregulated in 2003 and new entrants were positively encouraged through a revised regulatory framework.

The result a few years later is that everybody now pays for a service that was traditionally free, service standards have generally declined and there is widespread consumer confusion about the number to call as all service providers' telephone numbers are prefixed with the same three digit code, 118.

This cannot have been the purpose of the regulatory initiative. The same could happen with SEPA as it is very difficult to tell who is driving the agenda which makes it very difficult to be clear about the destination for the agenda. The respective European Commission's directorates, the ECB and the EPC, whilst having some common ground, clearly do not have the same agendas, despite any press releases to the contrary.

10.2   HOW THE CARDS WILL FALL

Despite this tricky background, it is possible to be fairly confident about some of the changes that are going to happen, and I think there are eight key predictions that can be made about how SEPA will impact the European card industry.

10.2.1   Major change will happen to almost all areas of the business

The structure of the European card payment industry has not fundamentally changed in the past 20 years. Almost all of the players and schemes that were around in 1985 were still around in 2005, although volumes had massively increased. Very few industries have shown such stability or rigidity over such a period of time. This stability will not be repeated, and the next five years will see major structural change in almost all areas of the business.

The change is both externally and internally driven. The banking sector that dominates card payments is undergoing massive change and is becoming increasingly competitive. Cards are now mainstream payment instruments in many financial institutions, and receive a great deal of boardroom attention. Therefore, the old ways of doing business are under intense scrutiny.

In addition, card issuance activity is no longer confined to banks, with non-banks already very active in the pre-paid and credit card sectors and, in some cases, even considering how to issue debit cards. Card acquiring is rapidly concentrating in the hands of a limited number of large players, with real scale economies of scale, and many banks have decided that a capital intensive, low margin business is not for them. I expect this trend to continue.

Meanwhile, the relatively benign regulatory environment with minimal regulatory intervention, has been turned on its head. It is not only the interchange that is under attack, the whole way the industry is organised is going to have to change because of concerns that there is insufficient real competition.

Even the regulators themselves are subject to change, as there is real debate about how best to govern and regulate the industry. So SEPA will be the largest maelstrom ever to impact the European cards business.

10.2.2 Interchange will survive but at a reduced level in many markets

Interchange fees are not an official part of SEPA and yet consistent interchange structures and rates are essential for a smoothly functioning single market. There would be a strong case for having a single European interchange fee rate, but no regulator is prepared to take the political heat that would come from raising interchange, and therefore merchant charges, in

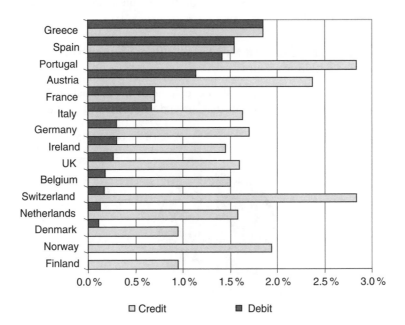

Figure 10.1 National card acceptances charges

those markets where card payments are currently loss-making and cross-subsidised by other activities. However, regulators are not going to sit idly by when MasterCard's interchange rates are substantially higher than Visa's, even though it is the same banks with the same costs at either end of the transaction. And when countries with relatively similar sophistication have such widely diverging charges for merchant acceptance of cards, the regulator will intervene.

So, expect the combination of the EU Commission and local regulators to:

- force average interchange rates decrease further;
- make MasterCard and Visa agree to similar levels; and
- reduce the high rates for debit in a number of national card schemes.

In this respect, Europe will be very different from the USA, where the pressure on interchange is upwards and not downwards. However, interchange is very unlikely to be eliminated because this would kill any new European card scheme at birth, and might leave the regulators being blamed for the re-imposition of card transaction fees that would inevitably follow such a move.

10.2.3   Many national payment schemes will disappear and MasterCard and Visa will become even more powerful payment brands

As many national banks become absorbed into European or global banks, the attachment to local debit schemes will massively reduce. Couple this with the need to invest heavily to make the schemes SEPA-compliant and the increased regulatory scrutiny over membership rules and interchange, and many schemes will just fold and give their cards business to MasterCard and Visa. MasterCard and Visa have built such strong consumer brands in the past thirty years that it seems inevitable that the local scheme owners will decide to accept the trend towards these mega-players. A majority of European bankers expect MasterCard and Visa to be major winners because of SEPA and, of course, many of the difficult regulatory issues can be left to these organisations to handle.

10.2.4   At least one European debit card brand will emerge and will take at least 15 % of the market within five years

There is an argument that if national brands are replaced by the international brands, then the market will become a duopoly between MasterCard and Visa. This will not happen. In the same

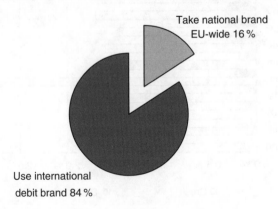

Figure 10.2   EU bank plans for debit card brands *Source:* PSEL/First Data survey, 2006.

way that Pepsi- and Coca- Cola do not control the total market for fizzy drinks, MasterCard and Visa will grow as a result of SEPA but will not achieve the 100 % market share domination that they crave. There are enough organisations around Europe who do not like doing business with these firms and SEPA, by removing technical and competition barriers, will create a situation where establishing more schemes becomes possible.

It will not be an easy task but the willingness of key industry players, especially in the old eurocheque markets, to build alternative card solutions to those of these global players should not be underestimated. Having said that, many banks do not share the ECB's enthusiasm for a new scheme. There is still quite some unease that that payment brands being in the hands of quoted companies could force prices up in the long-run. This fear, whether justified or not, is clearly there for MasterCard following their IPO and there are similar concerns about whether the Visa will follow the same route.[1]

10.2.5   Many national processing companies will become uneconomic and will cease to exist in their current form as a commercially driven pan-European processing sector develops

In many countries, there has been a shared card payments processing utility responsible for most of the transaction processing. The result is that there are at least thirty card processing organisations operating in Europe. In an industry that has a heavy technology component and where scale matters, this is simply too many for the market and concentration is widely predicted. National processing companies that were owned by national banks with close links to national card schemes were viable in the past but do not work today.

When banks are no longer national and schemes have been converted to European or Global brands, where is the persuasive logic for the banks to run their own shared processing utility?

There can then be some debate about how fast such consolidation will occur. How many survivors will there be, and who will they be?

In the past few years, banks in Austria, Belgium, Germany and Sweden have all sold national processing companies and there have been significant ownership changes in Italy, Poland and UK. This trend will continue. In the same way that many national airlines are in their death throes, we can expect a future where countries no longer have a national payments processor.

Longer term, there are likely to be no more than six large card processors in Europe within the next seven years. As banks become more and more cost and service level driven, we can expect that commercially driven business models for processors will become the norm, as the shared utility model will become less easy to sustain.

10.2.6   The card schemes that also provide processing will find their business model endangered and will have to chose what they want to be

One of the key requirements for SEPA is that payment schemes separate their scheme brand activities from their processing activities. This is clearly bad news for both of the international card schemes, MasterCard and Visa, because their whole strategy depends upon being in both the scheme brand and processing, and then making them work together.

---

[1] Visa announced they would also IPO general operation from November 2007. However, this does not include Visa Europe, which will remain bank-owned for the forseeable future.

Senior bankers do not believe that MasterCard and Visa will voluntarily comply with this new regime. This was demonstrated by a survey in 2006 performed by First Data with the firm PSEL. This survey showed that only a quarter of the senior bankers interviewed felt that the card schemes would voluntarily separate their processing activities, with most believing that they will try to only make cosmetic changes to demonstrate compliance.

This approach is likely to fail, as the anti-competitive nature of tying scheme and brand and processing has already been clearly identified by both the European Commission and the ECB as an issue, and they are unlikely to ease off. Similar principles of separation have already been successfully implemented in the securities and telecommunications sectors and they are likely to apply the same principles to the cards markets.

This is going to create an unpleasant dilemma for the card organisations. At their heart, they are branding organisations intent on getting maximum consumer uptake, and yet they often make as much or more money from the processing of transactions. Nowhere is this truer than for debit cards, where both MasterCard and Visa have failed to make significant revenue from the brand and therefore rely on processing to support their profitability.

Managing this conflict whilst keeping the regulator happy will be a major challenge.

10.2.7   Increased regulatory intervention will happen, as self regulation will not deliver results fast enough

A stated objective of both the European Commission and the banks is for SEPA to be a self-regulated initiative. Whilst the banks absolutely subscribe to this principle, the Commission's view is really that self regulation is OK as long as the industry makes the required changes quickly enough. And therein lies the rub.

Many industry participants would argue that they cannot comply with SEPA until the cards requirements are more fully defined. The SEPA Cards Framework is generally thought to be weak in a number of key areas and the Payment Services Directive will not be enshrined in national law until the end of 2009 at which point the SEPA cards transition can begin. So, some feel there is very legitimate reason to wait. Others, especially those who see no obvious role for themselves in a single European market, intend to carry on doing business the old way regardless.

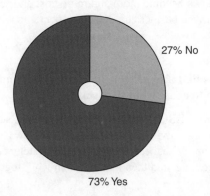

27% No

73% Yes

Figure 10.3   Will the EC legislate anyway, to enforce compliance? *Source:* PSEL First Data survey 2006.

Whatever the reason, a sizeable majority of bankers believe that eventually the Commission will decide progress is too slow and will regulate anyway, and most industry players think that the imposed regulations will be less advantageous to them than the self-regulatory framework.

10.2.8 Some large banks and some non-bank market entrants will prosper from aggressively exploiting SEPA freedoms and opportunities.

There are very many banks that see the cards requirements for SEPA as yet another compliance burden that has to be endured. The reasoning is that this is creating unnecessary changes and costs to an industry structure that has worked well for over twenty years. Combine this with associated reductions in revenues from lower cardholder and merchant fees, and SEPA delivers a generally negative impact.

There are however an increasing number of banks taking the attitude that if the changes are inevitable, the question is how to exploit them. This means adopting a smarter strategy than competitors.

Therefore there are already signs that some banks are well advanced in planning to rationalise their processing arrangements into a pan-European model, and they are looking in detail at the market opportunities that could be achieved through a pan-European operation. If these institutions create first mover advantage in areas such as pan-European co-branded loyalty programmes, pan-European corporate card programmes or in merchant acquisition for pan-European retailers, then significant gains will be made at the expense of institutions that were less responsive. Equally, many non-bank players are looking at these new market opportunities also.

10.3   JOKERS IN THE PACK?

Every pack of playing cards has a minimum of two jokers. In contemplating the future of cards under SEPA, it is worth thinking about the potential jokers that could change the course of events and derail some of the above predictions.

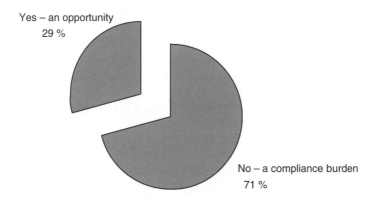

Figure 10.4   Will SEPA bring business opportunities for your bank? *Source:* PSEL First Data survey 2006

There are probably three jokers in the payments card pack:

- A decision by the European Commission to outlaw interchange for card transactions would take the industry into new territory. Nobody has any confidence about how the industry would develop after such a move, including the retailers who are continually asking for interchange fees to be abolished, and the effects would be seismic.
- Rapid convergence of card processing with ACH processing would change the outlook for both debit card schemes and for processing. Such a move would seriously weaken both MasterCard and Visa, and would make new schemes much more likely. The eventual processing survivors would be different from those in a cards-only scenario.
- If either of the card schemes proactively spun-off their processing organisations to create truly European operations willing to process all brands on an equal basis, the effect would be very substantial. Such an organisation would stand every chance of becoming the dominant card processor in Europe and would be a feared competitor. However, to achieve this, they would have to abstain from favouring their former owners in any way, which would require an enormous shift in mind-set.

The cards industry will be changed substantially and permanently by SEPA. It is now too late to stop the initiative although nobody is quite sure where it is leading.

SEPA for cards is perhaps best thought of as a snowball careering down a hill. It is gathering size and momentum. Its' precise course is not sure. It could deviate at any moment. It is very difficult to stop. If you decide to stand your ground and ignore it, there is a grave danger that your business could be flattened.

Life in the cards business is going to be very interesting in the next few years.

11

SEPA and eCommerce – the Consumer is King

René Pelegero, PayPal

German grandmother, Hannah Kolb, lives in Munich and is an enthusiastic collector and active trader of attic finds, or 'dachbodenfun'. She attends collectors' fairs and flea markets and scours newspapers and magazines for bargains. It's more than just a hobby for Hanna, since she relies upon it to supplement her pension.

Hanna keeps up with technological developments and so recently started to buy and sell items on the internet. She is keen to explore ways in which she can grow her business across Europe.

When she traded solely in the physical world, she confined her activities to Germany. Now that she has internet access, she has expanded her outlook internationally, taking advantage of recent changes introduced by the European Union. For example, she no longer has to worry about import duties when buying and selling within the European Union, or about currency conversion since the introduction of the Euro.

Hannah recently located a 75 year old Steiff sitting dog rattler, offered for sale by a French collector, that would complete her collection of old rattlers. The seller only accepts credit cards as a form of payment, but Hanna does not have a credit card, and besides, she likes to complete all her trades via bank transfer and direct debit, the preferred way for German consumers to pay for internet purchases.

Though she may be willing to share her bank account details with the French seller, he cannot debit her bank account in Germany from France because the seller is not equipped to handle these payments and, besides, French and German payment and clearing systems don't 'talk' to each other.

Fortunately, recent developments allow Hanna to initiate the purchase and pay by debiting her bank account. The French seller can receive payment into his own bank account for the same fee as if he had received a local payment without having to make any changes to his infrastructure.

Is this how things would conceivably operate post 2010, in the SEPA era? Possibly. However, this scenario is typical of millions of payments carried out daily by PayPal. PayPal is in a position to offer a unique perspective on the SEPA vision as it already operates a model that treats all transactions within the Eurozone as borderless.

SEPA's vision is to create common international banking standards and interoperable payment systems. Although the macro-economic benefits associated with SEPA are clear, the specific benefits to consumers or merchants are less so. The hope may be that the emergence of a simpler way to do cross-border transactions will encourage innovation focused on meeting customer needs. It is unlikely, however, that regulation or infrastructure changes alone will make it happen.

Banks and payment services providers that seek to win consumers and merchants will need to craft innovative solutions. That is not likely to result from a focus solely on harmonisation and cost reduction, but would be a response to consumer and merchant needs and intense competition between innovative and existing payment methods.

PayPal's experience in Europe gives it a thorough understanding of the online habits of customers within the Eurozone. If this is representative of behaviour in the wider world, it reveals some of the challenges for SEPA.

11.1   THE BENEFITS OF SEPA

There are undoubtedly a number of positives brought about by SEPA. SEPA harmonises national rules to create a simplified, standardised payments back end infrastructure. It envisions a secure, convenient and inexpensive means for national and cross-border payments, whether by credit card, debit card or money transfer, that incorporates new protection guarantees for consumers. It provides added assurance that, for example, by 2012 an electronic payment will be made within 24 hours, or 48 hours if made in paper. That compares with the current wait of up to seven working days to complete a transfer within Europe.

As national boundaries will no longer be an issue, merchants will be able to buy their services from any EU provider and increase competition between service providers at all levels of the value-chain. There could also conceivably be more financial services providers, as non-banks and private labels credit issuers provide bespoke services for merchants to purchase, creating greater opportunities for price negotiation. It should also help both bank and non-bank payment providers expand their businesses, and this competition may lower prices and improve efficiency for all users.

11.2   WHAT ABOUT CONSUMERS?

What is less clear is how harmonisation will affect the choices of payment methods available to European consumers. PayPal's experience has shown that the online needs of consumers and merchants are not that different from those in the physical world. Online consumers want to choose between familiar payment methods such as bank accounts, credit, debit, store and prepaid cards. They also want to know that they can use that method in a safe and convenient manner everywhere they shop.

Local consumer and merchant habits inevitably emerge from the distinct set of payment instruments developed by each country. These do provide some barriers to a one-size-fits-all strategy. For example, in the UK and France, cards dominate both online and offline. In Germany, there is a distinct preference for bank payments such as direct debit and credit transfers. Cash On Delivery purchases have traditionally been a popular method of payment for eCommerce purchases in Italy and Spain. Unfortunately, instruments designed to work in the physical world and which suit local preferences are not necessarily able to perform equally well online.

Many consumers are already familiar with the need to provide credit card and personal details online. Yet the process is cumbersome and some users are concerned that this may potentially expose them to fraud and misuse of personal information. Bank transfers may be cheap, but there can be delays before the merchant receives payment confirmation. In Germany, direct debits expose the merchant to a high level of risk. And while the debit card is a popular electronic payment instrument in Europe, outside of the UK it is usually not broadly enabled for online usage.

Equally significant is that many of the instruments most popular for online payments in their home country cannot be used to shop abroad. A German online shopper can buy a new mp3 player at a local electronics site such as http://www.technikdirect.de and pay by providing their German bank account details. If they want to make the same purchase at http://www.darty.fr they need to pay by card. But in Germany today, only 15 % of all payment cards in circulation are enabled to support purchases on the Internet.

Conversely, merchants set up and define their back end processes and fulfilment pipelines in support of the prevalent method of payment. Merchants supporting card payments, for example, can ship merchandise upon receiving approval to their authorization request and can recognize revenue at that time. Merchants supporting bank transfers must decide whether to ship the merchandise upon placement of the order, risking non-payment and a collections issue, or wait for the arrival of the payment before shipping, negatively impacting the consumer experience. In either case, the accounting treatment to these scenarios is different. This genuinely restricts online shopping choice for consumers and the addressable market for merchants. It is a real barrier for the SEPA promise of a single domestic market in Europe.

11.3   WHAT ARE THE ALTERNATIVES?

A number of possible solutions already exist. One of these is the online 'wallet' that PayPal offers to our consumers and merchants.

This wallet is a multi-function payment account that enables its owner, who might be an individual or business, to send and receive payments online. The wallet is usable across different internet sites and channels including internet and mobile, and its owner is able to store and re-use multiple payment methods and shipping addresses, with no need to retype personal or card details. None of this information is shared with the merchant. Most importantly, a cross-border wallet insulates consumers and merchants from each other's preferences with regards to local payment methods and processes.

This style of wallet is an example of a complementary service that covers the 'last mile' in the eCommerce purchase continuum. Wallets do not compete with bank accounts, but extend their reach. They connect to global card and bank networks and allow any merchant to accept – and buyer to choose – any relevant card or bank payment method. All transactions are acquired and processed by major banks, with a high level of security. The bank retains full control over the account balances and earns the same level of transaction-related revenues that would apply if the payment instrument had been used directly.

Cross-border online wallets already fulfil the SEPA ideal as they give consumers a safe and simple way to use locally available instruments, online and globally. The wallet also addresses several major e-commerce problems, including consumer fears of identity theft and desire for fast, convenient and familiar checkout experiences. As a result, more than 25 % of Europe's online shoppers now use them.

11.4   THE MERCHANTS' PERSPECTIVE

Merchants are also consumers of payment services and their needs must also be taken into account. Merchants care primarily about the cost associated with the form of payment and whether it brings additional sales.

As in the physical world, a merchant is at an advantage if shoppers can use their chosen payment method and enjoy a seamless checkout experience. Merchants also need a system that provides instant confirmation of payment, quick access to funds and limited risk of roll-back of transactions. It will have added appeal if it also minimises any upfront investment in new systems to integrate new payment methods and limits transactions charges.

The addition of a popular payment method enhances credibility, particularly for sellers that are too small to offer credit card payments. This typically results in a significant increase in sales. For example, consumers can already use their PayPal wallets at over 100 000 merchants in Europe including major online stores such as Boots, Harrods, Pixmania and Blume 2000.

As eCommerce grows and cross-border trading becomes commonplace, consumers and merchants will continue to gravitate towards methods which offer the greatest safety and convenience, and this is likely to be the case post 2010. Although PayPal expects the core principles of SEPA to have been implemented by then, local mechanisms are unlikely to be phased out for a few years at least. It is, for example, quite difficult to establish just how consistent support is for SEPA at a national government level. That increases uncertainty over the phase out of local instruments.

11.5   HOW WILL PAYPAL FIT IN THE FUTURE?

PayPal intends to continue playing a leading role in the provision of secure and efficient payments. From PayPal's perspective, SEPA is broadly positive. It improves access to many national markets and brings about operational efficiencies. However, it also creates an environment where innovation will be possible and PayPal expects to remain at the forefront of payments by exploring how to meet needs of consumers, merchants and the financial community.

PayPal has already been part of major changes in areas such as micro-payments, where the greatest innovation has come from outside the traditional banking industry. PayPal is simiarly at the forefront of other advances such as payment via mobile handsets. This is something of a return to roots, as the company's original premise was to facilitate payments between PDAs. PayPal mobile was launched in the US and Europe in 2006. It allows customers to text funds to each other and expects to benefit as mobile telephones become increasingly popular as a payments mechanism.

There are a number of roles we are well-placed to provide in the post 2010 environment and, working directly with the banking industry, could also help banks transition into the new SEPA environment. For example, European banks outside the Eurozone could funnel their consumer payments into SEPA countries through PayPal. This could provide their consumers with a gateway into SEPA payments, but without those banks having to make any investment in building a SEPA infrastructure.

Banks within the SEPA zone could equally leverage PayPal's infrastructure and consumer interface and use it as the vehicle to initiate SEPA payments. This may be of particular interest to banks in countries where consumer initiated bank transfer (i.e. countries where card based payments dominate) are not common.

Finally, it may be possible to take advantage of PayPal's extensive risk management infrastructure. This is designed to prevent, identify and detect fraudulent activities such as money laundering. As the speed and volume of cross-border payments increase, banks in the SEPA area, particularly the smaller entities that have not thus far had to deal with a large volume of non-domestic payments, could leverage this infrastructure in partnership with PayPal.

PayPal is not necessarily in a stronger position than other participants to divine the future. The views represented in this chapter represent educated guesses. But a focus on consumers and merchants' needs suggests that between now and 2010, consumers will increasingly adopt new services that help them take better control of how they manage their funds. Convenience and safety, in that order, are increasingly important considerations likely to lead them to select payment vehicles that are more attuned to their requirements. Such payment innovations will help keep Hanna Kolb happily in business.

Part 3
The Views of the Banks

- Citi
- Barclays Bank
- JPMorgan Chase
- The Bank of Ireland
- The Bank of Finland
- Nordea
- Banca Popolare di Verona

12

The Payment Services Directive – a critical view

Ruth Wandhöfer, Citi

The Payments Services Directive (PSD) is a significant regulatory challenge, which needs to be carefully assessed by all existing and future players in the European payments market.

For the last five years the PSD, formally known as the New Legal Framework for Payments, has been in preparation and was finally published on the 5 December 2007. Despite the long negotiation process and the fact that several hundreds of amendments were made to the European Commission proposal by the European Parliament and the Council, the text is far from straightforward and starts to trigger more questions than answers.

At a time when banks have to cope with European and global regulatory requirements (MIFID, Basel II, FATF and more) as well the imminent launch of the SEPA (Single Euro Payments Area), the PSD constitutes a very significant additional challenge for the industry.

Whilst many estimates have been made on the costs and savings of SEPA, the PSD has not yet been considered in its own right and compliance costs are likely to reach unexpected dimensions.

This chapter attempts to provide a critical analysis of the PSD, its roots and goals, highlighting the key elements that need to be carefully assessed by the industry.

12.1 BACKGROUND

With the introduction of the Euro there was a clear expectation by politicians that cross-border Euro transactions would significantly increase as a response. Furthermore, Regulation 2560/2001 made cross-border Euro payments more attractive by limiting their price to domestic transaction pricing. However, reality proved slightly different with cross-border Euro payments remaining at a mere 2 % of total retail mass payments in Europe. In order to achieve a more consistent integration of the European payments market, a payment system for the Euro was needed and banks began developing SEPA. In this context, the European Commission was approached to provide assistance in harmonising key areas such as rules on refunds, which is very relevant for direct debits, the removal of Central Bank Reporting and the establishment of unique identifier primacy to enhance straight-through-processing (STP).

While banks took care of designing the SEPA schemes that standardise inter-bank practices for euro payments, the European Commission was to complement this work by regulating the relationship between payment service provider (PSP) and payment service user (PSU). The resulting PSD however developed into a far more complex and rather confusing piece of legislation, combining the creation of a new type of non-bank payment service provider, called 'payment institution', with the general legislation of payment services across all providers, capturing all electronic payment services within the single market.

12.2   SOME ISSUES TO CONSIDER ...

The PSD is divided into four broad pieces covering:

* scope and definitions (Title I);
* the regulation of payment institutions (Title II);
* conditions for transparency and information for payment services (Title III); and
* rights and obligations of users and providers of payment services (Title IV).

The one-size-fits-all approach to payment services and payment service providers does not always fit with the detailed elaboration of provisions, particularly as this confuses the reader as to how to apply certain articles to the various payment instruments. This means that guidance and clarification for PSPs is crucial to allow for a clear understanding and implementation of the provisions.

For example, some of the definitions in Title I need further qualification. Some examples include the definition of 'payment account' in connection with the definition of 'payment transaction'. The current definitions would mean that every account to and from which money could be moved would be caught. This could have the unintended consequence of hugely increasing information requirements for mortgage and savings accounts, for example. Definitions like 'scriptural money' are also still unclear, whilst other terms like 'payment card' are not even defined.

Whether the implementation of supervisory standards for payment service providers will be coherent is still an open question as Member States have the choice in Title II to appoint any 'competent authority' to look after the new payment institutions, which might therefore in practice be different from banking supervisors.

The defined degree of information to be provided to customers before, during and after transactions under Title III is slightly excessive, translating into potential information overload.

While the PSD governs the customer-to-provider relationship, certain provisions of Title IV, the heart of the PSD, also touch the inter-bank or inter-PSP space. Uncertainties persist regarding a clear understanding of the concept of 'receipt of a payment transaction' and the rules on execution times for payments. These provisions dive deep into the operational domain of payment service provision, where the European Commission's aim of translating a political vision into detailed rules can hardly be considered a success. Furthermore, this title adds additional complexity by stipulating several opt-out possibilities in relation to non-consumer users, which is welcome in practice but should have been a default rule. It is therefore still unclear how national regulators will interpret these options and whether all PSPs will be required to actively approach their business customers to negotiate the opt-out.

Key opt-out options cover the burden of proof of PSPs in relation to the authentication and execution of payment transactions, the liabilities of PSUs for unauthorised payment transactions, refund rules, irrevocability of a payment order and rules regarding non-execution or defective execution. The radical shift in liability towards PSPs not only has the potential of increasing fraud on the PSU side, but also creates a number of important legal questions in the inter-bank and inter-PSP space.

The mandating of rules including execution times and the definition of receipt of a payment are so stringent that one cannot but assume the European payments market to be currently in a state of market failure, which is of course far from reality.

In addition, there are a number of instances where the interplay of the PSD with existing EU legislation, such as Anti-Money Laundering and Terrorist Financing or the E-Money Directive, is still ambiguous. Finally, Central Bank Reporting has not been removed, still constituting a barrier to the integration of the European payments market.

12.3   THE PSD FAILS TO MEET THE 'BETTER REGULATION' BENCHMARK

Over the last few years, the European Commission has further developed and refined its Better Regulation policy, which focuses on high-level principles aimed at improving the quality and flexibility of the regulatory architecture. The four cornerstones of Better Regulation are identified as:

1. Simplification
2. Dialogue
3. Impact Assessment
4. Ex Post Evaluation

In practice, the PSD does not entirely measure up to this benchmark. Instead of a principle-based approach, the PSD is a very complex and detailed construct of rules, which neither supports simplification nor reduces the administrative burden or business compliance costs. In fact, the PSD can be best described as a Chameleon. You are never really sure of what you see, and it keeps on changing!

The choice of the instrument of a Directive, instead of a Regulation, is in itself problematic as it allows for variations in transposition across Member States, leading to the classical risk of 'gold plating'[1]. This is amplified by the fact that twelve explicit provisions allow for national derogations[2] in addition to Article 86, which relates to full harmonisation. This permits PSPs 'to grant more favourable terms to payment service users'. Some Member States already consider 'more favourable terms', for example longer refund periods for direct debits, which could have a negative impact on SEPA migration.

Furthermore, the wording of a number of additional articles seems to suggest even more options for derogation, where those would not be required to be reported to the Commission. This will create significant implementation challenges for multi-country banks, and we could end up with 27 or more mini-PSDs. A coherent payments product proposition across the region might therefore be under risk.

A practical problem could arise, in terms of transparency, if Member States choose to transpose the provisions by updating several existing laws, instead of creating one new coherent legislative text. This could have been avoided in the case of a Regulation.

We also, of course, have the general problem of translations where, for example, the Swedish definition of 'business day' became 'banking day'. There is a clear potential for misunderstandings and wrong interpretations to grow exponentially.

---

[1] Gold-plating is where a domestic regulator adds extra provisions, which go beyond the basic requirements, or alternatively follow an overly prescriptive interpretation.

[2] Derogation is the partial revocation of a law or a legal provision in a law, as opposed to the total abolition of a law.

Dialogue during the preparation phase of the Directive was indeed regular and intensive. However, the breadth of different stakeholders' views made effective dialogue very difficult, and factual technical analysis provided by the banking industry was often ignored in favour of political views. The fact that the PSD provisions dive deep into mandating operational rules means that a sufficient understanding of the workings of payment systems was necessary. Reality showss that some provisions do not live up to those requirements making, compliance a difficult exercise

The Impact Assessment, which was published with the legislative proposal, unfortunately fell short of providing a clear cost-benefit analysis or a proper risk assessment. The choice of policy option (Regulation, Directive, Recommendation or 'no-action') was not made on the basis of the conclusions of the regulatory Impact Assessment, but instead taken on purely political grounds in advance of even drafting the Impact Assessment. This, again, is not in line with the European Commission's own guidelines on Impact Assessments that form part of the Better Regulation policy.

12.4   CONCLUSION

While banks have long considered the PSD and SEPA as one project, it now becomes clear that the PSD is a far bigger exercise than anticipated; affecting all existing electronic payment instruments in each EU country, in addition to the new SEPA payments. Banks will have to carefully review all of their existing payment products, as well as contractual terms and conditions. Whilst the PSD will definitely impact the legal environment, by creating a payment specific contractual element, payment products might also require adaptations to become PSD compliant.

The solidity of the legal basis provided by the PSD is unfortunately not a given today. The complexity and partly unintelligible content clearly creates difficulty of comprehension in the first place, while the additional administrative burden constitutes yet another barrier to achieving the Lisbon Agenda.

2010 is approaching and, despite the European Commission's reduced law making activity, Europe is still burdened with considerable regulatory compliance management, limiting the use of creative capital so necessary to achieving the Lisbon goals of global competitiveness.

13

SEPA – The Implications for banks

Mark Hale, formerly Barclays Bank and now PricewaterhouseCoopers

SEPA means significant change for banks and it introduces a lengthy period of business and operational uncertainty with new payment schemes co-existing with national schemes, new rules to understand and operate, euro and non-euro product changes, electronic and non-electronic impacts. Banks must now act rapidly to successfully navigate the obvious challenges and also to avoid the less obvious risks.

The advent of Economic and Monetary Union and, in particular, the introduction of the euro in 1999 followed by euro notes and coins in 2002, was a major step forward in the creation of an efficient Single Market. The single currency removed currency risk within the euro area: it enabled a broader, more liquid and more effective capital market to be created; and it promised a larger, more competitive and easier retail market for consumers.

There have been notable successes in the journey to create an effective Single Market, as can be seen in many markets such as euro-area derivatives, euro money markets and bonds trading, and as clearly evidenced in reduced spreads and reduced price variation.

Today, the euro is accepted as a global currency. It stands as a peer of the historic reserve currencies, and the Eurozone interest rate compares favourably with other regional competitors. This pace of change and level of integration is however not evident in the European retail banking sector, where:

- domestic players typically dominate the primary concentration measures of their national markets;
- customer choice is often limited to domestic providers; and
- apart from a few notable exceptions such as the acquisition of ABN AMRO by the Royal Bank of Scotland, Fortis and Santander consortium, M&A activity predominantly takes place within national boundaries.

The European Commission and the European Central Bank therefore both continue to work to accelerate the development of a more homogenous Single Market, with a particular focus in the area of retail banking.

A core dimension of this focus is the creation of a Single Euro Payments Area (SEPA) across all EU Member States, extending to the three European Economic Area countries and Switzerland. The vision of a SEPA is essentially that:

- customers will be able to make payments as easily, cheaply and conveniently anywhere within SEPA as they do in their national market;
- businesses will be able to undertake their cash management on a SEPA-wide basis and using standardised SEPA-wide processes, platforms and solutions; and

- payment institutions will more easily be able to offer their propositions, products and services throughout SEPA, which will provide customers with more choice and therefore lower prices.

The creation of SEPA is not happening in isolation and, to fully understand its impact, the broader market context needs to be taken into account.

13.1   THE BROAD MARKET CONTEXT

By most measures, recent banking sector performance has been impressive. Substantial increases in market capitalisation have been achieved with many institutions delivering record year-on-year operating profits. Total shareholder returns by the banking sector compares well against most other sectors. However, recent times have seen an end to the benign financial market conditions that have been a feature of the preceding decade.

Market instability, rising commodity prices, consumer uncertainty and increasing regulatory intervention, will all have their challenges in the coming years. The underlying performance implications of these new global market conditions will also be influenced by the economic performance in the new economies, as well as by the impact of new and emerging technologies. Indeed the maturity of recent 'new' technologies, the maturing of 'Generation D'[1], combined with the maturing of both Internet and mobile technologies, allow almost every aspect of the payment supply chain to be redefined.

In Europe, the custodians of the Single Market vision will continue to progress various initiatives to deliver greater integration in all aspects of financial markets. This is regarded in Brussels as essential to cope with the process of enlargement, to deliver the vision of the Lisbon Agenda, and to make the local economies of the European Union collectively more competitive in the broader global economy.

'Programme Europe' therefore continues full steam ahead, relentlessly looking to the next development, as each current development is completed or as they identify new problems or challenges that need to be overcome or confronted. This strategy will of course impact many industries but clearly has a disproportionate impact on retail banking in general, and payment infrastructures in particular. This is because of the nature of banking, its role in society and, most importantly, its ability to deliver political policy objectives across the broader economy

There are of course other players who will shape the general business environment. Regulators will increasingly co-operate, both regionally and globally, to increase market efficiency and safety through the Basel II Accord, AML, FATF and others. Competition authorities will more proactively act to open up markets and to increase competition in established markets. An example is the European Union Regulation 2560/2001 on cross-border payments in Euro and the Payment Services Directive. And customers will demand an easier, better and more accountable financial services experience using the European Union Payment Services Directive and other instruments.

The beginning of 2008 will also see the launch of customer oriented payment innovations in both retail and commercial euro payment markets, as part of the Single Euro Payment Area process, and it is a process.

Once the initial SEPA schemes and services developed by the European Payments Council are launched by the banking community, their absence will no longer be a barrier to implementing other ideas that will change the economic scope and nature of banking:

- Channels (e.g. online);

---

[1] The generation that has grown up with, and is completely at home with, digital devices and digital culture.

- Services (e.g. online card payments), and;
- Business scope (e.g. Electronic Invoicing).

Together, these business challenges will shift the balance of power in established business relationships, change the identity of some market providers, and will redefine established ways of doing business. With so many demands on investment and operating capital, with so many dependencies between related change initiatives, and with so much inherent business and delivery risk, the high performing banks of the next decade will need excellent performance improvement strategies to prosper.

The success of these strategies will depend upon outstanding market insight, confident and calm leadership, and an entrepreneurial vision.

13.2 THE CREATION OF SEPA IS A PORTFOLIO OF CHANGE

Often confused as a 'simple' or 'single' initiative of the European Banking industry, under the leadership of the European Payments Council (EPC), SEPA is best seen as a process and a portfolio of related and proactive initiatives by a number of different stakeholders.

Examples of these are:

- **Vision and drivers:** the EU Lisbon Agenda 2000; EU Green Paper on financial services policies 2005–10; The SEPA White Paper 2002; DG Competition's sector enquiry into Retail Financial services; current accounts and related services; DG Internal Market Success factors for a single payment market; the series of ECB SEPA Progress Reports;
- **New standards and practices:** the EPC Scheme Management Internal Rules; EU Payment Services Directive; UNIFI ISO20022 XML; EPC SEPA Data Model; etc;
- **New schemes and frameworks:** the EPC SEPA Credit Transfer; EPC SEPA Direct Debit; EPC Cards Framework; EPC Online Payments; EBA Priority Payments; etc;
- **New infrastructures**: the EBA Clearing Company PE-ACH; ECB TARGET2; etc; and
- **New governance:** the creation of the EPC Scheme Management Committee; the UK Payments Council; etc.

The SEPA programme also consists of a number of reactive market responses:

- **New capabilities**: for example, the investment in new operational platforms such as by VocaLINK Ltd; the creation of new commercial infrastructures such as STET;
- **New operating services:** for back-office processing, electronic mandate management, electronic bill presentment and payment by VocaLINK Ltd; and e-invoicing by the European Banking Association;
- **New alliances:** for example, infrastructure consolidation such as between Interpay and TransactionsInstitute AG to form EQUENS or Voca Ltd and LINK Interchange Network Ltd to form VocaLINK Ltd;
- **New proposition extensions:** for example, the use of TARGET2 to improve securities clearing and settlement under the TARGET2-Securities Programme; and
- **New market requirements:** for example, the CAST Programme of the European Association of Corporate Treasurers; the impetus for electronic invoicing by the European Commission, DG Internal Market / DG Enterprise.

These activities are many in number, managed under different governance structures and, although they are related, they are not integrated in either design or scheduling. This creates a number of performance challenges for banks:

- **Single:** the new payment schemes will co-exist with the national schemes that they displace with no universal deadline for their withdrawal;
- **Euro:** some of the new rules apply to non-euro currency activities;
- **Payments:** a number of the changes impact non-electronic payments activities such as current accounts, cash management and risk management;
- **Area:** the impact of SEPA extends beyond the Euro-zone and impacts all Member States, the three countries of the European Economic Area and also Switzerland.

The development of SEPA is also creating pressures for change in other global regions such as North America, the Middle East and Southern Africa.

13.3 THE SEPA BUSINESS CASE

At one end of the spectrum, some commentators describe SEPA as the most significant event ever to affect European banking, and much more significant and complex than the introduction of the euro. At the other end of the scale, its introduction is sometimes described as an example of economic madness by the banking industry, European bureaucracy at its worst, or as a non-event created by the supply-side of the market for which there is no corresponding demand.

As with most things in life, the actual business case is relative and depends on your existing mandate, mission or circumstance. On the one hand, you may be a committed European; have little legacy information technology constraints; have an agile and proactive product development capability; have a diverse and European customer base; have limited existing revenues at risk; and have a strong entrepreneurial risk appetite. On the other hand, you may regard Programme Europe as something to be mitigated; particularly worry about the cost and risk of changing legacy systems; have a local and national customer base; have business models founded on the market inefficiency that SEPA intends to remove; have a poor new product capability or an aversion to straying too far from established business models and practices. Wherever you sit on this spectrum determines how you hear and respond to the common SEPA headlines summarised in the European Central Bank's occasional paper about the Economic Impact of SEPA:

- Introducing SEPA will cost an average low of € 5.2 billion to an average high of € 7.7 billion.
- The number of ACHs will consolidate down to three or four.
- After 2010, payment revenues across the EU will decline by between € 18 billion and € 29 billion.
- Banks can increase additional revenues of € 8 billion by displacing cash costs.
- Some 'polls' suggest that 74 % of banks believe that SEPA will bring new opportunities.
- The EU needs to create a third 'SEPA' debit card brand.
- Average payment revenues will fall by 4.4 % following SEPA.
- Average payment costs will increase by 4.8 % following SEPA.
- A SEPA e-invoicing solution will save businesses well over $100 billion per annum.
- Inefficiency in the EU payments accounts for 2 % of the EU GDP.

Of course all of these 'headline' figures have flaws in their basis.

Little consideration is given to the costs of customers generally and, of course, consumer costs are usually treated as a free resource. They also have different accounting bases, making comparison difficult.

However, what they do have in common is predictions of significant revenue reductions, significant investment capital requirements, and significant revenue opportunities for new e-SEPA products and services.

Regulation 2560/2001 restricted a bank's ability to charge different cross-border prices for transactions with a domestic equivalent. The Payment Services Directive prohibits value dating and reduces float opportunity by mandating a D+1 end-to-end clearing cycle. DG Competition is likely to establish cost based practices for interchange. SEPA Online Payments will cannibalise card revenues. Corporates will demand SEPA-wide aggregated volume discounts and transactional revenues will move to lower cost providers.

Therefore, if you are a new entrant you will be optimistic. If you are a bank with an investment budget unburdened by mandatory change related to Faster Payments, SOX, BASEL II, etc, or you have an ability to innovate, then you will be fine. If you are a bank with a new, modular and up-to-date IT and Operations capability, with effective business development capabilities, then you will also probably relish the prospect of SEPA. Equally if you are a bank with global ambitions, then the enlarged scale and greater simplicity offered by SEPA should have a clear strategic fit too.

What if you are not in one of these positions? What if your efforts are focused upon 'keeping the lights on'? What if your investment focus is dominated by a compliance agenda? What if you have a sourcing arrangement with providers unable to respond to the challenges of SEPA, and unable to cope with certain change of an uncertain nature? What if you have insufficient people who know how your systems fit together and work? What indeed.

13.4   INTERVENTION IS INTENDED TO CHANGE MARKETS

Accepted wisdom is that banks will segregate into a variation of the following three tiers: regional transactional banks, own processing banks and niche service providers. If this is the case, then what does this mean for the payment processing activities of the 8000 or more banks that exist today across Europe? Given that the current market size for payments in Europe is around 75 billion electronic credit and electronic debit transactions, then sufficient size for a scale player would be in the region of 3–5 billion transactions. This means that the SEPA market will only support 15 to 25 transactional service providers, down from the over 100 that exist throughout the various countries today.

In conversation with members of various national competition authorities, it is clear that policy makers believe that at the macroeconomic level, the market is insufficiently competitive and therefore underperforming its capability. Several themes emerge from these discussions:

• European banking is over-supplied.
• Bank to customer relationships tend to be too stable.
• Information asymmetries between customers and providers inhibit the ability to choose.
• There are too many barriers to entry for new suppliers.

Disrupting the status quo is therefore the objective.

This means change. To be more specific, it means the demise of existing players and the enablement of new ones; the displacement and re-employment of staff; different premiums on existing and new skills; changes in ownership; and, of course, new business models. The Payment Services Directive contains provisions to specifically encourage this.

Charles Darwin said that, "It is not the strongest of the species that survives, or the most intelligent, but the one that is most responsive to change". This will be a good description of the evolution of SEPA once the market settles.

Policymakers are not in the best position to design the future structure of the market, of course, and should not try to do so. That is the function of the market itself. Where policymakers can add value is in either the enablement or the instigation of market-led structural change.

Market results are in many cases not determined solely by the nature of the change itself, but often by the simple fact of change unleashing market forces. The key thing is not to stimulate competition with any regulatory intervention, which may stifle innovation or could jeopardise the proper functioning of the financial system in general, and the payments system in particular.

13.5   THE CUSTOMER DIMENSION

One of the political goals of SEPA is to increase competition amongst banks in existing national markets. A key means of achieving this is to make it easier for new payment institutions and bank entrants to offer their products and services within national markets, outside their own member state. There is no doubt that many of the various aspects of the SEPA programme make this easier. However, there are other important success factors that remain unaddressed for the delivery of the full SEPA vision, in terms of fiscal, language, cultural and behavioural barriers.

In theory, multi-national corporations (MNCs) have the most to gain from the creation of SEPA. However, their size, sophistication and corporate capabilities mean that many already have business and operational solutions in place to deal with today's market imperfections. This is evident in their supply-chain integration, the use of electronic data interchange and the application of sophisticated treasury and cash management solutions. This means that for many existing MNCs in the market, the benefit for SEPA lies in stripping out complexity, cost and risk from their current operating structure and supply chain, rather than changing their business model.

Companies in the medium, small and agricultural sectors that are not predominantly integrated into the supply chain of an MNC, typically have a business model that focuses on their national market and local geography. These customers would need to radically alter their strategic scope and business models to benefit from SEPA. This may indeed happen and no doubt many entrepreneurs will do exactly that, but the major part of this segment will retain a local focus in the medium term.

The retail impact will in many ways mirror the corporate impact, in that it is primarily those customers that have complex and multi-national affairs that will see a significant opportunity from the SEPA vision. SEPA will therefore be relevant to the second homeowner, high net worth segments of the market, and it will also provide opportunities for supporting migrant labour within the European Union. For the majority of consumers however, they will continue to purchase within a small geographic footprint, near their place of employment and with brand names that they understand, trust and can easily communicate with.

Ask a customer in isolation whether they would like to see lower prices for almost any economic activity and, in almost all cases, the answer will be yes. However contrast the demand for lower cost payment activities with lower cost airlines. Headline costs for low-cost flights are sometimes very low and indeed in some cases zero. Add in all of the costs for the items that the provider has unbundled, and that the customer then pays for as extras, and the final price can be much higher than headlined.

Many commentators hail this as a form of economic democracy in action, with power being in the hands of the consumer. Talk to the customers themselves and they will regale you with a very different perspective. Customers want simplicity, ease of use, things to do what they claim to do, a simple means to fix something when it goes wrong and at a reasonable price. In short they do not want the sort of unbundling that many advocate, because their lives are simply too busy and difficult as it is. This should be the focus of taking SEPA to the consumer.

Also, as environmental issues move up the political agenda, consumers are under increasing pressure to be more local in their demand patterns. SEPA is not therefore the only item on the political and economic radar.

Much is made of the role of public authorities in stimulating demand and migration to the new SEPA instruments. Given the political drive for SEPA it is reasonable to expect the public sector to adopt the new SEPA instruments early, if not from the outset. If they did so, this would lead to an immediate migration of 29 % of the market and would familiarise the wider public with the new instruments, as well as helping the banks to accelerate a wider migration.

However, any significant movement in the public authority market to the new SEPA instruments will likely remain with existing providers in the short term. Why add to the risk of changing instruments with the risk of changing suppliers at the same time? Public authority tenders are usually won on price, and rarely is a premium paid for value added services.

This means that a third of the payments market is really only open to the large-scale transactional providers. Potentially this provides more choice for each public authority department, but sourcing of services across-borders in this market remains rare.

A further factor is that SEPA is likely to have the greatest initial customer impact in the application of technology and digital-based businesses in the first instances. The Internet channel will be essential to the success of SEPA as will be the development of new SEPA wide standards in such areas as:

- electronic invoicing;
- electronic bill presentment and payment;
- online payments, and;
- contactless cards payments.

The issue for banking as an industry is whether it can innovate effectively and quickly enough in this space.

13.6   THE STRATEGIC IMPACT

Acclaimed strategy is largely determined by some mix of insight, timing, leadership and luck. Effective bank strategy processes, and particularly those that involve significant infrastructure questions, should therefore focus on these elements.

For banks to succeed in SEPA they need to be clear about:

- where they think the market will develop;
- the pace at which this development will take place;
- the role that they wish to take; and
- the optimum way of delivering this to maximise returns on investment.

This will mean critical business decisions about each stage of the banking supply chain; where to redefine the operating boundaries, who are the most appropriate partners to work with, how and where to organise and govern, what propositions to offer which customers. Some of these decisions may be very uncomfortable indeed.

13.7   DEALING WITH REVENUE PRESSURES

A number of standard options exist to replace reduced revenues including increasing market share from existing products and services, developing new products and services, re-packaging and re-pricing existing services, or re-selling services from other providers.

Banks can also diversify their business lines which, in real terms, mean one or more of the following:

- improving the operational processes to drive up customer satisfaction and viral marketing;
- acquisition of banks serving other geographies or segments to acquire new customers;
- new product innovation to create new revenue; or
- product swaps with other banks to focus on relative competencies and improve cost income ratios, etc.

For all of their efforts, banks find it hard to innovate. There are many reasons for this including the retail banking sector DNA with regard to risk taking, innovation being crowded out by regulatory demands in the investment portfolio, and distraction from the external market reality because of the priority of the internal agenda. As one very successful new entrant put it to me, "we don't really worry about competition from banks, because new ideas don't move their investment needle".

13.8   THE NEED TO REDUCE INTERNAL COSTS

Inside banks the main thing that they can actually control is cost and, for many banks, this will be their primary focus. Re-engineering and automating operational processes, consolidating and rationalising infrastructure, moving costs to lower cost centres of production, improving the delivery cost and risk of change portfolios, improving internal scale economies and shifting costs off balance sheet to third party suppliers are all some part of the SEPA solution.

Where there may be less ambition or risk appetite is in using M&A as a mechanism to displace hugely complex and outmoded architectures and infrastructures. The M&A route should be particularly attractive because of the way that the cost of restructuring can be accounted for and reported. However, payments and SEPA is often driven out of the wrong part of the bank to recognise and instigate this route.

SEPA will also bring internal infrastructure and operations into sharp relief by, for example, the need to reduce all electronic clearing to a maximum D+1, and the requirement to make cash deposits immediately available. This will challenge many processes related to payments such as fraud management, credit risk management, account management and information management, particularly where they are founded on batch oriented systems.

It is likely that many of the current cost projections of SEPA also under-estimate these impacts and implications by only taking into account the transactional elements. This will change.

13.9   THE NEED TO IMPROVE THE EXTERNAL SUPPLY-CHAIN

Many bank executives find it hard to come to terms with their inability to control the full financial supply chain. Many factors cause this discomfort and the nature of being in a network business is at the heart of the problem.

Change requirements to retain scheme membership, to retain access to payment clearing and settlement mechanisms, and to support oversight and regulation, cannot be prioritised in the same way as the requirements to change a proposition of an internal strategic business unit. It may simply be that such changes have to be accepted even if they are not desirable to the institution concerned.

In SEPA, where the consensus of so many countries and banks is needed to create or change the rules, these decisions are almost necessarily out of kilter with internal financial planning lifecycles. Complex industry change activities, increasingly involving many new stakeholders, means that the nature of the change is uncertain for longer and longer periods. This makes planning and resource allocation difficult and, for those banks that have outsourced IT development activities, it makes supporting such changes cumbersome and expensive.

One of the expected outcomes of SEPA is that the number of clearing and settlement mechanisms will reduce, because reach can be provided through a single Pan-European ACH. This means that banks will also need to carefully assess the number of connections that they need, decide which of their existing investments they want to support with further capital, and therefore determine where to place their bets for the future clearing environment.

There is a general expectation that a small number of Pan-European ACH's will emerge, and this is supported by the experience of the evolution of clearing in the securities business. Whether this happens with payments is a different matter, and new models are both possible and potentially more attractive.

13.10   CONCLUSION

In conclusion, the European market is entering a period of uncertainty, and one which challenges all banks and businesses operating in the SEPA Markets. The change is driven by the political desire to accelerate the delivery of an efficient Single Market and by the intent to increase competition. The challenge that this creates for banks is exacerbated by developments in the global economy; increasing cost of capital, a higher premium on liquidity and more prudent investment decision making and risk appetites.

Today, many bank services overcome market inefficiencies However, as these inefficiencies are removed, new services must be developed to replace lost revenues and offset fixed overheads. Banks will increasingly be forced to compete on efficiency rather than on inefficiency and to move up the value chain. Combined with developments in technology, this will mean a shift to electronic processing on a more real-time basis with greater customer interaction and communication.

There are plenty of strategies available to banks to avoid a general atrophy in their performance, but some of these this will require bold and insightful leadership. Initially the market may be slow to develop, and therefore provide additional time to act, but a number of leading banks have been preparing for this change for several years and so the time to act is now.

SEPA is like a stone thrown onto the European banking millpond. Its purpose is to change the status quo and its effects will ripple on for many years to come.

14

Bring on the benefits, a SEPA success story

James Barclay, JPMorgan Chase

SEPA has been slow to arrive but has potentially major benefits for not just European business, but also European banks. There needs to be more determination to work together towards standardisation to make it happen.

Launching the Single Euro Payments Area (SEPA) has been like lighting a slow action fuse. Regulatory expectations are that, through this ignition, Europe will foster competition and innovation for retail payments across Europe by aligning international with domestic practices, and thereby encouraging cross-border trade. In reality SEPA spluttered into life in January 2008 with the launch of a basic Credit Transfer scheme, expanded its horizon with the introduction of Direct Debit services by the end of 2009, before striding towards a single market with migration of national payments services by 2012.

SEPA's origins date back to 2002, when banks drew up the White Paper on 'Euroland our Single Payments Area', but the actual benefits of SEPA will only be realised by consumers and corporate customers after there has been general migration to the new standards to support the integration of new or innovative services.

Before Europe reaches full migration, payment service providers will have absorbed the considerable development costs of adapting their systems to the new standards. This is estimated to be € 3 to € 5 billion[1] for each medium to large sized bank alone over the next five years. Some of this pain will be assuaged for the front runners, who should benefit from the fall-out of financial institutions that cannot establish a business case for the investment. The industry is also likely to see those players only participating indirectly in the SEPA schemes, as well as an increase in payments outsourcing.

SEPA's success is dependent on a series of parallel actions over the next few years, when corporates and public administrations of the EU's member states migrate their internal systems to the new SEPA standards. Of course, customers will only move to the new standards once banks develop the innovative products made possible by the new SEPA environment. In addition, the drive for these migrations needs to come from regulatory pressures, as well as the increasing benefits derived from moves towards e-commerce. The particular challenge that payment service providers are facing is how to make their conversion to new standards worthwhile, and the success of SEPA depends upon these standards.

---

[1] Figures from ECB Paper on the Economic Impact of SEPA August 2007 extrapolated from Accenture/PSE Consulting analysis 2006.

Until Europe reaches full migration, its fragmented payments market will remain a battle-field of expectancy. Additional SEPA challenges include the redundancy around the European theatre that could slow large-scale movement towards SEPA standards by end-users. The front line infrastructure providers are bedded down in the trenches, crouching behind multi-million euro investments in domestic retail payment services. They have dug in, set the national stan-dards, rely on efficient and cheap communications networks, and offer specific services that make it very difficult for users to route payments elsewhere.

These users, who tend to be owner banks, are confronted with a dual challenge: first, max-imising internal development investments in legacy systems that link to the national infrastruc-tures whilst, second, integrating the new SEPA standards by interfacing enhanced systems to be SEPA-compliant CSMs and PE-ACHs. At least they can do the former with some confidence in the cost effective payments processing services that underscore their previous investments. The latter integration with SEPA standards gives more cause for concern.

Banks still process around 98 % of their payments business within national boundaries. The transaction cost for doing so is minimal. National Automated Clearing Houses (ACHs) continue to offer the lowest prices outside bilateral file exchanges, which are largely volume dependent. The financial advantages of routing domestic transactions through a national ACH may come into question, as banks review the new SEPA processing opportunities alongside bilateral arrangements. However, it would be a brave decision to reroute vol-ume through more expensive SEPA infrastructures offering less functionality in the short term.

From a regulatory perspective, the SEPA endgame outweighs the advantages of cheaper, existing solutions within individual Member States as outlined in recent ECB papers:

> The Eurosystem supports the creation of the Single Payments area . . . . Changes are needed to move towards a more integrated payments market, which will bring substantial economic benefits"[2] Following the successful introduction of the euro, the Eurosystem is looking to "foster further development and modernisation of the financial system. . . achieved when three conditions are fulfilled: (1) singleness of the market, (2) market participants' equal access to the market, (3) market participants' equal treatment in the market." [3]

In response, the major payment processing banks have, with limited enthusiasm but consider-able effort, accepted their obligations to deliver SEPA and provide a single market with fair and open access. The wiser players are taking the opportunity to modernise their payment processing systems at the same time as, before 2010, they will need to demonstrate to their customers the value of migrating their own systems to realise the cost benefits of a harmonised market. The real issue therefore lies with the fact that, at this time, the same pressure that has jumpstarted banks into action has yet to be applied to end-users.

Herein lays the SEPA challenge. Banks must produce innovative SEPA products and obsolete the long-term costs of legacy national infrastructures. Yet even leading edge products cannot force migration on their own. Without a truly focused push from the regulators to encourage end-user take-up, the SEPA success story in 2010 may look very different from the unified European landscape we are envisioning today.

---

[2] ECB paper July 2007 SEPA 'From Concept to Reality', Fifth Progress Report.
[3] ECB paper August 2007 'The Economic impact of SEPA'.

14.1   THE EUROPEAN PAYMENTS ENVIRONMENT FROM 2010

14.1.1   Bank Products

In 2010, SEPA is a reality. The single market can swagger under the mantel of its own success. The European payments market is in full transformation. Good progress is being made by the European Commission in harmonising national interpretation of the invoicing and digital signature Directives[4], and public administration acceptance of secure electronic VAT reporting has been obtained, thereby removing the most significant barriers to electronic commerce.

The Euro Banking Association – on behalf of its membership of commercial, savings and cooperative banks – is promoting business practices for e-invoicing, using standards that enable innovative solutions to work across Europe.

Domestic communities in France and Italy are aligned with government e-reporting obligations, using interoperable certification schemes for digital signatures. This has started to facilitate electronic commerce from one end of the financial supply chain to the other, albeit on a national basis only. Meanwhile, the Nordic communities are technologically still in advance of the rest of Europe, and operate on a one click for everything basis.

Elsewhere, banks and service providers have joined forces to deliver individual e-solutions for their own customers, from the initial order through to end payment. A standard for on-line secure payments is in the EPC pipeline, based on the four corner model and using the SEPA schemes for the underlying payment, and European direct debits are finally on the market. The mobile payment industry has taken off in Europe as consumers delight in the simplicity of making person-to-person payments over the phone, whilst talking to their friends and family. Consumer confidence is high and the banking industry is well positioned. The future is bright and a single payments market is beginning to deliver the anticipated benefits.

However, all is not perfect in 2010.

14.1.2   Payments Infrastructures

From a European perspective, rationalisation of the payments industry should lead to consolidation amongst the key players. As the European payments industry slowly migrates to single processing standards, the requirement for separate national infrastructures that are all basically doing the same thing is diminishing. In addition, national defensive strategies and differing value added services are still limiting the financial advantages of a single market.

Banks offering payment services across Europe are beginning to minimise the central processing costs, either through bilateral arrangements with high volume counterparties or through participation in a single market infrastructure, processing sufficient volumes to offer comparable financial conditions and full reach across Europe. Meanwhile, consolidation in the banking sector is expected to increase, partially driven by smaller banks finding it harder to sustain sufficient payment revenue in a more competitive market.

Yet, by 2010, payment processing infrastructures have barely reduced in number. The essential services offered in different countries have yet to be incorporated into a central processing engine, and interoperability between service providers continues to improve.

---

[4] Directive 1999/93/EC on a community framework for electronic signatures; and Directive 2001/115/EC, amending Directive 77/388/EEC, with a view to simplifying, modernising and harmonising the conditions laid down for invoicing in respect of value added tax.

The hub and spoke model has been adopted where the EBA STEP2 system is used as the hub for cross-border payments, with national infrastructures processing domestic transfers whilst directly linking to this European hub to route cross-border transactions. The situation is clearer in Luxembourg, where all non-urgent payments are routed centrally; and in Italy, where the majority of national transactions are now processed through the same system. Consequently, payment service providers continue to support multiple investments in different processing engines.

Future enhancements to the STEP2 service promise to deliver domestic service levels across Europe on a single platform, and infrastructures continue to discuss migration commitments with most national communities delaying decisions to wind down domestic services.

14.1.3   Corporate and Consumer Benefits

In 2010 in the end-user space, the first steps towards faster payments processing have been taken.

Value dating has disappeared, with revenue from float, and maximum timeframes for all payments processed in European currencies are appreciated, as is the SHA charging principle.[5] Priority payments have become the standard for urgent payments, with funds availability in under four hours temporarily meeting corporate expectations. Increasingly, however, corporates are looking to automate the full financial supply chain and European e-invoicing initiatives are replacing paper-based services. Unfortunately it is not yet enough to rationalise the investment in SEPA standards for the majority, and take-up remains slow. Retailers continue to lobby to their own advantage, putting pressure on interchange fees, whilst notably failing to guarantee the ensuing cost reductions to the consumer.

Consumer benefits are minimal. Only for the selected few who have physically emigrated to or work in another country, or who have opted for international utility suppliers, are the harmonised European conditions for processing a payment of any real advantage.

Therefore, although SEPA is seen to be an on-going European success, its impact will only be really understood by the next generation of payments users and practitioners. The cost of a payment for an individual has not come down, though the PSD has ensured that there is greater clarity on when a cross-border payment will be credited and under what conditions.

Most importantly, the increase in cross-border trade is barely perceptible. Companies continue to transact in established manners under the 'know your local supplier' principle. Most internationally-focused companies have still not streamlined their banking arrangements, as they are just beginning to integrate the SEPA standards.

Companies that are particularly active in a few different national markets maintain their national banking arrangements, and have no intention of migrating services to SEPA standards until internal systems upgrades dictate the investment. The real advantages of the single market are perceived to be too intangible.

In order to resolve these issues, there is increasing corporate involvement in governance and working groups as the value of the UK model, which separates payment schemes from payments operators, is acknowledged.

---

[5] The EPC published Interbank Charging Principles (ICP) as part of their response to Regulation 2560/2001. The ICP will guarantee that the full amount transferred by the originator will be credited to the beneficiary's account, leaving both the originator's and the beneficiary's bank accountable for charging their own customer (the so-called "SHARE" or "SHA" charging option).

14.1.4   The Regulators' Response

In 2010, in light of the progress to date, the latest ECB progress report on SEPA displays quiet satisfaction with the general situation, but regrets the slow progress and lack of general migration in the corporate and public sector. This is despite extensive communication on the benefits of SEPA by the banking community.

Supported by corporate representatives and consumer bodies, the ECB report encourages bringing forward the date for adoption of the D + 1 maximum timeframe for payments processing. The report also expresses concerns over the absence of even one alternative pan-European debit card scheme, and on the perceived US-centric card services offered by Visa and Master-Card that increasingly dominate the market. The report raises questions as to the existence of real European competition.

The European Commission continues to evaluate the difficulties underlying consumer account mobility, with research indicating consumer dissatisfaction in relation to the difficulties of changing bank accounts and the lack of information on how to do so. Bankers continue to refute the findings, stating that national account switching arrangements are improving daily and that the ease of multi-banking and the minimal demand for cross-border switching removes any need for account portability.

The PSD has not quite delivered the hoped-for range of innovative payment solutions and there is little evidence of increased competition or new players in the market, although niche markets for mobile payments are beginning to emerge. Interchange fees are still discouraged, although the consumer benefits are imperceptible in models where retailers have taken full financial advantage of their removal.

14.2   THE GLOBAL SITUATION FROM 2010

14.2.1   Leading the Industry

Mark Garvin, International Executive for JPMorgan Treasury and Securities Services said in Rome that: 'We are on the brink of a new order in the payments industry'.[6] He was referring to Machiavelli's observation that 'there is nothing more difficult to take in hand, more perilous to conduct, or more uncertain in its success, than to take the lead in the introduction of a new order of things'.

Mark was also reflecting on the need for leadership to meet the new challenges of a united financial Europe. Stepping into the breach of change as a global leader and succeeding in a competitive market, driven by fast return on investment, requires a steady nerve. By 2010, players seizing the opportunity are well placed to capture business and improve revenue streams and an increasing number of smaller banks are actively working towards outsourcing their payments activity.

The result is that competition is fierce for SEPA compliant service offerings.

14.2.2   Harmonising the European and US Markets . . . and Beyond

If Europe has set the standard for harmonisation, the slow rate of progress has highlighted the difficulties inherent in changing standards in a competitive market. Migration to SEPA has not

---

[6] EBAday Rome June 2007 keynote speech.

been painless, but is making good progress whilst standards evolution in the US runs at its own pace.

In the 20 years leading up to 2005, the 130 ATM suppliers have consolidated down to less than thirty, with the top four non-bank owned companies handling over 80 % of the US market, according to Tower Group estimates. Tower Group also indicate that in 1990 three privately owned ACHs competed for 10 % of the market, with the Federal Reserve taking the rest. Today the Federal Reserve shares more or less equally the market with EPN, after the closure of AZCH and VISA ACH at the beginning of the millennium.

Discussions of aligning global standards with Europe or providing interoperable global interfaces, starting with the euro and the dollar, are taking place. Meanwhile, European banks are largely preoccupied with meeting their SEPA obligations but, by 2010, a major part of the underlying investment in SEPA, both technically and at the level of intellectual resource, will be in the past. Opportunities for taking advantage of new standards that can be adopted at a global level will become more apparent, and payments practitioners will find more time for closer examination. Additionally, as Europe migrates to a limited number of CSMs all using the same SEPA standards, a clearer picture will emerge as to who the key players are.

Visionaries see opportunities to link the dollar, yen and euro clearing onto a single platform, even extending netting systems such that they operate 24 hours a day five days per week, only settling at the end of the week.

They also see mobile payments picking up a rapidly increasing percentage of low value payments, and becoming the standard in developing countries where large populations are confronted with low bank account accessibility. In more technologically advanced countries, improved near field communications (NFC) terminals are being rolled out to merchants, as the younger customers make increasing use of their mobile phones for financial transactions. Cooperation between banks and telecom operators is still in its infancy but active pilots are demonstrating the opportunities, and banks are beginning to provide the underlying financial services.

Payments practitioners with the clearest views see fully automated, e-initiated, end-to-end processing along the financial supply chain. In this world, an electronic purchase order can be matched on-line to end delivery and payment and banks play an increasingly important role in the financing and security of the operation.

14.2.3 The SEPA Inheritance

Europe has provided a clear example of how progress can be made, largely around a long term vision. Without regulatory encouragement the banking standards and products that make up SEPA would not have been possible. In any other environment, the lack of immediate return of investment would have held back developments.

By 2010 SEPA will be in place but still needs to prove its real value. The new products can provide real benefits to end-users, but they alone may not encourage full migration or force full rationalisation of the payments infrastructure. Regulators should also be mindful that their responsibility to the European marketplace, as this will not end once the SEPA Credit Transfer becomes a reality. If they give the proper encouragement to end-users, the next generation will benefit from cheaper and more efficient payment processing. They may well be blissfully unaware of and indifferent to the challenges that the banking industry had to surmount.

With an efficient European market now established, a global integration of the standards is clearly the next step. Let's hope it is not a bridge too far.

15

The Impact of SEPA on the Irish Payments Industry

Brenda O'Connell, Bank of Ireland

Ireland has had a very effective domestic bilateral system for years, with cross-border payments a relatively small part of the whole but, as SEPA becomes mature, Irish banks will be faced with strong regional and global competition. Can they keep up?

A post-SEPA Ireland will be an attractive market for payments providers, with greater competition as entry barriers are removed. This means that Irish businesses will be able to make payments electronically rather than by cheque, and enjoy a richer range of services. This will also lead to the use of cash by consumers falling significantly, replaced by convenient and innovative electronic alternatives.

Post-SEPA, the current European domestic clearing arrangements will be consigned to history; cheque volumes will reduce drastically; the cards market will be transformed by both new entrants and new technology; and the volume of cash-based transactions will be significantly lower and falling. Of even more importance is that customers are likely to have access to a far richer suite of related value added payments services, whilst also enjoying very competitive pricing. The marketplace will become far less national and much more European, with some of the current players likely to no longer exist.

SEPA will be the primary driver of this change. As one of the primary objectives of SEPA is for Europe to become a huge domestic market for euro payments, most of the member states that have adopted the euro as their national currency will obviously be impacted.

As a country that has traditionally been very committed to European matters, Ireland was one of the first Member States to complete and submit a National SEPA Implementation Plan to the EPC in December 2005. This plan included not just a commitment to develop and launch SEPA-compliant products for 1 January 2008, but to deliver the migration of national payment schemes to SEPA schemes. The Irish Payments Services Organisation (IPSO) subsequently set a target date of December 2010 for this national migration.

While the later than expected arrival of the Payments Services Directive (PSD) may ultimately challenge the timeframe of this National Implementation Plan, a successful migration to SEPA will ultimately deliver increased value in payments services for Irish businesses.

15.1 CLEARING ARRANGEMENTS

Unlike most other European countries, Ireland does not operate a domestic automated clearing house (ACH) but relies on a system of bilateral arrangements between member banks, with electronic files being exchanged and settlement taking place daily through the Central Bank of Ireland. While there are some set-up and maintenance costs associated with this system, the main attraction is that banks do not charge each other for transactions processed. Therefore, the migration of this current domestic payment system to the new SEPA pan-European ACH (PE-ACH) environment will present a significant financial challenge to Ireland's banks. Participants will be faced with challenges to continue to offer, and indeed enhance, existing services to their customers in an economic and efficient way.

A decision not to change the existing bilateral arrangements to cater for SEPA credits transfers means that from January 2008, payments between customers of Irish banks would be settled through mainland Europe, rather than locally. It will be interesting to see if all of the current domestic traffic will hence migrate to a PE-ACH solution, or if some bilateral deals are agreed between the larger domestic players instead.

Of course the ownership of these domestic players could change anyway. For example, two of the main clearing banks have been taken over by non-Irish parent institutions in recent years and this is likely to continue. The continuing trend for consolidation in the industry combined with the continued high level of economic growth and the attractive high level of banking profits in Ireland, means that the remaining indigenous players could well become targets for multinational players looking to increase their geographic spread across Europe.

Such a move would have a significant impact on clearing arrangements, as local bilateral arrangements would be less likely to be attractive to large volume participants of PE-ACH clearing arrangements. These participants would seek to avail themselves of bulk discounts for their payment processing, and such a scenario would likely result in all transactions being processed through a PE-ACH.

15.2 MIGRATION TO SEPA

Ireland is keen to adopt a realistic timeline for the full completion of the SEPA project. A critical mass of payments instruments should have migrated by end of 2010. A realistic timeline is needed for the phasing out of the 'old' national payments products along with the migration of customers to the widespread use of new SEPA products.

For Ireland a vital public confidence exercise in the SEPA process is needed to ensure the success of this early mass movement. Banks in Ireland need to create a positive climate amongst their business and personal customers for such an early migration to succeed within tight timelines. Creating this climate will clearly mean strong leadership from the Irish banks and payments organisations to promote the price and performance characteristics of the new SEPA products. Any misplaced perceptions that SEPA product performance may be slower or more costly than the existing Irish domestic systems, will need to be publicly overcome by the banks and government in their planning to assist with customer migration to the new payment products.

Moreover a proactive national approach that enables easy migration of mandates is key to the success to SEPA. If SEPA is to reach a critical mass in Ireland by end of 2010, then national management of the existing mandate structure and system migration of legacy payments systems and instructions is needed.

A key dependency in all of this will be the appetite of public institutions and government departments to incorporate early adoption of SEPA, and the support from central government to kick-start the migration process.

An additional complexity for Irish migration to SEPA is electronic mandating, or e-mandating as we refer to it here. E-mandating is not yet recognised in a SEPA world and may take a number of years to achieve, even though it is commonly used throughout Ireland and the UK. A return to using paper mandates for domestic SEPA direct debits in Ireland would certainly be viewed as a retrograde step for originators who have successfully migrated to electronic mandates.

This lack of consideration of e-mandating within SEPA may become a major barrier to national migration for the larger originators and it is interesting to note that much of the current Irish direct debit functionality would be viewed as SEPA Additional Optional Services (AOS) elsewhere in Europe. There are many opportunities open to Irish Banks to offer such AOS service to both domestic and cross-border originators, based on current Irish offerings. Another solution would require local or European legislation to encompass the domestic concept of e-Mandates within the SEPA cross-border mandate management and returns processes.

Whatever happens, Irish banks and their business customers will need to work closely together to ensure that this migration takes place as smoothly and economically as possible.

15.3   THE TRANSITION FROM CASH TO ELECTRONIC

Ireland is currently one of the highest users of cash per capita in the European Union, and is the third largest user of cheques per capita of the euro countries after France and Portugal.[1] In order to be consistent with the aspirations of SEPA – that participants should enjoy the economic and other benefits of more efficient payments – Ireland has established a National Payments Implementation Programme that aspires to convert as many cash and paper transactions as possible to electronic payments. In fact, the introduction of SEPA is regarded as a catalyst for advancing this aspiration. As businesses see the benefits of efficient electronic payments, and the expected valued added services that will evolve, it is reasonable to assume that there will be a natural migration away from cheque and cash usage.

Consolidation at the European level combined with increased competition at the local level should see a significant enhancement to the range and value of payments services being offered to businesses. International businesses will especially see the benefits when products such as the SEPA Credit Transfer and the SEPA Direct Debit are introduced, as it will enhance their cross-border payment options. The benefits of the SEPA direct debit are also obvious for a multinational biller, such as a mobile operator, who will ultimately be able to issue direct debits to all of their Eurozone customers from one single originating bank, located in any of the SEPA countries.

For domestic businesses, however, there may be some initial costs to bear before the expected benefits of a fully developed SEPA can be realised. The scale benefits of SEPA will be achieved when there has been a significant shift of domestic payments to SEPA schemes. This migration from the existing domestic standards to the SEPA equivalents will also require changes to the financial systems of domestic businesses, which will inevitably carry a cost. However, early migration to SEPA payments in Ireland is vital for domestic businesses, in order to realise the benefits of their investment.

From a consumer perspective, such migration may take a bit longer as significant change in consumer behaviours is generally slow. This is especially true with financial services, where the payments business in Ireland has a few other complications.

---

[1] IPSO Annual Review, 2005/06.

Firstly, card products are subject to an annual government duty charge of € 10 a year for debit and ATM cards, € 20 a year for a combined debit and ATM card, and € 40 for credit cards. This is seen as a 'tax on plastic' and is widely regarded as encouraging the use of cash instead of electronic payments, as well as discouraging consumers from using a card product at all or discouraging their use of multiple cards from competitive providers. This also has a dampening effect on innovation in the cards business, with very slow progress in areas such as prepaid cards, contactless cards, card-based micro-payments and mobile card payments, in comparison to Ireland's European counterparts.

A second issue is the number of adults without bank accounts, which is currently estimated at 11 %[2] of the population.

These issues may have been resolved by the time that SEPA is fully deployed. A review of the tax on plastic is likely, in light of the expected and welcomed increase in competition in financial services within the country and across the Community. Significant progress will also have been made in relation to bank accounts, as institutions such as the post office and credit unions increase the range of financial services that they provide to their customers, including money transmission accounts. There is also a significant effort being made by the State to deliver social welfare and other payments electronically, which should close this gap further.

The third area where Ireland will be impacted is through the development of a SEPA debit card, which is of key interest to the Irish business community. Similarly to many other European countries, Ireland has a closed national debit card scheme. This scheme has universal domestic acceptance, is low cost to the consumer and the merchant, and is a popular product nationally and across-borders. The development of a SEPA debit card has raised concerns that, under current market developments, the increased SEPA functionality will come at the cost of increased market concentration and a more expensive payment card for the merchant.

The possibility of a third card scheme may ultimately be the catalyst that encourages this mass acceptance of a SEPA debit card but, for the moment, it is a key challenge for the Irish migration to SEPA compliant products.

15.4 AN ATTRACTIVE AND COMPETITIVE MARKET

Ireland is an attractive and exciting place for the payments business in the post-SEPA environment. The current rate of corporation tax for trading income is 12.5 %, which is considerably lower than most of the rest of Europe and the cost of doing electronic business in Ireland remains amongst the lowest in Europe.

Post-SEPA aims to see the general cost of European electronic business reduce to norms established in the rest of the world. This is a key success criterion for a market that is up to 21 % more costly than its world counterparts.[3]

Economic growth in the country ran at 6 % in 2006, which is the highest level since 2002. 2007's growth is 4.75 % with 3.5 % growth anticipated in subsequent years, which is still considerably ahead of growth predictions for Europe as a whole.

All of these factors make Ireland a very attractive market for mainstream financial institutions, niche players and other payments services providers. The provisions of the proposed PSD will make it easier for non-banks to compete with the established payments service providers, leading to greater competition. The trend for consolidation in the financial services sector

[2] IPSO Survey, August 2006.
[3] Charlie McCreevy, Speech, Paris 18 September 2007.

is likely to lead to participation by multinational players, further enhancing the competitive environment.

15.5 CONCLUSION

In conclusion

- Although payment service providers are likely to be facing ever-increasing competition for customer business, they should be able to generate attractive returns for the provision of efficient, attractive and innovative payments products and services.
- Business and personal customers can look forward to the benefits of this increased competition leading to greater choice, efficiency, security and more importantly value, following the implementation and transition to SEPA.
- Businesses can expect to be conducting most of their payments business electronically, not just domestically but across all SEPA countries. Consumers can expect a significant reduction in their cash transactions, driven by the delivery of convenience, security and value through the innovative use of technology.

The challenge of SEPA for the Irish banks is to provide these services to their customers before the competition does.

16

After 2010: Will the Customer become King?

Harry Leinonen, the Bank of Finland

In a global world that is technologically turbo-charged, is SEPA the challenge or is the customer and their needs the challenge? As the customer becomes king, the world of European payments post-2010 will be far more revolutionary than just an expanded PE-ACH.

'Cash is king' and 'The customer is king' are two old and frequently used sayings. In many cases, the former still seems true while the latter is hardly true at all when it comes to payments. What will happen after SEPA in 2010, is that the first statement will become less true and the second statement will become truer. Nevertheless, changes in payment conventions have traditionally occured slowly. Although the speed of developments has accelerated, we will most probably have to wait for major payment habit changes from 2013 and onwards. SEPA can be as an important stepping stone however towards a Single International Payment Area. This kind of development would be in the general interest, but:

- Why is the customer not the king in payment services?
- What would be needed to make the customer king?
- What would happen if the customer were king?
- How will the new king rule after SEPA in 2010?
- What riches could the king reap?

16.1 WHY IS THE CUSTOMER NOT THE KING?

Most industries, and especially service industries, put a lot of effort into developing services focused upon the customer's interests. They are keen on know their customer's preferences in order to improve their offerings. Market players in other industries try to make their services as efficient as possible, in order to attract customers with better service at the best price. For example communication and telephone service providers have shown enormous growth in content and quality, coupled with decreasing pricing, due to efficient employment of modern technology. The payments industry seems to work according to different rules.

Whilst other industries have introduced real-time or nearly real-time delivery, the European payments industry conducts lengthy discussions on whether a delivery time of three days would be satisfactory. Other industries generally show a time-to-market for product improvements of six months, while six years does not even seem to be enough for most banks to introduce improved payment features. While most industries have found that the implementation of global standards is beneficial to all, the banking industry seems to prefer national or proprietary solutions. The payments industry appears to be moving in the same direction as other industries, but considerably more slowly.

Why is the payment industry so different? There seems to be four main reasons for this situation:

- complementary products;
- network externalities support natural monopolies;
- hidden pricing rather than transparent pricing; and
- outdated regulations.

None of these would be able to create the situation of too little competition and very slow development speeds in the payment industry by itself. Equally, some other industries face the same situations. Mobile telephone carriers contain the same kind of network externalities, most transportation industries are heavily regulated, and other complementary products show fierce competition. The problem seems to be that the combined force of all these together is so strong that the normal rules of market competition do not work.

16.1.1   Complementary products rather than independent demand

The complementary status of a payment means that nobody is interested in making a payment just for the fun of paying. Payments are just a part of financial dealing. Therefore, the volume of financial dealing completely determines the demand for payments, in the same way as the demand for champagne determines the demand for champagne corks. As part of this process, in payments, everyone has a budget which puts a limit on their financial dealings and hence the amount of payments to be made.

An example of how irrelevant the numbers of payments are within this overall budget is when there is a large payment which could be split up into smaller payments, often in the customers' interest. In most cases however, it would just increase work and administration, and so payments are made in full, just as part of the financial transaction process.

The result is that payment processing is a zero-sum game. Any new instrument just redistributes the current volumes. The result is that the industry cannot calculate the growth of payments revenues and profitability based upon improved offerings through volume increases. Equally, nobody wants to arrange more commercial deals just because the complementary payment component has become more efficient.

16.1.2   Network externalities support natural monopolies

Payment services are a typically networked industry, and thereby contain dependencies on internal networks, which lead to monopolistic tendencies as everyone moves towards the largest scale operator.

In a network, the users are better off the more participants there are, because the reachability will be better. For example if there were more than one e-mail network, without a bridge between them, users would need to keep e-mail accounts in several networks in order to reach the necessary e-mail addresses. This would result in the larger network attracting more customers, due to its larger value for the users. This external benefit for the largest network results in a natural monopoly easily, as everyone is attracted to the largest network for convenience, cost and ease-of-use.

Payments are the same as all payment methods, including cash, are essentially just fund transportation services. Funds are transferred from the payer to the payee, and the start and end destinations are payment accounts. The banks and other payment service providers constitute a large payment network for making these transfers and, in order for the customer accounts to be reachable, these banks and service providers need to be connected via interbank networks and clearing systems. In most cases, this introduces monopoly structures into the payment networks due to the externalities described. Maintaining parallel infrastructures, trunk networks between banks for the transportation of the same payments would just increase the overall fixed costs.

Most of the national interbank payments are therefore transferred via a national clearing centre. Its payment service content will determine the general payment services available to customers, as customers need to be able to make most of their transfers to customers using the services of other banks. The service level of the industry is thereby determined through interbank cooperation among the service providers within clearing centres, bankers' associations and other organisations, without any customer involvement. Therefore, this creates collaborative networks rather than competition.

16.1.3   Hidden pricing rather than transparent pricing

Cash is the world's dominant payment method. Historically it gained this position because, at one point of time, it was the most efficient payment instrument compared to bartering valuable metals, tobacco, man days or other measures of value.

This status of case is today based upon a hidden pricing structure, involving heavy cross-subsidies and, as a result, customers experience cash as a free service. Banks provide most cash services for free. There are seldom charges for ATM or branch teller withdrawals. Merchants get low cost cash services from their banks.

Because cash is seen as a free service, it is difficult to introduce more efficient services to the market. New and more efficient payment services will not be able to thrive on their cost efficiency therefore, as there cannot be any price competition among non-priced services. The new services can only rely on customer convenience improvements.

This has created an interest to bundle services, like credits and bonus points, with new payment services in order to increase the visible customer benefits. However, this has just increased the hidden pricing convention, as the credits and bonuses are paid by merchants via high merchant fees which they then embed in the prices of their goods.

The hidden pricing also introduces a barrier for new entrants as they cannot make a business out of being solely efficient payment processors, but have to rely on cross-subsidisation synergies with other products. Hidden pricing reduces the possibilities for customers to select the most efficient instrument and service provider as it reduces price competition and therefore customers generally pay excessive hidden prices, which is confirmed by the high profitability of the payment industry.[1]

---

[1] See the European Commission's Competition DG Sector enquiries on Retail Banking Interim Reports, Part I, Payment cards; Part II, Current Accounts and Related Services; and Final Report on the Retail Banking Sector Inquiry.

16.1.4   Outdated regulations

Banking and payment industries are heavily regulated. Non-bank service providers have therefore had difficulties to enter the market. Some of the regulations, from the cash and cheque era, have been promoting the use of old fashioned paper instruments.

The typical regulation of most Member States promotes the use of cash as a legal tender for example. At some point of time, this needs to be updated to encourage the use of electronic solutions.

There are other examples of accounting laws and practices, invoicing, taxation rules and archiving requirements, which need to be updated in order to support more efficient payment solutions. Different kinds of grey and black market activities, tax evasion, money laundry and so forth, employ cash due to its high degree of anonymity. There are many rules in the market which, in different ways, support legacy payment operations.

16.2   WHAT WOULD BE NEEDED TO MAKE THE CUSTOMER KING?

The customer can only become king, if the market structures above are changed. The three later ones – network collaborations, hidden pricing and outdated regulations – can be changed, but the complementary status of payments is a basic fact.

Network externalities are part of any network service but their impact can be reduced by requiring network structures to support open competition. This would imply:

- separating payment scheme management and standards from network operations, as it can reduce legacy solution protection and increase competition in networks;
- maximising the service area of service providers and minimising the area of the common inter-service provider networks and centres, as it would increase true customer choice by preferring customer service to be provided by individual service providers, instead of provided by joint customer service centres of all service providers for example;
- requiring openness of the infrastructure for all service providers on equal terms, as it increases the probability for new entrants;
- requiring transferable account addresses as it would support customer mobility, which in turn, is essential for real competition;
- establishing common technical standards and rules for payment instruments, as it reduces lock in to proprietary standards and supports customer mobility;
- facilitating customer involvement in the development of user services and standards, in order to promote development of the interest of customers; and
- reducing considerably or abolishing any subsidies, as it increases competition and efficiency.

Increased competition would make current service providers more interested in developing services based on customer needs, because of increased risk of competition among current service providers and also from new entrants. The bigger the benefit gap between current services and potentially improved services, the greater the opportunity for new entrants to grab a slice of the market. Competition authorities have increased their interest for competition issues and barriers in network industries, including payment scrvices, during recent years. For example, roaming charges on mobile networks. These issues and remedies seem to be common for all these industries.

Transparent pricing reduces cross-subsidising and would move the industry from embedded pricing to volume-based pricing. The current lack of these pricing conventions is due to underlying barriers and old non-transparent conventions:

- cash is heavily cross-subsidised due to its historical status as legal tender, and this has required other payment instruments to follow suit;
- cheques are still used regularly for payments in some countries due to preferential pricing because, in countries where cheques have been priced transparently, customers have moved swiftly to more efficient instruments;
- card payments are often bundled with other services, especially credits and bonus point schemes, in order to provide visible incentives to cardholders to use them; the high fees embedded in the merchant prices of goods and services, especially in combination with non-surcharge rules and traditions, result in an increase in hidden pricing;
- inter-service provider interchange fees, when the acquiring service providers are required to transfer income to the issuers, increase the pressure for high merchant fees which then increases the non-transparent embedded pricing in goods and services; and
- the 'float' based on value days and long delivery and processing times, has been a traditional non-transparent pricing mechanism in the payment industry.

Transparent pricing would increase price competition and make it possible for the customers to select the most favourable instruments. Comparable pricing structures and parameters would simplify customers' selection processes. Increasingly transparent pricing will also probably require regulatory authority involvement. For example, the Payment System Directive (PSD) contains an abolition of value dates and reduces float to a maximum of one day for interbank transfers.

Regulations need to be updated to promote competition and modern payment services, especially as new technology and economic structures develop rapidly. Allowing new entrants to enter the markets increases competition and should be encouraged, as long as these are promoted under sufficiently safe and stable conditions. The regulations should not maintain a safe haven for inefficient legacy structures and solutions.

The customer will not be crowned king overnight. It will take time, because past experience shows that customers change their payment behaviour very slowly and need several separate reasons for doing it. In fact, customers need to become more mobile and begin to consider moving service providers on a more regular basis.

Low customer mobility reduces competition and has been another factor in the industry's poor responsiveness to customer needs. There is a need for more activity to support increased customer mobility and the lowering of the barriers to changing service provider, such as reducing high close-down costs, avoiding proprietary standards, abolishing undue bundling and so forth.

A final cautionary note is that too much Competition might induce service providers to take too many risks in their attempts to keep up, which could, in turn, jeopardise customers' payment funds and the general trust in the system. Therefore, supervising authorities need to ensure that increased competition will not have negative effects on the overall stability of the system.

In summary, an efficient balance is needed between competition, cooperation and stability, with the aim of promoting the total efficiency of the payment scrvice supply. These competition increasing proposals are unlikely to be introduced by the industry itself, and hence regulatory authorities will need to step in to be kingmakers.

16.3 WHAT WOULD HAPPEN IF THE CUSTOMER WERE KING?

The customer as king mantra drives the developments in other industries towards increased customer benefits. In payments, the main benefits will be found in:

- lower payment costs and fees;
- improved delivery speed;
- a suitable security level;
- convenient customer interfaces; and
- efficient customer-to-bank systems integration.

The main bulk of payments is already handled electronically today, and will be even more so in the future. In line with Moore's law,[2] ICT costs have decreased continuously, by 25–30 % per year. Already today, the average cost of data storage, data communication and data processing of single transactions, such as payments, are just millicents.[3] This development can be seen in the prices of e-mails and short mobile phone messages (SMS). An e-mail account closely resembles a payment account. Both have incoming and outgoing messages. In payments, the balances of the accounts have to be updated with each transaction, but this is purely a trivial computational task. Keeping payments accounts is essentially the same as registering payables and receivables and, in the future, customers will view their e-accounts over the internet using their PC or mobile phone or other device.

Real-time processing is the ultimate delivery speed, and it has already been reached in several data-based industries. In fact real-time, or near real-time, will become the most efficient delivery convention. For example, where are the savings in providing e-mails or short messages the next day? When payments are processed in real-time, error handling and corrections can be made directly. Customers will be able to control their transactions and liquidity better. There will be no payments in transit. Payment processing can then be better integrated with other real-time events and transaction driven business activities, which creates a processing convention which will be used more and more in internal corporate systems.

Strong customer remote identification and transaction security features are needed in this context, as almost all payments after 2010 will be initiated and processed electronically over networks. Customers will need secure hardware devices for storing their electronic credentials, with secured interfaces. The more money there is within this internet environment, the more criminals it will attract. Future e-criminals will have both technical know-how and large budgets. The current PCs and smart phones appear to be far too open to Trojan horse viruses today. These can be used to seize customers' identities and money if they are not protected by more secure, tamper-proof devices. Customers will expect easy-to-use, standardised and reliable security solutions.

The identification service providers need to also construct a trunk network amongst them, in order to provide identification reachability. In the same way as payment networks make it possible to send payments from one bank to any other bank, the customer identification network would make it possible for any customer to identify themselves to any other person or necessary party in the internet environment. Secure e-identification will again require regulatory interventions to create more control over internet accessibility because, without such

---

[2] Computer processing power doubles every eighteen months whilst the price of processing power halves.

[3] For example a high performance 1 TB disc-drive, which can store 1 billion densely packed payments, sells for around € 1000 and a 2 Megabyte broadband connection. which can carry more than five million transactions a day, costs less than € 20 per month in September 2007.

measures, the risks will be too high. Sufficient web security is a basic requirement for e- and m-commerce in the future.

E-mails and SMS messages have simple interfaces that are accepted and used by most customers. Today, more e-mails and SMS messages are sent than payments. This is why payments will also need simple easy-to-use interfaces. Both e-mails and SMS messages could provide the starting point for such modern electronic payment interfaces. This is in fact what some new service providers have implemented. They have re-used the e-mail system by adding a payments balance field or introducing payment balance fields into SMS messages. This is in effect what PayPal has implemented, for example.

Customers can intuitively relate to these added options, as they are made to familiar services. These service providers have even simplified the account number addresses, by using e-mail addresses or telephone numbers as account identifiers. Customers will expect that tomorrow's payments are easy-to-understand and have convenient interfaces. For example, current plastic cards will become digital cards in mobile telephones, and the card payments will be accepted by phone through the use of a simple keystroke or PIN input. The basic structure of e-mails will change to incorporate a main body for payment transport details, and separate enclosures contain information about orders, invoices, guarantees and other information related to the underlying deal. Near-field-communication (NFC) using blue-tooth and Radio Frequency Identification (RFID) will be used to transfer payment contents between customer payment devices, such as mobile telephones, PCs, point-of-sale terminals, vending and ticketing machines. Making payments will become as easy as possible.

However, the greatest customer benefits can be found in the potential for integration.

All payments need to be connected to an underlying business deal, and nobody wants to have to use extra resources to pay attention manually to payments. At best, payments should just flow automatically between the different systems, with as little manual intervention as possible. In particular, corporate customers are interested in integrating payment data, based upon process-to-process integration with payables, receivables, ordering and invoicing systems. This will require reconciling information such that each payment will need a unique transaction identifier for error handling and control. Increasing customer-to-customer data using fields for reconciliation and other payment enclosures is the basis for future integration.

However, payment service providers can also provide integrated value-added services for customers, based upon this expanded data content. Private customers especially would be interested in e-archives of payments, which they could browse in the same way they browse e-mail accounts; find all payments received from or sent to somebody; find all payments sent on a given day; find all payments with details including things such as the word 'camera', and so on. One rapidly growing area will be combined payments and electronic tickets, as it can provide large cost-savings and increased convenience. Tickets would become digitalised and stored in the telephone or retrievable by telephone.

The developments described[4] have already started to happen, but mainly in other industries or by new entrants interested in payments services such as telecommunications firms, internet service providers such as PayPal, or retail trade companies. There are four basic reasons for the new entrants' interest, as they:

- have employed the new technologies in their main business areas, and are now interested in synergies available in the under-developed payment industry;

---

[4] A more detailed description of these trends can be found on the website http://www.bof.fi/sc/payhabits2010, which contains the results of the Payment Habits 2010+ project of the Bank of Finland.

- can make large profit margins by employing the new low-cost technologies without the legacy burdens of existing providers by reusing their main services and systems;
- have the same customer base as the banks and can reuse their own identification systems and customer databases;
- can provide added value to customers via new integrated payment services and through synergies with their main business, for example using mobile phone accounts as payment accounts; and
- can cross-subsidise or embed the payment service charges with their main services in a profitable way, and thereby compete with the hidden pricing policies of bank payment services.

For the customers, payments are near enough a utility service. It should be there, it should function rapidly and it should function without problems. The costs should be low and its usage should require a minimum of effort.

Who will be the future e-payment bulk service providers: the banks or the new entrants?

16.4   HOW WILL THE NEW KING RULE AFTER SEPA IN 2010?

In industries with open competition, new digital services have conquered the markets. Low cost digital calculators replaced mechanical calculators, typewriters have been replaced with PCs and word processor applications, analogue and line-based telephones have been replaced with mobile telephones. These changes have pushed the old service providers out of the market although, in some cases, the old service providers have had enough innovation to ensure a strong market position in the new environment.

Another feature for change has been the consolidation and globalisation of service provision. Local and regional service providers have been replaced by multinational companies providing standardised services worldwide.

Open competition combined with the introduction of a versatile e- and m-payments world would, if it follows the pattern of other industries, change the current payment markets rapidly and profoundly. This will result in the banking industry facing a major restructuring as customers will move their payment accounts and funds to large international payment service providers, as these can provide the most efficient solutions.

This development has already started because some of the new entrants, such as PayPal, report over a hundred million customer accounts already. These figures are so big that it looks as if the new entrants have reached critical mass. If the traditional banking industry is unable to create more drive for internal change, it will lose the payment business as the change to fully digitalised payments occurs.

There are therefore two main scenarios for post-SEPA developments:

1. the European banks determine to innovate and become the forerunners for the true digitalisation of payments and the emergence of a Single International Payment Area (SIPA); or
2. the new global entrants grab the market and introduce the SIPA.

The result in both cases is a SIPA, rather than a SEPA. There is no economic backing for regional solutions in our network-based global village of post-2010. SEPA can therefore best be viewed as an efficient step towards this end objective.

Just as we have one global e-mail system or one de facto mobile telephone system, one basic, real-time, network-based, payment infrastructure service and concept will be sufficient.

The new king will be harsh. You serve me or you are out of the market! There is no possibility for inefficiency in a highly competitive market. The focus must be on delivering maximum benefit to the customers.

17

The implications of SEPA for e-invoicing

Erkki Poutiainen, Nordea

E-Invoicing is the first step towards achieving a SEPA for supply chains which, by incorporating corporate needs across the flow of commerce, achieves the real SEPA dream; rather than the narrow view of just using SEPA for cross-border payments.

In the current debate in the payments industry, e-invoicing has taken a very visible position. It is linked both to the hopes of the future SEPA world and to the build-up of supply chain related value propositions. However, it is clear that the basic SEPA service will not include e-invoicing in its first implementation phase. What are the considerations for this?

First, in order to reach a break-through for any new market-wide service, there is a need for strong community support, vision and a drive to create supporting infrastructure with a sound motivational pull. In other words, there needs to be a business model.

The means of achieving widely used e-invoicing infrastructures definitely requires collaboration amongst all stakeholders and a number of banks have already proven that the payments industry is one of the important players in this. A strong unified effort from the banks is weakened however by the massive investment and attention to they have had to give to the basic SEPA implementation. Some regulatory actions have also been adding to the challenges of collaborative[1] work around new services.

With some recent activation in the collaborative work, we may see an emergence of a widely used e-invoicing solution within five years from now although there are some critical pre-requisites for a successful outcome.

In this chapter, I shall discuss the lessons to learn from SEPA design, its elements and further necessary ingredients required for developments on the way to the successful creation and implementation of pan-European e-invoicing. I shall not discuss e-invoicing solutions nor technical standards, but rather the biggest challenges on the collaboration.

17.1 WHAT DOES THE SEPA INFRASTRUCTURE STAND FOR AND CAN IT BE AN ENABLER FOR FURTHER SERVICE INNOVATION?

The creation of the basic SEPA infrastructure provides a historical shift to a pan-European platform on which more efficient and modern payment related services can be built. In choosing and fixing the direction, the solutions should produce an efficient platform and space for future innovation in the market. In the worst case, an infrastructure can create bottlenecks for sound

---

[1] Here I refer to the fuzzy line between collaboration and competition, and some actions have more impact to business models and earnings logic than others.

evolution by locking too much rigidity into the system. In my view SEPA, as it is today, provides features on both sides in that it provides huge opportunities but also unfortunate bottlenecks.

The excessive collaborative effort to work out the SEPA roadmap has proven the strength and success of the productive organisation and processes of the European banking industry. The basic SEPA, with its rulebooks and adoption of new XML standards, is an encouraging achievement for the market. It is an encouraging showcase for the work on further infrastructure and standards development, as demonstrated by the interest rising on other continents in the work of the European banks to implement this process.[2] SEPA is an example of successful implementation of an unforeseen large and complex project.

Unfortunately there is also the restrictive side of the initial SEPA implementation. Even if some very clear road-signs for modern user requirements for payments were presented by some forerunners, such as Rosettanet and other e-commerce pilots, SEPA has resulted in a kind of payments industry 'back-office' development.

The SEPA end-to-end vision is very modest in the documented form designed by the banks in the European Payments Council. Originally there was no proper dialogue between the stakeholders, and this was during the critical times of fixing the overall directions for the SEPA journey. The vision of SEPA was therefore developed as supporting the EU Single Market objectives, but no widely shared practical goals were produced for SEPA. There was very little clarity on what to expect from this process as an outcome, in the form of end-user services. This in turn has resulted in voices being raised later in the day by some end-user communities.

We know that the corporate, SME and public administration users expect simple and harmonised services and support for automated payment-related processes. These services include standardized interfaces and payment-related messages, e-reconciliation and e-invoicing. None of this has been part of the basic SEPA agenda however, except for mild recommendations on customer-to-bank standards. Although SEPA's design scope starts from payment initiation and ends in payment reporting, something is missing in between. This is due to those designing the process resisting too rigid a definition in between, with statements such as: 'this is not the space for core banking'; or 'this is a competitive issue'. In my view, this creates the whole problem whereby the current SEPA infrastructure does not support real end-to-end straight through processing; instead, the chosen approach creates some bottlenecks.

We have learned from various reports how heavy the exercise is, in terms of the investments that have had to be made to get to the basic SEPA for the payments industry. The implementation phase is also ongoing, and very few banks can afford to think of new service innovations during this phase, as resources are unavailable during this early implementation phase.

By the same process, the revenue perspectives on traditional payment services are declining. A sound reaction would be the creation of more positive visions and roadmaps but this is not reflected in the community. The EPC has no activity for thinking further beyond the implementation of basic SEPA. For the sake of exception, there are some developments for online and mobile payment scoping activities, but these are in their early phases and still struggling for broad support.

---

[2] By way of example, Middle Eastern and African countries are using SEPA to create their own strategies for currency convergence with the Gulf Cooperation Council (GCC) agreeing to a common currency for Bahrain, Kuwait, Oman, Qatar, Saudi Arabia, United Arab Emirates and Yemen around the same time as SEPA's implementation.

17.2   MODERN INTEGRATED BUSINESS REQUIRES A SHIFT FROM LINEAR AND BILATERAL TO NETWORK THINKING

The firm foundation of bank created payment infrastructure is a strong proof of a good network service. Everyone can be efficiently reached now as the SEPA elements will be in place. But this network is designed to only serve the banks, and yet the service value chain goes beyond that on both ends of the payment. We need to extend the scope to contain more of the value chain.

Furthermore, alongside the creation of the end-to-end scope, the SEPA payments cycle should incorporate a circular chain-style concept. After all, where does the payments process really start and where does it end? Taking the commercial perspective, a buyer makes a tender, chooses to order, checks the delivery, accepts the invoice, updates accounts payable, initiates the payment, etc; and there is a mirror function on the seller's or supplier's side. When we add the various counterparties and their service providers to this process, we have a sizeable number of service networks where bank services are just a part of the overall cycle.

This is what we have learned from our corporate and public administration customers. Does our current service infrastructure provide a platform for these real-life business requirements? The truth is that a lot remains to be done and developed. For example, the global standards on ISO20022 were truncated to SEPA messages and this is a bottleneck which disregards well founded standardisation work on global business requirements performed earlier.

Even if there are a number of opportunities for new business developments, building on natural and obvious synergies, banks have remained passive as a community. Conversely, there are also a few quite advanced individual banks and some national communities who are active in this business, and who have achieved success. Nevertheless, as this is a network business, neither a single player nor a restricted community is able to provide satisfactory reach to their customers' networks of counterparties.

A SEPA for supply chains is required. For sure it will not be created in a short time but we need a new SEPA White Paper and roadmap, this time in collaboration with all stakeholders.

17.3   A SEPA FOR SUPPLY CHAINS: AN OPEN CALL FOR A EUROPEAN FORUM?

The discussion of integrating the physical and financial supply chains was raised in conference vocabulary some years ago. Learning about SEPA from banks and European authorities, the corporate community have placed their hopes on having a response to the requirements of financial supply chain automation. This was of course an unjustified expectation, as described above, and led initially to an unfruitful debate with no resolution.

What has happened as a result, however, is that the thought barrier for SEPA for the supply chain has been broken, although this is only an early start. The speakers in the current conferences have started to introduce terms like 'SEPA 2.0', 'e-SEPA' or 'Full SEPA' for example, but still without really defining them in more detail. There is hardly any collaborative activity beyond SEPA 1.0 on European forums. There is no big picture or high level roadmap existing for future developments to align collaborative innovation. There is no home for this discussion, which would lead to constructive forward-looking collaboration.

We have some activity in the marketplace, as described below, but an organised discussion and process to achieve roadmaps is missing right now and is needed if we are to provide the supply chain automation that the corporate community would wish us to deliver.

17.4 THE EUROPEAN AUTHORITIES AS PROMOTERS FOR FURTHER EVOLUTION

From the early days, the European Central Bank and representatives of the European Commission have encouraged the banking industry to construct a progressive plan for taking best-of-breed payments practices to the European markets. This is easy to say and recommend, but the reality creates some challenge. We must understand the impact of tradition, user habits, and consequently differences in basic infrastructure, such as internet adoption, to the process of importing new innovative services. The difference in applied revenue elements across the payment instruments is another important hurdle in adopting best practices along with the 'not invented here' syndrome.

Nevertheless, the aims of the authorities seem to be determined. The ECB signals its views on developments through their regular SEPA Progress reports and the processes in the EU Commission to drive further the Lisbon agenda are becoming very influential to in the market. The 2010 initiative with pilot programmes on e-Government, and especially interoperability targets for e-Procurement and e-Identification, seem to proceed faster than some of the collaborative actions in the private sector. Furthermore, the initiative on e-invoicing will very likely lead to, as it is targeting, a speeding up of collaborative actions across all relevant stakeholder groups. This is because it is aiming to commit the public administrations in the Member States and the Commission itself to this initiative, as well as corporate and SMEs in the private sector.

However, feasible business models need to be agreed among the stakeholders first. If the economics are not driving, there be no service providers to realise the mass market solution.

17.5 THE MARKET NEEDS TO FIND ITS SOLUTIONS WITHOUT FORCING REGULATION

The slow progress in collaborative action for advanced infrastructures in payments can partly be explained by the unsuitable organisation of the service providers, banks and other relevant players. The challenge of organising and aligning the political will of complete industries behind new initiatives is demanding. It is simply unrealistic, with the fragmentation and different kinds of specialisations of the service providers.

What ways could be more suitable for innovation-oriented collaborative design and development? The European Payments Council through its Charter has ruled out its participation at least for the time being, even if a large number of its members are active innovators. The problem of the EPC is the mandatory nature of forcing its members to commit to actions. How about a voluntary forum then, with inclusion of relevant stakeholders?

17.6 E-INVOICING IS THE FIRST STEP ON THE ROAD TO 'SEPA FOR SUPPLY CHAINS'

As discussed above the 'SEPA for supply chains' needs to be taken in steps. There is no time to be wasted on broad discussions only, but to take the first practical steps in parallel to the overall visioning and plan. Besides, the interest and demand for e-invoicing is already there and, with convincing signals on near future developments, even broader masses of users can be encouraged to prepare themselves for the new opportunities.

There is of course the danger of creating bottlenecks if the overall vision is still missing. However, with supply chain automation there is nothing very new as such. Standards bodies and business communities have progressed quite far in conceptualising the global context, as well as the details related to both physical and financial supply chains. What is missing is the remaining infrastructure, particularly the common business rules and the network.

It is only natural to start with e-invoicing however. The e-invoice is in the middle of the whole supply chain. It links sales and procurement. It links physical and financial processes. It can support automatic integration of the different processes.

17.7   CURRENT MARKET NEEDS A EUROPEAN SOLUTION AND PRACTICAL EXPERIENCE IS AVAILABLE

Large corporations are early adopters of these innovations with their strategic supply chain partners, and have faced the problems in the cross-border reality and the challenges of making the SME suppliers integrate to their chosen invoicing practices. The European Association of Corporate Treasurers (EACT) has also worked extensively to put together user requirements for pan-European and global e-invoicing.

The SME sector has a similar target to reduce the administrative burdens and automate processes towards all of their counterparties, but in a simpler, more easily accessible way, and on acceptable investment cost level.

The public administrations have similar efficiency goals, especially in light of the pressure to deal with increasing budgetary constraints, and have launched a number of public e-procurement programmes aimed at end-to-end automation and integration of the functions in the procurement and invoicing process.

Among the most experienced service providers are the companies performing integration, message handling and large volume communication hub operations, typically for the large corporations. This group of service providers have established links between each other based on the geographical needs of their customers. Another model of service found in the market is a portal for a community or company, serving the invoicing and other related document exchange with its own network of suppliers or customers.

Another domain of e-invoicing experience exists amongst some banks and bank communities, for example in the Nordic countries, Austria, Belgium and Italy. Bank-driven solutions are based upon some payment supply chain synergy effects, which should also be considered to be taken into the European level solutions. These effects include trust networks, wide reachability, e-channels to customers, financing of payments, and collaborative design expertise for standards and infrastructures. These are especially beneficial for achieving wide reach in the consumer invoicing and SME sector as senders and receivers.

17.8   SHINING A LIGHT ON THE EUROPEAN INNOVATION SCENE: e-INVOICING, THE COMMISSION INITIATIVE

Best practices, experiences and synergies need to be place upon a common table. The challenge starts from the scoping to an optimal outcome which can best benefit the wide range of stakeholders.

The European Commission called in an informal task force on e-invoicing in December 2006. The task force was composed of representatives from users, service providers, standards bodies, legal experts and public administration. The work resulted in a report which recommended the EC establish a steering committee to govern the process to address the issues raised.

The novelty in the EC initiative on e-invoicing is not in the e-invoice itself, but in the aim for a design of a European-wide infrastructure through which the widest reach can be supported, in a similar manner to the way in which SEPA supports reach for payments. This does not only call for technical standards but also for rules for service provision and harmonisation, combined with diminishing administrational and legal complexity in the cross-border environment. Furthermore, this calls for collaboration across the variety of end-users, industries, public and private sector, service providers and public authorities.

17.9   BANKS ARE PUTTING THEIR ACTION TOGETHER THROUGH THE EBA ASSOCIATION

As discussed above, pan-European e-invoicing is a service requiring development of infrastructure, standards, business rules and removal of some barriers. Building on the success and experience of the SEPA rulebook and implementation, banks have an asset to bring onboard in the work for e-invoicing but, as the EPC has scoped its activities narrowly upon the basic payment infrastructure and instruments, another forum is needed.

The EBA Association of banks recently decided to raise its activity from the e-invoicing working group, established in 2006, to a higher level. The new plan includes an analysis and market description document which will set out the key questions to be addressed, the drivers, constraints and a range of possible solutions. It is also intended to conduct a series of productive dialogues with all other stakeholders, including the corporate and SME communities, public administrations, standardisers, other service providers, banks and the Commission. This will be performed using appropriate forums and consultative processes.

By mid-2008, the EBA Board plans to produce a Roadmap or White Paper providing proposals as to how an electronic invoicing solution could operate, and how it could be taken forward as part of an overall market evolution. The EBA is totally open as to the nature of such a solution and has no preconceptions as to the governance and cooperation model that may be required. In other words, the EBA sees e-invoicing as a good possibility for the future.

17.10   CONCLUSIONS

In summary, I see the next phase of SEPA already emerging, with the broad support of the community towards e-invoicing solutions, not to mention the local or community services that are already running.

Many people say that technical standards are the key for making e-invoicing popular but I have not discussed standards at all in this text. The reason is that I see other, more primary issues to be addressed, such as governance and a committed vision with the scope and objectives for the whole framework. When a good collaborative framework for design is in place, I am very confident that solutions around technical and business requirements can be found.

The most important factor right now is to keep up the positive spirit of collaboration and progress. We must not let the dead-lock on competitive issues lead to a zero or null discussion of customer and end-user needs. In the actual work we deliver, we need to keep the focus on doing things, and not in listing and inventing new challenges for an ideal model. Before we can take a second step, we need to take the first.

The biggest effect will be in models where the widest possible participation can be achieved, especially the inclusion of the SME market. This is the primary target in the scope of both the Commission and the EBA. Of course this also fits well the overall political goals in the

EU. Economic growth and employment can best be achieved through supporting SMEs and entrepreneurs and, with e-invoicing, we should contribute to make it as simple as possible for the SME and entrepreneurs to automate their commercial processes.

In summary, e-invoicing has all the chances to be a successful next step on the way from a basic SEPA to a SEPA for supply chains. This can be achieved by merging the broad stakeholder participations and SEPA design experiences together, which will benefit the creation of a smooth transition process.

Few community things happen in an instant. In the best case, with the activities we can witness today, the design phase for pan-European e-invoicing can be completed before 2010. There are then some legal and tax administration actions which will take a little longer but, with decisive promotion, we should see a critical mass of interoperable solutions and active users from 2012 onwards.

18

Banking after SEPA: 2010 and beyond

Daniele Danese, Banca Popolare di Verona

Banks will need to innovate in the new world, whilst corporate customers will initially be disappointed with SEPA's products as they are designed for simple retail transaction services. However, these products will soon migrate to more sophisticated, faster and cheaper services and the question will then be how long it will take the corporate client to use them.

The consequences of SEPA and the PSD on banking are going to be extensive and far reaching, and will impact in some countries far more than in others. We can view SEPA as a catalyst. A point in time when some international trends including standardisation, globalisation, electronic interchange and others, get real.

How will banking be affected? The following predictions will be patchy, as countries move at different speeds and some will need to move more than others. Equally, some developments seem obvious whilst others are not. Read on . . .

18.1 MORE COMPETITION – TO THE BENEFIT OF THE CUSTOMER?

The first result of SEPA will be increased competition between banks. SEPA will make it easier to enter into somebody else's market as all instruments, rules and standards will be the same. In quite a few cases, you will not even need to enter the market as the international corporate customer will bring the market to you. There will be more and more payment factories, and less 'foreign' or 'collection' accounts – accounts opened to a company resident in a different country – as 'one account is enough'.

Multinational groups comprising local companies located in different countries may still need local accounts and access to local credit lines, but will increasingly handle liquidity and payables and receivables out of one main account. If they keep more than one account they may want to move the orders instead of the money, as in make payments for all the group out of the most liquid accounts.

Concentration will mean better prices, and possibly more shopping around so expect many more RFPs from corporate customers. In short, payments and direct debits will become a commodity, with large users able to drive down costs for all payments, both SEPA and international ones. Retail customers, on the other hand, will probably see only limited benefits.

18.2   MORE TECHNOLOGY = MORE COSTS – CAN THE CUSTOMER WORK FOR THE BANKS?

With each new regulation, banks have to keep investing just to stay in the business. The larger players will therefore be better positioned, thanks to their larger pockets, to provide new services and to make life easier for the customer.

However, this will come at a cost as the pricing gap between STP and NON-STP will widen, with manual paper handling becoming so expensive that every customer, çorporate or retailer will need to move to the electronic presentation of orders. Remote banking, ATMs, mobiles, credit cards will all be promoted heavily, as long as you do not bother the teller.

Standardisation will help as there will be no need for the bank to invest in different systems and standards for each country, but banks need to invest to make sure their services are easy to use, shielding the customers from their complexities.

In short, the customer will do the work of the bank, entering the data of the order and sending to the bank pre-checked STP order files. Customer support will be crucial to make sure this business lifeblood keeps flowing without disruptions, as non-STP payments will become very expensive.

18.3   MORE CONCENTRATION TO REDUCE COSTS – CAN WE HELP YOU?

From the corporate customer's point of view, concentration of payments means lower prices whilst, from the bank's point of view, lower revenues. Hence, the need to reduce costs again by concentration.

SEPA spells the end for national, incompatible payment systems and the birth of pan-European infrastructures with a much wider potential market: the Eurodomestic one. For the banks, this means the possibility to choose and to reduce costs, by concentrating their European operations on fewer infrastructures, possibly just one or two.

But if your volumes are small and you operate in just one country, then maybe you are already using just one infrastructure so there is not much room for improvement, is there? According to the pundits of outsourcing, there actually is. By joining forces with a bigger player, you get to share part of their cost reduction as long as you do not mind losing some control on part of your business.

In short, there will be a concentration on the use of infrastructures, and many cases of outsourcing of payment processing by smaller banks to larger banks.

18.4   PROPRIETARY IS DEAD – MOVING TOWARDS A EUROPEAN REMOTE BANKING STANDARD?

In the past, one way to keep the customer tied to the bank was through the use of proprietary standards for connection, message formats, processing rules, and so on. This is even truer where the number of players is limited to a few big institutions.

With SEPA, and more in general ISO20022, the format for giving orders to the bank and getting information back is standardised. What we need now is a way to standardise the connection between the corporate customer and the bank.

There are quite a few examples in Europe of countrywide systems – CBI in Italy, Isabel in Belgium, CFONB in France, Multicash in Germany and Austria, to name but a few – but they are not interoperable and none seems capable of becoming a truly European system. The SWIFT alternative, on the other hand, seems more suited to large multinationals and not attractive enough for medium-sized European companies.

Market pressure will be the driving force here, not regulation, as everybody stands to gain from a European remote banking standard in the end. However, the current trend towards 'national flavours' of the customer-to-bank payment initiation standards is an indication that the banks still prefer to go the other way, as in protection of the home market rather than open standards.

In short, notwithstanding market pressures, banks will resist the request for a European remote banking standard, although corporate customers should be able to redirect SEPA orders from one bank to the other with minimal changes.

18.5   EVERYBODY CAN PLAY = AN ENDING OF POSITIONAL ADVANTAGES IN RETAIL BANKING?

In Pre-SEPA Europe, to make a local payment a bank needs to have access to the domestic payment system, either directly or through a local bank. The same goes for direct debits, where you need to be connected to the local system to be able to receive requests to debit your customer's accounts.

SEPA will fundamentally change this, as being part of the local clearing system will no longer be necessary. A Frenchman will be able to have the electricity bill for his Italian house debited to his German account. Clearly, a local presence will no longer be enough to get the retail business, and no longer a prerequisite.

The internet may be a further vehicle for delocalisation, and we have already seen a number of significant services move to the web from airplane tickets to car insurance. Nevertheless, the bank on the web has so far always been a domestic one.

With SEPA debit cards to get cash locally, SEPA credit cards accepted all over Europe and SEPA credit transfers and direct debits, will you still need local accounts?

In short, a full European banking service over the web, offered by a bank to potential customers all over Europe, will become reality sooner than we think.

18.6   BANKING CONCENTRATION: THE EUROPEAN SUPERBANK(S)?

To say that SEPA and the PSD will bring about further concentration in the banking industry is probably far-fetched. In theory, bigger is better in the SEPA and PSD environment as larger volumes means lower cost per transaction; being competitive in the market place; getting more market share; increasing your volumes; and so on. But to reap these advantages, you need to rationalise your systems, re-engineer your processes, concentrate your volumes, and so on.

Given the effort required by the current large mergers, integrating SEPA processing in just one place is not likely to be one of the major initial priorities, but it will come. Multinational banks can reap the benefits of a single processing point with single access.

One word of warning however: don't centralise customer support but keep it within each country, otherwise you risk alienating your retail customers.

In short, the major European banks will gradually create central processing centres and single-point connections to infrastructures, and further consolidation in the industry will accelerate this process.

18.7   FINDING ALTERNATIVE REVENUES – MORE FRILLS TO THE BASE PRODUCTS

Finding new sources for revenue is already a priority for European bankers and the increased cost of SEPA compliance will be accompanied by a decrease of payments revenues. In addition, payments will become a commodity with no real differentiation between the offerings. This means payments will move to whoever and wherever it is the cheapest. There will also be a further negative impact in this situation for the countries that are still paying interest on the accounts, as the PSD eradicates the use of value dating.

As a consequence, revenues of the basic SEPA products will be severely depressed. How do you recover lost revenues? Two strategies come to mind: either go for better products such as faster payments, or offer additional services on the basic products such as electronic invoicing. If bankers can figure out a way to offer real additional value to their customers, they might be able to give away the payments for free. For example, think about ink-jet printers where a couple of sets of replacement cartridges often cost as much as the printer. You make money on the cartridges, not on the printer.

Within banking, to make another example, handling the customer's sent and received invoices, automatically preparing the payments or the direct debits, reconciling incoming and outgoing funds to the invoices, and so forth, all gain significant value. In short, banks will start to insource some of the customer's business and get paid to do the job.

An example for the retail business would be the launch of a mobile advisory service providing end-of-day balances of the account, notices on large credits or debits which can be configured by the end-user, and so on.

Another service may be to go directly to full real-time payments such as instant transfers, reporting and balances. These are the treasurer's dream.

The road from the initial basic SEPA instruments which are suited to the retail market to services more suited to corporate companies such as priority payments will be a long one, especially as these are not part of the SEPA rulebooks.

In short, with payments becoming a commodity, banks will need to find useful premium or additional services that the customer is willing to pay.

18.8   FROM BANK PAYMENTS TO ALTERNATIVE PAYMENTS

Migrant payments, web micro-payments, mobile payments, credit card corporate payments, rechargeable transport cards; these are just a few examples where the banking sector has gradually lost hold of potential business in favour of outsiders. With the PSD, the Payment Institutions will be recognised, and will become a force to be reckoned with.

So far alternative banking channels has mostly meant web and telephone but, to keep hold of their retail market, banks need to develop interfaces that are channel independent and as ubiquitous and simple to use as a mobile telephone or an ATM.

On the one hand, competition to banks will come from convergence of technologies, such as mobile telephones used as a prepaid cash wallet to make micro-payments. On the other hand, competition will also come from new entrants who are able to operate from a much lower cost base as well as being able to tap into the unbanked markets. Banks have become more and more data processors, and are therefore more vulnerable to this kind of competition.

Banks will need to rethink their payment strategies by concentrating on large-volume corporate clients; keeping a toe in the traditional retail payments business; getting into new, innovative payment systems; entering into partnerships with payment institutions; or maybe a combination of some or all of these strategies.

In short, payments are the lifeblood of many banking businesses, and banks cannot afford to lose this market to outsiders. However, to stay in the business, they need to ride the innovation train or find a partner able and willing to do it for them.

18.9   REALITY CHECK: IS THIS WHAT THE CUSTOMER WANTS?

If you talk to corporate customers about SEPA, you get either a blank stare or the start of a lively lecture on banks failing to cater for the customer's needs, by giving priority to optimising their own internal processes rather than coming up with interesting and useful products. Up to a point, this is true. For example, working together on SEPA has been difficult enough for the banks. The idea of then getting a bunch of corporate experts to criticise these efforts would probably have been too much for many banks.

If you ask a corporate what he wants from SEPA, the answer is quite straightforward: cheaper, simpler, faster payments up to a point, although the corporate will be willing to pay more if the proposed SEPA products are going to save costs.

The fact is that most corporate customers are disappointed with the initial SEPA offerings but they tend to forget that SEPA was mostly intended for the retail market. This is why the basic SEPA instruments are just that: basic!

Considering that the domestic systems have taken years to mature, it is not surprising that harmonisation has been only possible at the lowest level. Given time, market demand will push the banks into developing new SEPA products suitable for the wholesale market.

In conclusion, customers need to overcome their initial disappointment with SEPA products as these products are likely to be cheaper and simpler than the existing products, thanks to increased competition and the fact that the same formats and data for payments and direct debits will be used across all of Europe.

The big question will then be: when will the customers migrate to SEPA?

Part 4
The Views of the Corporates

- Doctor John Ryan, European Business School
- The European Association of Corporate Treasurers
- TWIST

19

SEPA: an introduction for corporates

Doctor John Ryan

The Single Euro Payments Area (SEPA) was introduced on January 2008; it aims to bring a number of advantages for corporates. It is these new opportunities that will encourage corporates to make the necessary changes to their systems and operations, and also justify the investment needed.

Over the last fifteen years the European Commission has pushed to create a Single Payments Area (SPA). The Internal Market DG of the EC defines SPA as an area 'in which citizens and businesses can make cross-border payments as easily, safely and efficiently as they can within their own countries and subject to identical charges'.

The Regulation (2560/2001/EC) passed in November 2001 by the European Parliament and the European Council mandated charges for ATM withdrawals and cash transfers to be no more than domestic levels by 1 July 2002 and 1 July 2003 respectively. Since 1 January 2006 it has also applied to transfers in euro of up to € 50 000 in value made between two euro-denominated accounts within the EU.

It was this experience that opened the eyes of the banks. Their inertia at preparing for the SPA showed that the regulation, which ordered domestic and intra-Eurozone payments to be priced equally, would change things. In particular, the fact that it was favourable to banks in countries with relatively inefficient domestic payment systems meant that banks working in efficient systems rightfully complained.

Transfer systems in countries such as Italy and France are much more costly to run than their equivalents in Germany, the Netherlands and Belgium. As a consequence banks in the former set of countries were charging higher prices for domestic transfers than elsewhere, before the directive came into effect. Cost and pricing of international transfers are of course at the same level, in both cases high.

Given this situation, the equal pricing directive meant that banks in north-west Europe had to increase domestic fees significantly in order to bring international and domestic prices to the same level and not lose money. In Italy, on the contrary, banks only had to raise prices a tiny amount.

Thus, the undesired effect of this regulation was that customers of efficient domestic transfer providers were punished heavily in the short term, as overall cross-border inefficiency became the standard benchmark for pricing across the EU. Indeed, the creation of a level playing field should have preceded the measure, with inefficient systems forced out first. However, this can be attributed as much to banks dragging their feet, as to the EC not providing sufficient time.

Under the threat of further regulatory action of the same sort as the pricing regulation on transfers, Europe's banking community reacted. The three major banking associations of the European Banking Federation, the European Savings Bank Group and the European Association of Co-operative Banks created the European Payments Council (EPC) in June 2002.

The clear objective of the EPC was to take the creation of a Single Payments Area (SPA) into the banks' own hands. Soon after inception therefore, the EPC issued, in August 2002, a White Paper outlining its intention to create a Single Euro Payments Area (SEPA) by 2010:

'SEPA is the integrated market for payment services which is subject to effective competition and where there is no distinction between cross-border and national payments within the euro area'.

The EC has charged the EPC with overseeing the delivery of the SEPA programme and meeting the agreed dates. To facilitate this process, the EPC has produced the SEPA Cards Framework (SCF), which lays out the timelines and requirements as well as the main principles for stakeholders to become SEPA compliant.

SEPA is consistent with the aim of the European Commission's financial services policy over the next years to further the integration of the EU's financial services markets, and contributes to the Lisbon Agenda which aims to foster the competitiveness and development of the European economy.

19.1 MAKING SEPA HAPPEN

SEPA will be delivered by the banking industry in close conjunction with all stakeholder communities – consumers, SMEs, merchants, corporates and government bodies, and supportive public authorities. The community of European banks is strongly committed to this ambitious programme of action, based on self-regulation and a full recognition of the role of market forces and competition. Commitment and support from all parties involved in the payments process is essential to make SEPA a reality.

Most companies believe that the construction of a fully functioning SEPA for payments by cards in particular will bring benefits to European cardholders and consumers and, by opening up the European payments market, will reduce costs and increase efficiencies for banks and processors. The successful implementation of SEPA within the timescales laid down by the European Commission depends upon the resolve, understanding and active commitment of Europe's banking community. Without industry support, implementation timescales will slip and delivery of the benefits of SEPA will be put at risk.

In July 2003 the EPC published its 8-pillar strategy, which outlined its plans for implementation of the 2002 white paper. The pillars address fraud, licensing, standardisation, safety of usage, the organisation of the processing industry, interchange, the place of the bank card schemes and regulation. The latter explicitly states that it is the group's intention to become a self-regulating body.

The eight action points were produced in response to the strategic interests of the banking industry, which have been laid out within the same document. Besides removing borders and implementing common standards the banks state that they will:

- seek to uphold their franchise over payments and ensure common card schemes remain aligned within bank objectives; and
- acknowledge processing as an independent business, which also means that they will review the role of card schemes within this, given the statement above.

19.2   THE OPPORTUNITIES

Automation, centralisation and reduced costs. These are the buzzwords in the corporate world and what every treasurer and cash manager works hard to achieve across their organisation. Through the standardisation and harmonisation of processes and payments instruments across Europe, SEPA will accelerate all of these trends.

Transaction costs will be reduced and corporates should be able to use more standardised formats in their communication with banks, such as sending payment instructions to banks and receiving information related to inflows. Companies will also benefit from easier and faster transfer of funds, as well as the ability to more easily centralise payment processes through payment factories and to close local bank accounts in some countries.

For instance, corporates will be able to perform all of their financial transactions centrally from one bank account using the new payment instruments. The handling of payments will also be simplified, as all incoming and outgoing payments can use the same format. This will significantly reduce current complexity in Europe in terms of the number of payment instruments and their unique features from country to country, alongside data format specifications and bank and bank account identifiers, accounting platforms, legal framework and clearing systems. By consolidating their payment and liquidity management into one location, corporates will not only save costs, but also time and effort.

SEPA will improve conditions for large corporates and multinationals, because setting up a payment factory is really the first step for any corporate that wants to become more centralised and improve efficiencies. For instance, SEPA will allow them to much more easily consider the option of consolidating bank accounts and moving accounts to a central location. It will also enable smaller corporates, who do not currently have the economy of scale, to establish their own payment factory.

Finally, SEPA will create the right environment for value-added services as banks leverage the core SEPA payments rules and standards, such as e-invoicing and reconciliation, which will help companies to further optimise their end-to-end handling of accounts payable and receivable.

19.3   PREPARATION

Of course, in order to enjoy these benefits, corporates must be ready for SEPA, so what do they need to focus upon?

One area is changing the use of cheques to credit transfers and changing their national collection instruments to SEPA direct debits, which depends upon the clarity around the legal provisions of the EU Payments Services Directive, commonly known as the PSD and approved in April 2007.

There is also full account consolidation to consider, which is not possible in countries where specific national instruments continue to be used. In these cases, usage of SEPA instruments to the fullest possible extent will be the only option, with partial consolidation of accounts for these countries.

Secondly, corporates should start to assess the use of dedicated reference data fields and structured remittance information throughout their financial supply chain, in order to benefit from efficiency gains as soon as possible.

Thirdly, corporates should now be at the stage of completing their international bank account numbers (IBANs) and bank identifier code (BIC) databases for all their European business partners. For national payments, IBANs and BICs will eventually become the only account identifier and, therefore, the relevant data of each business partner will have to be completed to enable this. The importance of this cannot be stressed enough, as corporates may face penalty charges if they do not supply the correct IBAN and BIC information in their payment messages. Banks and technology providers can offer support in this area, as getting suppliers and vendors to cooperate is recognised as a difficult task.

Finally, corporates should conduct a first analysis to determine which systems are likely to be affected by the new formats and data elements and also which ones will be compatible with them. While electronic banking systems, ERP and treasury software will be adapted by technology providers and banks to accommodate changes, corporates should be aware that there might be proprietary developments that require adaptation on their side.

In order to make sure they take the necessary steps forward, cash managers and treasurers must stay informed and updated on all SEPA-related developments, and this is why corporate awareness around SEPA is growing. Corporates want to structure their business in order to be SEPA compliant and they expect their banks and business partners to help them do this.

While it is clear that there is a lot that corporates can do now in their preparation for SEPA, we must also acknowledge the fact that there is still uncertainty around SEPA, which hinders progress to some extent.

19.4   WHAT WILL THE PAYMENTS BUSINESS LOOK LIKE POST-SEPA?

There is a consensus that there will be consolidation in the payments business as a result of SEPA, and this is a factor that is also contributing to corporate uncertainty around their preparation for SEPA. Who do they partner with or outsource to, for example?

Post-SEPA, two types of cash management bank will exist in Europe: transaction banks and distribution banks. A transaction bank will continue to perform sales and services for cash management, but also product management including development of cash management products, processing and clearing. A distribution bank will focus on sales and services, but outsource its back-office functions to a transaction bank.

19.5   MAKING THE TRANSITION PAINLESS

Despite the uncertainties and challenges described above, as of January 2008 SEPA is a reality and banks must help clients get on board. So what should a corporate expect from their bank in their migration to SEPA?

A SEPA bank should ideally have a worldwide banking network that covers Europe and the rest of the world – not just the SEPA countries. Expertise in different regions, and therefore understanding payment specifics on a country-by-country basis, is a definite advantage. If a bank operates in various countries across Europe, it can already support existing delivery formats and build upon these capabilities to transform domestic delivery formats into the new SEPA formats and minimise the impact on customers.

Corporates should also expect their SEPA bank to invest in technology and facilitate the transition by providing value added services. A number of banks will be SEPA compliant as of January 2008 and the bank's pan-European SEPA platform will also be fully functional.

In addition, corporates will expect their bank to have the scale and cost efficiency to provide them with competitive pricing, as well as high service level standards in order to maintain customer loyalty. Underlying all of this, a real SEPA bank must take a holistic view by creating value across the whole financial supply chain.

19.6   WHAT LONG-TERM INDUSTRY CHANGES WILL SEPA BRING?

The combination of SEPA and the PSD – and it is the combination – will exert even more pressure to use economies of scale and straight-through processing (STP). There is also potential convergence of individual payments and Automated Clearing Houses (ACH) mass payments, where I would expect that the consolidation we have seen in the individual payments' euro clearing market will extend to ACHs too.

SEPA will act as an accelerator of these trends, particularly the drive to centralise functions. It will reduce the complexity in Europe in terms of clearing systems, accounting platforms, legal framework, and the number of payment instruments out there. It should reduce the need to maintain local bank accounts for payment purposes and it could eventually mean just one bank connection in Europe to handle local and cross-border transactions. By standardising and harmonising processes across Europe it creates further efficiencies and allows for greater economies of scale, which will mean an increase in the use of in-house banks, payment factories and other centralised cash management structures, and the related strategic cost benefits.

In addition, the harmonisation of the SEPA Direct Debit (SDD) Scheme will bring about new opportunities for centralisation, which will be highly beneficial for corporates in business-to-customer industries like telecoms, insurance, and utilities. Indeed, for the cross-border collection business, this scheme marks a significant development in the creation of a true domestic market in Europe. SEPA should also create harmonised pricing across Europe for the instruments covered. In Southern Europe for example, where prices are relatively high, they will be reduced to levels equivalent to those in the Northern European countries, which again should provide benefits to corporates.

It is important to remember, however, that SEPA does have certain limitations both geographically, as it does not cover the whole of Europe, and also from a currency perspective since it does not incorporate all currencies used throughout Europe. Furthermore, not all instruments are encompassed by SEPA. For example, cheques as well as some bills of exchange are not supported. It also fails to deal with corporate-to-bank connectivity, which is a critical issue in the payments world. These limitations could affect centralisation projects, which usually include the whole of Europe, and the related instruments used in each market.

19.7   CONCLUSION

Corporates should act now, especially large companies, because SEPA will radically transform payments in Europe, and it will be the front-runners who benefit most and in the shortest time-frame. In order to make the right decisions, corporates need accurate and timely information about SEPA, and all parties involved with SEPA must play their role in this:

- banks competing in the single open market with SEPA-wide products should be informing their clients about SEPA;
- the EPC should maintain and enhance consistent SEPA rules and standards and develop stringent governance fostering market forces;

- the ECB should ensure a level playing field, especially where central banks are involved in payments and reporting requirements, for ensuring that public authorities adopt SEPA quickly; and
- the European Commission should focus on the PSD, the abolishment of reporting requirements and ensure that governments and administrative bodies actively support SEPA.

The introduction of SEPA is a challenging and exciting prospect for Europe. With the right strategy in place, the migration to SEPA need not be a daunting task for corporates.

20

SEPA: The Corporate Perspective

Gianfranco Tabasso, EACT and Tom Buschman, TWIST

The way in which SEPA has been developed has missed a number of vital areas, particularly the inclusion of all stakeholders: corporates, citizens, governments, banks and infrastructures. As a result, critical standards required for SEPA's success are missing and this will need to be addressed if SEPA is to be successful.

With SEPA's initial implementation, there is growing excitement about achieving the political objective of a Single European Payments Area. To help achieve this objective and to ensure widespread adoption, more work is needed.

The original SEPA design and the achievements by the European Payment Council (EPC) demonstrate indeed that immense efforts have already been made by the banking industry in making SEPA happen. This chapter now identifies a number of obstacles that still have to be overcome if we are to achieve the full potential of SEPA and to meet the expectations of all the stakeholders.

Firstly a deeper understanding of SEPA is still needed. Secondly, a more collaborative effort between the various parties in the payments industry and financial supply chain would greatly help to realise true end-to-end straight through processing in payments.

With the SEPA initiation in January 2008 there is still too much uncertainty, ambiguity and confusion that makes the dialogue between banks and their customers ineffective and deters corporations from making a clear commitment to SEPA. This means that a potential delay in the SEPA start-up is of less concern than the lack of a serious dialogue between the banks, their corporate customers, and public administrations about the removal of obstacles and the planning of SEPA.

To help kick-start this dialogue, this chapter identifies both the barriers to SEPA and possible solutions. It is written based on the belief that only the effective collaboration between the stakeholders will guarantee that the right investments are made and that those investments will achieve the SEPA common benefits, which go beyond the scope of the SEPA payments instruments.

20.1 THE SITUATION AT SEPA LAUNCH

After the approval of the Payments Services Directive (PSD) and the EPC Rulebooks, a number of significant SEPA issues are still unresolved. This causes confusion amongst banks and corporations alike throughout the European Union. In turn, confusion leads to corporations adopting a wait-and-see attitude.

In addition, many financial institutions view the introduction of SEPA as a compliance issue. This leads to doing the minimum that is necessary to comply with the new rules, such as adapting the national payments and reporting standards.

National implementation of SEPA is a necessity but, without close central monitoring and a strong guidance, it will deliver fragmented SEPA markets. At the moment, if all EU states implemented their SEPA solutions, the effect from a customer perspective would be little change from today's landscape of local solutions and will limit SEPA both in its immediate and long term impact as a European alternative. Therefore, the situation needs to be addressed as a matter of urgency at the political, service provider and end-user level.

20.2   THE SITUATION FOR THE BANKS

The general sitation for the banks is that there are three major SEPA risks they are facing:

- diverging national SEPA implementations;
- limited adoption of the Direct Debit Scheme;
- limited end-to-end Straight Through Processing (E2E STP).

20.2.1   Risk of diverging national SEPA implementations

As nobody wants to waste a historic opportunity for Europe like SEPA, the banking sector is putting much energy and commitment in overcoming the particular problems and high costs of the current fragmented European payments infrastructure, whilst achieving the objectives of both the PSD and SEPA.

However, the PSD leaves much room for interpretation and gives Member States much leeway for exceptions. Therefore, national implementations need to be watched very closely to make sure they do not create situations inconsistent with the objectives of the PSD and SEPA, and do not create barriers for cross-border interoperability. Indeed, the ball is back in the camp of the national banking communities as they are planning for SEPA National Migration Plans. From a point of view of the end-users, this creates a loss of 'visibility' and central control.

The EACT (European Association of Corporate Treasurers) has pointed out that there are few countries where treasurers associations and other stakeholders are seriously involved in SEPA national committees. Corporates are at the sending end and receiving end of the vast majority of payments. Given that corporates generally have strict operational procedures around payment processing, and are using tightly tuned systems for it, the absence of corporate engagement incurs the risk that national migration plans will not be supported by corporates. The consequence is that they will not be implemented, or only with significant delays and after additional investments by the banking sector.

Corporates generally will act cross-border, which means that they will seek internal consistency between multiple national SEPA migration plans. This means that monitoring and comparison of SEPA national plans should be done in depth before they are implemented by national banking communities, to avoid internal inconsistencies that may lead to higher costs and different levels of attractiveness of national SEPA implementation plans for the users of payment services.

This activity could be performed by a European SEPA Steering Committee that includes representatives of all stakeholders. This is similar to the planned creation by the European Commission of a Steering Committee to oversee the work in e-invoicing at a European level.

20.2.2   Risk of limited adoption of the Direct Debit Scheme

Although Banks are implementing the SEPA Credit Transfer there is still great uncertainty over the final configuration of the Direct Debit Scheme. More specifically, it is doubtful whether in its current form it will be widely adopted by corporations.

Moreover, little discussion with corporations has taken place on the Additional Optional Services (AOS), which together with the pricing of SEPA payment services are key drivers for adoption by corporations.

20.2.3   Risk of limited end-to-end Straight Through Processing (E2E STP)

Given that the EPC has been constrained by its mandate to limit itself to the design of inter-bank payment processing, the resulting solution carries the risk that end-to-end straight through processing is unlikely to become a reality. Therefore, careful consideration should also be given to addressing the customer-to-bank (C2B), government-to-bank (G2B), business-to-consumer (B2C) and business-to-government (B2G) spaces.

20.3   THE SITUATION FOR THE CORPORATIONS

It has been recognised that corporations have only belatedly been engaged in the design and implementation of SEPA and, even though engagement has now been established, it has happened at a stage where much of the technical solution was already completed.

The success of SEPA is largely dependent upon uptake by the end-user community and, like the banks, corporations are facing huge changes to systems and processes. Therefore, they need to be able to increase their influence over how a number of hurdles that are still in place will be overcome.

It is key that the electronic message communication standards are mutually agreed and used between the banks and their corporate customers. SEPA needs a more formal and recognised structure for this to become an efficient mechanism for controlling implementation and managing future changes.

Corporations are willing to engage in the development of industry message standardisation and to adapt their organisation and procedures to the new services. At the same time however, they would like to work with banks on an equal footing and have a say in deciding mutually beneficial solutions.

20.4   THE SITUATION FOR THE SOFTWARE INDUSTRY

For many years, the software industry has been fundamental to the success of the financial services industry. SEPA has created a very sizeable commercial opportunity for the software providers and consultancies to offer systems and advice that enable their customers to achieve SEPA compliance as well as to attract new business.

However, to maximise success, the software industry in particular needs to be engaged to enrich the debate on effective solutions. In addition, they should be encouraged to take part in working groups that are formulating technical specifications. Finally, the software industry should also have access to information about all the facets of SEPA so as to prevent concentration of knowledge leading to competitive imbalance.

20.5   THE SITUATION FOR STANDARDS, TECHNOLOGY AND SEPA

There are many unresolved issues concerning the agreed use of ISO20022 and the fields within the message standards. There is also a need to agree XML and its use between corporations and their banks. Many of these problems can be resolved by a concerted effort of all parties.

Corporations and ERP vendors should support the ISO20022 standard and put pressure on banks to offer payment initiation and reporting services based on the new XML standards. European authorities should facilitate the effort and give the market a clear message in this direction. The market can then produce a market practice process that begins to bring together standards that will eventually fuel adoption.

There is no need to develop new technology for SEPA as there are already many good off-the-shelf solutions. Firms wishing to develop their own systems face inevitable delays in meeting SEPA deadlines.

TWIST and the EACT's CAST (Corporate Action on Standards) project are cross-industry initiatives that include corporations, banks and solutions providers. They deliver best practices designs based upon the participants' in-depth experience in financial supply chain dematerialisation. They have the potential to mobilise the industry for ISO20022 and XML standards as well as developing the cooperation with the banking industry to develop new value-added services, organise and monitor pilots, help introduce the new standards, communicate benefits to the wider audience of treasurers associations and stakeholders representative organisations.

SWIFT can be an important agent in SEPA's successful implementation because of its competence and deep involvement with the EPC and the banking industry. The only reservation about SWIFT is its governance, possibly limiting the extent to which SWIFT can cooperate with corporations on new standards and open solutions.

20.6   THE INDUSTRY MANAGING SEPA

SEPA is a European-wide payments industry project with clear objectives in harmonising the payments industry and bringing benefits to corporations and by extension to all retail banking customers.

These objectives are under threat as the finance industry has difficulty in managing collaborative projects. Indeed, too many banks see SEPA as a threat to their competitive position and view it as a compliance issue that must be met with modifications to legacy systems at minimal cost.

If this is the case, then the best possibility for advancing SEPA is an alliance of those banks and corporations that look at SEPA as a strategic opportunity. SEPA would then be viewed as an essential stepping stone to move to a higher technology platform, enabling new value-added services, better end-to-end integration and drastic cost reductions in the processes of both banks and corporations.

If this were the case, SEPA would enormously benefit from the establishment of an alliance of influential stakeholders, whereby a number of key industry participants demonstrate leadership in the successful implementation of SEPA and the specification of well-designed AOS.

More specifically, a strong SEPA Steering Committee in which all stakeholder groups are represented should be set up quickly and should be empowered by the European Commission (EC) to:

- centralise information on national implementations;
- monitor developments with implementations;
- identify divergence between in particular national migrations and the objectives of the PSD and SEPA; and
- present proposals for corrective action to the EC and ECB.

It should have much the same composition as the envisaged European e-invoicing Steering Committee. Given the interrelationship between e-invoicing and e-payments, it could even be considered to set up only one European Supply Chain Management Steering Committee and have two sub-groups: one for e-payments incorporating SEPA, and one for e-invoicing. This would then mirror a similar stakeholder engagement as has been set up by the financial services industry for the implementation of MiFID (Market in Financial Instruments Directive) in the securities industry.

The e-payments incorporating SEPA Steering Committee should have high visibility and should give a clear message to the market about the determination of the EU, and the industry, in supporting and guiding SEPA as a successful pan-European project.

20.7   THE EUROPEAN ASSOCIATION OF CORPORATE TREASURERS (EACT)

The EACT has been raising issues on SEPA with other stakeholders during numerous meetings and has held consultations with various European authorities. Notwithstanding those efforts, EACT is concerned that no serious discussion has followed this major effort and that the banks and the EPC keep focusing solely on meeting their deadlines for the SEPA project.

Whereas it is of course recognised that the financial industry is under huge pressure to implement SEPA, it should also be accepted that EACT's request to establish mixed working groups will produce better result than the current bank-only groups.

Furthermore, SEPA is suffering an implementation delay because of the PSD, disagreements over direct debits and other unresolved issues. This delay is not necessarily unhealthy, and indeed provides an excellent opportunity to pause and regroup and start a different type of cooperation between banks and other stakeholders.

This pause for reflection should be used to create the much needed proper governance model, to resolve any unsettled issues, eliminate uncertainties, and launch a credible implementation plan which includes the changes and the AOS that are considered necessary for the acceptance of SEPA.

The commitment of corporations and other stakeholders is vital for the success of SEPA. This commitment is not there today and will not emerge if banks, corporations and the European authorities don't succeed in establishing real cooperation on the issues, and a modus operandi which involves banks and corporations together in a meaningful way.

Corporations do not expect that all of their requests will be accepted and executed in a short period of time, in other words not in the original SEPA Master Plan between 2008 and 2010. It is much more important for corporations to see that their requests are taken seriously however, and that they are discussed and filtered at a European level, that they are compared with alternative solutions and that decisions are made in a democratic and transparent way, with input from all interested parties.

In the absence of such a collaborative process at the European level, it is likely that individual banking communities will resist switching to SEPA products and develop community-specific AOS instead.

Unless compliance, change and innovation are governed at a European level, there is a substantial risk that there will not be a SEPA, but a series of national SEPA-compliant systems. However, those different national systems would then have to be made interoperable which, in turn, would require additional complexity and cost. That prospect does not encourage corporations to invest in SEPA.

The thought process behind this chapter therefore recognises that the financial services industry has to meet its challenges in running the interbank payments infrastructure. It does not dispute in any way how the industry manages the issues of a pan-European interbank infrastructure. Instead, this chapter puts forward an expectation that corporations would like to be involved in the shaping of the payments schemes, and the banking services that are based upon them.

A concrete example of this expectation is that standardisation be carried out end-to-end from the payer's operational processes and systems to the payee's operational processes and systems and not be confined to the bank-to-bank domain only.

20.8   THE EUROPEAN PAYMENTS COUNCIL

This chapter is intended to draw the attention of key stakeholders of the SEPA project, including the EC and the ECB, to the problems that exist today. It is also a plea for assistance to provide the payments industry with the governance tools to ensure SEPA does not fail.

The approval of the PSD is welcomed as a very positive step, but its benefits will not be achieved if its transposition into national law by the Member States is not closely monitored. This monitoring should be performed centrally to avoid any attempts by Member States at putting measures in place that conflict with the sprit and the letter of the Directive.

It is hoped that the various participants in the payments chain will be able to constructively co-operate with the EPC in the future. To make this happen, it may be necessary to enlarge the mandate of the EPC to include the entire payments chain. Alternatively, the proposed possible Steering Committee for e-payments could establish a working relationship with the EPC in its current form, where the EPC focuses on the inter-bank implications of wider payment issues.

Once again, corporations feel that addressing the issues that stifle a pan-European implementation of SEPA that includes corporate engagement is far more important than meeting the original SEPA deadlines.

20.9   THE SEPA IMPLEMENTATION

Corporations have four concerns regarding the implementation of SEPA:

- Corporations still do not know what kind of services will be offered by their banks and at what price.
- Corporations do not know what changes they will have to make to their systems, organisations and procedures to adapt to these services.

- Corporations do not know when individual countries will move to SEPA, nor when old payment systems will be dismissed.
- Corporations do not know how internal consistency is ensured between national SEPA migration plans and how migration costs will be minimised for multinational corporations.

This uncertainty clarifies why corporations have not acted upon SEPA yet in any significant way. Hence, it will also hinder a rapid take-up of SEPA, which might then be perceived as a political and industry failure.

20.10   THE SEPA SELF ASSESSMENT

The resolution of issues around SEPA at a pan-European level should not hamper those banks and corporations that would like to progress with SEPA-based implementations. For these organisations, it will be important to ensure that early implementations are in line with what can be expected to be the outcome of further discussions between banks and stakeholders, especially with regards to end-to-end designs for payment services.

In order to enable these institutions to continue their path towards SEPA implementation, the EACT and TWIST collaborated with BISS Research to produce a template to benchmark the functionality of SEPA service offerings and system designs from a corporate requirements point of view. The template will allow firms to assess whether their SEPA offerings are aligned with the corporate requirements, and detailed specifications that underlie the TWIST standards which include the ISO20022 message range used in the SEPA rulebooks developed by the EPC.

There are two benchmark templates. One is for banks wishing to test in-house developments and third party vendors; and the second is for software vendors anxious to prove their systems functionality. These templates can be found on the websites of TWIST (http://www.twiststandards.org) and BISS Research (http://www.bissresearch.com).

20.11   THE TOP TEN SEPA ISSUES LIST FOR CORPORATES

The remainder of this chapter documents ten problem areas that require specific attention and resolution. These are all serious issues that need to be agreed between the banks and corporations if SEPA is to be a success.

20.11.1   SEPA Direct Debit

At the implementation stage in 2008, this is SEPA's major stumbling block as a number of countries in the European Union do not want to adopt the basic SEPA Credit Mandate Flow (CMF) scheme. This situation is unlikely to change if the CMF Scheme is not improved to the overall industry requirements and made more secure. If it is left unchanged, there will not be more certainty about the finality of collection, and direct debits will continue to be performed under current national schemes.

The EACT found a basis of consensus for a reinforced CMF scheme. However, a number of countries (such as Italy, Spain, Portugal and the Nordic countries) would also like to have a Debtor Mandate Flow (DMF) option as part of the same scheme, as well as a separate scheme for mandates. The EPC is adamant they will not change the core CMF scheme as detailed in Rulebook Version 2.2, as banks have already implemented this scheme in their software applications. Unfortunately however, such intransigence will cause SEPA fragmentation.

At the EPC's Plenary in June 2007, the proposed e-mandate solution was approved for submission into the national consultation process. The EACT's position is that whereas the e-mandate scheme could meet the requirements for a stronger CMF, a CMF Plus, it still leaves a number of issues unresolved such as the treatment of old and new paper mandates, the optional nature of the scheme for the banks and the lack of a DMF option where debtor banks receive and stock the original paper mandate.

A number of legal and related issues associated with the new e-mandate scheme also still need to be verified, and the EPC has been prepared to engage with the stakeholders in tackling these issues together before a final decision is made on the scheme.

Informal discussions with the EPC have indicated that the e-mandate scheme could be extended to include dematerialisation of old and new paper mandates, provided the banks are ready to offer such a service. Although this extension is out of scope of SEPA, corporations may insist it is put on the agenda for banks to act upon.

In addition, the National Treasurers Associations (NTA's) are requesting more clarity on the volumes of B2C and B2B DMF mandates in the various countries, on the relevant legislation in the various countries, on corporate practices, and on the banking conventions.

In order to address this need for more information, the EACT is sending a questionnaire to a number of European corporations that use Direct Debits and to their NTA's. Once all the information from the corporations has been received, banks and stakeholders will meet to determine and define the actions and plan for the development of common AOS to handle these e-mandate requirements.

20.11.2   Renewal of DD mandates

The PSD does not state any position with regard to the resigning of mandates for direct debits, and left it up to each country to resolve. In the transposition of the PSD into national legislation countries such as Italy will probably pass a one-line article saying that these mandates maintain their validity in SEPA. This is provided as long as there is a simple authorisation by the debtor to their bank to accept direct debit on their account from a specific creditor, and provided they do not contain other clauses that are in contrast with the PSD. However, wider action across all European Member States is called for as there are inconsistencies. For example, Germany is understood to be orientated towards a resigning of old mandates. The end result will be that some countries will require renewals of mandates whilst others will not. This will obviously create a difficult problem for SEPA and the European community at large.

Even at this late stage, every NTA should be lobbying its government, Ministry of Finance, Central Bank, Banking Association or whoever is charged with drafting the transposition of the PSD. Again, the lack of central planning of the SEPA implementation is a severe impediment to successful execution.

20.11.3   IBAN and BIC

The usage of IBAN and BIC is a major issue for the whole payments industry. Although the IBAN and BIC combination is preferred by many banks, it is not a simple solution. In addition IBAN and BIC on their own, as well as in combination with each other, have been long debated by the financial industry in terms of their usage and standardisation, but are yet without an agreed resolution for usage within corporations.

Collecting many millions of IBAN's in different formats from all clients' suppliers and employees is a nightmare for corporations. This creates the need for banks to develop and devise systems and schemes to allow a file transfer of IBAN's from banks to corporations under an agreed standardised format.

BIC holds a different problem for corporations and therefore the success of SEPA. Corporations should not be forced to acquire and store BIC's in their Enterprise Resource Planning (ERP) systems. This is a burden that corporations should not be hampered with. A solution would be that Banks automatically apply the BIC in their payment applications based upon the IBAN of the payment order. For banks that do not adopt this solution, a BIC database should be made available to corporations as a free service.

20.11.4   Additional Optional Services (AOS)

SEPA will struggle to achieve its objectives until improvements are made to existing rulebooks. Additional instruments also need to be recognised and standardised according to the SEPA XML and ISO formats.

Rather than studying national AOS for the same instruments such as Riba's, LCRs, Recibo's and other non pre-authorised DDs, Italy, Spain, France and Portugal should unite and present a single multi-community AOS that other countries can use if they want. This would at least produce momentum towards a European-wide solution.

Only the NTA's can put the pressure on their banks to do this, especially in countries like France, Italy and the UK, where they directly engage with banking associations or government bodies in SEPA Migration Plans.

There is also a great deal of uncertainty about what constitutes an acceptable AOS. Specific proposals would clarify this point for all in the industry and a mapping of the desired instruments to the existing rulebooks is required, using the same format and data sets and showing the differences and similarities between each, especially the additional data fields required.

The EPC has decided not to play a proactive role in the AOS developments. This however creates a situation where there is no central point of information and coordination. This vacuum will be filled by others, such as TWIST and the EACT, in order to avoid a situation whereby AOS could proliferate out of control.

20.11.5   BOP Reporting

BOP Reporting is a recurrent issue with the ECB and the EC regularly advocating the elimination of BOP Reporting in its current form. Instead, it has been proposed that there be the introduction of more standardisation among countries to create solutions that would facilitate true STP. However, this has not yet happened.

It has been proposed that there be the creation of a stakeholder group of experts who understand how different systems can coexist across the EU, and who would provide information on best practices to resolve this.

20.11.6   Pricing of SEPA products

The pricing of SEPA products is one of the greatest uncertainties holding back corporations from a commitment to SEPA, and is indicative of a lack of communication by banks with their corporate customers.

Bank pricing of SEPA products has been a well-kept secret. It is hard to understand why, when the corporations need this information as part of their decision making process with respect to the implementation of SEPA. The only reason this could have been the case is that this unnecessary impediment was created by bank-based competitive pressures.

There does seem to be a trend however towards *à la carte* pricing, with a minimum base service and everything else being considered an extra AOS.

It is obvious that corporations will not invest in SEPA as well as having to pay more for SEPA services from banks. The sum of basic SEPA services combined with AOS that simply bridge the gap with existing services, should not cost more than it has previously. This should be a basic principle and objective of SEPA where the EC and ECB should clearly state that 'SEPA payments should be at least equal to existing ones and should not cost more for the same level of service'.

Pricing is a competitive issue for banks but must also be within the specifications of the PSD. Otherwise, it would make the issuing of these directives from Brussels worthless. Although the EC does not like to interfere in commercial pricing, it did intervene on cross-border payments with Regulation 2560/2001 ('... must not cost more than domestic ...') and the PSD mandates that a minimum set of information should be given free of charge.

The solution should not call for a legislative act. A statement on SEPA pricing by the EC and ECB should give banks the direction they obviously need. If established in this manner, this principle would be difficult for banks to ignore in negotiations with their clients, and it would have a very beneficial effect on the implementation of SEPA.

20.11.7   End-to-End (E2E) Straight Through Processing (STP) in SEPA

At this stage the payments industry will not achieve real E2E STP, which is the primary objective of SEPA. The EPC Rulebooks only standardise the interbank space, whereas a wider solution is called for.

The EPC's recommendation to the market to use the ISO20022 standard for payment initiations and bank statements went unheeded, with the exception of a few banks that will accept and generate ISO20022 formats – Italy is the only country in fact which, in the new version of its CBI solution, will adopt only ISO formats. Elsewhere banking communities are adapting their domestic standards to support SEPA data and PSD transparency requirements.

This means that a multinational must change its current multiple bank interfaces and, after that, it will still have multiple bank interfaces to maintain. This is also therefore failing to deliver the primary objectives and benefits of SEPA once again.

Certain ERP suppliers, such as SAP, say that they do not support full ISO20022 formats for payment initiation, only for the reduced SEPA subset. The 140 characters remittance information space and, more importantly, standardisation in the first and last steps of the payment chain – payment initiation and e-reconciliation – needs urgent agreement between the payments industry and the corporations. This is absolutely key to the successful realisation of E2E STP in SEPA.

ERP solutions providers are critical to creating more standardisation in the corporate-to-bank space which means using ISO20022 in its original design to enforce a payments industry standard.

In the past a de facto standard was established with IDOC. This could be achieved once again with ISO20022, especially if it is strongly backed by corporations and their organisations.

In the bank-to-corporate space, which is vital for reconciliations, the banks generate the bank statement out of their own applications. This should also be geared toward usage of the standard bank interfaces in ISO20022, especially when the reconciliations procedures of ERP systems adopts this standard. Any other format will then be considered non-standard, entailing additional customisation and additional costs.

The corporations and their treasurers associations should be lobbying with their banks to force this issue.

20.11.8   Governance of SEPA

The EPC published its draft proposal for consultation, but only a few treasurers associations responded. It seems strange to us that the body that designs and operates the system as a legal monopoly should also be the same body that regulates itself and settles disputes. Logic and prudence require that an independent trusted third party should regulate payment systems. If it is too complicated to create such an independent body, the ECB might be a better candidate than the EPC.

If the EPC is left to regulate itself, for political and practical reasons, the governance should ensure adequate participation by other stakeholders with absolute transparency in all internal procedures, especially in the areas of litigation and resolution of conflicts. The presence of a few independent members in the Committee who rule on disputes may not be enough to ensure equanimity of decisions. Independent members are not there to represent the interests of non-bank stakeholders, but are chosen because they bring special competences. Their name can be proposed by anyone, but they are elected by the EPC. Non-bank stakeholders would feel more confidence in these members if they were appointed by the EC and the ECB.

In the other vital areas of change and innovation within SEPA, end-users can submit proposals but, once again, are not part of the evaluation and development process. Stakeholder Forums are the only form of cooperation envisaged, and experience has shown that the current approach is focusing more on broadcasting and consultation on finished products rather than on joint development of these solutions.

20.11.9   Transposition of PSD into national legislation

The PSD is transposed in national laws by November 2009. This is a delicate process because the PSD is deliberately flexible and leaves enough leeway for national states to define laws or regulations. The result of this flexibility is that the PSD is vague or even omits to cover a number of important points.

It is vital that the industry keeps a close watch on how these points are translated into national laws. Different interpretations will lead to confusion in the market, damaging SEPA implementation and creating the same fragmented payments landscape we have today.

The PSD will be implemented by the Ministries of Finance with the support of banking associations and central banks. Corporations' end-user associations should seek to be consulted and keep a close watch every step of the way.

20.11.10   Unique Entity Identifier (UEI)

The creation of a unique code identifying each corporate and individual in every electronic transaction, should be a goal of the payments industry. With the massive increase in on-line banking, at an individual and corporate level, this should be extremely achievable.

Banks have created and use standard codes and formats, such as BIC, because this is in some part enabled through the collaborate network operation of SWIFT but, for corporations, it is different as there is no organisation like SWIFT operating a network.

Italy has chosen the Tax ID for identification purposes and has made it freely accessible through a public database. Other European Member States have chosen a different UEI. An international standard should be developed, with its application and accessibility mandated.

The use of the UEI would give enormous benefits in terms of simplification of internal procedures for e-certificates and e-reconciliation for example, as well as for the security of transactions.

An table of experts should be created at EC level to examine the results of previous studies, consult Member States and agree a Roadmap to introduce and establish a UEI in Europe.

NOTE: The seventh issue listed is particularly worrying due to the lack of centralised information, which is not yet perceived as a danger.

20.12   CONCLUSION

The success of SEPA and its ultimate objectives are in doubt because there is no standards basis yet for end-to-end straight through processing and because the current process for defining and implementing SEPA products is sub-optimal.

Furthermore, the fact that the implementation of SEPA has been left to the national banking communities, means that there is a loss of SEPA visibility and a perceived lack of direction and leadership.

A European SEPA Steering Committee including all stakeholders should be in place. It should be given the means to closely monitor the execution of national SEPA implementation plans, suggest corrective action where appropriate, and help the EC and ECB to keep SEPA on course.

This Steering Committee should be selected by the EC in agreement with the ECB, taking into account the necessary independence and geo-political representation. The relevant experts with the required skills and market knowledge are already part of existing market groups and committees.

The Steering Committee should have official status and clear governance rules. The mission of the Steering Committee is to ensure that SEPA be kept on course by ensuring compliance with the letter and the spirit of SEPA.

In addition, an Industry Leaders Group of banks, corporations and solutions providers should set the example by implementing the complete family of XML ISO standards and setting up pilots for SEPA products and AOS. This group could be informal, and include those banks and corporations that are committed to using open standards for the whole of the financial value chain with the aim of creating real E2E STP.

TWIST, TBG 5, EACT and SWIFT could all participate, draft the programme and manage the implementation, provided there is prior agreement on the overall guidelines and the specific projects to be pursued. Participants should also agree to a high degree of transparency and publicity for the results of the projects. It is assumed that these pioneers will find their own benefit from their implementations, but must not forget the overall objective which is to create a following and, in due course, the critical mass that is the key success factor for any standard.

The more innovative banks and corporations will be attracted by this initiative and will accept to commit the money and the resources.

Part 5
The Views of the Observers of SEPA

- Gartner
- David Doyle, EU Policy Advisor on Financial Markets
- the SEPA Consultancy
- Ernst & Young
- Hervé Postic, UTSIT

21

Will the promises of SEPA come true
for corporates?

Juergen Weiss, Gartner

In 2010, SEPA has delivered some benefits for corporates in terms of their organisational structures, capabilities and operations. However, it has not delivered the promise of rationalisation of standards, formats and processing.

According to the European Payments Council, the Single Euro Payments Area (SEPA) will deliver many benefits to European businesses, independent of their size and industry. The most important ones are:

- lower costs for payments;
- fewer bank relationships;
- lower total cost of ownership (TCO) because of fewer formats, better reconciliation and unified payment processes;
- an increased potential for cash management centralization; and
- increased payment flow transparency and better cash management forecast.[1]

Let's take an imaginary trip into the year 2011, putting ourselves in the position of a German mid-sized corporate with a couple of production and sales subsidiaries abroad, and analyse whether the promises of SEPA came true or not.

21.1   LOWER COSTS FOR PAYMENTS

Before the SEPA implementation began in January 2008, Germany had been one of the biggest and most efficient markets for payment services within Europe. Almost a quarter of the entire cashless payment transactions could be attributed to the German market in 2003[2]. The average fee for a record-less transaction in Germany was € 0 03, while corporates in other countries had to pay significantly higher fees. According to a study by the European Commission of the impact of regulation 2560/2001 on bank charges for national payments in 2005, this was as high as € 0 90 per transaction in Italy for example.

These prices haven't changed a great deal in Germany since SEPA started three years ago, although SEPA has led to major changes in some other European countries, especially in the Southern European states where transaction fees did adjust to a level which is now comparable to other countries with more efficient and advanced payment systems. Several subsidiaries of

---

[1] EPC, *Making SEPA a Reality*, 2007.
[2] ECB, Blue Book, 2006.

the German enterprise gained tremendous benefits from these developments, and were able to achieve significant savings in bank fees.

21.2   FEWER BANK RELATIONSHIPS

While some of these savings can be assigned to lower transaction fees, due to increased competition between financial institutions, others have different root causes. When SEPA was introduced back in 2008, the German company decided to re-evaluate their banking landscape. Before SEPA, the corporate had to maintain at least one correspondence account for each of the foreign subsidiaries. This was mandatory for the German company, in order to properly serve its business partners abroad and to provide them with local and familiar payment services.

This demand became redundant when SEPA, and its two predominant payment instruments credit transfer and direct debit, were introduced on a pan-European basis. Both credit transfers and direct debits put the German corporate in a unique position, as it was suddenly able to reach almost every one of its business partners with only one account. This fact led to increased competition between the 56 house banks used by the German headquarters. Very soon one of them, a leading German bank, decided to provide additional payment services outside its home turf, and entered into a number of strategic co-operations with a various European financial institutions. This collaboration created new and progressive products for customers in the corporate banking space.

The German company was among the first to grasp these new opportunities and decided to leave a major part of their payments business to the German house bank. As a supporting measure, the Germans also opted for a consolidation of its banking relationships.

Today, three years after the SEPA launch, only three of the former 56 banks are still employed. Each of these banks covers one of the main geographical regions where the German company is present and doing business: Americas; Europe, Middle-East and Africa (EMEA); and Asia.

21.3   LOWER TCO

The reduction in banking relationships provided two key benefits. Besides reducing the number of bank accounts, and the associated administrative overhead, the company strengthened its bargaining position towards the remaining financial institutions and realised significant savings from bank fees and other costs.

SEPA also delivered on its promise for better reconciliation of open items in the company's Accounts Receivable (AR) and Accounts Payable (AP) departments. Before SEPA, reconciliation rates were only at a level of 74 % of all transactions. Although the corporate had implemented a state-of-the-art Enterprise Resource Planning (ERP) and Treasury Management System (TMS), the IT department was unable to increase straight-through-processing rates. This was largely due to missing and meaningful reconciliation information.

The Cash Managers were unable to process incoming bank statements because reference data was either lacking or cut-off by the banking systems. SEPA changed this by introducing 140 characters of reference data, which was transported without any changes by both financial institutions and payment service providers. The introduction of powerful and systematic master data schemes including the International Bank Account Number (IBAN), Bank Identifier Code (BIC) and Unique Creditor Identifier (UCI), had an amazing effect on reconciliation rates within the ERP system and drove them to a level of almost 100 %.

The German company was able to reduce the workload of its AR and AP department by almost 50 %, and could assign more productive tasks to its staff. Business processes that had previously been handled in different ways in the various European subsidiaries were harmonized and created additional efficiency gains. For example, users no longer had to take care of different local payment procedures, processing time lines and cut-off times anymore.

On the other hand, the costs for these improvements were considerably high. Corporations willing to adapt to the new SEPA framework had to invest huge amounts to convert existing bank account master data systems. Since banks were neither willing nor able to provide unified European-wide conversion tools, the result was ineffective, sometimes manual and often error-prone activities to gather IBAN information. It took the German company almost two years to convert the domestic bank data of its 15 000 vendors, 100 000 customers and 5000 employees.

Another drop of bitterness was the way in which different payment formats emerged after the introduction of SEPA. Initially, SEPA created only two payment formats: one for the SEPA credit transfer and one for the SEPA direct debit. Both of them were defined by the European Payments Council as sub-sets of the ISO20022 standard for electronic payments. However, it turned out very soon that the various SEPA member countries defined their own interpretations and deviations from the EPC implementation guidelines for the SEPA formats. Some countries even abused additional optional services (AOS), which were initially planned as competitive differentiators for banking services, and made them an integral part of the SEPA payment formats.

These format differences continue to create headaches for the Cash Management and Treasury departments within many businesses, with the result being that the original idea of a unique payment format across Europe remains a chimera. The German enterprise had to implement additional middleware to react to the challenging fact of these mini-SEPAs across Europe, converting outgoing payment instructions into the local SEPA flavours. Although all formats are based on XML, the lingua franca of the Internet, adaptation costs were significant. Some critical employees even doubt that SEPA delivered a greater value compared to the pre-SEPA era, with its diversified national payment formats.

21.4   CASH MANAGEMENT CENTRALIZATION

While SEPA never delivered on its promise of simplified formats, the German enterprise did realise another huge benefit: the unification of internal business processes and the reduction of bank relationships resulted in a fundamental shift of the company's organisational set-up. This meant that after a year from SEPA's launch, the German corporate voted to centralise its treasury operations and started implementing a payment factory.

This organisational change had many implications and created a lot of internal, sometimes painful, discussions circling around the right balance between centralisation and decentralization. Before SEPA, the treasury departments acted independently of the headquarters, and maintained individual relationships with their local banking partners. Today, these local networks no longer exist because all payment transactions are routed via the central payment factory. The result is that the parent company took over the role of a head office, and is processing all payments for the group through the three remaining house banks.

The subsidiaries no longer maintain local bank connections and replaced them with internal bank accounts within the payment factory of the headquarters. This payment factory and its house banks are processing all incoming and outgoing payment transactions on behalf of the subsidiaries.

Overall, the new set-up has a number of positive implications:

- Physical cash transfers between subsidiaries were reduced and replaced by internal netting via the payment factory, which also lead to shorter netting process times.
- Float and value date losses were decreased, which resulted in additional bank fee savings.
- The concentration of cash and exposure to capital risks resulted in fewer hedging deals and associated hedging costs through economies of scale. Another consequence was an improved competitive position through the external money markets, which reduced refinancing costs.

The implementation of the payment factory was actually only the first step for the German company, as the management are currently considering whether to outsource their entire payment business to one of the remaining banking partners.

21.5   PAYMENT FLOW TRANSPARENCY

Besides cash management centralisation, SEPA provided additional benefits for the German company. The use of unambiguous reconciliation data and harmonised master data reduced both the number of defective payment instructions as well as the number of returns. This could also be attributed to the structured processes and processing timelines, as they were laid out in the rule books and implementation guidelines of the European Payments Council.

Another positive effect was an increasingly transparent payment flow within the corporate. Unique error and transaction codes, as well as the introduction of new XML-based status messages, helped the cash managers to gain better insight into the current status of their payment instructions. As a consequence they were able to further mitigate capital risks and to deliver better cash and liquidity forecasts.

21.6   BOTTOM LINE

The balance of SEPA is a positive one after the first three years. The main improvements are of a more indirect nature though, and not an immediate consequence of the Single Euro Payments Area. On the contrary, some of the expected benefits such as lower costs and fewer formats did not materialise at all, or only to a very limited extent. Companies were instead able to reap benefits from the different set-up structures allowed by SEPA generally. New organisational models such as payment factories, or better internal business processes because of increased straight-through processing, are just some of the disruptive changes created by SEPA.

22

The Single European Payments
Area – the user and supplier perspectives

David Doyle, EU Policy Advisor on Financial Markets

*SEPA has benefits for corporates, merchants and consumers alike, but the two phase introduction
by banks to begin with and then across the EU could create a dangerous mix of limited short-term
benefits requiring a second phase renewal to achieve SEPA's true aims.*

With the adoption by the European Parliament in April 2007 of the EC proposed Directive on
Payment Services (PSD), the basis of a Single Payments Area became a reality. First proposed
in December 2005, the PSD aims to allow businesses and citizens to make electronic payments –
credit payments and transfers, e-payments and direct debits and so forth – in total security and,
more importantly, on an evenly low-cost basis across the EU.

Member States have until 1 November 2009 to transpose the Directive into national law,
although the Commission has been urging the banking industry and other payment institutions
to be ready with the first SEPA products since 1 January 2008. Thereafter, the Scheme has to
be fully operational for clients across Europe by the end of 2010.

The stakes are high. A total of € 52 trillion of payments are processed each year, representing
some 231 billion payment transactions. The Commission believes that given this magnitude
of payment activity, 'the potential savings linked to the use of efficient payment services are
enormous'. At the European institutional level, the charges for transferring money across EU
borders is seen as a significant burden, and a barrier to the efficient single European financial
services market.

Escalating and sometimes opaque transaction costs, coupled with lengthy processing times,
constitute two crucial issues. The EC's data shows that it can presently cost anything between
30 and 55 eurocents per transaction for a normal cash transaction in Europe, compared with
an efficient electronic payment service costing only a couple of eurocents per transaction. In
addition, citizens and small business owners travelling in the European Union face daunting
problems when trying to pay for goods and services: cross-border acceptance of payment cards
remains less than universal and, even when they are accepted, anomalies such as transaction
costs for making withdrawals and ATM usage are imposed. Similarly, at an anecdotal level, a
growing number of Europeans owning a holiday home in another EU state find that they are
unable to even pay local utility bills from their bank account in their home state. Extra cost is
thus entailed in having to open a bank account in the country where the bills fall due.

Research undertaken in 2007 for *The Daily Telegraph* by the personal finance website
Moneyfacts showed that banks charged £ 726 million (€ 1 billion) last year for credit and debit
cards used outside Great Britain. This works out at an average of £ 37 (€ 50) for each trip

abroad by a UK family embarking. EU citizens travelling to another EU Member State face two levels of charges when using credit and debit cards: the first are front-loading fees which apply every time the card is used in another EU state; and the second are for those outside the Eurozone related to currency conversion costs.

The PSD attempts to address these two issues by:

- ruling that, from 2012 onwards, cross-border transfers made by credit and debit cards must be processed within one day after the payment order is placed with the bank or payment provider; and
- opening up competition to a wider spectrum of payment service providers including alternative providers such as retailers, telecommunication companies, and money transmission agencies, thereby boosting competition in favour of lower cross-border payments vis-à-vis established banks. This comes on the heels of a 2001 EC Regulation (2560/2001) giving citizens a guarantee that when they transfer a payment in euros to another EU Member State, it should cost the same as a domestic payment. The EC claim that the costs for cross-border transfers has since fallen from an average of € 24.00 in the pre-2001 period to an average € 2.50 today.

The Directive also sets out a series of harmonised rules to strengthen consumer rights, in areas such as where cards are stolen or lost, and where payments are mislaid or delayed. This new legal framework also covers other stakeholders too, including retailers, large and small companies and public authorities. Appropriate prudential rules for all new entrants to the retail payments market will be a central part of the Scheme.

22.1 THE BANKS' PERSPECTIVE

Whilst applauding the New Legal Framework underpinning SEPA, the EU banking community remains concerned about certain provisions in the directive particularly those related to the additional requirements to provide client information and liability coverage. Such issues should not be ignored if market confidence is to be sustained in the corporate to bank relationship.

One potential area of litigation is the shift of responsibility of an unauthorised payment from the user, the corporation, to the supplier, the bank. Banks believe that it is impractical to hold payment providers liable for losses that may fall outside of their control. For example, a cardholder claims the unauthorised use of their card, but has acted with negligence or fraudulently. Whilst it may not be right that the user suffers all the losses incurred, moving the burden to the payment service provider is not a solution.

A balanced system for determining the burden of proof must be found as, if it is not, the risk of loss from fraud could rise sharply resulting in higher costs for the bank and, ultimately, will be reflected in higher prices for the users.

A further complication arises in that banks are expected to upgrade their IT systems and replace existing manual processes with automated ones to force costs down. Some bank sources say that to accelerate progress towards lower transaction costs, they must be in a position to set prices for the various payment methods to match their true costs. Nevertheless, in some EU Member States, banks are prevented from doing this.

With efforts focused upon banks to force consolidation of the payment infrastructures within the tight timeframes of 2010, bank analysts are predicting that increased pricing pressures will lead to four outcomes:

- a more rapid pace of consolidation of market infrastructure;
- increased levels of bank acquisitions and mergers to create entities with much higher payment volumes in order to generate economies of scale;
- opportunities for outsource payment processing activities and, in other cases, the strategic necessity to do this; and
- increased short-term transactional and compliance costs.

Overall, SEPA should be viewed as an opportunity for banks to review a number of areas:

- the re-evaluation of legacy systems to determine if the timeframe is right for replacing or upgrading the systems;
- the cost/benefit analysis inherent in weighing the profitability of continuing to carry our every permutation of payment processes for all payment types. There will surely be distinct payment types and segments that are dependent for cost economies on large volumes and economies of scale; if these are also associated with limited competitive advantage then they constitute key targets for outsourcing, enabling the bank to re-deploy resources towards more profitable products and services; and
- the development of innovative products and opportunities to penetrate new markets and win new relationships, as has been predicted by the European Payments Council.

22.2   BANK-CORPORATES PARTNERSHIP

The prospects of opening up new opportunities are not lost on some of the more established pan-European banks with cross-border client bases. Banks are under huge regulatory pressure and are keen to identify areas where they can add value to their client bases. Corporates have long sought standardisation of payment systems as they pursue their efforts to centralise their treasuries. Both banks and their corporate clients are beginning to recognise that facilitating and financing the financial supply chain from procurement to pay is a big area of opportunity. With the right technology in place, the SEPA mechanism could further drive this new phenomenon as financial supply chains enlarge and globalise.

Some banks have formed work groups with their key corporate clients involving treasurers, key buyers, accounts payable and receivable and logistics, to map out the procurement to pay and related processes. Within corporates, SEPA is also helping treasurers to focus on cash management. Cash forecasting can be improved immensely, allowing companies to release and deploy surplus cash through better integration of the payments systems in co-operation with their banks. Uncollectible receivables and premature payments to suppliers are two areas of particular focus in building a more coherent financial supply chain.

At the other end of the corporate scale, the European small business community has greeted the PSD with cautious optimism. SMEs are fundamental to EU growth as they represent two-thirds of private employment in Europe, representing 75 million jobs and one-half of total corporate turnover in the EU. SMEs remain sanguine around the Directive's potential to simplify payment rules, increase competition and cut burdensome costs for the 26 million small business owner-managers in this sector across Europe. However, analysts believe that SMEs based in the Eurozone will particularly benefit in the long run from SEPA, led by the market concentration of processing as a result of higher volumes and potential economies of scale made possible for euro payments. This is backed by a 2005 Deutsche Bank analysis that found some 70 % of the total cross-border payments made by private and SME payment users were euro-denominated, with both legs of the payment transaction made in the EU.

This must be balanced with the reality of the SMEs payment culture. Most micro-enterprises operate on a very localised and regional basis, and thus may not process more than a handful of cross-border payments per year. A 2005 study carried out by VISA, *The Internal Market for Payments,* revealed that the vast majority of debit card payments are extremely localized. 'It has been said, for example, that 98 % of all debit transactions take place within a 30 kilometre radius of the cardholder's bank branch'.

The fear is also that micro-enterprises[1] will not opt for the SEPA system. This is because SEPA concentrates on providing more efficient and less costly cross-border transactions which may be at the expense of dearer, and potentially compensatory, national payments structures.

There is also some concern amongst the SME constituency that the task of harmonisation will be protracted given that the current national payment systems differ significantly in terms of transaction times, as well as the provision of additional optional services and card payments. SME representative organisations are urging Member States to ensure workable transition measures to smooth the entry of end-user SMEs into the new systems, and provide more tailor-made solutions directed at the small business sector.

Governance is another issue that needs to be carefully thought through, involving all stakeholders. The FIN-USE Expert Forum, the high-level advisory group to the EC, was established in 2004 to help improve policymaking in the field of financial services with special reference to European consumers and small businesses. The result has been that this forum has helped to raise the governance debate surrounding the management of the SEPA scheme.

For example, in its 2006-2007 annual report, FIN-USE calls for serious consideration of the following safeguards:

- separation of the Scheme and Processor of payment systems, with the appropriate mechanism put in place to ensure compliance;
- pricing of services provided by infrastructures to be determined through more than just self-regulation alone; and
- information-sharing structures, such as payment systems bodies, may constitute platforms for infringement of article 81 of the EU Treaty prohibiting agreements which have the object or effect of restricting competition in the internal market.

FIN-USE underlined that 'good, reliable and unambiguous information about products and services on offer has to be provided to users if the latter are to benefit from competition'. The expert group suggested that 'users continue to receive insufficient information regarding the payment instruments available to them.'

Attention is also being given to how SEPA will affect the financial services industry, especially their back-office payments processes. The goal should be to take an in-depth review of existing back-office payments operations, with the inevitable change over in mind, and reconfigure for enhanced cost-effectiveness. It clearly makes little sense to introduce major changes to integrate the SEPA measures, and then yet another some months or years later to streamline the process.

---

[1] Micro-enterprises are important in this debate as they represent some 91 % of the total small business sector in Europe, and are defined as companies with less than 10 employees, generating turnovers of less than € 1 million and having a balance sheet below € 500 000.

The investment asset fund industry in Europe, traditionally held back by a lack of technical connectivity and limited open-architecture, could usefully view SEPA as the catalyst needed to accelerate the pace of cross-border investment transactions and encourage the more powerful institutions to move away from their own transactional solutions. These solutions provided them with an immediate incentive not to take part in any co-operative scheme that would deprive them of a competitive advantage.

Cross-border transactions are estimated to have grown from around 50 million a year to nearly 200 million a year in less than five years, raising the question as to how long the present insular, institutionally driven, transaction model can sustain itself. Some analysts speculate that the co-operative mechanism enshrined in the SEPA mechanism could galvanise the European fund industry towards more appropriate co-operative solutions, embracing interconnectivity and open-architecture.

In summary, SEPA has benefits for consumers, merchants and corporates alike, as outlined below:

Benefits	Consumers	Merchants	Corporates
More options for making payments	X	X	X
One account serves all Europe	X	X	X
Transparency and clarity of charges	X	X	X
Common processes with reduced costs/complexity	X	X	X
Predictable execution times	X	X	X
New SEPA Direct Debit Scheme	X		X
EU-wide acceptance of payment cards	X	X	
Reduced fraud	X	X	
Increased choice of processing services		X	X
Lower cost standard software and services		X	X

Adapted from the European Payments Council report: SEPA Benefits and Implications (2007).

23

SEPA – It's Trench Warfare

Ashley Dowson, the SEPA Consultancy

Who will be winners in the post-SEPA world? The banks that provide outsourced payments processing services, or the banks that use those services?

Looking at the banks involved with SEPA, one can visualise two trenches deeply dug and far apart. The left trench is heavily populated by banks beginning to understand that market forces is making them think about payments outsourcing to the banks on the right. The right trench is more thinly populated, and consists of a noisy bunch of banks loudly proclaiming their payments and SEPA prowess.

The left trench is deeply dug in, and hopes that the current wave of change will evaporate and that the national implementation of the PSD will instead offer a chance for further stagnation. The right trench are meant to provide the left trench with a SEPA service, but seem unable to articulate a proposition to help the banks on the left regain level ground without threatening their customer franchise.

All around the banks on the left are new competitors created by the newly licensed Payments Institutions[1] categorisation. The banks on the right suffer from the fact that there are just too many of them, given the potential for further regulatory interference and the available economic value of this marketplace.

The opportunity is there however for banks to take advantage of a marketplace in which more and more banks are actively seeking an outsourced payments solution to handle their payments processing and, in addition, seek a supplier of best-of-breed payment related services.

Meanwhile, the corporate clients of these banks are seeking help with improved straight through processing (STP) from buyer to supplier, not just from bank to bank, as well as the integration of the financial supply chain with the physical supply chains. Instead, they watch, bemused by the lack of tangible value being offered in their direction.

23.1 THE RATIONALE FOR CHANGE

As mentioned we have two trenches. The left trench looking for outsourcing payments to service providers, and the right trench comprising service provider banks who seek to be outsourcing payment processors.

---

[1] Title II of the Payment Services Directive will allow non-banks and money transfer companies to move further into the payments market. This will put yet more pressure on banks trying to retain volumes and maintain revenues. These Payments Institutions will come into the market unencumbered by legacy-based operating environments!

The rationale for change for *the banks in the trenches on the left* is:

- reduce total and unit costs;
- substitute fixed costs with variable;
- minimise strategic investment spend in this business;
- improve customer experience in basic payment delivery;
- gain accessibility to improved and emerging services;
- focus on access channels, especially of the self-help variety.

The rationale for change for *the banks in the trenches on the right* is:

- cost leverage through consolidation and scale;
- a compelling business case for strategic investment;
- achieve sustained economic profitability;
- design future solutions and shape market behaviour;
- re-draw the line between co-operation and competition.

The point is that doing nothing is not an option. If banks do nothing, they run the risk of marginalisation within the payments industry and will find themselves presiding over a deteriorating P&L and delivering negative economic value to their bank.

Therefore it is a board-level issue, and market consolidation is inevitable as the upward pressure on unit costs is given a further push during the period that SEPA runs in parallel with legacy systems. And all of this takes place at a time when the credit and liquidity squeeze is causing investment constraints and pointing the way towards more income being derived from fee-earning activities, rather than less.

M&A activity is again in the headlines as the 'Royal Bank of Scotland Consortium' works out how to dismantle ABN AMRO and integrate the pieces into their various operations. Interested market watchers now look for similar signs of other cross-border deals in Europe. Regulation and the ever increasing cost of compliance will stimulate those who design such asset sales and mergers, whilst geographic scale is needed to combat reduced income and increasing over capacity in the market.

Bank executives are also viewing payments activity through a different lens as they see payments as a critical capability which is very painful if things go wrong, but a non-core activity for an increasing number of players. Indeed, recent dialogue suggests that Europe's community of ACHs will grow fatter as the industry consolidates. The demand for these ACHs offerings will increase with the advent of SEPA as banks demand more shared services around direct debit mandate management, data reference services, back-office processing facilities, and so on.

And, of course, customers are demanding a step-change in their experience and the range and depth of services offered, particularly if domestic boundaries start to whither in this new Single Payments Area.

23.2   SCT CREATES TACTICAL MARKET DEMAND

The SCT is a near term market driver that should create demand, although the banking market recognises that volumes will be low and there has been little evidence of corporate customers having a business case to move to the new standard in 2008. Therefore, those banks that want to comply need only invest in a small scale, low tech solution. This solution will be available to those banks that do not have the appetite for continuous improvement or the desire to answer big questions, such as, should my organisation have an XML strategy?[2]

This has its advantages for all parties as it buys 12 to 18 months in which strategic choices can be identified/assessed and reduces the investment 'tag' to manageable levels. For some banks it means very little change to their existing payments environment and short term solutions will be readily available from their nearest ACH (or card network).

Banks will aim to contain SCT within their interbank world and will not be in a rush to ask their customers to adopt this new payment standard based on the ISO20022 XML format.

23.3   SDD CREATES STRATEGIC MARKET DEMAND

The SEPA Direct Debit ('SDD') has a more strategic impact and the market will demand richness and reach.

There is evidence already that major insurers and utilities are looking ahead to a pan-European offering that allows them to overcome multiple standards, albeit with significant upheaval when mandates have to be replaced with their SEPA versions. Banks coming forward with a market offering will need to have a proposition that delivers economic value in the near term. These offerings will need to be designed to be available in a way that will increase both their richness (what they offer) as well as reach (connections through to the client's corporate customer base).

A bank that wishes to acquire significant market share must build on its low-cost payments processing service to offer a suite of payment services based on a coherent XML strategy, which is extendable out to its customers and their counterparts. I anticipate this will be executed and managed through an integrated middle-office capability. This middle office will support the principle of self-service customers become more selective in the menu of services they require, the type of information demanded, and when that information is provided to individuals whose profiles are managed at business unit level. This middle office would bring together core skills required to interpret future customer needs, adapt product features to meet those needs, and leverage event and static data to match customer information requirements.

As suggested earlier, there will be plenty of scope for collaboration, as the remaining industry players seek common solutions for AML screening, fraud detection/prevention, mandate management, etc. The dual running of SEPA and 'legacy' payment instruments will equally demand higher levels of data management to facilitate STP for both banks and their customers.

Supplemental capabilities are also likely to be in demand in areas such as liquidity and investment management, consulting & system integration for 'onboarding' – preferably through a partnering agreement with market specialists with proven depth in the payments space – and enhanced 24x7 multilingual customer call centre support.

Finally, recent discussion with the players to the left and right has suggested that business integration and set-up concerns must be identified early, understood by the party looking for a sourcing solution, and addressed by the chosen service provider. For Europe, this is a relatively new interface between banks that have traditionally been competing over their payments business to one that will be more cooperative, and will grow in scale as SEPA matures into the strategic thinking space.

---

[2] XML is the Extended Markup Language, a technology interface standard adopted by the SCT.

23.4   CONCLUSION

It is very evident that the banks that market themselves as being 'winners' in the post SEPA landscape have not yet determined what comprises a compelling market offering to the banks on the left. Each proposition seems to have an interesting feature or two – track and trace, real-time billing, online queries, data repair, BIC/IBAN validation – but none was sufficiently robust to offer a business case of mutual benefit to both parties.

The trench warfare will eventually end, choices will be made and, either way, banks will need to invest to realign their payments business and extend their capabilities to offer the business and information services required of this emerging Single Payments Area. Either way, new ways of thinking and new skills are needed to steer a way through to 2010 and beyond, when the real battle for volume and value adding services will begin.

24

Payments Operations – Building to protect the franchise

Robert Bradfield, Ernst & Young

Banks across Europe have tough choices to make in the forthcoming SEPA world. They need to focus upon value-add services and outsource payments or, if retaining payments inhouse, they must make sure they are fit for this future. Many banks will not be unless they undergo complete business transformation.

By 2010, banks within the European Union will be faced with a payments market that is radically different from the one that exists today. A combination of European Union and country-based payments directives are contributing to a major upheaval in the payments market, the like of which we have never been seen before. The two main powerhouses for change are the creation of the Single Euro Payments Area (SEPA), which focuses on euro denominated payments within the Eurozone; and the Payments Services Directive (PSD), which is driving change within the competitive landscape across the entire European Union. Alongside these pan-European directives, there are also regional and inter-regional drivers for change. Some examples include the creation of a new domestic payments infrastructure within the UK as a result of the Faster Payments scheme, and the Euro Alliance of Payment Schemes (EAPS) drive for a new debit card processing capability across Europe.

Understanding how the market will change in response to these and other drivers, and what the payments market will look like across Europe, is essential for all market participants. Each market participant of the payments cycle needs to build an appropriate payments agenda that will encapsulate their strategic objectives and drive the road map for change. For many organisations who have not been investing in their payments capability, this payments agenda will need to be fairly radical if it is going to protect the existing business, let alone support new business opportunities.

This chapter looks at some of the key components of the payments cycle that will be impacted by the changes in the payments market, how competition will evolve, some of the responses that should be considered, and the relative merits of pursuing different change methodologies. Whilst the focus of this chapter leans towards electronic payments, the discussion points are predominantly generic and, where necessary, reference is made to other payment instruments as appropriate.

24.1 PAYMENTS – A COST CENTRE OR REVENUE GENERATOR?

Accurately determining the cost burden and revenue contribution of payments to a bank's overall profits is often very difficult. Over the years parts of the payments process have become embedded within numerous systems, deployed across a multitude of channels, undertaken by most business units in some capacity and integrated within a range of different product offerings. It has been rare for a bank's payments operations to be viewed as a business within its own right and is far more usual for payments to be viewed as a cost centre. Even where payment processing costs can be determined in some shape of form, the same is not always true for the revenue streams that payments generate or the overall profitability of the operation.

The importance of the payments operation should not be underestimated as payments typically generates between 25 % and 33 % of the banks operating revenues. On the other hand, supporting the operation is estimated to absorb more than a third of the bank's operating costs. The result is that costs exceed income by anything from 6 % to 10 %.[1]

By far the greatest proportion of spend on payments is on regulatory compliance and meeting market infrastructure changes, and SEPA and the PSD are only going to increase this burden.

Whilst payments processing may be a cost burden on the bank, the ability to securely transmit funds from one entity to another is a major reason for relationships to exist between a bank and their customers. Historically, customers have looked at forming banking relationships that can provide local support across their operations. This local bank to local customer relationship is now under threat as, across Europe, SEPA and the PSD are going to challenge the need for relationships based on the bank and customer organisation being in the same geography. For the first time, customers can easily look outside their own geographic region for the best service provider to meet their needs, regardless of location within the EU.

This challenge will directly impact revenue generated from intra – Eurozone payments and indirectly impact domestic payments, as the markets become more commoditised. Furthermore, whilst the focus of SEPA is on electronic and card based payments, there will be some impact on cash and paper-based instruments. As new, cost effective payment instruments become available, and their acceptance increases, there will be a migration away from paper. Banks need to ensure that they have appropriate exit strategies in place, or face the cost of supporting an infrastructure that becomes an increasing burden as the fixed cost per transaction escalates whilst revenues decline.

24.2   PAYMENTS – A DWINDLING REVENUE STREAM?

Protecting revenue generated by payments within the EU will be challenging as the market becomes increasingly commoditised as a result of competitive and regulatory pressures. Figure 24.1 demonstrates how payments processing contributes directly and indirectly to five basic revenue streams, each of which will be impacted as the market evolves and changes as a result of the EU directives alongside the new, opportunistic market entrants and changes in customer behaviour.

Taking each revenue stream in turn shows where the pressure originates and some of the considerations that the bank needs to consider.

24.3   EXECUTION REVENUES

Historically the revenue generated from transaction charges and fees has allowed many banks to camouflage poor processing performance. The amount of charges and basis for levying execution fees varies across the EU, and all will be under pressure from the PSD and SEPA.

---

[1] 'European Payment Profit Pool Analysis: Casting Light in Murky Waters', McKinsey, 2005.

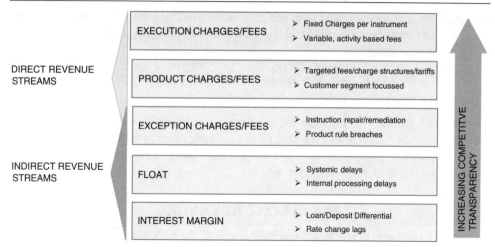

Figure 24.1   Sources of revenue attributable to payments

Poor performing payments processing operations will no longer be able to hide behind high charges.

Whereas a payment from France to Germany used to be treated as an international payment that would attract a cross-border charge, the PSD and SEPA now stipulates that if it is below € 50 000 only a domestic fee rate can be applied. As a result, we have already seen cross-border payment charges within the Eurozone reduce from an average of € 25.00 per transaction down to € 2.50. For UK banks, this may not appear to be a major issue as payment volumes may be relatively small, but the problem will rapidly escalate as moves are made to extend and centralise operations across the EU.

24.4   PRODUCT CHARGES

Closely aligned to execution revenues are the charges applied to specific products that have a payments element. Charges that banks apply vary across Europe and by market sector. Within the business-to-corporate banking sector, product charges tend to be tariff based as well as including value-added services such as lock-box and collections. In the retail sector, charges are transaction based with a set fee per payment instruction.

As the payments market becomes increasingly commoditised, banks will need to find new means of creating value. Knowing what the bank's customers really value in the payment cycle will become increasingly important, and will drive the emergence of new market entrants. Value-added services need to be matched to the need for increased transparency around the charging structures. This is already being seen as a specific requirement of the SEPA Cards Framework in the cards markets.

24.5   EXCEPTION FEES

Payment related exceptions fall into three broad categories:

- remediation charges: where the bank charges for the correction/enhancement of payment instruction messages;

- charges for alerting customers of specific incidents impacting their payments or account activity: this could be notification that overdraft limits are being approached to receipts of a payment transaction;[2] and
- Incident fees, especially referral charges: these have been estimated to be nearly as great as the revenue generated from overdrafts themselves, but these types of fee are coming under increased scrutiny.

Neither SEPA nor the PSD are expected to have a direct impact on exception fees although direct pressure may come from a regional level, as has been seen in the United Kingdom over current account charges and the need to treat customers fairly. Indirect pressure will be seen as the market becomes increasingly competitive.

24.6 FLOAT REVENUES

Historically, payments delays have been built into both the bank's internal processing capabilities and the external payments clearing and settlement systems for a variety of reasons. Some of these have been due to technological constraints, some have been risk related such as the need to accurately authenticate the payment instruction, and some delays have been due to a regulatory burden such as the need to undertake sanction and anti-money laundering checks. Dependent upon the payment instrument, the delay between funds leaving the debit account and being credited to the beneficiary's account can lead to the generation of float-based revenue, especially for paper based instruments.

SEPA is driving all of Europe's payments processors towards next business day settlement, referred to as D + 1, and the Office of Fair Trading (OFT) Faster Payments scheme in the UK is based on the provision of near real-time processing capabilities. Both of these drivers will effectively remove float revenue from e-payments.

Whilst D + 1 processing should not cause a major headache for most banks, as overnight batch processing can still be supported, near real-time processing will pose a greater problem as account balance data also needs to be updated on a near real-time basis. This is required to support the decision making processes to make pay or no-pay decisions at the point of capture.

24.7 INTEREST MARGINS

Interest paid by banks on current accounts is another major basis for interbank competition and is one of the largest revenue generators for banks, especially in the retail sector. There are regional variations but banks generally tend to offer low interest rates and high overdraft rates on current or money transmission accounts. Higher rates on savings accounts are often offset by restrictions, such as the number of withdrawals that can be made in any given period or a maximum value that has to be deposited.

The ability to define rules to automate the movement of funds from one account type to another will be an increasingly important value-added service for the customer in the retail sector, whilst becoming ever more sophisticated in the business and corporate sectors will be to the detriment of bank revenues derived from interest margins. Bear in mind that customers will also be able to access bank services outside of their regional domain to find the interest rates that are most advantageous.

---

[2] Note that fraud related alerts are not generally a charged for service.

Profit decomposition, € billions, 2004, EU9*

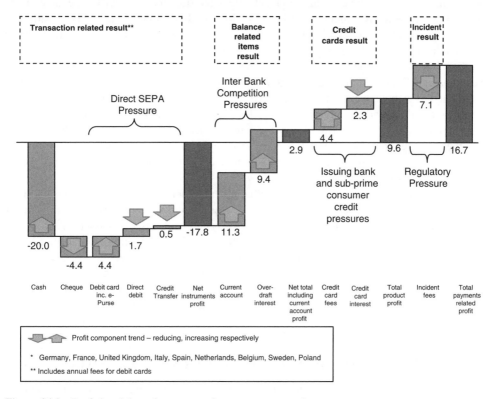

Figure 24.2   Profit breakdown by payment instrument type and revenue stream

Interest margin returns are also maximised by ensuring any changes in amount and time are as advantageous to the bank as possible. For example, borrowing rates and lending rates of bank products are rarely changed at the time of announcement or by the same amount as the central bank lending rate changes.

Credit cards also tend not to carry credit customer account balances, but do generate significant revenue streams from interest applied to unpaid balances.

Each revenue stream and its subsequent contribution to profits face different challenges as a result of the changing payments market across Europe and, based upon work undertaken by McKinsey[3] and our own insight at Ernst & Young,[4] Figure 24.2 shows the breakdown of payments profits, the trends in the contribution that they are making, and the pressures that each stream faces.

There is a high degree of interconnectivity across the drivers and the trends that are being seen. For example, as revenue and profit diminishes from debit and credit transaction processing, banks will start to look for increased margins from balance related activities or develop new means to apply charges.

[3] 'European Profit Pool Analysis', McKinsey, 2004 and 'Payments in Europe: a Tower of Babel with Construction Problems', McKinsey, 2007.
[4] '2006 Cash Management Services Survey, 23rd Annual – Participant Report', Ernst & Young, 2006.

This revenue breakdown model is by nature fairly generic, and there are marked differences across the EU regions and customer segments. Revenue streams are heavily dependent on the prevailing payment instruments used in the region, the bank's payments charging structure and the market infrastructure. What we do find is that France and the UK along with the more cash and paper oriented regions such as Italy, Spain, Austria, Hungary, Portugal, Poland and the Czech Republic, tend to be more reliant on fees to generate payment revenue; whilst the Scandinavian, Benelux and German regions are more focused on process efficiency. As already mentioned, it is those banks that rely on high fees to cover operational inefficiencies that are going to face the greatest challenges, especially if they have a substantial European footprint.

In summary, so far we have seen how revenue is generated from payments within the bank and the pressures they face. Some banks and geographic area have a greater reliance on fees than others, which can be indicative of processing inefficiency and/or a prevailing use of cash and paper products within the region.

As SEPA products become accepted and competition across SEPA matures, fees will reduce, margins will be squeezed, and inefficient processing infrastructures will be placed under pressure. Cost reduction will be a necessity for survival or increased cross-subsidisation will be required, however this will most likely be unacceptable to competition authorities as the PSD shows a clear tendency towards direct charging for services rendered.

On the other hand, there are those regions where processing efficiencies are very high and costs are low. Whilst in a strong position, they will still need to remain competitive and attract transaction volumes to increase economies of scale and look for value-add services.

The next section looks at the options banks have for their payments operations.

24.8   PAYMENTS – POSITION WITHIN THE ORGANISATION

Improving the cost-revenue ratio within payments operations requires a full understanding of how the costs are derived, the sources of revenue and the resources needed to bring about the changes needed to meet the organisation's payments agenda. Performance improvements employing Six Sigma type techniques is a start, but it may not be enough to meet the demands of a commoditised payments market as processing excellence is but one of the components. There are two other prerequisites: accurately knowing and managing the cost-revenue streams and having a very clear vision for the bank's payment strategy. These components should then form the basis for the organisation's investment in its payments operations.

24.8.1   Know your payments business

Maintaining the efficiency of any process requires a full understanding of the end-to-end operation, as well as continually monitoring internal and external performance. This includes all the payments functions and supporting applications used throughout the processing cycle. This should include the entire suite of inter-relationships with other business functions, such as fraud and anti-money laundering, security, channel management, limits management, treasury, and so on.

To obtain the clarity needed, a full process flow should be mapped out and costs for staff, licences, maintenance and so on, allocated to each element. Overlaying the processes and functions with the supporting applications, physical locations and business units, will assist in both the impact assessment and change management process. It will show who, what, where and how impacts will be made. Part of the definition process should also include a benchmarking to peer groups where full objectivity is essential to avoid misdiagnosis of gaps, and hence requirements.

Even understanding where the current benchmarks lie, and aiming to achieve process excellence to the prevailing market norm, will only maintain the existing status quo in terms of market position. The wolves of competition will still be at the door and so developing a payments strategy to meet the demands of the post-SEPA payments market will often require a major step change, along with an appropriate supporting business model.

24.8.2   Knowing where you are going

European payments market developments will not stop with the adoption of the SEPA products and compliance with the PSD. There will be increased competition from banks and other new market entrants, looking to provide value-added services both within and from outside the EU. This competition is expected to lead towards a reduced number of market participants, a smaller number of banks that support their own payments capability, and a contraction in the number of regional payment switches and processors.

To survive in the payments market, banks have three options they can follow, which are summarised in Figure 24.3 below.

Common to all options is the need to clearly demarcate the payments process within the organisation. This will help define the operating model, the functions and the supporting technology, as well as facilitating any sourcing options going forward.

Option 1:

Payments business

- **Key Driver:** To be a global payments player or, a major regional player with global reach

- **Market Positioning:** Dominant market share and position in a least one market. Volume based growth and scale are critical

- **Servicing Option:** Payments business stays a bank owned asset, operations maximised for in-sourcing opportunities

Option 2:

Centralised payments process

- **Key Driver:** To improve cost to income ratio through processing efficiency only

- **Market Drive:** Not looking for market advantage via payments, value add services are maximised

- **Servicing Option:** sourcing options high on the agenda

Option 3:

Cost driven payments service

- **Key Driver:** To keep cost to income below 100 percent

- **Market Drive:** Does not wish to carry mandatory spend needed to remain in the payments industry

- **Servicing Option:** Outsourcing is the only option with access 'white label' payment products

Figure 24.3   Payment agenda options

The aim should be to create a core, standardised processing function that is common for all inbound and outbound payments across the bank, in effect a horizontal business line that can meet the common needs of the vertical business units. This core payments processing function should form the 'vanilla' payments service for which the cost structure is fully defined and can be viewed as a business in its own right. Balanced against this is the need for the payments operation to earn its position as the payments processor of choice for the bank. Therefore it has to be responsive to the bank's business unit demands to support a full range of products. If this entails any change to the vanilla service offering, there has to be some form of impact assessment, and the cost of support of the non-standard service determined. These costs can then be factored into the product capabilities and the profitability assessed.

Ensuring that the supply side of the payments process is managed as a business within the organisation also facilitates the ability of the bank to attract additional payment processing volume from other organisations. Like outsourcing, insourcing requires absolute clarity around capabilities, cost structures and supplier-customer interfaces, which is simpler to manage if the payments processes are already clearly demarcated within the organisation. All too often alternative sourcing ventures fail due to unforeseen costs, unclear rules surrounding the relationship, and the inability to rapidly meet changing demands because the operating model has been compromised.

Building a vision as to how the bank is going to run its payments operations, aligning the organisation and actually making this vision a reality by delivering the target model, can be extremely challenging. The complexity of existing payments operating models combined with the need to effect change across the entire organisation, presents some major cost consider- ations. How much is the change going to cost and can a low-cost with maximised revenue balance be achieved?

24.9   COST OF CHANGE

Dependent upon the organisation's current payments capabilities, level of processing efficiency and strategic intent, the degree of change required will vary enormously. This can only be ascertained correctly through a thorough assessment of the current environment in relation to strategic intent.

Again, there are three broad options open to the organisation and each has cost-benefit potential which needs to be considered in relation to the payments agenda. The cost savings that the change needs to bring about has been estimated to be as high as 50 %[5] but, in our experience, these levels of savings cannot be achieved by process optimisation or even through process re-engineering. If organisations are to achieve these levels of cost savings then a far more involved business remodelling exercise is required.

24.10   COMPARISON OF TYPICAL DEVELOPMENT
APPROACHES ACROSS THE INDUSTRY

Figure 24.4 illustrates the relationship between development approach, potential benefit re- alisation and scale of investment needed to support each approach and the typical delivery timescales.

---

[5] 'World Payments Report', CapGemini, 2005.

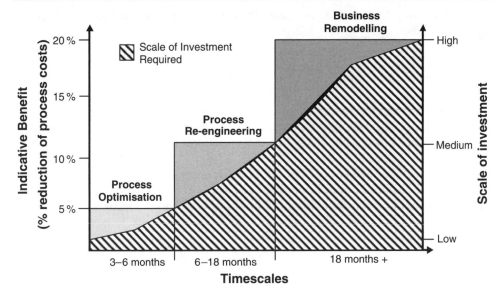

Figure 24.4 Balancing investment cost and benefits

The characteristics of each approach can be summarised as follows:

24.10.1 Process Optimisation

Ideally used in a post-change environment to ensure that benefits are being realised and the processing environment strives to reach more demanding performance tolerances. The cost savings that can be achieved through this approach will suffer from the law of diminishing returns. As a result, this approach cannot be used if the existing processes and supporting architecture are not fit for purpose.

Driver: Cost reduction or specific process failure

Methodology: Six Sigma approach. Typically small scale with very focussed, piece meal projects. Reviews of existing processes with the aim to make improvements with minimal change. Systems may be impacted, but usually limited to minor ad hoc changes or implementations

Outcome: Treats the symptoms but may not affect a full cure. Initial benefits gained will typically be eroded over time; process will need to be revisited. End-to-end STP still compromised.

Saving: Short term, 10–15 % of process costs

24.10.2 Process Re-engineering

Where the bank's existing technical architecture can support the bank's strategic direction, and the bank has a proven ability to deliver change within very tight time scales of less than ten months, it may be feasible to reorganise the payments operation and the core payments processing skills.

Driver: Cost reduction, new product/function/activity support or a need to meet specific regulatory demands or changes to market infrastructure.

Methodology: 'Sweat the Assets' approach. Programme maximises existing infrastructure. Business case developed in support of medium/large scale projects. May require the development of additional functionality and will require operational change.

Outcome: Extends the return on original investment, maintains the current business in a recognisable format. End-to-end processing achievable but is often compromised by any further functional demands coming from different business units or market directives.

Saving: Medium term up to 20 % process costs

24.10.3   Business Remodelling

More often than not existing payments processing capabilities have evolved over time with the existing technical architecture being a result of mergers and acquisitions, unilateral business decisions and other legacy applications running on various platforms. In fact, it amazes me what applications are still in existence and what they are running on. It may well be that the degree of change needed across the entire bank is just too great or too disruptive. In this case the option of creating a *green field* payment processing capability should be seriously considered. This approach can have the additional benefit of facilitating the migration to the new business model, as it breaks the ties with the legacy world.

Driver: Threat to market position or revenue stream due to operational and technical constraints.

Methodology: Wholesale business reorganisation to standardise core common services and processes. A defined business strategy that separates the value chain into products and services. Service lines aim to be 100 % STP with exceptions controlled and viewed as potential sources of revenue. Full board level ownership and governance. Requires a full return on value-based business cases that are integral to the bank's strategic direction. May need green-field site and structured migration.

Outcome: Repositioned organisation that fully understands how value is derived. Clear cost models can be applied to support longer term decision making processes. Facilitates sourcing options.

Saving: Long term in excess of 20 % process costs

In summary, regardless of which route the bank decides to pursue, absolute clarity around the future payments operation is required. This has to be detailed enough to align all the stakeholders and show them exactly how the operation is going to work and their role within the new operation. This needs to emphasise the importance of payments processing to the bank, and that the bank has to change as existing business practices may no longer be supportable going forward.

24.11   IMPROVING PAYMENTS PERFORMANCE

As each bank has different processing infrastructures supporting their payments operations that have developed as the bank has grown, there are no panaceas that would apply equally across all organisations but there are some key considerations and principals that can be adopted. The following section looks at some of these key principles and the considerations that need to be taken into account.

24.11.1   Product and Instrument Support

As a baseline, the payments processing infrastructure will need to provide the following information to support operations, management and customers alike:

- knowing how many payments have been received, made, failed, etc;
- details of what postings to/from customer accounts have been made;
- updating of balances, limits and product usage details;
- triggers for secondary transactions as a result of account and cash management mandates;
- sending alerts and notifications; and
- transparency around product and service costs.

All of these payments activities have to be managed on a real-time basis and will contribute to the core service offering. Demand for operational and payment related information is also required by the bank itself, not only from a performance perspective but also to manage its own treasury and liquidity management functions.

The challenge from a technological perspective is to ensure that the core processing environment can support both the volume of transactions, and yet be flexible enough to support existing and future products developments. An assessment should be undertaken to ascertain the bank's current support capability and projected requirements for the future. Not only should this cover the reporting processes but also include complaints handling workflows and tracing and tracking capabilities.

24.11.2   Channel versus Core Services

Payment channels, and how they are supported by core payment services, will become increasingly important across the Eurozone. With the appropriate channels in place, there is no reason why a bank domiciled in Ireland cannot provide a full range of payment products to customers in Greece. No longer will there be any great advantage for a merchant acquiring bank to be domiciled within the merchant's own region. Likewise card issuers do not have to be in the same country as the customer.

Whilst the channel may need to support specific regional requirements, such as language, product names and limits, the core underlying payments service should remain totally agnostic to the channel. A payment instruction submitted at a branch or over the internet or via a kiosk or ATM, should follow the same acceptance criteria and logical process flow.

The role of the channel should be to support the customer interface with the bank and provide a similar experience across all access points, so that a corporate submitting a bulk payments file or a single payments instruction will have each instruction validated to the same set of rules sets and will be able to track or trace payments through any supported channel. This includes host-to-host services where the customer's Enterprise Resource Planning or Treasury Management System interacts directly with the bank's core payments service.

24.11.3   Automated and standardised processing

Straight-through-processing and processing performance has to be at the heart of the core payments operation to be cost effective. This requires that once the payment instruction has been captured, it can be executed. If the payment cannot be validated at the point of capture, it should be rejected and the instruction originator informed as to why the payment cannot be accepted and processed. Acceptance rules should include all aspects of the payment instruction and the customer's ability to fund it.

Managing the instruction acceptance and the downstream payment processes inputs and outputs for many internal and external channels, product types, business units, payment instruments and infrastructures, requires clearly defined rules. The rules should control the initial payment instruction validation for data and instruction completeness and acceptance, as well as the end-to-end logical process flow. Where exceptions are permitted, they should be on a revenue generating basis.

Rules governing the process flow will determine which payments are used across which channels, in accordance to customer type, product, limits and the routing mechanism for the instruction itself.

The importance of achieving STP, without the need for intervention, is also critical to reduce the internally originated fraud. If repair or remediation is allowed, where alterations can be made to the original payment instruction, full audit trails and secondary authorisation process will need to be in place, especially as internal fraud is one of the fastest growing types of payments fraud being perpetrated.

24.11.4   Single customer view

Existing payments processing capabilities within an organisation often touches a large number of applications. Perhaps the greatest challenge will be the ability to make the pay or no-pay decision at the point of capture, and subsequently reflect the impact of that decision for that transaction across the entire organisation in as near real-time as possible.

An inability to provide real-time balances and funds availability will generate opportunities for fraudulent instructions to be generated, where instructions are submitted, processed and credited before account balances have been updated from alternative payment instructions from alternative payments channels.

24.11.5   Customer expectations

The ability to accept a payment instruction at the point of capture, and provide the surety that the payment will be credited to the payee's account within a given timeframe, should be the goal of all payments processes. Expectations should be set in line with transparent pricing structures, including prevailing FX rates, so the customer knows what service can be expected. Wherever possible, the bank should clearly state its terms and conditions for normal processing times, the cost of processing the instruction and how this is broken down, and when the beneficiary can normally expect to have the benefit of the funds transferred. The bank should also aim to exceed these without fail.

24.12   CONCLUSION

There are no hard and fast rules as to how any given bank should structure itself to compete in the post-SEPA world. What is true is that payments revenue is at risk, processing costs need to be reduced and transaction volumes increased, to offset the loss of margins if the bank wants to compete as a payments processor. The alternative is to build value-added services and look for an appropriate payments processor to outsource operations.

Competition is also being derived from new market entrants who do not have the legacy baggage that banks have built up over the years. They have a clearer view of the role that they can play in the payments processing value chain, and how they can derive value from the transaction flow. Banks cannot afford to be complacent. Complacency and inertia will lose the bank's existing payments franchise.

For those banks that want to protect their payments franchise, improving payments performance is critical. Functionality should endorse STP with instructions rejected at the point of capture if they cannot be processed. If an instruction cannot be processed, it should not be accepted unless the bank believes there is a revenue stream to be tapped into, such as charging for any repair or remediation work. In this case, exception queues will be essential to manage workloads.

Where business units or products require bespoke processing capability, charges for any non-standard services should be applied. Working on this basis will assist in protecting the core processing capability of the bank, continually allowing for alternative sourcing options to be evaluated, and helping with product and customer profitability evaluations.

This is just the starting point. Striving for operational excellence will not be enough if the bank wants to compete in the future European SEPA market and not lose its customer base. What is needed is a payments agenda that incorporates a clear vision as to what payments mean to the organisation. The serious market contenders will need to consider re-modelling their payments capabilities around a supply and demand business model, where there is absolute clarity around what the supply side will offer. Defining the target business model and ensuring it is fully described and documented is the bed-rock for future development, as well as providing the basis for insourcing work from other institutions and driving sourcing decisions for non-strategic processing components.

If the bank works on the basis that payments will be a commoditised service, the true basis of competition will be the value-add products and services that are supported by the core service. However, these services reside outside of the payments operation and experience has shown that building a business model, and re-aligning the business around these functional areas, requires a degree of expertise and objectivity not normally found within a bank's change teams, let alone within their payments operations.

Understanding how to develop a new business within existing businesses to be able to manage and drive complex, mission critical transformation programmes, and ensure all stakeholders across all business units and geographies are aligned to the payments agenda is critical. This is where the organisation should be looking for skilled resources to provide objective advice, assistance and assurance, in order to help ensure the transformation process is as rapid as possible and benefits are fully realised.

25

SWIFT for Corporates, a channel to SEPA?

Hervé Postic, founder, UTSIT Paris

SEPA will dramatically change the way corporates work with their banks. This will happen not only because of SEPA itself but also initiatives such as the new ISO20022 standards and 'SWIFT for Corporates'. Whilst these are not directly linked to SEPA, their success will help SEPA to take off in the corporate market, making SEPA a laboratory for the new payments world.

Reading the EPC document released in April 2007 '*Making SEPA a reality*', you will probably note the lack of details regarding the necessary change in Corporate-to-Bank relationships. For the EPC SEPA will be an occasion to set up shared service centres and standardise Bank-to-Corporate relationship:

> Corporates (...) will be able to create (and receive) a single aggregated file for all payments (domestic and cross-border) and submit these to a single institution within standard clearing and settlement timeframes. There will no longer be a need for multiple files prepared to different standards. This will remove costly multi-country payment platforms and enable a migration to one common, consolidated system ....[1]

Nowhere in these statements do the EPC answer critical questions such as:

(a) which standard will be used to create these '*single aggregated file for all payments*'; and
(b) which channel will be used to send and receive files instead of the '*costly multi-country payment platforms*'?

In fact, although the EPC decided to force the use of ISO20022 standards in the Bank-to-Bank space, it allowed Corporate-to-Bank transactions to stay in the competitive space with each bank proposing its own proprietary solution to become the corporate's sole bank for cash management in SEPA.

This clearly goes against a second objective of the EPC:

> Major savings will result from improved and simplified exception processing, automated standing data set up and improved and guaranteed remittance ... Entities with large volumes of direct debits and credit transfers will be able to shop around for banks able to clear and settle at best service, and lowest costs, inclusive of additional bank services, in any country.[2]

In order to ensure clear competition between banks, corporates not only need common rules and standards for clearing and settlement, but also common standards and rules for payment initiation and reporting. Only in this way can we place a clear and strong bank-independent

---

[1] *Making SEPA a Reality*, p. 36.
[2] *Making SEPA a Reality*, pp. 16 and 36.

offering between corporate IT environments, based upon Enterprise Resource Planning and Treasury Management Systems (ERP's and TMS), and the banking world.

25.1   CHALLENGES FOR CENTRALISATION

When large companies decide to put in place shared service centres in Accounts Payable (AP) or Accounts Receivable (AR) on a European basis, their major challenge lies in harmonising payments and collections. Not only local practices often differ from one country to another but, more importantly, IT solutions are too distinct.

Bank reference data, such as account numbers and bank branch identifiers, vary from one country to another, and the way they are used also varies according to the payment means. For a German domestic payment you need a BLZ and a 'Konto Nummer', but for a cross-border payment you need an IBAN and a BIC code.

For many corporations the nightmare starts when they intend to use the same supplier account number for two different subsidiaries hosted in the Shared Service Centre (SSC) as most ERP systems cannot have two ID's for the same 'object', such as the supplier's account number. Moreover, training people in SSC's is hampered by the use of different names and usage for the same object. For example, a German invoice would have the BLZ, Sort Code, CAB-ABI, which are all different names for more or less the same bank branch identifier. A German invoice with several bank account numbers at the bottom is a problem for French staff.

This is why IBAN and BIC are so important in the SEPA project. As IBAN and BIC become mandatory for national and domestic payments, this will dramatically simplify the bank data maintenance and allow for true rationalisation.

Payment processes are also dependent on country specifics and format issues. Most corporates have been forced to put into their processes and IT developments some pieces of the chain which connects them to their bank. For example, the integration of channels has involved lengthy and specific developments which are only applicable to one bank or a national group of banks. Some corporates tried to struggle along in this environment through the use of EDIFACT but, even though the syntax is common, implementations were too different from one bank to another and channels were often different too. This resulted in a small financial EDIFACT world where very large corporates and banks were linked to each other at very high cost.

The challenge is clear to all involved: benefit from the EDIFACT experience to create common standards at not only a syntax level, but also in depth of implementation; and add a channel which is accepted by a large number of banks to ensure their transportation in a common way across the industry.

25.2   SWIFT'S ROLE IN THE CORPORATE-TO-BANK SPACE

The bank-owned cooperative, SWIFT, stands at a crossroads as the armoured vehicle of the banking community in three main areas: data references, standards and channels.

After becoming the BIC ISO registration authority 30 years ago, SWIFT has now been chosen to become the IBAN registration authority. It provides, with its Data Reference programme, a common directory for all the information necessary to validate BIC and IBAN, allowing corporates who will use it to ensure a 100 % STP rates in their payments. This removes the need for 'payment validation' at the bank level, and makes EU cross-border payments as easy as national payments. All of these efforts will also benefit other cross-border payments, such that the SEPA project will have a strong impact in all payment markets by allowing the automation of a large number of simple cross-border payments which are currently manually processed.

SWIFT's role in standardisation is at the heart of the mission banks gave to it in 1973. Its standards department, which employs more than thirty people, is probably unique in hiring such a large number of staff to co-ordinate and drive a common standardisation effort made by the whole community. In recognition of this fact, ISO chose SWIFT as the registration authority for ISO20022 standards, and invited all stakeholders to contribute to the initiative.

Banks, corporates and software providers gather on a regular basis at SWIFT's premises to create and maintain the standards. More than this, the EPC has asked SWIFT to centralise implementation guidelines and manage the need for specifics. Looking back at the EDIFACT experience, the whole community will appreciate this methodology.

Since the outset, financial messaging has been SWIFT's core activity. After focused on payments and Bank-to-Bank relationships, SWIFT is slowly but certainly moving to become the standard in financial messaging. This is regardless of the area – payments, securities and treasury – or the players – banks, brokers, asset managers and many others.

This was first attempted in 1997, although it was not until 2002 when SWIFT finally opened its door to corporates, further progressed and achieved through its offering in 2006 by the standardisation of bank offerings through the SCORE model. The next step for this organisation is to focus on its customers, whatever their status, in addition to its shareholders.

A solid and increasing numbers of corporates have already found their way to the nirvana of 'single-connection to many banks' via SWIFT's current connectivity solutions and their new CEO, Lazaro Campos, made it clear in his introductory speech at SIBOS in October 2007 that this opens a new area. This speech raises the hope amongst treasurers to see a brand new connectivity solution, based on a web interface accessible through the internet, which could also be fully automated at a truly affordable price, making SWIFT for Corporates available for a large number of SMEs and mid-caps.

For corporates, the use of SWIFT is not only the way to use a common channel for a large number of banks but, moreover, it opens an age of collaboration with banks to define the way to exchange between themselves. This means that they will benefit from each euro invested by banks in their strategic core business system.

Beyond cash management, a number of other areas will be explored together to find opportunities to increase STP, reduce costs and finally increase transactions.

25.3 CONCLUSION

In conclusion, ISO20022 standards cover the whole of the payments chain, from payment initiation to payment reporting, in the Bank-to-Bank environment. For the first time in payments history, standards can now be common, defined and maintained by users. ERP providers included in this standardisation initiative will provide their customers with the ability to incorporate all of these standards. For these reasons, corporates will have to ask their banks to use these standards also in the Corporate-to-Bank space, even if the EPC has not made them mandatory.

Full SEPA benefits will not be achievable if the frontier between collaboration and competition does not move to include Corporate-to-Bank standards and channels in the collaborative space. SWIFT's hard work to increase its value proposition for both banks and corporates in this area helps both parties to understand their common interests in dismantling this frontier. Furthermore, with the release of new ERP systems, gathering in the same software Bank Data, ISO20022 standards, combined with a direct link to all banks through the SWIFT network, will definitely help corporates in getting the maximum returns and benefits from SEPA.

Part 6
The View of the Implementers of SEPA

- IBM
- Sentenial
- Eiger
- The Reference Data User Group
- IdenTrust
- TietoEnator
- BT
- Sterling Commerce

26

The most critical technologies for SEPA

Neil Burton, IBM

Banks can exploit SEPA opportunities by using a component based model for the renewal of their payment services, introducing XML and ISO20022 through gradual change, rather than a big bang replacement of their total payments factory systems.

The driver for SEPA was originally to achieve the Lisbon agenda[1] which seeks to make Europe 'the most dynamic and competitive knowledge-based economy in the world'.

Inefficiencies in the banking and payments system could, if rectified, save the EU economy between € 50 billion and € 100 billion a year. The banking industry's response, represented by the European Payments Council (EPC), was to set about ensuring that 'making and receiving payments will become as easy, reliable, competitive and efficient as currently in the domestic context.'[2]

The investments made to date by the banking industry, including TARGET2, consolidations between and innovations within the national ACHs, as well as SEPA, go some considerable way to reducing costs, driving out inhibitors to change and enabling the market.

However, it is well known that the fees levied by interbank payment systems represent only 10 % to 15 % of the total costs of processing a payment. This means that the anticipated reduction in clearing and settlement tariffs will not compensate for the revenue shortfalls. Banks can do more; payment processing within the bank's back-offices, where the major costs lie, is typically fragmented across different lines of business. Each legacy system has evolved over many years in response to differing national standards, rules and practices, and this silo structure has been further compounded by mergers that have made it more difficult to implement unified architectures and processes in a secure and phased way.

SEPA will therefore no doubt accelerate the trend to concentrate back-offices into shared service centres, and the quest to find cheaper operating locations. Applications can be simplified in a number of ways; for example, fewer interfaces to clearing systems will be needed.

Banks typically face three options in restructuring:

- migrate current domestic platforms to SEPA: XML can be difficult to implement for older applications, and they may need renovation to become more efficient;
- migrate international platforms to SEPA: however, these systems are usually not scalable to sustain the combined domestic and international volumes as migration to SEPA schemes gains momentum; or
- create a new SEPA platform: with the flexibility required to process all payments on a more modern, scalable architecture.

---

[1] http://www.europa.eu/scadplus/glossary/lisbon_strategy_en.htm.
[2] http://www.ecb.int/paym/sepa/html/vision.en.html.

To date, many banks have addressed SEPA Credit Transfer (SCT) through the implementation of format converters which convert between ISO20022 and the format of the bank's internal systems, whilst reach is achieved through a veriety of CSM's including the EBA STEP2. Through this approach, in simple terms, compliance is achieved.

Whilst this approach is challenged by some SEPA purists, it does minimise the investments required during the initial period. However, 28 January 2008 is by no means the end of the journey. The standards and processes dictated by the SCT rules should be expected to improve with usage. As SEPA evolves, further investment will be needed; many analysts argue that the bulk of the investment is yet to come.

The next major challenge, SEPA Direct Debits (SDD), is much more substantial than SCT for most banks. Few banks will be able to meet the requirements of SDDs through minor enhancements of existing systems and processes. The investment necessary may well absorb the best part of a bank's available resources over some years. The outcome of SDD alone – if separate from initiatives such as e-invoicing – has doubtful commercial benefit, and may lead to indirect consequences as other investment projects and innovations must inevitably take lower priority. Indeed, a healthy groundswell of opinion is developing, challenging whether SDDs is the best next step.

Nonetheless, the advent of the Payments Service Directive (PSD), which will be transcribed into national law by of all EU states by 1 November 2009 will undoubtedly result in substantial changes to legacy payments systems and processes. The scope of the PSD is wider than SEPA; it covers payments in all EC currencies where both payment service providers reside in the European Community. It also applies to payments of any value, and to payment orders requested by any type of customer. After 1 January 2012, the maximum settlement period become $D + 1$. It will be interesting to see whether banks, once forced to transform, will voluntarily elect to aim for best-can-do rather than simple compliance – as is the case with the UK Faster Payments service, due to launch in May 2007.

Whilst some banks are treating SEPA as a compliance issue, other banks see SEPA as an opportunity to renovate and differentiate. Andrew Long, the Head of Global Transaction Banking at HSBC, said:

"The impact of the emergence of new models and standards, such as XML and ISO, is being built into the infrastructure of banks like HSBC, which is firmly committed to remaining as one of the core providers in the payments business. Mass payments corporate clients are saying to HSBC that the SEPA business case only really makes sense to them if file formats are completely standardised, e.g. strictly one size fits all XML. In light of this, and noting that industry margins are being squeezed, HSBC remains committed to significant ongoing investment in state of the art technology for high volume payments processing to deliver the lowest unit costs of processing. This is critical to keep us at the forefront of technology innovation in payments, a core business for HSBC, and ensure we pass on these benefits to our customers through differentiated propositions."

Ann Cairns, CEO, Transaction Banking, ABN AMRO commented that regulatory changes are costing banks upwards of $40 billion a year to remain compliant. The investment should be thought of as not just being the cost of compliance, but in terms of how it can be used to provide more value to the client. In this case, SEPA is an example of a regulation that could drive differentiated offerings.

This view is common amongst the bigger banks. A further example is Deutsche Bank who state that they have already over-delivered on SEPA, by making comprehensive SEPA clearing and settlement services available to their international financial institutions customers. They are

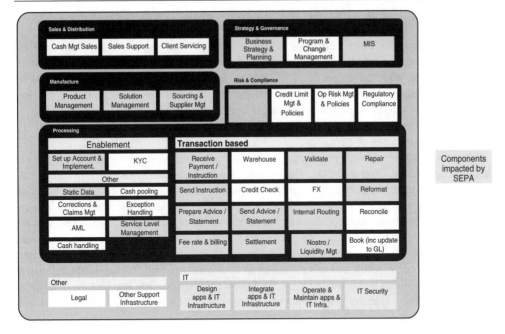

Figure 26.1   Component Business Model for Payments

helping other banks achieve SEPA compliance through outsourcing parts of their processing to Deutsche.

A successful response to SEPA therefore demands a business-oriented enterprise view of payment messaging that is standards-based, with a flexible architecture using a defined common data and process model. This is a departure from the past. For the last quarter of a century, the payments environment has been relatively slow changing. Post-SEPA, banks face a period in which change will be the norm. Outsourcing, white-labelling and other models, in which investments are shared across more than one institution, are fast maturing and will become far more prevalent. Agility to adapt to new opportunities will become a survival issue, not a nice-to-have, and all to be achieved through and in parallel with a migration from the current legacy environment. This requires a rethink, not only of the way systems are designed and built, but also in the way that change projects are approached.

The first step is to take a hard look at the shape of the current environment, breaking the operating processes into components. In this context, a component is a group of cohesive business activities supported by appropriate information systems, processes, organisation structure, and subject to performance measures. The figure above shows the Component Business Model (CBM) for Payments, where payments are one component of the overall CBM for the entire bank.

Banks should then appraise their own capabilities and identify components driving effective competitive differentiation. Some activities are dependent on large volumes and economies of scale to reduce costs, and offer little competitive opportunity. These are clearly prime targets for outsourcing to other institutions or shared service centres operated by bank consortia or third parties. So too are those components for which the bank is unwilling to invest in re-engineering, or lack the technology and skills required to achieve the relevant critical success factors.

For components yielding competitive value and retained in-house, the bank should examine whether they can be re-used across other geographies and payment instruments, or even other lines of business. With the advent of SEPA. it is perfectly conceivable to centralise operations and IT whilst retaining sales, advisory services and first-line customer support locally. Process modelling and simulation enables optimisation from a cost and/or execution time standpoint.

Many banks are adopting middleware-based enterprise architectures as the basis for this flexibility, with reusable components.

In recent years, middleware has progressed from being a relatively new category of asset to being commonplace, Over the years, vendors have made substantial investments in functionality, which is relatively common across many IT systems and processes. Through the provision of common formats and process orchestration previously complex tasks. such as interfacing to legacy systems, have been accelerated and de-risked. To an increasing degree, middleware is commoditising and substituting the old systems integration tasks. Many, if not most, banks are therefore using middleware technology in very high volume, business critical applications.

When designed correctly, today's systems can be scalable and flexible using the minimum amount of IT resource and contributing to the lowest possible cost per transaction. The wider the design, the more types of traffic that can be supported on a single system. The more scale, the more economy.

The flexibility to re-orchestrate existing functional modules and process steps also has a measurable benefit. For example, one bank's system costs for compliance with the new UK Faster Payments initiative were understood to be half those of other banks, as a result of a prior investment in a well-architected system.

This kind of architecture is often described as a SOA (Services Oriented Architecture). SOA provides the flexibility to treat elements of business processes and the underlying IT infrastructure, as secure, standardised components and services. These components can be reused and combined to address changing business priorities. SOA can then be defined as architecture that is based upon a collection of business processes that rely on reusable standard interfaces to integrate applications within a company, as well as externally with customers, partners and suppliers.

SOA helps transform applications into component business processes called services. Services can be quickly manipulated, combined and new ones can be added. The business process is no longer confined to a specific platform or application. It can be treated as a component, and reused or changed. SOA thus allows businesses to become more agile while avoiding the old style of rip and replace legacy IT systems.

The roadmap to SOA can be gradual through a series of small projects, each with a tangible business value aligned to banks' resources and priorities, rather than a big bang replacement project. In this context TowerGroup, the research firm, recently identified a major conceptual split between product vendors and framework providers of enterprise payments solutions, with the vendors recommending gradual transformation of technology rather than a big-bang approach.

Unlike many legacy systems, today's frameworks are native consumers of the emerging ISO20022 standard. The EPC's SEPA Rulebooks mandate that ISO20022 is used for bank-to-bank communications, and highly recommended it for bank-to-corporate communications. In order to self-certify for SEPA compliance, only the ability to communicate externally is necessary. However, ISO20022 is being imposed by SWIFT, which is controlled by banks and by the EPC, again a bank-dominated organisation. It is therefore self-imposed upon the industry, and presumably will become a cornerstone of new services such as e-invoicing.

Vendors are increasingly delivering new features and functions that make the processing of ISO20022, and its underlying XML syntax, more efficient. Hardware devices compress and accelerate. Databases can read and write native XML, thus avoiding the cost and overhead of shredding into other formats, and improving agility through enabling new schemas to be adopted more quickly. The old Message Type (MT) formats have been around for a long time, and the means of processing them has become well tuned over the years. It will take time for SWIFT's new formats to catch up in terms of processing efficiency, but agility is an increasingly important prize.

However, the full benefit of the investment cannot be captured by banks acting alone. The real question right now is whether not just the banks, but also the other key stakeholders, are tracking towards optimising their systems and processes for post-SEPA economics?

In order to capture the full benefits, governments and the corporate sector need to take a more active role. The EPC has recently declared e-invoicing to be outside the scope of SEPA; if e-invoicing is to proceed, other groups will need to lead the way. The EC's initiative around e-invoicing[3] may go some way to drawing in a wider community. But there are relatively few firm deadlines; the Spanish government's drive requiring government institutions to adopt e-invoicing by 2009 and other companies by 2010,[4] is an exception.

26.1   ALTERNATIVE MODELS

It is by no means only the banks who can provide payments services addressing the goals of the EC. In fact, the new regulations provide active encouragement to new entrants. The Payments Services Directive (PSD) provides for:

- enhanced competition by opening markets to all appropriate payment service providers; and
- harmonised market access requirements for non-bank payment service providers, payment institutions, ensuring a level playing field and at the same time encouraging innovation.

Banks, faced with a large legacy infrastructure and burdened with a plethora of regulatory challenges, are not as agile as new market entrants; but banks are also the custodians of the characteristics of payments, safety and reliability, which must be encompassed in any new service.

Banks have been relatively slow to adapt. Several bankers have observed that the correspondent banking model is becoming an increasingly weakened value proposition, especially for lower value payments.[5] However, it is by no means only banks which can deliver against this objective. New entrants typically face a lower regulatory burden than the banks, and one view is that banks should lobby the regulators to impose the same levels of oversight on all market participants. An alternative view is that banks offer a range of services, not all of which should face the same levels of capital adequacy and other governance.

New entrants can appear to inherit the hard-won reputation of the incumbent payments providers without necessarily paying the dues. Whilst people often think of the mobile device as the cornerstone of ubiquity, in fact ubiquity derives from the global service which the

---

[3] http://www.ec.europa.eu/information_society/eeurope/i2010/docs/studies/eei-3.2-e-invoicing_final_report.pdf.
[4] http://www.red.es/prensa/pdf/factura_electronica.pdf.
[5] For example, Tom Isaac of Citigroup in the Journal of Payments Strategy & Systems, Volume 1, Number 3/April, 2007.

telecommunications firms have developed. It is, in some ways, analogous to the correspondent banking clearing network offered by banks. But it is not seen by consumers the same way. Market research clearly shows that consumers are prepared to pay for payments services involving mobile devices (where typically they expect payments ervices to be free if provided by banks). The common estimate is that consumers would be prepared to pay around € 1 for a person-to-person local transaction and up to € 20 for a cross-currency international transfer. Telecommunications firms and others are increasingly exploiting this.

Of course, at the end of the day, banks are eventually involved for services such as the holding of deposits and the settlement, but these services are either commoditised or are perceived to have little value. On a value chain assessment, they are relatively non- profitable and non-differentiating components.

The most often cited example of a new entrant is PayPal. Simple in concept, PayPal has grown to become multi-service and ubiquitous. Onc banker at SIROS 2006 dismissed PayPal as being 'just a convenience thing' whilst, at SIBOS 2007, another banker commented that his bank would never have launched a mobile payments service like PayPal's, unless it met the bank's rigorous security and audit procedures. This is understandable but beg the question: so who's taking the income?

Perhaps the most significant incursion into banking is trust and brand name recognition. PayPal seems to get more airtime in general conversation and internet chatrooms than the average bank for example. There is no reason to assume that innovators such as PayPal are any less well run than banks (who are themselves not immune to problems, the recent Northern Rock experience (in which where there was a major run on a bank is an example). PayPal's new banking licence will be passported throughout Europe under the PSD. This new brand seems here to stay.

26.2   CONCLUSION

Ultimately, it may be that payments is too narrow an objective. Returning to the original Lisbon goals, the end-goal is to drive out costs, drive up efficiency and deliver on GDP growth. Banks' payments and cash management businesses can only contribute to that agenda in part because the business problem to be solved is not payments, but e-commerce. Most of the technology needed to achieve an efficient e-economy is readily available. Technology has improved hugely over the last decades, by almost any measure. Technology is not the major inhibitor; the real challenge is to get a large and diverse enough community of stakeholders to adopt the appropriate technical and business process standards – for which technology is an enabler Changing an interdependent, networked economy is a challenging task; but it would be disappointing if the current period of incentivised and inspired change results only in the same services, run faster and cheaper.

Whilst additional bank-centric initiatives. such as supply chain financing and e-invoicing, will help to drive market adoption, the true value of the banking industry's investment in SEPA will only be realised if ambitions, and hence the scope, is raised and the other players in the economic model are incentivised to participate and fully contribute.

27

Compliance: Friend or Foe?

Sean Fitzgerald, Sentenial

Financial institutions that treat SEPA as a compliance project will gain little benefit and will be late to the opportunities it presents. Institutions should instead focus upon a strategic transition to a post-SEPA world which meets the customer's needs.

Since the late 1980's, compliance and regulation have been the burden of the financial institution. This has taken many guises and, more recently, we have seen the mandated TDES[1] requirements and the EMV or Chip and Pin requirements for cards. Along with trying to accommodate the regular business requirements, institutions are in a constant state of compliance projects.

Continuing this trend, SEPA has brought a new raft of requirements and regulations. Its aim is to level barriers to free trade across Europe and, overall, the new SEPA holds much promise in terms of the reduction in the cost of monetary transfer in Europe. This will open up new larger markets to many parties, including Financial Institutions. However, it seems that financial institutions will struggle to realise their full potential in this new emerging SEPA. The reasons for this are many.

For some, SEPA is seen solely as a compliance issue, and these institutions will invest significantly just to become the same as others. This is hardly satisfactory as surely the aim of any institution is to compete through differentiation. For others, those who have the vision to look beyond compliance to the emergence of a larger and more competitive payments landscape, their visionary strategies are impeded by their legacy silo-based architectures, compliance costs and time restraints.

Indeed the fast approach of SEPA deadlines, and its ever-moving goalposts, challenge even the most forward looking of banks on the compliance front. Compounded by the complexity of core banking systems, which require huge budgetary investments to reach compliance estimated at 70 % to 85 % of the total budget, it is hardly surprising that innovative and strategic solutions do not emerge.

Nevertheless, SEPA will bring about significant market changes. The existing landscape or ecosystem consists of key players including financial institutions, the corporates and the payments processors. As the market has developed, it has opened its doors to other players and as such a crossover has emerged. The result is that it is no longer appropriate to speak in terms of verticals as we must also factor in organisations such as online providers, the amalgamation of larger players, corporates as well as the larger financial institutions. The larger entities

---

[1] TDES, or Triple DES, is in cryptography a block cipher formed from the Data Encryption Standard (DES) cipher by using it three times.

have the ability to carry the risk through scale, infrastructure and capability and enter the new landscape confidently and the advent of the service aggregator is all too prevalent.

So what does this mean for the future? With most institutions investing solely in compliance, the real challenge is to meet the demands to become compliant, and to take on the new conditions and use the changes SEPA creates to innovate. Compliance is not the only game in town and those organisations that believe it is will be swept up with the tide and miss the wave. It is important for organisations to recognise and see the greater landscape: they should aim to combine short term compliance investment with the adoption of an architecture which will meet their longer-term strategy objective.

At present, three strategies are being adopted among Financial Institutions

- Addressing SEPA as a short term compliance issue and leaving it at that. In this case, SEPA compliance is viewed as a sunk cost where all the boxes are ticked but there is no product differentiation. This will result in greater investment downstream as the bank will inevitably have to revisit the infrastructure and investigate how to meet new demands and remain competitive as the landscape changes.
- The late starter who plays the wait-and-see game and then sprints to catch up. In this case, a looking-over-the-fence approach is used to see what others are doing about SEPA with little or no planning. When the decision is taken to go, competitors have a head start.
- The long-term view which is measured, structured and flexible, taking compliance as part of the project. This is the approach that the winners will take and it is important that adequate planning and investment is undertaken to ensure that all factors are considered across the wins, risks and targets.

Options one and two are reactive short term approaches and, despite the significant investment involved, they will not leave organisations well set to enter SEPA. Those adopting these approaches will be faced with competition from organisations taking the strategic view. The strategists will be looking beyond the requirements for SEPA compliance, viewing these only as the preliminary part of a much more market-focused project. With the lid already off existing infrastructures and systems, these organisations see the opportunity to take a closer look at processes, procedures and systems, and make the changes to turn SEPA compliance into an advantage. It is important that any institution engaging in such a project should see the long-term view, and search for new competitive opportunities and increasing revenues through methods which develop and capitalise upon new business initiatives.

So the need to invest is unarguably mandatory although the size of investment is far more debatable. It is probably true to say that the extent of the investment can be proportional to the return. If investment is provided to achieve compliance, then compliance will be achieved and nothing else. A strategic, long-term investment will bring greater benefits but why not wait and see what the market does first? After all the future is uncertain so why risk investing heavily in a less than guaranteed solution? Predictions can be wrong, consolidation may not occur, competition may not increase, and customers may stay loyal to their national banks.

The problem with sitting on the fence is that it does not absolve banks of risk. Playing it safe is, in itself, a risky strategy. There is a very real risk of being left behind in the race or even being disqualified. So it seems banks, crippled by financial, architectural and time constraints, must move forward at an ill afforded cost and, no matter which route they choose, the risk is great.

So what is the path forward? How can banks and financial institutions minimise their initial investment but still keep their eye on future goals?

Flexibility is the key. What is needed is a step-by-step approach through an incremental investment towards a strategic end-goal. Seek flexibility, scalability and room for growth, with speedy adaptation to the new market as it emerges. This will be critical to gain first mover advantage. The approach should be measured and can be taken in phases. For example, not all investments need be deployed up-front but can be managed through three phases:

1. **Compliance**: use this phase to build the infrastructure to address the immediate requirements around compliance and to future proof your organisation from the ever-moving goal posts.
2. **Strategic:** build on the existing platforms to launch new initiatives and ensure a competitive position, whilst searching for additional revenue streams and reducing costs.
3. **Returns:** use the products, services and infrastructure put in place by the initial stages to diversify into new areas.[2]

One item to factor into the research is the benefit of many of the componentised and modular solutions available to organisations today, enabling them to adopt an evolutionary or bolt-on approach to building the infrastructure. Those institutions already working alongside vendors or integrators may well be aware of this, where modern solutions are developed in such a way as to facilitate this building-block approach. A distinct advantage of this approach is the ability to phase the delivery by taking mandatory components at the beginning, with ease of deployment of additional components at a later stage. This also has the advantage of spreading the investment costs in line with the strategy and the project. This approach also has the advantage of suiting organisations of different sizes and complexity.

In the case of SEPA, organisations will spend early to address the compliance requirements. If this is carried out in parallel and complimentary to a strategic project, the bank will automatically see complimentary areas where crossover is achieved. This can already be seen with the advent of new payment initiatives, such as eInvoicing and Electronic Bill Presentment and Payment (EBPP), two services which are greatly facilitated by the oncoming single payment process and CSM in Europe. Financial institutions are already stating their case and positioning to leverage strength through their existing presence, scale and infrastructure. They see SEPA as a product that can be diversified into disparate business areas and many are looking to position themselves as service providers to non-associated or smaller organisations, and also to corporates, thereby enabling full utilisation of their SEPA infrastructures.

The race is on. Organisations must ask themselves: will they be the early sprinter who tires early in the marathon through lack of tactics or strategy; or will they be the marathon runner who sets milestones at each stage in the race, measures progress, and can take comfort of their preparation and approach to ensure that they will reach the finish line even thought they cannot see it.

27.1   HOW CAN THIS BE ACHIEVED?

This can be achieved by using the three R's approach.

- Revenue
- Reusability
- Reduction

---

[2] The new landscape will see organisations amalgamating to provide new services. The third phase of the project can be used to deliver on these, e.g. the provision of processor services in the new environment through the outsourcing and hosting to smaller entities.

27.1.1 Revenue

Revenue potential exists and organisations must look to develop and deploy value-added services around the compliance project. This is to ensure a greater level of service to customers, and thereby increase potential and opportunities within the customer base.

Growth in revenue should be seen as the objective, and not just as a by-product of the investment. The growth can only be gained as a result of the definition and delivery of new products and services, for example through service provision such as hosting, or new product offerings such as e-invoicing.

SEPA will also bring increased potential in the corporate marketplace through the delivery of services around management of mandates, hosting services, validation of payment processing and so on. Larger organisations can look to scale as payment acquiring providers and to bring services to the smaller players that wouldn't otherwise exist.

It is also important that there be a return on investment approach obviously, so that the sunk costs of implementing a compliance-only project are minimised.

27.1.2 Reusability

A common approach is to do the obvious and not ask the question: 'how much of the existing infrastructure can be reused?' We all agree that investment is essential. However, before running out to buy new infrastructure, an evaluation of the existing infrastructure should be carefully undertaken.

Certainly, the license or purchase of new solutions cannot be avoided. New technologies, new developments and the latest gizmos are fine but most institutions will already have infrastructure supporting existing systems. This will need fine tuning to ensure its ability to support the demands of being compliant as well as the ongoing strategic approaches for the future. Through careful planning, the utilisation of an existing infrastructure can be taken into the project.

Utilisation of industry expertise and vendor knowledge should also be part of the project. Software vendors, consultants and systems integrators have the advantage of taking a holistic view of the landscape, and can use experience and skills to assist in ensuring that all aspects of the project and end goals are addressed.

Reusability covers three areas:

- Infrastructure
  - o Existing processes and procedures
  - o Localisation
  - o Integration and relationships with external processors
- Technologies
  - o IT infrastructure
  - o Applications
- Skills
  - o Business
  - o Industry
  - o Technology
  - o Consultative

Any organisation that embarks carefully on an approach will gain maximum advantage from the investment and should perform the following steps:

- identify areas where change is necessary or where there is a requirement for the deployment of new solutions;
- plan the approach and the project; and then
- focus upon the key deliverables around this.

27.2   REDUCTION

Investment in SEPA should not be a throwaway cost and so institutions should strive to ensure that the investment can deliver in three areas:

27.2.1   Cost reduction

The deployment of new process and procedure should have the added benefit of reducing costs across many areas, especially IT and operations. For example, through the deployment of systems to manage a payments process, institutions can ensure that the correct validation and data integrity procedures are implemented. This will result in a reduction in the amount of exceptions and rejections during payments processing, two items that pose a high cost element to any institution. SEPA will draw attention to these particular areas.

27.2.2   Overheads

In line with a reusability approach, overheads and logistics costs should reduce also. An efficient approach to the project will look at all aspects, and will bring with it a focus upon areas where efficiencies can be implemented across the spectrum.

27.2.3   Risk

De-risking the deployment and subsequent solution is of paramount importance. Organisations should look at negating the inherent risks associated with the payments infrastructure and, although risk is not the main focus of this text, it is worth spending some time on it.

We are all aware of the identified risks around SEPA. These include:

- *Credit Risk*: ensuring that the processing of rejected or returned transactions is handled properly, and that the mechanisms are put in place to reduce the volumes of 'r' transactions so that validation, checking and so forth is reduced. Also this should ensure that the risk to the creditor institution is reduced in the event of the creditor failing in any way.
- *Operational Risk:* negate the exposure to fraud or processing problems.
- *Reputational Risk:* ensuring that the reputation of the parties, including the scheme, is upheld.
- *Currency Risk:* reduce the currency exchange exposures when customers and institutions are transacting outside the Eurozone.
- *Financial Risk:* ensure that the exposure to incorrect processing of amounts or dates is mitigated such that no party is exposed during the process.
- *Commercial Risk:* reduce the exposure of the debtor bank to the effects of poor service or other interferences, which would reduce the confidence in the Direct Debit payment instrument.

In addition to the elements outlined above, new areas are being highlighted. These include:

- *Systemic Risk:* with the increased demand for greater efficiencies around fraud, risk and KYC, Institutions need to be ring-fenced against losses through the system. These losses may be as a result of failures in the processing network and the exposure to the greater geographical and market regions.
- *Crisis Management:* there is a need to implement proper and trusted mechanisms to cater for failures in any part of the payments infrastructure through networks, communications, or through the failure of any player in the chain.

Even the best intended and planned projects will suffer if the end deliverable is not secured against risk and clearly identifying the potential risk areas is important to ensure that anyone embarking on the SEPA compliance project does so with a clear and open door approach, factoring in all aspects of the scheme, the win potential and the risks.

27.3 THINKING ACROSS THE SPECTRUM

SEPA is the first step in an ongoing project. Using this analogy, if the first step is uncalculated or shaky, then the second one will be carried out based upon the uncertainty of the first insecure feeling and so on, bringing with it an overall lack of confidence. Where the first step is safe, secure and carried out confidently, then each subsequent step can be measured against this.

SEPA provides us with a means to achieve an end to end STP across a spectrum that has three basic elements: pre-payment, payment processing and post-payment. Each element brings with it a new set of requirements and deliverables. If these elements are addressed with the three R's approach, then it should deliver an enhanced payments compliance process. By opening with this approach, institutions should look for potential at all stages in the cycle.

This brings me back to my opening paragraphs regarding the emerging, or emerged, landscape. The new landscape opens doors for many existing players. There is the opportunity to implement new strategies around existing payment instruments. A single payments infrastructure reduces the barriers that would otherwise restrict new initiatives and the potential for the delivery of new products, services, hence restricting growth. Combining all of the elements of the new payments infrastructure into one cohesive plan allows organisations to plan to effectively take advantage of the opportunities available. This can only be done if there is a clear strategy in place at the start.

Post-SEPA, we will see the emergence of new players. These will take the shape of larger processors, central acquiring providers and service providers. There will be a shuffling and positioning in the market. The end result will be a much more competitive environment and positioning to take advantage is critical, hence early adoption is important.

Leveraging an existing competitive advantage is something that many institutions already have the power and resources to do. With the SEPA framework nearing completion, many players are late coming to the table and, as of yet, have failed to implement a clear strategy or project. They are the late starters taking the first shaky steps.

One method which can alleviate this is the emergence of specialist vendors who, through their skill, expertise and solutions, will assist the late starters. Many such organisations exist in the shape of systems integrators or software vendors. They can work closely alongside the organisation, thanks to their strong reputations in the marketplace, to ensure that not only is compliance addressed but that the approach taken is both strategic and will come close to addressing the three R's.

What is usually missed when considering the use of a third party is the ability for the third party to manage the end-to-end project, addressing the requirements and the strategy of the target organisation whilst also allowing them to carry on their day-to-day operations. Specialist vendors have the advantage of taking a holistic view of the entire landscape and can provide a measured and strategic input into process. Institutions can maintain control of the project, while using the vendor in partnership to deliver. More often than not, the reach of the institution is extended through the expertise, market knowledge and delivery of key components in the strategy through trusted third parties.

Although the approach by larger institutions would be to bring the compliance project in-house with, in most such instances, compliance being met. However, the bigger and more strategic rollout could be missed through this approach, thereby implementing a compliance-only project rather than something strategic. More than this, the institution will take on the ongoing maintenance and support for all additional and associated compliance requirements that might come in the future as a result. Therefore, taking a longer and more measured approach, the institution can dictate the requirements in line with their strategy and take input from vendors to maintain a clarity and targeted approach to the market.

No matter what approach is undertaken, it is certain that SEPA will bring with it opportunity and challenges. SEPA should be seen as a journey. Without belittling the size and scope, I cannot emphasise enough the opportunity that it presents to the market. When the new landscape evolves, new payment instruments, products and the potential for growth will expand to fill the needs and requirements that will emerge.

The seeds of this growth have already been sown and the drivers are not compliance or regulation, but customer demand. The corporate marketplace is already demanding newer and more streamlined methods to bill and settle payments. It is the responsibility of the financial institutions to meet this demand. However, as I have repeatedly stated, it is important to think long-term and to capitalise at each step on the journey. The early adaptors will take the first steps and will win out whilst the latecomers can only hope to take the scraps that might fall from their table.

28

SEPA: How the technology requirements for SEPA will help it evolve

Jonathan Williams, Eiger

This chapter considers the technological requirements to support a Single Euro(pean) Payments Area, how they change from 1 January 2008 and to the SEPA end-game after 2020. Through this process, it investigates how these technology needs influence the direction of SEPA and its speed of widespread adoption.

As discussed in earlier chapters, the European Union has pushed through a significant programme of change within banking and payments, affecting potentially all of the EU citizens, companies and governments. But the SEPA of 1 January 2008 and 2010 is as far from the SEPA of 2020 and thereafter as the horse and cart is from the racing car. Looking back from 2020 through the fog of historical perspective, I am sure we shall wonder what the issues were that delayed this fundamental part of our banking system. And if we cannot recall our motivations and impediments, surely we shall have forgotten the technological challenges we faced.

At the start of SEPA there are three key stages: compliance, coexistence and conversion. The compliance stage finished on 1 January 2008, and left most banks fully compliant with the mandatory elements. There is then a period of coexistence where banks maintaining both new and legacy systems. Conversion, the final and more painful process, can be undertaken only with the involvement of bank customers, both retail and corporate.

It is clear that SEPA at its introduction is a product developed by banks for banks at the political behest of the European Commission and under the auspices of the European Central Bank (ECB). In order to minimise discussion and disagreement, SEPA has delivered products for the banking members of the European Payments Council to offer to their retail and corporate customers, but with little direct involvement from or with them. In order to really gain traction with the payment initiators themselves, SEPA needs to become both more personal and more effective for businesses.

SEPA is primarily a domestic market and, looking at the history of domestic markets, suggests that planned developments generally take longer and end up at a different destination than that which was originally envisaged.

The question often asked then is, 'Where does SEPA go from here?' I believe there is a more informative way to look at this problem. If we consider what the SEPA end-game must be, can we answer the question, 'How do we get there from here?' If we can extrapolate what the long-term goals of SEPA are, can we interpolate the decisions and developments necessary to get there?

The European Payments Council defines SEPA as 'SEPA will be the area where citizens, companies and other economic actors will be able to make and receive payments in euro, within

Europe, whether between or within national boundaries under the same basic conditions, rights and obligations, regardless of their location.'[1]

Taking a long term view, this has a number of key implications:

- **Inclusion:** SEPA is for everyone including citizens, governments and businesses, not just banks and payment industry bodies.
- **Entirety:** SEPA must encompass how individuals and organisations initiate payments, as much as how banks process those payments on their behalf.
- **Ubiquity:** SEPA must cover the all key payment methods the citizens, governments and businesses want to use, wherever they want to use them.
- **Parity:** there is no difference in payments between countries for SEPA to the extent that national processes do not exist or, if they do, they have no bearing on how the SEPA payment is initiated, processed, settled or reconciled.
- **Efficiency:** the system must be the most efficient possible otherwise there will inevitably be a 'New SEPA' programme to replace it, or payment initiators will move to other, more attractive payment offerings.
- **Uniqueness:** there can be only one set of payment mechanisms within the area.

This sort of complex problem with multiple constraints, some of which appear esoteric or at least impenetrable, is not new to physicists. Although physicists use very different language, the analogy with the long-term challenges for SEPA can be viewed in this way. For example, for many years, physics has been trying to come to terms with viewing the universe in two fundamentally different ways: quantum mechanics or relativity. Perhaps this is best embodied in the question: 'Is light a particle or a wave?'

However, with SEPA we have one additional problem that the physicists do not: economics. The difference between physics and economics is famously characterised by the saying 'physicists hope to create one theory using many experiments; economists use many theories but have only one experiment'. This explains why it is so difficult to predict exactly how a situation in the payments industry will evolve, as it's impossible to know all the variables in play and all the different theories being applied.

It is therefore necessary to consider each of the key long-term implications to understand what technological solutions are required.

Inclusion: *SEPA is for everyone including citizens, governments and businesses not just banks and payment industry bodies*

Considering the long-term SEPA, how do we define inclusion? Governments are rightly concerned about citizens' participation in banking services today, with many investigations through various financial-inclusion task forces, but the capability to buy goods or services is more fundamental than the ability to own a bank account. In the long-term, inclusion must mean that every citizen has the facility to make SEPA payments, either with the benefit of an EU bank account or based on their status as a citizen.

The technological challenge is to empower every citizen to make at least one form of SEPA payment, in a way that is acceptable for all the goods and services he or she might reasonably consume. This means that payments must become personal. In the same way that individuals

---

[1] Realisation of the Single Euro Payments Area, European Payments Council, 2004.

use cash today, a personal payment mechanism is a fundamental building block of the SEPA. Individuals will still have a desire for anonymity whilst engaging in their private business, but increasingly governments will want to scrutinise every transaction. In this context, it is not clear whether payments will still be made incognito.

One thing is for sure, the drive for efficiency must make these payments automated and therefore related to some set of unique features of the individual, based upon a unique token that the individual has which may be the descendant of today's mobile telephones and PDAs, or a combination of both.

In addition individuals with accounts which can make payments, including but not limited to bank accounts, will want at least as efficient methods of making payments from wherever they are. Business will similarly need to make payments and, while the method of initiation will differ, the basic necessity of trust between the payer and payment service provider must be ensured.

There is significant demand from government and business, in addition to that from consumers, to allow billing organisations to control when and how payments are collected from consumers. While the various direct debit schemes are extremely successful in Europe, with over 24 billion transactions processed in 2005, it is not the only mechanism for payee-originated payments. Credit and debit cards can provide similar services, although direct debit is certainly the most cost-effective method.

However, the simplicity of the direct debit schemes may prove to be their major weakness as they start to be targeted by organised crime. Only by mitigating this risk can direct debit schemes continue to be offered. In the medium term, it is therefore inconceivable that SEPA should not fully support direct debit transfers. However, the demands of managing risk will mean that organisations will need increasingly sophisticated mechanisms to control operational and credit risk in this environment. The technological need is for reliable, pan-European data on all accounts and mandates which exist in the system.

SEPA must also cater for foreign nationals and multinational businesses at least as effectively as it supports its citizens. In this area, and this alone, SEPA cannot decide how its payments will be made and must interoperate with other regional payment areas, to some extent, such as those created by the potential Asia-Pacific, North American, African and South American agreements. The technological challenge here is to learn the lessons, select wisely and benefit from the technologies developed elsewhere.

SEPA must also tackle the issue of payments made in currencies other than euro, although taking a long-term perspective almost certainly makes these currencies irrelevant, or at least an historical anachronism.

In summary, to satisfy the needs of inclusion, more than one payment method is called for. What SEPA must therefore offer are schemes which solve the same problems as cards, cash, credit transfer and direct debit, but it is more than likely that those mechanisms will be more secure, more reliable and more automated.

Entirety: *SEPA must encompass how individuals and organisations initiate payments as much as how banks process those payments on their behalf*

End-to-end is a phrase which has frequently been misused when discussing payments, and this disagreement as to the application of the term is at the heart of the problem of entirety. Different parties have a different expectation of where their role starts and finishes, and therefore have

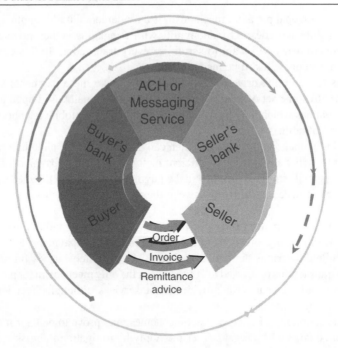

Figure 28.1   The starts and finishes of the end-to-end process

different end-points. This is probably best demonstrated by considering a purchase of goods and services using an electronic credit transfer (see Figure 28.1 below):

- A buyer places an order with a seller.
- The seller processes the order delivers the goods or services and sends an invoice.
- The buyer processes the invoices and initiates payment, at the same time sending a remittance advice.
- The buyer's bank takes the payment instruction from its customer and initiates the payment, typically through an automated clearing house.
- The ACH passes the payment information to the recipient's bank and passes the information for settlement.
- The seller's bank receives the payment and passes it on to the seller's account.
- Finally, the seller receives information on the received payment and can attempt to reconcile it against both the original invoice and the remittance advice.

So where are the ends of the process?

- For the seller, the process starts when the invoice is sent and finishes when that invoice is reconciled against the incoming credit transfer and remittance advice.
- For the buyer, the start is either when the invoice is received or when the order is placed with the seller, and the end of the transaction is when the seller acknowledges receipt of the payment or when the seller's bank has not rejected the payment.

- For the buyer's bank, the start is when the buyer gives it the payment instruction and the process finishes when the payment has been received, or at least not immediately rejected, by the seller's bank.
- For some banks, merely sending the transaction to the ACH is enough to classify as an end point.
- For the ACH, the start is when the buyer's bank sends it the instruction and the finish is when it passes the instruction on to the seller's bank and the settlement mechanism.

Each party has a clear idea of where the process starts and finishes but they cannot agree where the endpoints are. Given this fundamental disagreement, how can SEPA hope to cover the entirety of the process?

The key to solving this technological requirement is within the phrase that defines it: end-to-end. Only by looking at the requirements at the extreme ends of the process can SEPA hope to cover the entirety of the process. This means solutions to the problems of payment initiation and reconciliation so that the organisations involved, the buyer and seller respectively, can achieve their goals from efficient processing.

The buyer must have the ability to initiate payments and while banks provide a number of solutions, it is likely that the full efficiencies and clear division of responsibility cannot be achieved without more direct access to the clearing system for the more trusted initiators of payments.

Similarly the seller must have an ability to reconcile successfully and the technological needs are for sellers to make is easy for buyers to ensure that the reference information in their payment information is correct and complete, for reference information to be sufficiently complete to allow complete automated reconciliation and finally for exceptions to be handled effectively with a single end-to-end reference for each payment. This will have most impact on the buyer and seller systems. As noted during the conversion to the euro, progress was slow until the software vendors were engaged, this cannot happen without the full involvement of the software vendors including all sources of payments.

We shall not achieve the goals of covering the entire process without the first target, inclusion, but these two aims have the potential to get the citizens and businesses of the EU to drive SEPA forward quickly.

Ubiquity: *SEPA must cover the all key payment methods the citizens, governments and businesses want to use, wherever they want to use them*

Given the initial focus on SEPA products for SEPA banks, it is not clear at the outset how customers will want to use SEPA payments. What may seem to be an unlikely or inappropriate transaction may just be awaiting the right business model to put it into context. For example, it is common in Austria and Germany to purchase rail tickets using direct debit, an idea which might appal a consumer in a different country.

Consumers and businesses will want to make the payments they must make, when they want to make them, and in the easiest way possible. Any service which supports this ability is likely to find customers, even advocates. For some payment mechanisms there are still problems to be solved around risk and ease of use upon which SEPA will have little effect, such as internet cardholder-not-present transactions where the cost of security currently outweighs the risk. Can SEPA resolve some of these issues by using regional agreements to implement appropriate technologies? Perhaps, but it is more likely that innovative commercial solutions will arise to solve or mitigate these issues.

At its outset SEPA appears to cover all the payment instruments required by the population it serves, and only time will tell whether the SEPA evolution matches the needs of its citizens.

Parity: *there is no difference in payments between countries for SEPA to the extent that national processes do not exist or, if they do, they have no bearing on how the SEPA payment is initiated, processed, settled or reconciled*

The initial intention of SEPA to be the superset of the best of all national schemes, has been compromised to allow it to become little more than the lowest common denominator. In fairness, this is the only way that the national political bodies could take up such a radical notion as SEPA, and still remain popular with their own supporters. Whilst this has led to the single Payment Services Directive, for example, it has also led to multiple national implementations and interpretations.

National payment industry bodies have made decisions on almost mandatory 'additional optional services' for their own nations, in order to maintain each country's level of efficiency, rather than trying to achieve a common level of efficiency for the SEPA area and to build upon that. It is unsurprising when the common expectation of SEPA among companies is that is should be 'just like our national system, only better and cheaper'.

This disparity between countries only serves to highlight the need for a real SEPA end-game. Until we can reach that goal, however, the industry will need solutions to paper over the cracks between the national schemes and to promote conversion to common standards and rules.

One of the areas where disparity is most obvious is within data standards, with many countries setting standards for the International Bank Account Number (IBAN) based upon different assumptions and arbitrary local choices. In some cases banks have chosen not to comply with the common method of implementation because they know that none of their branches or customers fall into particular categories. For example, if all bank accounts are unique across a branch network then the branch code is irrelevant, and therefore a bank could put the head-office branch code into the IBAN. This bank-by-bank interpretation of a national standard has led to confusion and data quality issues, which undermine the standard nature of IBAN and impede the conversion of domestic bank data to SEPA-compatible formats.

Some countries have plans to assist their corporate customers with migration of their account data from domestic format to IBAN and BIC. In some cases manual web-based utilities have been implemented. The business need is for a reliable mechanism to covert valid domestic details to valid IBAN and BIC to minimise the costs of contacting existing customers, which some organisations have estimated as a cost rising up to € 10 per customer.

Data is not the only area. The handling of mandates is another area for inconsistency between countries, with both debtor- and creditor- mandate flow being acceptable in some countries, although only creditor mandate flow is preferred. In this case it is likely that the proposed mandate management solutions discussed in the next section will impose a degree of standardisation.

For SEPA to be truly successful the disparities between the countries and banks must disappear. During the co-existence phase, this may be acceptable but convergence must be driven actively by the SEPA stakeholders to realise the main benefits. Technology can help iron out the differences but, ultimately, only political agreement can solve this problem.

Efficiency: *the system must be the most efficient possible otherwise there will inevitably be a 'New SEPA' programme to replace it, or payment initiators will move to other, more attractive payment offerings*

The main challenge to ensure an efficient SEPA is the huge investment in legacy systems that the banks and corporates continue to maintain. It would be impossible to schedule but if all customers and banks could switch across in one day to the new, more effective data formats and schemes then, at a stroke, SEPA would make business sense.

Banks have learnt that the best strategy for long-term survival is not leading but being a fast follower. This has informed their SEPA adoption strategy so far, in that the general reaction has been to do as little as necessary as late as possible. Some banks have seen SEPA's potential, and have invested to replace legacy systems and develop new services, although these are a small minority. In order to achieve the long-term SEPA we all want, it will be essential to take a strategic decision that SEPA is in banks' best interests and that the migration, painful as it may be, will be worthwhile.

What is therefore needed is a means of enabling the coexistence of the legacy systems with the new standards. Converting legacy data in real-time to meet new rules and formats will be essential to minimising the costs of migration and evolution. As new systems are developed to take advantage of more efficient SEPA payments, care must be taken to provide those mechanisms to legacy users in as cost-effective a manner as possible. Banks will have to wean their customers from pre-SEPA products, and assist them in integrating the new schemes into their business processes. This will be a painful task, but banks may find that the increased understanding they gain from their customers more than makes up for the costs of developing these consulting services.

There are also a number of key improvements which will further improve efficiency and prove the SEPA business case. For example, the consolidation of direct debit mandate handling is an area in which a number of banks are expressing interest. A single direct debit scheme across the entire SEPA region, linked to multiple clearing and settlement mechanisms (CSMs), is possibly a recipe for disaster. The issue arising will be one where no individual or organisation will know exactly which CSM might be used to provide the direct debit transaction on a given day, especially given business continuity plans which may rely on more than one CSM being available.

Direct debit mandate management should be straightforward because it is part of every direct debit scheme in existence nationally but, inevitably with new rules, country-specific additional optional services are likely to be key, especially with the unfamiliarity of IBAN and BIC codes. In addition, with more than one mandate management entity, we are in the position that some countries are in with credit reference data: companies use more than one to get a complete picture. Finally, by verifying the existence of the direct debit mandate at the start of the process, an organisation can eliminate a great proportion of transaction failures through cancelled or amended direct debit instructions.

e-invoicing is held up as a potentially huge saving for accounts payable and receivable. The EU estimates that this could represent many billions of euro's saved through the chasing of missing and misapplied payments. This is likely to be implemented as a federated scheme, with country-by-country invoicing and billing reference formats or even actual invoice numbers, if taken to the extreme. By giving the originator of a payment a higher confidence of success through e-invoicing, a number of working capital practice improvements could be made in addition to the savings. Meanwhile, it is unlikely that a single organisation could provide the sole database for all invoice formats in use, but multiple national organisations could maintain lists of invoice issuers and their formats to improve efficiency, in the same way that billing data exists for a large number of UK billing organisations.

Related areas which require single technological solutions to improve efficiency are single SEPA anti-money-laundering solutions alongside anti-fraud, credit reference checking and anti-terrorist funding solutions. Inevitably these will be driven by the large data processing organisations that provide national schemes. Perhaps, under the impetus of SEPA, these products can be harmonised and consolidated into regional or worldwide solutions which they should be.

Ultimately the greatest potential gains for users of SEPA are in the areas of operational and credit risk minimisation. By identifying problems with payments at the point of data capture, cost and risk can be eliminated. In the SEPA environment, the challenge around data is complicated by the different national IBAN formats and the multiplicity of banks participating. Further benefits could be gained by a more robust validation of payment data, in particular verification of the identity of the individual making or receiving a payment. This solves some anti-money-laundering problems and minimises the potential for fraud in the system.

Banks have also historically closely-guarded the process of payment submission and routing, as an area in which they provide additional value. As the euro clearing and settlement mechanisms consolidate, grow and harmonise, this potential to add value will decrease. This leads to two interesting implications: trusted organisations submitting SEPA transactions directly to the CSM; and the abolition of the need for BIC routing information to be provided alongside the IBAN. The first is a need for businesses to be able to take control and responsibility for their own payments processing. The second is a simple efficiency improvement though companies asking for the minimum address information, such as postcode and house number, and inferring the rest.

Businesses who submit their own payments to a CSM will benefit from being in control of what payments to submit and when, their approval process and, more importantly, their own data extraction and conversion systems.

SEPA has the potential to create great efficiency benefits, some through industry change and some through innovations created outside the banking industry. In essence many are not truly new, but developments of discussions within the payments industry. This does not, however, devalue them and, with some of the transaction cost benefits already provided, businesses will need sound commercial reasons to use SEPA. Efficiency promises financial benefits.

Uniqueness:*there can be only one set of payment mechanisms within the area*

Finally, it is assumed that all of the EU will use SEPA and that there will be no competition. While there is no restriction on a service provider setting up and competing through non-SEPA schemes within the provisions of the Payment Services Directive, it is unlikely that the investment required could be made by such a player across the whole of the EU. However, it is possible that a disruptive technology might change the way that a single country or group of countries chooses to use, or not to use, SEPA for its payment instruments.

Finland is good case in point to consider. Finland has a highly technically literate population with no professed plans to take up the SEPA Direct Debit, but to maintain its own high levels of efficiency using some form of comprehensive e-invoicing or e-billing solution as discussed in its national SEPA migration plan. For one country to support, but not to use, a SEPA scheme will not undermine the solution and yet it may set an interesting precedent.

Perhaps there are those who, unsure of migrating to the euro, decide to take up other currencies and other countries' payments mechanisms. This would create a situation whereby interchange between the two systems would become increasingly important, up to the point where the external system might threaten the stability of the SEPA system. In this case, the central banks would have to oversee it as a systemically important payment system for their country.

In reality this scenario is unlikely to occur. However, if SEPA does not take off, then there is the danger that banks may band together to provide and use new services which are more cost effective. How these services might be presented as a single payments window to the world is a simpler problem to solve than developing the commercial relationships necessary to support them.

28.1   CONCLUSION

Today we ask ourselves: 'Where is SEPA going?' We should ask instead: 'How do we get to the SEPA we want from where we are now?' The answer is in complete harmonisation and therefore greater efficiency. Only a willingness to fundamentally change will achieve this, and tools to convert formats and co-existence rules and standards are essential. Benefits can be derived from these key technological solutions, to balance the business case, and it is therefore up to vendors and banks to boldly implement these solutions to enable the full SEPA.

29

The relationship between SEPA and Anti-Money Laundering (AML)

Anthony Kirby, Chair Reference Data Subject Group and Member of the Executive Committee, ISITC

In this chapter, we return to a critical and basic foundation premise for the financial markets: banks must remember the laws of money laundering in their SEPA implementations and the issues therein. This is particularly the case as the Third Anti Money Laundering Directive has been implemented in the EU in tandem with the launch of SEPA.

With the additional superposition of the SEPA measures under the Payments Services Directive, which takes complete effect for all payment processing by D+1 by Q4 2012, it is highly advisable that money-laundering measures be treated hand-in-hand with identity management under SEPA, if banks are to save money. This is because the current focus is upon the institutions and business processes, and less on the forensic, psychological or convergence aspects.

The issues around Money Laundering are critical because the prevention of fraud lies centre stage for any government or competent authority wishing to maintain confidence in the sound working of any financial system. This proves the financial system is fit for purpose, not least against cyber attacks or in the face of determined international crime and terrorism, and should be an essential part of any banks' or Member States' SEPA plans therefore.

Money laundering is also cited as the area where the financial services industry really feels the heat according to the 2007 Kroll Global Fraud Report (see Figure 29.1).

According to the International Monetary Fund (IMF), an estimated $ 1.5 trillion of money is derived from illegal activities and is laundered through the world's financial systems each year. The cost to British businesses for fraud in 2007 was estimated as £20 billion per annum according to Ecomnet, slightly higher than the £13 billion estimate from the City of London Police in 2002. According to the research firm Celent, the five-year CAGR for identity theft costs incurred by US financial institutions grew at a staggering 29 % between 2001 and 2006. This is also corroborated by the 2007 Kroll Global Fraud Report, who found that more than 600 000 consumers become fraud victims each year in the US alone with four of the top five techniques involve financial services: opening new credit card accounts, using existing ones, opening new deposit accounts, and obtaining loans.

All of these facts and figures demonstrate the critical nature of money laundering activities in the financial industry, and the reasons why these should become an integral part of SEPA's infrastructure changes and not just an adjunct. After all, being compliant with regulations such as the PATRIOT Act in the US or Money Laundering measures in Europe doesn't make an organisation secure. In fact, the opposite is true: being secure from financial crime and identity fraud will generally make a firm compliant with regulations as a by-product. So the correct

This heat map shows which sectors feel themselves to be vulnerable to particular fraud threats. The point it makes is simple: not every industry (or even company within an industry) will face the same issues. Some threats are seen as "industry problems".

Financial services is the only industry that is perceived to face a high risk from money laundering. But it also faces high risks from regulatory and compliance breaches, information theft and conflict of interest.

High / Medium / Low	Corruption and bribery	Theft of physical assets or stock	Money laundering	Financial Misman-agement	Regulatory compliance breach	Internal financial fraud/theft	Information theft, loss or attack	Vendor, supplier or procure-ment fraud	IP theft, piracy or counter-feiting	Management conflict of interest
Construction Engineering and Infrastructure										
Consumer goods										
Financial services										
Healthcare pharmaceuticals and biotechnology										
Manufacturing										
Natural resources										
Professional svcs.										
Retail, wholesale and distribution										
Technology media and telecoms										
Travel, leisure and transportation										

Based on data from the EIU survey

Source: Kroll Global Fraud Report commissioned via Economic Intelligence Unit 2007.

Figure 29.1 Money Laundering is a key area where Financial Services Firms are most vulnerable to Fraud *Source:* Kroll Global Fraud Report commissioned via Economic Intelligence Unit 2007.

approach is to spend money on amassing a business relevant security programme, not just a compliance programme.

Furthermore, in July 2006, the US Federal Trade Commission released a proposed new rule, commonly known as the 'Red Flags Rule'. If implemented, the proposal would require banks to evidence a written identity theft programme emphasizing the detection, prevention, and mitigation of crimes which could signal the potential for identity theft, with policies, controls and procedures to address these risks. Again, these sorts of rulings are expected to come through into Europe and may be part of full SEPA, so should be considered in these early phase implementations rather than being reverse engineered later.

Current estimates behind the costs of preparation for SEPA spanning activities, such as the above in the EU and EEA, range from anything up to US$ 6.5 billion as a cumulative figure, and these preparations are inclusive of preparations for client on-boarding, transaction management and identity management if firms are to make the best use of automation.

Therefore, it is clear that financial institutions will generally absorb much of the economic loss from this kind of fraud and factor these losses into the costs of doing business. This is why banks should focus upon minimising their exposures as they introduce their SEPA products and services.

However, this may not be enough as there are challenges from new forms of interactions including e-commerce breaches, mobile payments, and easier access to customer information through services such as Skype and Facebook. The result is that banks have to find better methods to enable trust and authentication with the basic questions: 'are you who they say you are?' and 'are you authorised to do what you are trying to do?'

The good news is that innovations in IT have made it easier to exchange, store, cross-reference and retrieve information. Just as identity management and authentication is mission-critical to the workings of SWIFT and IdenTrust, it remains clear that identity management and evidencing will be equally critical to mitigate theft and fraud from individuals and companies, and the banks that serve them in the e-sphere.

This is why the top 100 European Banks were expected to pay over € 3 billion to comply with SEPA's measures according to Accenture in 2006, with 40 % of bank respondents expecting to invest between € 11 million and € 50 million for ACH-type capabilities over the next five years. What banks did not necessarily bargain for is the cost of revamping their identity management systems to cope with retail and private clients, so the above figures may well be understated in relation to the total spend required under SEPA.

The scope of this chapter therefore focuses less on the detailed changes to processes or systems under the various stages or SEPA, but the fact that the staging of SEPA allows for harmonised approaches to credit transfer, direct debits and card schemes. The mandated changes will be staged, starting with revamping of BIC and IBAN codes to coincide with moves to further connectivity between the central banks as part of TARGET II.

SEPA also requires a class of unregulated entities to be authorised as payment service providers, which resonates with the need to reinforce identity management per the Third Money Laundering Directive's procedures. Payment service providers are likely to include not just banks and electronic-money issuers, who are currently authorised, but also businesses that are at present unregulated and who would be required to be authorised under the Payment Services Directive (PSD).

29.1   WHAT IS MONEY LAUNDERING?

Before we launch into detail, we need to first be clear on our definition of money laundering. Money laundering is a complex process involving at least three processes which must occur simultaneously:

- **Placement**: physically placing bulk cash proceeds;
- **Layering**: separating the proceeds from their criminal origins through layers of complex financial transactions; and
- **Integration**: providing an apparently legitimate explanation for the illicit proceeds.

At a high level, firms are most susceptible to risk in the wholesale markets from the 'layering' and 'integration' stages of money laundering. However, not all schemes are immediately obvious. For example, money laundering can be manifested as a series of unusually large international cash transactions or collateral transfers; suspicious account activities especially those involving tax havens; a desire for clearing and settlement arrangements outside the norm such as non book-entry transfers; or the sale of high-value, particularly illiquid, goods. In fact, even unexpected or inconsistent behaviours can be grounds for reasonable suspicion for the Money Laundering Reporting Officer (MLRO).

The historic approach to AML was rule-based, with procedures pioneered in the US. The Financial Action Task Force (FATF) was established in the early 1990's and established 40 principles covering the treatment of money laundering. Since then, there have been two EU Money Laundering Directives, and specific legislation brought out in the UK to counter money laundering and help firms manage their risks. These include the Terrorism Act (2000), The

Proceeds of Crime Act (2002) and the Money Laundering Regulations of 2003 and 2007 within the FSA's Handbook.

With industry guidance also emanating from both the Wolfsberg Group for private banking, the Joint Money Laundering Steering Group in the UK, and likely future guidance per the European Payments Council and the European Banking Federation to come under SEPA, the casual observer will be forgiven for feeling that the financial sector is over-burdened by needing to comply with an excess of overlapping measures.

29.2 WHAT IS THE THIRD MONEY LAUNDERING DIRECTIVE (MLD III) AND WHY IS THE TERM 'BENEFICIAL OWNER' IMPORTANT?

The Third Money Laundering Directive (MLD III), implemented on 15 December 2007, aims to deliver consistency under the banner of a principles-based regulation (see Figure 29.2).

MLD III introduces a new risk-based, proportionate approach across a list of sectors, replacing the Second Money Laundering Directive (MLD II) which was implemented as recently as 2003. MLD III makes transaction monitoring a mandatory legal requirement, with firms needing to scrutinise transactions and also keep documentation and customer information up-to-date.

Firms will most likely need to analyse system performance at a transaction-by-transaction level, and perform detailed mapping between the number of alerts they experience versus the number of suspicious activity reports they generate. On account of the principles-based nature of the Directive, firms will need to have a clear demarcation of responsibilities and benchmark themselves against their peers.

The Third Money Laundering Directive (MLD III) takes effect 15 December 2007. It introduces a new principles-driven, risk-based approach across a list of sectors, replacing the MLD II enacted 2003

MLD III Origins			
1970–1990s	2000–2002	2003	15 December 2007
US Bank Secrecy Acts 1970/1985; US ML Control Act 1986; US Crime Control Act 1990; FATF established 1993; MLD I enacted 1993	UK Terrorism Act 2000; Wolfsberg Group 2000 and Principles 2002; PATRIOT Act/N2 2001; US OFAC publication 2002; UK Proceeds of Crime Act 2002	MLD II applicable; JMLSG becomes company limited by guarantee	EU MLD III takes effect

Key dates

Source Accenture 2007

Figure 29.2 Third Money Laundering Directive (MLD III or 2005/60/EC) in Summary *Source:* Accenture 2007.

MLD III applies to financial and other key services sectors, as well as providers of any goods where payments are made in excess of € 15 000 in cash.[1] Those subject to the measures under MLD III are expected to co-operate in the fight against money laundering by taking various measures to establish customers' identities, assess the risks, monitor transactions, report suspicions and set up preventive systems within their organisations. Firms therefore will have a duty to 'recognise, resolve and report' suspicious activities involving transactions, and apply such measures to their branches and subsidiaries outside the territory of the EU/EEA.

New activities under MLD III consist of at least five factors:

- A principles and proportionate assessment approach which recognises differences between sectors, in contrast to existing rules enforced at national level. Financial institutions will need to apply EU/EEA standards to foreign branches and subsidiaries outside EU/EEA territory. These practices will need to be revised under any PSD/SEPA framework.
- A new governance, with senior management engaging in the process and 'owning' the risk-based approach. This means that management are accountable for the approval of risk assessment decisions. If there are interbank or third party processors in the loop, then these aspects will require revisiting.
- The emphasised role of the MLRO and the responsibilities of the same as part of the 'reliance' process within a dynamic Client Due Diligence (CDD) process, with on-going monitoring and record-keeping, although the responsibility for CDD remains with the firm that relies upon it.
- A strengthened focus on a risk-sensitive approach to AML procedures pre- and post-SEPA, including mandatory transaction reporting and correct entity identification through explicit formalisation of 'beneficial ownership', 'business relationships', 'reliance on other regulated firms' such as lawyers, accountants and other third parties.
- Government guidance with regard to published details of suspicious activity reports (SARs), prosecutions etc. These aspects will require continuous attention and review for retail, private and particularly corporate clients, once SEPA begins to take effect.

The fact that there have been two precursors to MLD III might have lulled banks into thinking this is more of the same. Other banks may dispute the connection between MLD III and preparations for SEPA. In both cases, these banks would be wrong. MLD III consolidates both prior Money Laundering Directives (MLDs) of 1993 and 2003 respectively so it's worth a brief review of those earlier Directives to understand the context behind MLD III better (see Figure 29.3).

The First MLD was implemented in the original 15 core EU countries, and covered Credit institutions, financial institutions,[2] and EU-based branches of the above including head offices based outside the EU. MLD I required firms to identify their customers when entering into business relations such as opening accounts or providing safe custody facilities, handling single or linked transactions of more than € 15 000, or whenever there was suspicion of money laundering irrespective of amount.

MLD I covered a wide scope from activities such as money transmission, lending and leasing, issuing and administering credit cards, trading on own account, providing advice to undertakings, and safekeeping and custody were all covered by its measures. From a legal

---

[1] This figure should be compared with the threshold figure of € 10 000 declaration limit under the 'Control of Cash (Penalties) 207' measures which came into force on 15 June 2007.
[2] As defined by the 1st and 2nd Banking Co-ordination Directives (77/780/EEC and 89/646/EEC).

point of view, however, it is interesting to note that in 1993, the term 'Money laundering' per se was limited by the definition of criminal activity in Article 3.1a of the Vienna Convention. This limitation restricted money laundering to activity involving the proceeds of drug-related offences, such as transferring property knowingly derived from criminal activity with the aim of concealing the origin of the property or assisting any person involved therewith, including the commission of such an activity, including the counselling, aiding or abetting any of the above.

As such, the definition did not capture activities funding acts of terrorism and was in urgent need of overhaul after 9/11. This overhaul was duly delivered by the Second Money Laundering Directive (MLD II) in 2003.

In July 2003 in the UK, for example, the FSA issued a statement on identification of existing customers as a part of risk-assessment and mitigation, and recommended that firms should consider the money laundering risks posed by existing customers who had not been identified. The FSA recommended that the approach taken to obtaining missing information should be risk-based and proportionate. Further preparations under SEPA will require that firms have appropriate systems and controls in place to monitor, manage and review changes to credit by 2008, debit by 2009 and Chip and PIN card arrangements by 2010.

Four years later, the Third Money Laundering Directive (MLD III) has the potential to create unintended consequences which could cause banks to question their modus operandi per MLD I and II, and could also trigger the entire debate into standardising Business Entity Identifiers (BEIs) because of the requirement to specify beneficial owner information where this is needed. More about that later. Meanwhile, it is clear that new Customer Due Diligence (CDD) mechanisms are needed, requiring institutions to identify and verify the identity of their customer and of the beneficial owner, for example, individuals with an interest in at least 25 %

	Firms Affected/Triggers	Activities in Scope	Timing/Countries	Definitions
Scope of MLD I 1993	• Credit institutions • Financial institutions* • EU-based branches of the above (including head offices based outside the EU) • Requires firms to identify their customers when: • Entering into business relations e.g. opening accounts, providing safe custody facilities etc • Handling single (or linked) transactions > ?15000 • There is suspicion of money laundering (irrespective of the amount)	• Lending • Financial Leasing • Money Transmission Svcs. • Issuing/Administering means of Payment e.g. Credit Cards • Guarantees/Commitments • Trading on Own Account or Customers in Treasury/ Transferable Securities • Advice to undertakings in capital structure or portfolio management • Safekeeping and Custody	• Implemented 1st January 1993 in the original 15 core EU countries – Member States to determine a) what Sanctions to be adopted and b) how to impose and enforce the obligations	• "Money laundering" limited by the definition of criminal activity in Art3(1)(a) of the Vienna Convention – restricted to activity involving the proceeds of drug-related offences • Converting or transferring property which is knowingly derived from criminal activity with the aim of concealing or disguising the origin of the property or assisting any person involved in the commission of such an activity • Concealing or disguising the nature, source, location etc. of property that is known to be derived from criminal activity • Acquiring, possessing or using property which is known to be derived from criminal activity • Participating in, attempting to commit or facilitating, counselling, aiding or abetting the commission of any of the above
Extra Scope of MLD II 2003	• Investment firms as defined by the ISD now expressly included in the definition of a financial institution e.g. activities above and receipt/transmission of orders in Financial Futures, Swaps, FRAs etc.	• CIV undertakings marketing their units/shares • Auditors, tax advisers, external accountants, real-estate agents, lawyers and notaries (certain activities), dealers in high value good, auctioneers and casinos	• Adopted 15th June 2003 • Followed implementation of CJA 1993, Terrorism Act 2000 and Proceeds of Crime Act 2002 in the UK	• Wider definition of "Money laundering" through changes to 'criminal activity' so it extends beyond drugs-related offences to criminal activity generally, including serious fraud and corruption • Express reference made to the activities of bureaux de change and money remittance offices
Extra Scope of MLD III 2007	• [The Beneficial Owner of a customer is defined as the natural person who ultimately controls the customer or on whose behalf a transaction or activity is being conducted. For corporate customers, the beneficial owner shall at least include the natural person(s) who ultimately controls the customer through direct or indirect ownership or control of a sufficient percentage of shares or votes in the customer (> 25% typically)]	• Applicable additionally to lawyers, notaries, trust and company service providers, and providers of goods to the extent that payments are made in cash in excess of ?15000	• To be adopted 15th Dec 2007 in EU 27 Member States including the 14 accession states from Eastern Europe • Member States required to establish appropriate penalties for breaches of national provisions	• Explicitly prohibits Money laundering and Terrorist financing • New Customer Due Diligence (CDD). Institutions to identify and verify the identity of their customer and of the beneficial owner (where applicable); institutions to also obtain information on the purpose and intended nature of a business relationship • Institutions to monitor transactions with the customer on an ongoing basis while taking into account a risk-based approach and conduct new checks where there are doubts about the veracity of previously obtained data • Institutions to report to the national authorities any suspicions of money laundering or terrorist financing • Institutions to take supporting measures such as recordkeeping, training of personnel and the establishment of internal policies and procedures

*As defined the 1st and 2nd Banking Co-ordination Directives (77/780/EEC and 89/646/EEC).

Figure 29.3 What has Changed between the various Money Laundering Directives? *As defined by the 1st and 2nd Banking Co-ordination Directives (77/780/EEC and 89/646/EEC).

of the capital of the company. This is not merely a static, once-off exercise to be completed at client take-on as part of Know Your Client (KYC) checks, but the monitoring of customer transactions on an ongoing basis, taking into account a risk-sensitive approach and conducting new checks where there are doubts about the veracity of previously obtained data.

29.3   CLIENT DUE DILIGENCE (CDD) – HOW MUCH IS ENOUGH FOR MLD III IN A POST-SEPA WORLD?

Some firms are already complaining that there is a fine line between serving the customer well and acting as a police officer under MLD III. This demonstrates that there is a need to balance the need to know to enforce the law against the right to privacy and confidentiality of customers. Given the breadth, complexity and range of products and customer types, it is not surprising that most firms experience particular difficulties when conducting risk assessments under their KYC and client on-boarding processes. These changes will necessitate that banks make changes to their core systems and internal operations, make changes to relationships with agencies and payments processors, and be implemented at a time when banks will face some revenue losses as a result of declines in both domestic and cross-border revenues.

KYC and client on-boarding are more than ticking boxes. They are an entire end-to-end management process to enable identities to be established and evidenced during any aspect of a transaction. Document management is a particular pain point. For example, banks spent over 30–35 % of their budget in preparing for MIFID on conduct of business and client classification measures, not including the recordkeeping costs. It is not unreasonable to assume that banks will need to commit a comparable level of budget under SEPA, to handle electronic transfer schemes such as credit transfers for their retail and corporate clients, especially weighted towards countries where the complexity factors are likely to be higher such as Italy, Spain and Germany.

Under SEPA, corporates located across multiple centres across the EU could need just one bank and, at least in principle, one format to cover all their Euro-based payments. As such, these corporates stand to be the biggest winners from SEPA in the short term. All corporates will be expected to make the necessary investments to adapt to new payment products and modify internal processes. As a result, many believe that there will be benefits if liquidity and payment operations are managed from one account as this will allow payment operations to be consolidated with greater efficiencies across the accounts payable and receivable processes, leading to likely reductions in payment prices. This will be particularly true if matching rates are higher in a SEPA-type environment through the use of common standards and market practices through the use of IBANs and TWIST.

From the banking perspective, things won't be quite so rosy. Typical banks take their corporate clients through at least three different kinds of checks before entering into a business transaction. Many corporate clients are not established household names with entities spanning various centres but are smaller corporates, where a considerable level of CDD is required. Another factor is related to establishing a commercial relationship that enables the bank to market to their customers, for example by gathering:

29.3.1   Basic details and investment objectives (commercial reasons):

- customer's legal entity details and proof of address;
- collecting client data to anticipate and personalise the customer experience with regard to evolving needs (e.g. trading or investment patterns);

- collecting market data to increase selling opportunities (e.g. expected turnover for companies, sources of wealth for private banking or retail clients, trading patterns) on an ongoing basis;
- collecting data to improve convenience, efficiency and customer loyalty.

29.3.2   Checks needed to protect the bank and the customer with regard to risk:

- detailed review of the customer's credit history (e.g. Experian ratings);
- ensuring the customer has sufficient collateral to meet its liabilities;
- validating the risk balance of the customer is maintained with regard to investments;
- ensuring that the customer has sufficient liquidity on call to meet investment commitments.

29.3.3   Checks needed for regulatory and/or compliance reasons:

- details of notarised passports as proof of individual identity, proof of address, certificate of incorporation and Articles of association (if a company/corporation);
- list of beneficial owners and List of who is authorised to transact (if a company or corporation);
- detailed checks on both management and shareholders to identify if the company appears on a sanctions list;
- details of investment objectives, e.g. suitability/appropriateness tests per the investment vehicle or the method of transacting respectively (MiFID L1 Arts. 19(4/5)).

Knowing the customer through correct authentication of their identity is a marketing advantage, and many corporates such as supermarkets or VISA are leading the way with loyalty and transaction card schemes. They are challenging banks given their greater respective understanding the dynamics of how supply chain management works.

On the other hand, firms can be forgiven for thinking that they are on something of an identity verification treadmill. For example, in 2005, Dunn & Bradstreet found that every hour:

- 63 new businesses open their doors;
- 4 companies change their names;
- 8 corporations file for Bankruptcy;
- 112 directorship (CEO, CFO, etc.) changes will occur;
- 240 business addresses change;
- 150 business telephone numbers change or are disconnected;
- 285 businesses have a suit, lien or judgment filed against them.

According to Dunn & Bradstreet, 17 % of business names will change, 21 % of CEO's will change, 20 % of all addresses change and 18 % of telephone numbers will change every year.

In such a pace of change in a post-SEPA world, banks can respond by using the regulatory challenges of MLD III and SEPA to raise their game by broadening their existing CDD programmes. This will involve obtaining and recording Know Your Customer (KYC) information on all customers, not just limited to identification documents but to also understanding the customer's business, expected turnover, sources of wealth, trading patterns, ownership, and so forth, on an ongoing basis.

Adopting a risk-based approach in relation to the categorisation, monitoring and authentication of customers will be required under MLD III and SEPA, with customers categorised into either higher or lower risks. Enhanced CDD will be required for those customers classified as 'high risk' and simplified CDD will apply for certain categories of customers deemed as 'low risk'.

Some of these ratings for companies will be obtained from the ratings or credit agencies, such as Standard & Poor's, Moody's, Fitch and Experian, and these ratings will need to be flagged and recorded for evidencing purposes, with the rating system maintained on an ongoing basis. Given the current climate in the markets, owing to the sub-prime and credit market crunch, extra vigilance seems particularly likely and on-going to monitor higher risk customers.

29.4 SANCTIONS – COUNTRIES, COMPANIES, POLITICALLY-EXPOSED PERSONS PER MLD III...

At present, the main means by which to identify and authenticate terrorist funds is for governments to identify those connected to terrorist activities and to provide lists, known as financial sanctions or terrorist lists, to financial institutions in order that the information on the lists can be checked against client databases. Where positive matches occur, the funds or payments must be frozen and the relevant external authority advised immediately. The mechanism for transposing the lists into financial institutions in Europe is by Council Regulations, which attach financial sanctions to named persons and entities.

Sanctions lists have been received by financial institutions following 11 September 2001, and are continually updated and republished at a country, corporation and person level. For example, Factiva reported in August 2007 that 'the US justice department and other authorities (had) stepped up investigations into several large European banks for violating US sanctions against Iran, Libya, Cuba and Sudan. A number of the banks, whose names (had) not been disclosed, came under investigation by authorities including the Treasury, when they alerted the government to potential violations after a landmark money-laundering settlement by ABN AMRO in 2005, according to people familiar with the matter. The Dutch bank was fined $ 80 million by the Treasury's Office of Foreign Assets Control, state regulators and the Federal Reserve, after it emerged that its US offices had processed wire transfers that originated from Bank Melli Iran and engaged in transfers involving Libya'.

Firms will need to conduct enhanced ongoing monitoring of their business relationships with their customers on an ongoing basis. Sanctions lists are maintained by competent authorities such as the Office of Foreign Assets Control (OFAC, part of the US Department of the Treasury), the Bank of England, the Commission de Surveillance du Secteur Financier (CSSF), the Hong Kong Monetary Authority (HKMA) or the Monetary Authority of Singapore (MAS) are there to help firms to do this.

Other watch lists are maintained on Databases such as Worldcheck or Factiva. These watch lists can assist banks evaluate whether they are at risk from risk to the activities from suspicious companies or from exposures to politically exposed persons (PEPs). This will include enhanced monitoring of the transactions conducted by PEPs and other 'high risk' customers, as well as conducting ongoing CDD to ensure that all customers are risk classified correctly, especially as their circumstances may change.

While some of this seems like business as usual, the requirement to check watch lists is not limited to the mere checking of client databases. MLD III requirements extend to the checking and mapping of the lists against remitter and beneficiary details on payments, as well as the principals behind non-personal relationships including directors, signatories, beneficial owners and more. Putting procedures in place to identify and monitor relationships with politically exposed persons is a particular challenge, as it is identifying beneficial owners where discretion has been the status quo especially within historic private banking practices in certain countries such as Lichtenstein, for example.

Enhanced CDD will need to be applied for those customers identified as politically exposed such that they will be treated as a high risk customer. In order to assist identification of these persons, a list of PEPs is required and needs integrating into matching tools for periodic reconciliation. It is also envisaged that a bank would need to perform an automated batch check to match names for all new customers against the PEPs lists within 24 hours of the customer's account being opened, as a minimum performance standard.

In summary, under MLD III, banks will need to raise their game to apply the appropriate screening and filtering checks at client take-on and during KYC checks. This is necessary for commercial, risk management and regulatory reasons, and better screening will also lead to downstream operational efficiencies for the straight through processing of information.

These are areas that should be incorporated into the systems refreshments that banks are undertaking for SEPA as the two go hand-in-hand. The danger otherwise is that banks will need to reverse engineer and incorporate these changes downstream, which will be even more costly and difficult to operate. By incorporating these changes now, banks can implement a one-change efficient new structure.

The facts are that banks need to record adjacent information, such as 'beneficial owner' and assess ancillary parties to the process including lawyers, whilst maintaining an audit trail. Firms will need to combine these KYC measures with credit and suitability and appropriateness checks, and it is sensible to approach these tasks holistically.

There are also downstream dynamic aspects to managing money-laundering with regard to tracking and reporting suspicions. These aspects are considered in more detail as below.

29.5   EXAMPLES OF SUSPICIOUS ACTIVITIES

It is generally agreed that a MLRO will regard the following types of activities as creating grounds for suspicion.

29.5.1   Incomplete Information Granted at Customer On-boarding

- A customer who opens an account without proper references,[3] or who refuses to provide any other relevant information the bank requires when opening an account.
- A customer who presents unusual or suspicious identification documents that the bank cannot readily verify.
- A customer whose home phone is disconnected or who provides mobile phone details only.
- A customer who includes no record of past or present employment on a loan application.
- A customer who has no record of past or present employment but makes frequent large transactions.
- A customer who is unwilling to provide personal background information when opening an account or purchasing monetary instruments above a specified threshold.
- A business that is reluctant to provide complete information or disguises information regarding the purpose of the business, prior banking relationships, officers or directors, beneficial owners, or its location.

---

[3] Proper references include proof of a local address on a utility bill as well as official identification papers such as a passport, foreign registration card, driver's licence or social security card.

- A company reluctant to reveal details about its activities or to provide financial statements.
- A company that refuses to provide information to qualify customers for credit or other banking services.

29.5.2 Suspicious Behaviours

- An account that is opened with sudden withdrawals, or behaviour such as receiving wire transfers and immediately purchasing monetary instruments prepared for payment to a third party including bi-directional arrangements.
- Activities in recently inactive or dormant accounts or excessive balance queries associated with the same.
- An account which shows several deposits below a specified money laundering threshold made at cash machines, or attempted repeated high-velocity ATM withdrawals.
- Deposits in high risk instruments, repeated loss-making trades or sudden requests to securitise loans as structured products, for example under Collateralised Debt Obligations.
- A customer who is reluctant to provide the information needed for a mandatory report, to have the report filed, or to proceed with a transaction after being informed that the report must be filed.
- Any individual or group that coerces or attempts to coerce a bank employee to not file any required record-keeping or reporting forms.
- A customer who purchases a number of money orders, or traveller's cheques for large amounts just under a specified money laundering threshold or without apparent reason, for example under $ 10 000 in the USA or € 15 000 in the EU.
- An increase in the amount of cash handled without a corresponding increase in the number of currency transaction reports filed.
- A company or new customer that asks to be placed on the bank's list of customers exempt from currency transaction reporting requirements.
- A customer who makes cash movements over agreed limits or frequently requests increases in exemption limits.
- A change of customer's address followed closely by an urgent request for additional or multiple credit cards.
- A company that presents financial statements noticeably different from those of similar businesses.
- Significant or sudden changes in transaction amounts, frequency, cash in/out, dormant accounts or currency shipment patterns between correspondent banks.

29.5.3 Cash Deposit or Money Transmission Suspicions

- Client or in-house company accounts, such as trust and escrow accounts, that show substantial cash deposits.
- Accounts that show frequent large bill transactions around deposits, withdrawals or monetary instrument purchases, without a business reason or accounts that show frequent large bill transactions for a business that generally does not deal in large amounts of cash.
- A single, substantial cash deposit composed of many £50 or $ 100 bills with frequent exchanges of small bills for large bills or vice versa.
- Large deposits from the cashing of casino chips or regular significant proceeds from on-line betting agencies

- Corporate accounts, where deposits or withdrawals are primarily in cash rather than cheque.
- Significant turnover in large denomination bills that are uncharacteristic for the bank's location, such as € 500 bills in certain accession states.
- A large increase in small denomination bills and a corresponding decrease in large denomination bills, with no currency transaction report filings.
- Rapid increase in size and frequency of cash deposits, without any corresponding increase in non-cash deposits.
- A customer who operates a retail business and provides a cheque cashing service, but does not make large withdrawals of cash against checks deposited.
- Unusual cash purchases of money orders and cheques or inconsistent change in currency transactions or patterns.
- Accounts with a large volume of deposits in cashier's cheques, money orders, and/or wire transfers, when the nature of the accountholder's business does not justify such activity.
- Retail deposits of numerous cheques, but rare withdrawals for daily operations.
- A business owner, such as a one-location store owner, who makes several deposits on the same day at different bank branches or sudden withdrawal transactions of similar amounts via credit card for example.
- An account that shows unusually large deposits of vouchers or other stamps, which are sometimes used as currency in exchange for narcotics.
- An account or customer that has frequent deposits of large amounts of currency wrapped in currency straps that have been stamped by other banks.
- A customer who suddenly pays down a large problem loan with no reasonable explanation of the source of funds, or a customer who purchases travellers' cheques or financial products with large amounts of cash.
- A customer that has frequent deposits of musty or extremely dirty bills.

29.5.4 Offshore and Overseas Suspicions

- The sending or receiving of frequent or large volumes of wire transfers or money transmissions to and from offshore locations, notably tax havens.
- Depositing funds into several accounts, usually in amounts below a reportable threshold, and then consolidating into a master account and transferring them outside of the country.
- Instructing the bank to transfer funds abroad and to expect an equal incoming wire transfer from other sources.
- An account that sends and receives wire transfers, especially to or from bank-haven countries, without an apparent business reason or when inconsistent with the customer's business or history.
- An account that receives many small incoming wire transfers or makes deposits using checks and money orders, and almost immediately wire transfers all but a token amount to another city or country, when such activity is not consistent with the customer's business or history.
- Regularly depositing or withdrawing large amounts by wire transfers to or from or through countries that are known sources of narcotics, or whose bank secrecy laws facilitate the laundering of money.
- Money transmissions or wiring the proceeds of a cash deposit to another country, without changing the form of currency.
- An account opened in the name of *a casa de cambio* (money exchange house) that receives wire transfers and/or structured deposits.

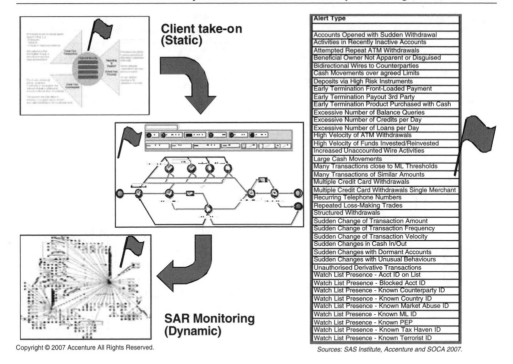

The table in the figure lists the following Alert Types:

Alert Type
Accounts Opened with Sudden Withdrawal
Activities in Recently Inactive Accounts
Attempted Repeat ATM Withdrawals
Beneficial Owner Not Apparent or Disguised
Bidirectional Wires to Counterparties
Cash Movements over agreed Limits
Deposits via High Risk Instruments
Early Termination Front-Loaded Payment
Early Termination Payout 3rd Party
Early Termination Product Purchased with Cash
Excessive Number of Balance Queries
Excessive Number of Credits per Day
Excessive Number of Loans per Day
High Velocity of ATM Withdrawals
High Velocity of Funds Invested/Reinvested
Increased Unaccounted Wire Activities
Large Cash Movements
Many Transactions close to ML Thresholds
Many Transactions of Similar Amounts
Multiple Credit Card Withdrawals
Multiple Credit Card Withdrawals Single Merchant
Recurring Telephone Numbers
Repeated Loss-Making Trades
Structured Withdrawals
Sudden Change of Transaction Amount
Sudden Change of Transaction Frequency
Sudden Change of Transaction Velocity
Sudden Changes in Cash In/Out
Sudden Changes with Dormant Accounts
Sudden Changes with Unusual Behaviours
Unauthorised Derivative Transactions
Watch List Presence - Acct ID on List
Watch List Presence - Blocked Acct ID
Watch List Presence - Known Counterparty ID
Watch List Presence - Known Country ID
Watch List Presence - Known Market Abuse ID
Watch List Presence - Known ML ID
Watch List Presence - Known PEP
Watch List Presence - Known Tax Haven ID
Watch List Presence - Known Terrorist ID

Sources: SAS Institute, Accenture and SOCA 2007.

Figure 29.4   Example of AML Monitoring Framework including 'Red Flags' *Source:* SAS Institute, Accenture and SOCA 2007.

- A request for loans to an offshore company, especially one located in a haven country, or for a loan secured by obligations of an offshore bank.
- An account to which money orders carrying unusual symbols or stamps are deposited by post.

The items above represent a dizzy plethora of the types of activities which MLROs need to look for in monetary transactions. In addition, the 'Red Flags' proposal touted by the US Federal Trade Commission should also be considered, as it covers over thirty patterns, practices, and suspicious activities which could signal – red flag – the potential for identity theft in connection with account opening, money transmission or credit and debit card usage (see Figure 29.4).

Fortunately there are numerous vendor solutions which can assist with tracking suspicious activities against pre-specified watch list criteria. There are also two sets of market practices and principles which can assist, issued from the Wolfsberg Group from 2000 and the Joint Money Laundering Steering Group (JMLSG) from 2003 respectively.

The merits of each approach are covered below.

29.6   THE WOLFSBERG GROUP

The Wolfsberg Group (http://www.wolfsberg-principles.com) is an association of twelve global banks, which aims to develop financial services industry standards and related products for KYC, AML and Counter Terrorist Financing policies. The Wolfsberg Group has emphasised the link between money laundering risk and corruption in private banking arrangements by

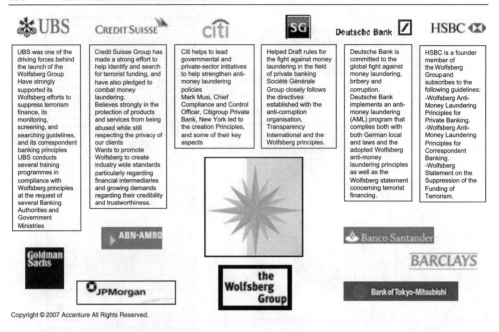

Copyright © 2007 Accenture All Rights Reserved.

Figure 29.5   The Wolfsberg Group's Founders

stating that 'transactions involving the proceeds of corruption often follow patterns of behaviour common to money laundering associated with other criminal activities'.

The Wolfsberg AML Principles for Private Banking were published in October 2000, and revised in May 2002. The Group published a Statement on the Financing of Terrorism in January 2002, and also released the Wolfsberg AML Principles for Correspondent Banking in November 2002. The Wolfsberg Group's most recent Statement, on Monitoring Screening and Searching, was published in September 2003. In addition to the 12 founding banks shown in Figure 29.5, Allied Irish Bank, DBS, Lloyds, TSB, SEB and Standard Chartered Bank have also participated in the development of guidance and rules.

Standards in a number of the particular areas have yet to be fully articulated by lawmakers or regulators although the Wolfsberg Group of banks has been actively working on four separate papers recently, all of which aim to provide guidance with regard to a number of areas of AML banking activities. The four papers are:

- Guidance on a Risk Based Approach for Managing Money Laundering Risks;
- Anti-Money Laundering Guidance for Mutual Funds and Other Pooled Investment Vehicles;
- FAQs on Correspondent Banking (supplementing the previous principles);
- FAQs on Correspondent Banking (supplementing the previous principles).

29.7   THE JOINT MONEY LAUNDERING STEERING GROUP (JMLSG)

The Joint Money Laundering Steering Group (JMLSG) is an industry-led forum created by 16 founding trade associations from a British Banking Association (BBA) committee. In late

2003, the JMLSG became a company limited by guarantee and, since then, the JMLSG has become an integral part of the UK scene for two reasons. Firstly, the JMLSG includes several specialists who know how the industry works; and secondly, the JMLSG has worked closely with both the FSA and HM Treasury during the drafting process for MLD III.

The JMLSG features a Money Laundering Advisory Committee (MLAC), an editorial panel, the communications committee, and other ad hoc groups. Fortunately JMLSG guidance is very detailed with regard to the recommended treatment of different groups of customers. The relevant JMLSG Sectorial Guidance is also detailed, and is available for firms through their website http://www.jmlsg.org.

Explicit guidance is provided on monitoring and how to establish beneficial ownership; how to conduct CDD on a risk-sensitive basis; scenario modelling to establish which cases warrant enhanced due diligence; and where to go to obtain statistics on the effectiveness of SARS, prosecutions and so forth.

Aside from these two groups, this leaves the paucity of case law as the only factor which is missing in assisting the MLRO in completing their duties. Again, it should be stressed that all of these factors and considerations are ones that I would promote as a part of a bank's SEPA implementation plans, as the MLD III and the PSD really go hand-in-hand. This is illustrated by the implications of both of these Directives on Reference Data.

29.8   THE REFERENCE DATA DIMENSION

Unambiguous identifiers for business and legal entity identification are essential across a wide range of pre- and post- trade operational and regulatory processes. These identifiers are needed, for example, to help identify and evidence activities such as due diligence during client take-on, KYC and AML compliance, legal agreements, counterparty and credit risk management, and counterparty identification for orders, trades, settlement, and reporting. As mentioned earlier, establishing and authenticating the beneficial owners of non-personal relationships, including the appropriate principals, needs to be identified, verified and recorded on the relevant client databases specifically for MLD III. Further reinforcement will be needed in a post-SEPA landscape.

The need to identify and authenticate business and legal entities, and parent and child hierarchies, is core to MLD III and other regulatory compliance measures such as MiFID, Basel II Pillar II and SEPA (see Figure 29.6).

Historically, the question of entity identifiers had been addressed by ISO, SWIFT, GSTPA, Omgeo, CLS and others. In 2000, for example, SWIFT worked on a draft proposal including the creation of new code to identify business entities, rather than using an envelope mechanism for already existing national or international identifiers as proposed in ISO 13735. Original proposals were put before the SWIFT Board to re-examine the case for basing the BEI on the BIC. The only problem was that this solution had been rejected by SWIFT itself earlier on, as likely to overwhelm the existing BIC scheme capacity. However, the future expansion of BIC codes is envisaged under current consideration, as the SWIFT community feels this to be expeditious.

These endeavours defined a 'Business Entity' as an entity that is either regulated or upon which due diligence is necessary under any jurisdiction. The scope of The Reference Data User Group's (RDUG's) work was limited to entities comprising institutional securities market participants such as broker dealers, clearers, custodians, investment managers, CSDs, exchanges, industry utilities, charities, local and national governments, supra-national bodies,

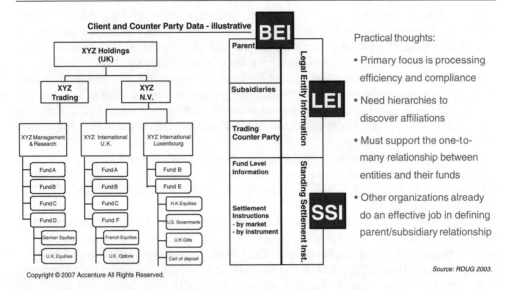

Figure 29.6   Sample Hierarchy showing parent and child relationships *Source:* RDUG 2003.

and corporate treasuries. Regrettably the scope of RDUG's work in 2004 and 2005 only touched on the subject of identity management, but the principles can be illustrated at a high level using the schematic shown in Figure 29.7.

With expertise in this field available from supplier constituencies, such as IdentTrust and SWIFT, more work can be done. For example, the work on Business Entity Identification (BEI) culminated in a White Paper issued by RDUG in 2004, which proposed approaches towards

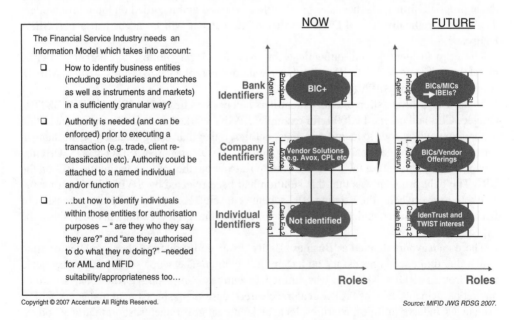

Figure 29.7   AML Fraud can be managed at a macro or a micro level *Source:* MIFID JWG RDSG 2007.

instrument and business entity standards ostensibly to meet the reference data needs of MIFID, rather than MLD III.

ISO's TC68/SC4 Working Group 8, referred to as 'ISO WG8' in shorthand, was subsequently tasked with defining the International Business Entity Identification (IBEI) thus: 'IBEI is a global scheme for uniquely identifying business entities playing a role in the lifecycle of, and events related to, a financial instrument'. ISO WG8 has published a standard entitled ISO 16372 in two parts: first, a scheme for identifying business entities through an IBEI code scheme, ISO 16732-1; and second, proposed management procedures for managing an IBEI database, ISO 16372-2. These ISO papers highlighted the fact that the generation and maintenance of IBEI records could involve several organisations cooperating with one another during the initial assignment of such records, as well as the long-term support of the IBEI registration and publication infrastructure. Examples might include the Registration Authority, Trusted Source, Sponsor, and Subscriber.

ISO 16372 proposed a code structure and a set of criteria such as a centralised database, but the open issue was who should be the registration authority and how would the facility best be funded. In the absence of an appetite to create a central registration agency, the next best step was to invite reference data facilitators to try to establish cross-referencing mechanisms. National numbering agencies (NNAs) also began to mobilise at the start of 2007, to produce BEIs for companies admitted to listing on regulated markets.

Despite efforts all round, there does not appear to be a short-term coherent approach towards specifying IBEIs in order to codify the beneficial owner information as required by MLD III and therefore, subsequently, SEPA. This is a serious shortcoming as the relationships between institutional business entities and the funds they manage, and between institutional parents and their subsidiaries and affiliates, can be tortuous.

The onus under the risk-based, proportionate approach is to rely on the firms to carry out the relevant reference data forensics. However, the real-world ownership of companies is complex, as the example for the ownership structure of Lazards clearly illustrates (see Figure 29.8).

How the identifier is used to create data structures and hierarchies will be largely up to the consumers of the data and is anticipated to be a commercial issue, based on considerations such as intellectual property rights (IPR) for the foreseeable future.

29.9 CONCLUSION

MLD III and SEPA both come into force in 2008. It will be interesting to see how each Member State implements the measures, not least because the onus will be on senior management, and not the regulator, to engage in the process and 'own' the risk-based approach. MLD III will raise the bar in terms of firms carrying out functions such as KYC, CDD and other client tests such as credit risk and suitability and appropriateness checks. The result is that firms will need to invest heavily in identity management technologies.

In the near- to medium term, the measures ushered in by SEPA surrounding the treatment of credit transfers, direct debits and other forms of money transfer will lay the groundwork for universal payment facilitation of D+1 by the end of 2012, as required under the Payments Services Directive. SEPA will require important revisions to client on-boarding processes, system monitoring and interactions with third parties, such as payment processing agents and automated clearing houses (ACHs). Given the falling margins combined with the need to manage greater complexity and effect system changes, it makes sense for banks to manage these risks by qualifying their retail, private banking and corporate clients under the most stringent means of due diligence affordable at the earliest stage.

- At least two perspectives:

  - The need to link companies with legal entities with issues for MLD III and risk management purposes and to precisely extract reporting, transactional and relationship information for other regulatory compliance requirements

  - The need to link investment programs and funds with counter-parties to promote processing efficiency when cross-referencing between proprietary internal identifiers

- IBEI (ISO 16372) was proposed as a global scheme for uniquely identifying business entities playing a role in the lifecycle of, and events related to, a financial instrument. A business entity is an entity that is either regulated or on which due diligence is necessary under any jurisdiction.

*Source ISO TC68 SC4 WG8 Feb 2005.

Figure 29.8   Business/Legal Entity Data – Problem Statement *Source:* ISO TC68 SC4 WG8 Feb 2005.

Banks will be challenged to design client on-boarding systems which integrate with their monitoring of suspicious transactions. This is because transaction monitoring will become a mandatory legal requirement, with firms applying due diligence measures in a dynamic sense. Banks will also be challenged to apply EU/EEA AML standards to their foreign branches and subsidiaries outside the EU/EEA territory, because of the need to address regulatory 'equivalence' issues. This particularly applies to areas which require the reconciliation of FATF principles with those of MLD III and SEPA.

MLD III also places greater responsibilities on the shoulders of the MLRO as part of the 'reliance' process. This will be even truer under real-time payments, the long-term aspiration of SEPA.

Finally, MLD III requires data to be evidenced and authenticated on 'beneficial ownership', 'business relationships', 'reliance on other regulated firms' such as lawyers, accountants, and other third parties, yet it is crystal clear that the standards for exchanging and reporting this information do not exist at the business entity level, much less at the individual level. With intermediaries such as the interbank processors like VISA assuming greater prominence in a post-SEPA world, adhering to standards is a short-term must for banks to remain in this space.

The good news is that innovations in IT have made it easier to exchange, store, cross-reference and retrieve such information, even if it is yet to be standardised. However, while banks in both the US and EU are pouring their security dollars into compliance with evolving regulations, this is not necessarily an automatic panacea. Firms should therefore consider the converse argument where being secure from financial crime and identity fraud will generally make a firm compliant with regulations such as SEPA and the PSD as a by-product. So the correct approach is to spend money on amassing a business relevant security programme centred upon identity authentication and evidencing, not an on-point compliance programme. At the core of the technology decisions then lie some very basic human and psychological questions such as 'are they who they say they are?' and 'are they authorised to do what they're doing?'

As mentioned at the outset, today's industry model operates at a macro level and features a preference for regulated financial institutions to intermediate to manage risk, rather than government institutions or through local enforcement at individual level. The likely continuum of payments processors, including mobile facilities and ACHs in a post-SEPA Europe, will mean that a firm's Compliance and Controls must assume 'centre-stage' if they are to tackle security breaches and reduce reputational risk effectively.

While the theory of building Management Information nerve-centres is well-documented, the requisite governance of situating a Chief Controls Officer in the midst of proceedings is further away. If firms are lucky, they will have a Chief Risk Officer, a Chief Compliance Officer or even a Chief Data or Forensics Officer, to support them when complying with the measures of MLD III and SEPA. If not, they will spend extra money trying to ensure their infrastructure is scalable and fit for purpose, while missing the transformational opportunities of MLD III, SEPA and the PSD.

As functions such as the Chief Risk Officer, Chief Compliance Officer and Chief Data Officer are sidelined or under-resourced and regarded as cost centres, rather than risk mitigation centres, so fortunately there are market practice forums such as the Wolfsberg Group or the JMLSG to fill some of the gaps. The European Payments Council and European Banking Federation dedicated a great deal of time debating the merits and de-merits of implementing SEPA without linkage to other directives, such as MLD III or Basel II.

The arrival of MLD III alongside SEPA and other major changes, such as the Markets in Financial Instruments Directive (MiFID), should allow firms to take a broader perspective to see where the lay of the regulation land is taking them. Banks need to do this at both a macro level through systems, controls and collaboration, as well as at a micro level through internal governance, the MLROs and identity management tools. For example, the functions above could easily morph into a Chief Controls or Forensics Officer overseeing not only money laundering transactions but equally collateral flows, if the governance so permits.

Complying with regulatory measures will mean that at least 45 % of a bank's compliance costs will be drawn from the IT budget to 'change the bank' over the next 5 years. This in turn will mean squeezing the innovation budget, unless regulatory-driven change is viewed holistically. If more firms are inclined to view regulations such as SEPA, MLD III and MiFID as transformative, we can expect to see fewer single-threaded approaches to regulation, and more instances of firms welcoming the arrival of regulations such as MLD III and the PSD in helping them raise their game. The time for beginning to think of regulation as business advantage, is now.

30

SEPA and identity: are you who you say you are, and does it matter?

John Bullard, IdenTrust

Infrastructures and their evolution are issues which have been with humans since the dawn of time, and show no signs of going away anytime soon. This chapter seeks to evaluate infrastructural implications connected with SEPA, particularly in so far as trust, reliability and authenticity of counterparties become more difficult to manage in a much larger ecosystem. Within this vein, how crucial will the role of identity be in the brave new SEPA world, where cross border equates with domestic and yet spans beyond a single legal jurisdiction?

In 2002, the leading banks across Europe established the European Payments Council (EPC) in order to spearhead efforts by the payments industry to put in place a set of pan-European conventions and legal regulations to support SEPA. These EPC rulebooks form the basis for credit transfer and direct debit schemes, and the cards framework. These are the applications which bring SEPA into reality. The next phase, starting in January 2008, consists of a migratory period lasting until the end of 2010. By 2010 time domestic payments systems, currently a patchwork of different standards and rules across Europe, will be replaced by a new, euro-domestic market using a single standard format.

30.1 WHAT DOES THIS MEAN?

To illustrate SEPA's overall impact take another industry in another era and look at the issues around transparency. This industry went through a revolution. This is the world's network of railways, one of the greatest eighteenth century infrastructures.

Even though they all carried fundamentally the same goods – passengers, raw materials, cargo and other livestock – they did so on railroad gauges that were of variable widths, as some still are, on a country and regional basis. These variations occurred for a number of reasons: some were for self defence to avoid the neighbours invading using the rail network for a lightning war; whilst some were for the protection of local vested interests and national monopolies; and some were simply because of terrain and local engineering practices.

The result was that any movement of goods became much more complicated, cumbersome, slow and expensive when it was across borders, and outside of the domain of one country's gauge.

Today, any railway publication will show that there is at least a standard gauge of 1435 millimetres, which translates to 4 feet 8½ inches in old school measurements. 1435 mm is used widely, if not ubiquitously, across Europe and around the world and it has been a long while coming.

We see the same process evolving as the electronic information networks proliferate at a much faster pace, to a degree undreamt of even at the height of the railroad expansion. This goes hand-in-hand with the adoption of standards, helping the move to interoperability and the physical movement of goods, material, information and people around the world.

So what relevance does this have to the evolution, and the ultimate success, of the Single Euro Payments Area and how does it connect specifically to the issue of identity management?

30.2   WHAT DO WE MEAN BY IDENTITY AUTHENTICATION?

A phrase widely used, identity authentication, often means different things to different people. In the context of SEPA, we mean Risk Management. Identity is essentially having a degree of certainty that our counterparty is who they purport to be, supported by one or more trusted intermediaries to whom or from whom a payment is being made across the SEPA network or beyond. To be truly "trustworthy", this risk management framework must allow those two parties to interact in an environment of privacy, authentication, message integrity, and non-repudiation, and through the provision of credentials which themselves enable authentication, encryption and digital signing.

30.3   WHY IS THIS DEGREE OF IDENTITY ASSURANCE NECESSARY?

Firstly, the drivers for identity transparency are the same as those for payment transparency. Disjointed, non-interoperable identities give rise to industry inefficiencies, additional costs and greater risk. A patchwork of different identity schemes that are ineffective across national or geographic borders, or are defined by an industry vertical or product delineation, is as inherently cumbersome as those railroad gauges. Efforts have been made to set up bi-lateral agreements between organisations and they can work within a small community, but they simply are not scalable on a pan-European basis, let alone in a global context. There is a need for a rules-based scheme approach, wherein one contract provides watertight relationships and liabilities for all members operating under the same scheme.

Secondly, whilst networks and messaging systems were controlled at each end by institutions, by which we usually mean banks, their entry and exit points could be carefully controlled. As these networks grew and their end-users demanded ever more direct access,[1] so there is a shift to identify those users. The requirement is essentially to identify who, as an individual as compared to a corporate name, actually initiates, signs for and executes a payment, and when.

Thirdly, and as a result of similar end-user pressures, we are witnessing the convergence of the physical and the financial supply chain. As the passage of information that flows between two parties[2] becomes increasingly network independent, the information eventually flows over whichever route is most ubiquitous, safe and economical.

For SEPA and other applications, who is best placed to provide this Risk Management framework for the issuance of and reliance upon electronic, and counterparty-not-present, credentials? Additionally, who is best to secure and control this confidential information?

---

[1] As evidenced by the need to provide direct corporate access to SWIFTNet, BACSTEL-IP and now some of the SEPA platforms.
[2] Contracts, invoices, logistical arrangements and initiating the movement of funds in settlement of the transaction.

At present, this is the financial institutions and therefore banks can issue and verify the identity credentials. However there are alternatives, such as governments, other types of financial institutions, or even the end-users themselves.

It is generally recognised that governments, although massive users of electronic networks in their own capacities, are not generally well attuned to managing the commercial risks between their citizens, the businesses which operate within their country and third parties. Where governments do issue electronic credentials, for example a passport, and third parties do rely upon them, government liabilities are strictly defined and are related to a specific application, as evidenced inside the front cover of a passport.

For corporations, or indeed for citizens as end-users, it is clearly impractical for each to be able to assert their own identities in making or receiving a payment, and to do so with non-repudiation and a dispute resolution process for multiple applications across multiple jurisdictions. Similar to governments, neither corporations nor end-users see themselves as managers of the operational risks associated with intermediation between parties.

It follows that the natural providers of this critical service, and the organisations whose structures are appropriate for this task, are the world's financial institutions, especially those who see a future for themselves in transaction management.

Indeed one might argue that for any financial institution that sees transaction management as a key strategy and core competence, including the management of payments in the SEPA environment, then the issuance and subsequent management of underlying credentials supporting the identity of their customer should be a foundation stone for their business.

30.4   WITHIN SEPA, WHERE WILL IDENTITY BECOME MOST CRUCIAL?

As noted at the start of this article, SEPA consists of three streams: credit transfers, direct debits, and the cards framework, with the latter still needing some clarification. Of these, many experts are seeing the introduction of SEPA Direct Debits (SDD), formerly known as the Pan-European Direct Debiting scheme PEDD, as the catalyst for widespread adoption of a cohesive, interoperable, underlying identity management framework. A framework based upon regulation and which carries with it a clear liability management dimension.

Take a practical example, a citizen of Ireland has a house in Spain. Today, that person has to have bank account in Spain in order for the local utility company to apply a direct debit for gas, water and electricity used at the property. Their bank in Spain will almost certainly have a relationship with the utility company or, at the very least, will recognise the direct debit as a routine transaction which takes place across its many customer accounts. However, as the SDD comes into effect, the Irish citizen will be able to use his local Dublin-based bank account for meeting the Spanish utility's direct debit demands, in exactly the same manner as if the Irish bank were a Spanish bank. It is highly unlikely that the Dublin-based bank will have any knowledge of who the Spanish utility company really is. Thus, the ability to prove identity and that the organisation is what it purports to be when a direct debit is applied to a bank account, becomes critical.

It follows that:

(a) a credential issued by the Spanish bankers to the utility company needs to be interoperable with, and to be able to be relied upon and trusted by, the Irish bank and its customer; and
(b) this credential must be capable of being authenticated/validated on-line and in real time.

Expand this example across different geographies, different customer sectors and different products and services, and one can quickly understand that multiple bilateral agreements between different disparate providers of "identity", is simply not feasible. There must be a scheme, a set of rules which define the rights and that are stronger than a code of conduct, obligations, responsibilities and liabilities, for each of the four parties described in this example. Such a scheme managing these identities needs to be capable of scaling across Europe and indeed globally.

For service providers of SEPA capabilities, it will be crucial to have a mechanism to manage the identities of the corporate organisations that will be performing direct debit creation and, more importantly, direct debit collection with organisations that they normally have no dealings with. What knowledge will the administration departments of banks, such as Barclays, AIB and BNP Paribas, require of the Estonian power companies and the Bulgarian telecommunication providers?

30.5 MULTIPLE USAGES

Whilst an important step in the evolution of the payments industry, SEPA is not the only issue within a networked world. A financial transaction between two parties is invariably preceded by a series of interactions which culminate in the movement of money. During each of these interactions, the need to know and to remain assured that the counterparty is who they say they are, becomes as important as the payment itself. In this regard, it is of no value to the end-user to have a separate electronic identity credential for each piece of a transaction, as being able to use the same underlying credential is essential. After all, one's identity does not change during this transaction, especially where its original issuance is based upon strong KYC practice and where a third party, such as a bank, can vouch for the identity of its customer.

The same identity that is used by a corporate to sign SEPA payment transactions with their bank, should also be used with SWIFTNet, the domestic ACH, the bank's e-banking platform, signing electronic forms through e-invoicing, and any one of many other transactions where a bank-backed identity credential would add value.

30.6 CONCLUSIONS

SEPA is happening. It will provide significant streamlining opportunities for the end-user: the corporate user, the government user or the citizen. It will cut costs and lead to much greater speed of money transmission, bringing both the physical and financial supply chains together into closer alignment. However, for SEPA to reach its full potential – not just with the Eurozone itself but across the EU and indeed worldwide – a framework for managing the operational risks associated with the issuance and reliance upon electronic identity credentials will become absolutely essential. A patchwork of solutions is not sustainable, as history has pointed out in other infrastructural endeavours.

As SEPA creates a consolidation of banking relationships, the banks that will gain most traction in this consolidation process are those that recognise this need and implement solutions for their customers. That is why the world's regulated financial institutions pooled their resources and skills almost a decade ago to create a scheme which, today, is called IdenTrust.

31

Why SEPA needs e-invoicing

Bo Harald, TietoEnator

Since the early days of SEPA there has been a desire to expand its remit to e-invoicing. It hasn't happened, but e-invoicing is the only way that banks can make money out of SEPA.

This chapter is based on my experience of establishing and marketing e-invoicing as a part of the payment services and e-banking in Nordea, starting from Finland and Sweden in close co-operation with TietoEnator, where I now work, and later to Norway and Denmark. Seeing that this should be a part of the European and global payment system, I have participated in many discussions and working groups also in Europe with the Commission and the European central bank.

The main conclusion is that only the complete SEPA will bring the needed business case for e-invoicing. The complete SEPA includes common open standards for payments linking into e-invoices and other commercial documents to and from both enterprises and consumers. If SEPA stops at purely consolidating payment clearing, then very little value will be created for enterprises. Luckily there is now a strong consensus that this will not be allowed to happen.

31.1 EARLY DEBATE

I participated in the early stages of the SEPA-debate in various meetings, arguing that e-invoicing should be the first stage of SEPA. This is for the simple reason that so many studies pointed out that e-invoicing is a good business case whilst it was difficult to find a short enough payback period for investments in other areas, such as credit transfer, direct debit and card consolidation. Furthermore, our own experience from the Nordic countries showed us that it was not particularly difficult or demanding investment-wise for banks to move into a natural extended payments role. With the banks' sales power it was possible to get tens of thousands of enterprises to sign up for e-invoicing right from the beginning.

We therefore came to the conclusion that banks should take their responsibility for producing this new value dimension of e-invoicing seriously and, by doing so, it would be possible to make it happen fast enough and with low costs. This is a critical factor, as customers always pay all of the costs of the banking system and investments that do not enhance their productivity should be made only when other areas have been completed.

There was also little support for my somewhat radical view however. The SEPA-train was already at the station and banks had not looked much into mass market e-invoicing at that point.

31.2   EU AND ECB SEE THE LIGHT

Nevertheless, fairly early on, there was a clear change in the message from both the European Commission and the European Central Bank: e-invoicing should be implemented as soon as possible and as a part of SEPA. The work of the EPC had already started however, and banks did not see it as possible to work on pan-European e-invoicing at the same time.

National banking community efforts did start to show up though and it became evident in more and more countries that both consumers and small businesses expect their banks to provide e-invoicing, both in their e-banking service and as a file transfer capability. Banks in Europe and the USA also started to see that the value created is a basis for generating income and a way to make more customers in the Small to Medium Enterprise (SME) segment become profitable.

31.3   THE EUROPEAN COMMISSION TASKFORCE, 2007

Another factor that started to demonstrate the value of e-invoicing came around when Finland ran the EU presidency in the latter half of 2006. The Finnish Prime Minister's office organised a high level conference titled 'Something Real for Lisbon'. Speakers were asked to list three concrete measures that would have a big impact on productivity in EU and be easy to implement. The audience then voted on the proposals and e-invoicing came, to no-one's surprise, out at the top.

This was documented in the Helsinki Manifesto which was handed over to Germany, the next presidency country. The Manifesto has been considered as an important tool when moving from producing only strategy papers and studies to real implementation of digital services, aimed both at large scale productivity improvements and better services.

As a result of this Manifesto, the European Commission established an informal task force in December 2006, with the task to describe a way to kick-start e-invoicing in EU. The European Electronic Invoicing (EEI) taskforce's work was supervised by DG Enterprise and DG Market, and involved representatives from banks, enterprises, the public sector, e-invoice service providers and the Commission. The final report was delivered in July 2007.

The surprising aspect of this was that the work was completed ahead of time and the deliberations, despite so many parties being involved, led to a unanimous result. The report even went into the details of how to make e-invoicing work, and is a firm foundation for implementation.

31.4   NEXT STEPS BASED ON THE EEI REPORT

The next step is in play with the European Commission now establishing a permanent steering group to ensure swift progress of the results. The Commission also took the responsibility for overlooking identified needs for changes in taxation and legislation.

For banks and other service providers, the next steps are to work out the needed rule-books. This will be coordinated by the EBA. Then, together with enterprise and public sector customers, these organisations need to identify a wide enough number of data fields in the e-invoice to make it possible for the 17 million European SMEs to send large enterprises and the public sector e-invoices, and other trade documents, that are sophisticated enough to meet most reasonable demands. In this respect, the experience with the Financial Invoice standard (Finvoice) in Finland and other Nordic countries has shown that this is not a very difficult task.

Both of the demands for sophisticated procurement value chains and user friendly presentment for consumers and SMEs, can be satisfied.

The core invoice once defined will then be taken by standards organisations and SWIFT to the ISO process, much in the same way as ISO20022 for credit payments was done.

31.5 STANDARDS DON'T HAPPEN OVERNIGHT

It should be made clear that the coming ISO-standard will not change the present fragmented format landscape overnight. Today there are many standards that need to be converted into each other's, to achieve automated end-to-end processes. Several banks are already offering an 'any-format-in & any-format-out-service', often with the help of service providers such as TietoEnator. This situation will continue for many years after the new global e-invoice standard is established although the number of standards, and the cost for reformatting and lack of interoperability, will start to diminish. Above all, the banking sector focused upon looking after the needs of the SME sector will start using the same standards, initially in the interbank space but also in the customer interface.

One of the most important arguments for banks is that payments-integrated e-invoicing provides the opportunity to seamlessly automate the payment and provide an extension to cash management services. Based on my own Nordic experience however, I would also consider the opportunity for banks to create a solution for SMEs that calls for no software solutions and no need for IT skills as the most important value add. It is not easy to come up with a solution that beats the numerous counterarguments and resistance which SMEs can come up with and this, the browser based e-invoice service, is one. For example, as most enterprises use browser based e-banking today, and all will soon, the Finvoice concept has a simple template form to fill in for sending e-invoices and other messaging, such as e-orders. It is this simplicity of approach that makes it work.

So e-invoicing really works like e-payments, and sits easily within the much used and trusted netbank services. As all banks are connected via the payment systems, every account holder can be reached with an e-invoice whether they are a consumer or an enterprise.

Other arguments for society at large to turn to banks for this service include the availability of bank security and, above all, a wide personal sales force. In any case, banks are obligated by law to protect society against money laundering, and the operative models thus established can also serve as a defence against fraudulent invoicing.

31.6 BANKS ARE GOOD AT STANDARDS

George F. Thomas recently wrote an article dealing with the needed enhancements of the US wire transfer systems and ISO20022.[1] His conclusion was as follows: 'Banks have demonstrated over the years that they will only act when forced to. They do not perform enough research; they do not listen to their customers very well; and have a reputation for milking the product until the bitter end. A prime example is the neglect of the wire transfer business...'

My reaction was that this is not a fair statement. Few industries have created more global and local standards, and thus created the basis for strong level playfield competition in a multitude of areas. Prime examples are the global payment system, card payments and acquiring, foreign

---

[1] 'Enhancing the US Wire Transfer Systems: ISO20022 or STP 820?' by George F. Thomas, Radix Consulting, GT News, 17 April 2007.

exchange, equity, bond and derivatives trading and trade finance. In the Nordic area we have seen that this approach has led to further dimensions of standardization with more 'radical sharing', which has created new corporate value through networked solutions. Prime examples are e-identification, e-signature, e-salary and above all payments-integrated e-invoicing. It has been very encouraging to see that the public sector has seen networking with the financial sector as the only fast and especially cost-effective way to further the e-society.

My second reaction to the comments Mr. Thomas made is that more should be done. The economy is moving faster to become networked on a global scale and banks need to expand their service scopes accordingly. To be successful this means more co-operation and investments in the standardisation field. Enlightened policy makers and enterprise customers realise that the immense new value created by the automation of business processes cannot be achieved without corresponding new income for the service providers involved.

Another recent article from Aite Group[2] stated that e-invoicing is likely to become more important for banks in the US over the next few years, especially as 67 % of small enterprises expressed some level of interest in the service in 2006. The Bank of America was the first bank to offer this service in June 2006, and others are likely to follow as 'winning the wallets of small business customers has become a top priority for most U.S. banks.' Small business is now seen as important potential revenue generators. 'Small businesses already spend US$ 353 billion on financial products. By cross-selling additional services like EIPP, banks will not only increase their spend, but they will better meet the needs of this important customer segment'.

This certainly corresponds to my own experience from launching e-invoicing as a payments and e-banking integrated service first in Finland and then in other Nordic countries. Once a common open standard was launched by the banks, it did not take long for IT-solution providers to adjust their ERP-systems for use by large companies. As the corporate mass market segment could join without any investments using e-banking templates an immediate take-off was possible. This was even faster than some expected thanks to the help of the massive sales force represented in the bank's branches.

For banks to make such things happen requires an open and innovative position towards the new opportunities and demands from new, increasingly interoperable, technology and globally networked businesses, as well as corresponding efforts to standardise the messaging. The public sector should naturally be a part of the networking and drive towards the re-use of existing, competitively based commercial solutions, instead of trying to build expensive separate ones for seldom needed services.

31.7   IMPLICATIONS OF SEPA FOR E-INVOICING

There is hardly any need to argue that SEPA, in its core version, is not a good business case. Certainly, SEPA has little business case in this version for banks and thus not for their customers or for Europe. Cross-border payments have already been speeded up and prices regulated to domestic levels. The rest of the improvements in productivity will have to come from higher degrees of automation in corporate reconciliation processes, more competition from standardised corporate to bank interfaces, and consolidation of clearing systems. This will be a slow process.

---

[2] '*Small-Business Banking: The Value Proposition for Banks to Offer Small-Business EIPP*' by Aite Group, published December 2006.

Full SEPA requires using this unique integration opportunity to also include e-invoicing. This will make the needed difference. The European Association for Corporate Treasurers for example states that yearly corporate savings in process costs could exceed € 200 billion. What other services could produce anything near this? This is why banks need to include this in their ordinary portfolio of standardized payment solutions.

My conclusion is that core SEPA can drive e-invoicing forward in many ways. The first reason why core SEPA needs e-invoicing is to improve the overall business case. There is also now a focus on standardising interfaces between enterprises and banks, to save cost and enhance competition. In e-invoicing it was the case from the beginning and ISO20022 for credit transfers is aiming at the same.

There is a focus on European productivity that can be taken to new levels, once the focus is in the payments standardisation field. The e-invoicing ISO process will, in the best case, act as a shoehorn to get fast alignment between the Universal Business Language[3] and the United Nations Centre for Trade Facilitation and Electronic Business (UN/CEFACT).

But there is one dilemma left. The billions of savings are so widely distributed and the daily business so hectic, that it will take far too long for enterprises to migrate to e-invoicing without some strong incentives. The Danish example, where the law permits only e-invoices to the public sector, is probably the best way forward; especially if banks and other service providers get the signal that this will happen in time to establish convenient, integrated and economical solutions.

---

[3] The Universal Business Language (UBL) is an international, royalty-free standard for business documents patterns in XML syntax.

32

The technology standards required
for SEPA

Chris Pickles, BT

SEPA is raising the need for banks to work with other industries and agree standards for technology interoperability across the payment schemes. SEPA will result in new, open standards as a result, enabling a level playing field for integrating payment technologies across Europe.

From a technological viewpoint, SEPA is driving a need for standardisation. If there is a business area that one would have thought would have been standardised by the banking industry years ago, it would have been how a bank sends a message to another bank to say, 'Here's some money'. If only the international payments industry was that simple and efficient but it is far from it. This is because the financial services industry makes money out of inefficiencies and risk.

If everyone was in a position of having *perfect information* – knowing everything about everything – then many business opportunities would simply not exist in this market. Arbitrage between currencies, instruments and execution venues would be a thing of the past. The risk of getting things wrong due to the lack of *perfect information* is therefore part of the DNA of the financial services industry.

However, the acceptance that there is no such thing as *perfect information* can lead to the mere acceptance of imperfection in all things, and therefore to a lack of impetus and momentum to improve the efficiency of the way that the financial services industry operates. As long as all service providers are inefficient to a fairly similar degree, there is little practical influence that customers can have to improve the situation, as moving from one inefficient service provider to another changes nothing. In addition, if the financial services industry still manages to make money out of such inefficiencies, and if there are no real competitive or regulatory threats that are likely to change the situation, the industry would continue to focus on issues that have a higher commercial priority.

The European Commission has given the first real impetus to change this situation, in the interest of investors and the public, through the threat and/or the reality of regulatory change.

In the securities industry, its first move was the Investment Services Directive (ISD) in 1993. As a result of this, national governments and some industry participants and regulators managed to erect barriers to mitigate the impact of the ISD which, in turn, has led to the Markets in Financial Instruments Directive (MiFID), which now removes many of these barriers in the securities industry.

Similarly, the Payments Services Directive (PSD) has been a key motivation for the banking industry to create the Single Euro Payments Area (SEPA) initiative. However, SEPA is an industry initiative and not an EU Directive or Regulation, and its success or failure is very much dependent upon the banks following through to the goals of this initiative. The PSD will change the landscape even further.

The result is a strong requirement to become interoperable through the implementation of standards between different technology infrastructures, but this is not as easy as it seems.

32.1   STANDARDS – WHERE THE USER MEETS TECHNOLOGY

To create a standard for anything, users have to define what they are trying to achieve. Most users hope that they push such a problem in the direction of their technology team and somehow it will be magically solved by the technology. Most technology people know that technology just tends to make problems happen faster, unless the technologists and the users work together to get the solution right.

Most technologists don't want anything to do with the data itself. 'That's the user's problem', is their usual cry. The technologists don't mind storing it, moving it or even processing it, but whether the data is actually correct or meaningful is the user's problem. So when it comes to defining messaging standards, such as the ones that are required for standardised message processing under SEPA, that's where the users have to get involved in the detail. They are the only people who understand the business process and the data that the technologists have to automate.

In the world of SEPA, there are two basic forms of standards user:

- the service provider: the banks, card processors and clearing houses; and
- the service user: everybody else in Europe.

As SEPA is an initiative of the banking industry, the service providers first define how they will communicate with each other, and then they define how service users will communicate with the service providers. As a result, the involvement in SEPA so far has been very much from banks, card processors and clearing houses, and very little from corporate treasurers, government administrations and citizens.

Most corporates consider SEPA to be a banking problem, and therefore see it as a problem for the banks to sort out. This has also been true of the development of the relevant standards, as corporates have started to involve themselves in the process of developing financial messaging standards only relatively recently via the TWIST initiative[1] and the work of the European Association of Corporate Treasurers (EACT).

Open industry standards are developed by industry participants, not by the standards bodies themselves. Though standards bodies, and vendors that are active in the standards space, are vital to the development of open industry standards, they are not the owners of these standards. The standards that have been prescribed for SEPA have been developed by participants from across a very broad spectrum of the payments industry internationally.

In order to really understand the challenges banks face in the SEPA space therefore, we need to review some of the history as to how banking standards were developed.

32.2   A BRIEF HISTORY OF BANKING STANDARDS

According to Moore's Law,[2] we are now some five generations of technology ahead of where we were when the EU Financial Services Action Plan was endorsed in 2000. Regardless,

---

[1] http://www.twiststandards.org.
[2] Computer processing power doubles every 18 months whilst the price of processing power halves.

most of the technology that is used by banks for processing payments today is little different from what was used back in the early 1970's, when the industry first decided how to process international payments more efficiently. This applies not only to hardware but also to software. Even as recently as 1999, one major UK bank discovered that many of its core systems still operated in UK pounds, shillings and pence, as a result of having to make changes to its systems for euro implementation. A quick and dirty fix had been made to its applications when the UK decimalised back in 1971 and, since then, it had never made or had the time for a full-scale changeover of its systems.

Banks typically dislike having to invest in doing something better or more efficiently if the current system actually works. Their money is already sunk into the current solution, and they would have to spend money to save money, something that banks are famous for not wanting to do. At the same time, no manager likes to admit that this is his or her own approach, as it fights against the business disciplines that we have all learnt. These disciplines go way back in time to the prehistory of SEPA.

The prehistory of SEPA stems back to the early 1970's. In 1971, the Bretton Woods Accord began to collapse. The Accord was the basis for fixing the relationship between foreign exchange rates and the price of gold. This collapse created the basis for today's foreign exchange and money markets.

At that time, banks were still using telex machines to send typed messages to each other to process cross-border payments. Telex was slow and messages were long and used free-format text. This meant that all cross-border payments were processed by human beings, rather than machines. The level of technology had been adequate in a world of fixed and stable exchange rates, but was totally inadequate for a new, riskier world of volatile and fast-changing financial markets. The banks judged that the costs associated with these new risks were potentially much greater than the costs would be of increasing their operational efficiency in order to reduce these risks. So began the push towards replacing the use of telex machines with computer-to-computer telecommunications and straight-through processing (STP) in the financial services industry.

At this point in history, it was only banks that were really using computer technology seriously. For example, new technologies back then for many stock exchanges, meant using overhead projectors to display hand-written prices on the walls of the trading floor. Financial data was delivered by paper-tape tickers, or was on a piece of paper pinned to the notice board in the stock exchange's reception area.

It was a different technological era. There were few recognised open industry standards and the hardware used proprietary standards, operating systems were proprietary, communications protocols were proprietary . . . everything was proprietary. Technology was comparatively expensive with a desktop calculator costing a month's wages and an office computer, with less processing power than one of today's mobile telephones, cost a year's salary. Data processing in banks was not in real-time on a transaction-by-transaction basis, but in batches of transactions and often on a once-per-day basis.

32.3   STANDARDISATION OF COMMUNICATION

With no global, secure and reliable networks that they could rely upon to interlink their computers, 259 banks across 15 countries agreed to create SWIFT, the Society for World Interbank Financial Telecommunication, in 1973. SWIFT became the bank-owned mutually cooperative organisation to manage their own virtual private network (VPN) for bank-to-bank communications.

SWIFT not only built a new communications network, but also defined a totally different approach to financial messaging. Standard computers were considered unacceptable for usage at the time due to secure communications concerns. As a result, computer manufacturers had to build special versions of their computers with additional security and communications capabilities, in order for them to be judged SWIFT-compliant. The banks had to define a new messaging protocol and new standardised data formats and, even though the banks operated some of the largest computer networks in the world, virtually nothing of what they used was considered to be adequate enough for the international SWIFT environment.

The original proprietary messaging standards that SWIFT developed in the 1970's gradually evolved and became a starting point for the development of the ISO7775 messaging standards in the 1980's. These, in turn, were the starting point for the development of ISO15022 message standards in the 1990's and ISO20022 message standards today. As a result, SWIFT and ISO became synonymous for many people, just as the vacuum cleaner became synonymous with the word Hoover. However, today's world is different and these origins are not necessarily the correct foundations for today's world.

32.4   TODAY'S WORLD IS DIFFERENT

Much has changed in the world over the last 35 years. Data communications is no longer a black art and many vendors now operate large international data communications networks that are used for financial messaging applications. The market generally considers that proprietary protocols are in the past, and that the future is based upon open systems standards. These are vital. The Internet has happened and created open standards. The cheapest personal computer today has more power as a communications device than any computer had thirty-five years ago, and is based upon open standards.

Today's businesses and their managers understand that increasing the size of user communities rapidly and achieving economies of scale are vital to long-term success and market share. In order to achieve this, market participants expect open industry standards, freeware, and instantaneous response times on data networks that cost them virtually nothing.

In comparison to these massive changes in the outside world, much of the banking side of the payments industry has stood relatively still, almost as though it is standing on an island protected by its old technology. The banking side of the payments industry continues to work with old practices dating back to the 1970's. Meanwhile, the card processing industry has raced ahead. Though a supermarket check-out can validate your credit card limit and post a transaction to your card account in a matter of seconds, it still takes days for banks to process those payments.

For many years now, much of the banking side of the payments industry has decided that it does not want to keep up with the technology that is used daily in the industries that it serves. In parallel, the card processing industry has adopted, and continues to adopt, some of the most up-to-date technology available, and new market entrants in the payments industry are specifically focussing on the use of technology in order to create and maintain a competitive edge.

One of the reasons for this stasis of the banking industry may be the way that it has tried to approach the standardisation of communication and, in today's globalised world and Eurozone integration, this is no longer acceptable.

32.5   INTEGRATING TECHNOLOGIES FOR SEPA: THE CHALLENGE OF DOMESTIC VERSUS CROSS-BORDER

The majority of financial services is domestic. Most of the customers of most banks are in the countries in which the bank is headquartered. Most of the members of any exchange are in the country in which the exchange is located. As a result, the number of cross-border payments is miniscule compared to the number of domestic payments.

In developed markets, domestic financial messaging systems work well. They do not necessarily, in themselves, need replacing. They are designed to do domestic tasks well, and to meet the specific characteristics and vagaries of the domestic market. One can therefore understand that banks have been unwilling to change domestic payments systems that work, and this has been a major barrier to the European Commission and SEPA. Domestic payment systems that meet the vast majority of the bank's payments messaging needs are already a sunk cost. Why throw this away in order to accommodate a minority of cross-border payments messages?

However, the ultimate goal of SEPA is to have one set of international-standard messages that can be applied both for international and domestic payments. As a result, banks are being forced to replace these domestic systems. In doing so, they will look towards new technologies and open standards. The problem they will encounter is the range of standards available. This is because there are many more standards for financial messaging than people would expect, largely because the standards evolved to meet the needs of each part of the industry, and do not necessarily recognise similar areas in other industries.

For example, banks are corporations at the same time as being banks. They have employees who need to be paid, they buy paper-clips and stationery, and they own premises and vehicles. These are all things that they have in common with other non-financial corporations. Whilst banks have been creating their own definitions of international messaging standards, such as SWIFT, other corporations and industry bodies have been doing the same. As a result we have SWIFT message standards defined by banks, TWIST message standards defined by corporates, Rosetta Net standards defined by manufacturers, and more.

The result of all of this is not a simple picture.

32.6   THREE KEY STANDARDS AREAS FOR SEPA

The messaging standards that are to be applied for SEPA relate to three different areas:

- how to format the overall structure of the messages;
- how to identify the banks and bank accounts involved;
- how to identify the originator and recipients of the payments.

32.6.1   How to format the overall structure of the messages

As discussed earlier, the payments industry has worked for decades to define an international standard through the International Standards Organisation (ISO), and these messages are now clearly defined in the ISO20022 standards which is today's generation of SWIFT messaging standards. However, these formats are not the ones that have been prescribed for SEPA.

ISO is a global standards organisation, and therefore the standards it defines have to meet a global requirement, and not just European or national requirements. The ISO20022 message formats for payments therefore include elements that are relevant to some countries, such as the USA, that are not relevant to Europe. Rather than using these standard message formats, the European banking industry has decided to use a sub-set of the ISO20022 standard within SEPA.

One argument for this approach is that, for business purposes, it is wasteful to have to process messages that are longer than necessary and that contain blanks in non-relevant fields. This would have been a particularly valid argument 30 years ago, when processing power, computer memory and storage were incredibly expensive. It may not be as valid an argument today.

A problem that this can generate is that the industry will have not only domestic standards and international standards, but there will also be a regional standard related to SEPA. We will have more standards, rather than converging and consolidating the relevant standards that we already have.

32.6.2 How to identify the banks and bank accounts involved

Fortunately, the payments industry has decided to use the international standard formats that it has already developed to address these two areas. The selected standard for identifying bank accounts is the ISO13616 standard, the International Bank Account Number (IBAN), and for identifying banks it is ISO9362, the Bank Identification Code (BIC).

The onus is now on banks to ensure that their clients know what the IBAN code is that relates to those clients' accounts, and equally it is on the clients to make sure that they and their creditors also know their IBAN codes. The structure of IBAN codes allows each bank to issue its own IBAN codes to its customers, making it easier to deal with the millions of accounts across Europe that need to be individually identified. The IBAN is a variable length of numbers, as the size of bank account numbers varies from one country to another.

The BIC is also variable length, and is either eight or eleven numbers. Whereas the IBAN is issued by each bank, the BIC code is issued by SWIFT. This is because SWIFT maintains the master database of all BIC codes due to the fact that these codes were originally developed by SWIFT as the network addresses for users of their network. Therefore, this information was vital to the operation of the SWIFT network.

However, not all of the institutions that will require BIC codes actually have one today, as not all banks are connected to the SWIFT network. This is why SWIFT has committed to issuing BIC codes to all parties that require one, irrespective of whether they use the SWIFT network or not.

32.6.3 How to identify the originator and recipients of the payments.

One of the key standards that market participants have been asking for is a unique and un-ambiguous identifier for each individual business entity internationally. To a bank, a client organisation can be traced via its account number, but the account number itself does not imply uniqueness. The client may have several bank accounts with one bank. Equally it may have multiple accounts with multiple banks, with each bank identifying the same client organisation in a different way.

As a result, ISO16372 has been developed as a standard format for an International Business Entity Identifier (IBEI). IBEI is a code that uniquely identifies the business, whichever bank and method is being used for payments. A major issue related to the use of ISO16372 however, is who will issue and maintain the individual identifiers?

One school of thought is that one central global body is required that can issue and maintain all IBEIs for all business entities worldwide. So far, no organisation is volunteering to take on this role. One reason for this is no doubt due to the daunting scale of such a task, likened to trying to boil the ocean. Another reason is that proponents of this approach frequently believe that such a global numbering authority should be a not-for-profit organisation, and no organisation is interested in or capable of making the necessary enormous investment on a not-for-profit basis thus far.

Another approach is that IBEIs should be issued by national numbering authorities to business entities in their own countries, which would appear to be more practical as movement has already begun. These issuers need not necessarily be the existing National Numbering Agencies (NNA), although such organisations might be well equipped to take on this additional functionality and this process has already begun in countries such as Germany and Switzerland.

One of the proposals by banks regarding SEPA implementation has been to allocate a BIC code to each business entity. This has been due to the time pressures and deadlines associated with SEPA implementation in part. Market participants are resisting this proposal for a variety of reasons including the fact that:

- business entities already have unique business entity identifiers, such as those issued by a state authority when their business is incorporated;
- BIC codes do not allow the flexibility in the structures that business entities want to have;
- BIC codes can contain an acronym of the bank's own name, for example UBS or BNP, so other business entities would like to have this same identification opportunity, such as ABB or BBC, and the BIC code structure does not allow for this flexibility; and
- once the banking industry use BICs instead of IBEIs, this would probably hinder the adoption and use of IBEIs for the function for which this standard has been originally created.

For these reasons, how to identify the originator and recipients of the payments is still a major challenge.

32.7   SEPA STANDARDS: OPENING UP COMPETITION AND NEW BUSINESS OPPORTUNITIES

In conclusion, a key benefit of the standards being developed for the SEPA implementation is that they are non-proprietary. This means that banks, clearing houses, card processors and corporates can use these standards with any relevant software that they choose, and can communicate with each other via any network approach that they wish. Banks can continue to operate their own private networks if they wish to do so, to communicate with their larger customers, or use the public internet, although they would normally add a layer of high security on top of any internet-based payments services that they offer. Equally, organisations can use any shared market infrastructure to communicate with each other. This is because these SEPA standards are network and vendor independent.

One of the greatest benefits that the adoption of open industry standards helps to create long-term is the added level of competition. One of the general goals of the European Parliament and the European Commission is to generate competition between service providers: a level playing field across all aspects of the financial services industry throughout the EU. The use of open, non-proprietary and network-independent standards for SEPA should generate these new levels of competition, as payments services providers seek more and more cost-efficient solutions for doing business with their customers, and as customers start to see pricing differentials between payments services providers and the technology that they use for delivering their services.

33

The most critical technologies for SEPA

Richard Spong, Sterling Commerce

It's time to learn a lesson. It's not a lesson that is unique to the implementation of the Single Euro Payments Area (SEPA), but SEPA implementation is certainly a market event that brings this lesson into focus.

It's a lesson that has been too easy to ignore and by-pass historically, in the scramble to devise low cost, just about adequate, just-in-time solutions each time there is a new financial instrument, market or regulation.

It's a lesson that in more recent years has been even easier to overlook.

What is this lesson? It will become clear, but we first need to review why it has become so critical and why it is so relevant to SEPA.

The lesson became clear with Y2K. The dawn of the new millennium was accompanied by intense and widespread suspicion of the viability of financial systems, many of which were needlessly replaced at phenomenal cost. As a consequence, business control of technology investments became mandatory.

The logic of business functions controlling technology investments is simple enough, and is eminently sensible for most purposes. The business is generating the revenue and therefore the business is best placed to forecast the real returns that may be expected from any given enhancement of innovation in supporting technology, in terms of increased profits, reduced costs, reduced operational risks or any combination of these. Therefore, if the business is best placed to assess the returns then they must also be best placed to assess the costs, and should accordingly have the final power to authorise any technology spend.

The historical allocation of vaguely substantiated budgets to autonomous technology groups has been overturned, and technology investment is now prudently managed on the basis of cost justification by business professionals.

So far, so good, but what lesson did the industry fail to take into account? With financial services technology investment now predominantly driven by business priorities, business revenue forecasts and business budgets, it follows that technology development schedules have become increasingly tactical.

This is a critical foundation stone that could jeopardise SEPA, because projects are being authorised and budgeted by different business divisions, operating largely in isolation and with divisional tunnel-vision. The resultant technology projects therefore result in random impacts on the overall technical infrastructures of the financial enterprise, and the budget allocated for each project accommodates only the system features and functions sponsored by that particular divisional stakeholder within the bank. The fact that very similar features and functions may be beneficially shared by other business operations is no longer generally assessed. The system requirements of those other potential stakeholders are not synchronised.

They do not collaborate to submit a combined business case that defines their shared needs. Finally, joint funding arrangements between two or more lines of business seem impossibly difficult to arrange.

These are all critical factors as banks implement new SEPA payments platforms and infrastructures. The enterprise-wide value and applicability of new and improved technology should be comprehensively thought through, and would have been in earlier years when technology resources were pro-active in serving all of their internal customers, rather than being largely reactive to today's individual business sponsors.

The lesson we have to learn therefore is around strategic investments in technology. The lesson says that it is critical to maintain a dedicated technology strategy group that has:

- the continuing mandate to step back from the tactical requirements of today, and to take a longer view of the strategic trends in business demands upon enterprise technology; and
- independent funding, enabling the group to develop responses to those trends.

This is critical because every system change is costly and many are operationally invasive, so it is essential to drive home the maximum value for each change of systems right across the business, and regardless of which single line of business was the initial sponsor. Has this been done for SEPA change projects and technology implementations? I wonder.

It has been illustrated time and again that central technology strategy groups represent a worthwhile investment, delivering:

- very significant medium-term savings in technology costs;
- increased business agility and flexibility; and
- innovation and operational benefits in areas where business sponsors had no awareness of technical capability, and therefore would not have sponsored change requests.

However, these illustrations are often retrospective and, without the technology strategy group, it is often realised that a tactical fix would have had much wider business value if only it had been applied in a slightly different way.

The lesson therefore is that the business-driven systems development model does not allow for sufficient funding for technology strategy groups. By definition, the model cannot fund initiatives that are undefined and intangible at the time of budget allocation. The model restricts opportunities to progress cohesive technology strategies, and in many organisations even the scheduling of prudent technology housekeeping and maintenance becomes increasingly difficult.

The scenario is further complicated by business decisions around hosting and outsourcing, which is another critical area that banks are grappling with in their SEPA transformation programmes.

In the area of outsourcing you have, on the one hand, the internal customer population becoming radically extended into multiple business domains where their needs are being serviced through remote enterprises, each having an alien systems infrastructure and a demanding service level agreement. On the other, systems that used to be in-house and relatively manageable are now fragmented into a range of local and remote hybrid operations, each of which present new challenges around performance, process visibility and integration.

The result of all of this is that, in recent years, the highest priority changes in financial services technology have tended to be at the edge of the enterprise. The focus has moved away from enterprise application integration and optimisation of processes that are internal to the organisation, to those systems and processes that exchange data and transactions externally. This may be with the organisation's customers, its outsourced service providers, or with its payments and securities communities. The case for a strategic approach to external data movement technologies at the edge of the financial services enterprise is particularly strong but, for the reasons previously described, the environment for efficient change management in this area is particularly weak.

All of this background conspires to make SEPA much more of a technical issue than it should be. In Europe, compliance with the first phase of SEPA is the dominant current case for change at the edge of the financial enterprise. It will not be the last as there is much more change to come as full SEPA comes into force. For the European financial services community, the task of implementing SEPA presents a much greater pain than it should.

SEPA has been for a long time, some would argue for decades, an entirely predictable industry event. True, it seems to have taken forever to nail down the political consensus between the European central banks and the regional regulators, and the common data standards that enable implementation. On this latter area, the debate still continues as agreement has not been reached for some payment instruments and documents that are captured within the scope of SEPA. You would think that this long lead time should have provided the banks with ample time to prepare appropriate technical solutions.

From the banking viewpoint, the first difficulty with SEPA is that it has no business sponsors in most of the Eurozone financial institutions that it affects. This is because SEPA is fundamentally directed towards consumer protection. For most banks, it does not increase their profits, nor does it reduce their costs or risks. Instead, it introduces a compliance cost for which there is no revenue return. Therefore, it is no big surprise that business professionals have deferred the decision to make the unavoidable spend for as long as they possibly could. This has thereby contributed towards additional slippage in the overall SEPA roll-out programme.

SEPA compliance projects have not been strategically planned and, yet again like other preceding European financial community initiatives, have been rushed through as just-in-time damage limitation projects on the smallest budgets possible.

There are some exceptions. The European financial services community contains a number of visionaries who are senior banking executives who accepted the inevitability of SEPA early on. These visionaries look beyond SEPA's initial operational inconvenience to the longer term opportunities for re-positioned industry activity in the post-SEPA European Economic Community.

The second difficulty with SEPA is that, just weeks before the start in January 2008, a number of operational logistics remained undefined, poorly-defined and speculative. For example, SEPA clearing and settlement mechanisms were not agreed. The Pan-European Automated Clearing Houses (PEACHs) were positioning themselves to provide this capability, but they did not know which banks would use which PE-ACH, nor did they know which would wholly or partially opt-out in favour of direct bilateral or multilateral settlement agreements.

The third difficulty is that the technologies that banks and other organisations need to deal with for SEPA are not just about complying with payments standards. Certainly, depending upon their size and their merger history, banks may have two, 10, 20 or more payments processes that generate value transmissions and that will have to comply with SEPA standards. That is a pain in terms of scheduling un-remunerative development priorities, deferring more profitable development initiatives, repetitive system adaptations and extensive testing.

Nevertheless, the deliverables of generating SEPA-compliant credit transfers and, in later phases, SEPA direct debits and other financial instruments, do not amount to an unachievable science project. The more serious technical problem arises from the changed revenue profile that SEPA will progressively enforce on community organisations.

It is these three difficulties that dictate the shape of the technology response to SEPA across the community. The fundamental nature of previous changes in the European payments landscape is that they have dictated changes in community processes and technologies. The difference with SEPA is that, unlike previous changes, some of its consequences are difficult or impossible to model or predict. This is because it is driven by regulation, rather than by traditional market forces, and SEPA introduces a number of fundamental unknowns.

It is these unknowns that banking technology must address. This results in a whole raft of strategic questions, of which the following are just a few examples:

- How do we standardise our domestic and pan-European pricing policy for SEPA credit transfers against unknown competitor pricing policies?
- If it transpires that we cannot sustain a sufficiently remunerative SEPA payments service, do we outsource our payments processing and, if so, all of it or part of it and who to?
- If we do outsource, how do we provide a robust and secure front-end service to our customers, who are already demanding faster payments and better process visibility?
- If payment processing still looks profitable, should we seek economies of scale by extending hosted services to other smaller banks and, if so, how many domains can we process in parallel and how scalable do we need to be?
- If we are comfortable to continue independently processing SEPA credit transfers, how will SEPA direct debits and other later instruments affect our revenue profile?
- If SEPA traffic increases and scales in the future and proves to be detrimental to our capabilities, what options should we design into our strategy?
- If we decide to outsource, we cannot be locked into one external service provider, as others may compete to offer better performance or more favourable fees, so how do we retain the ability to switch rapidly to alternative third parties?
- Which networks shall we connect over and which PEACH shall we connect to, and what if we want to change those selections?

All of these questions involve issues of multi-enterprise data communications technology. They are about moving transactions and associated service information between community enterprises who are collaborating in executing SEPA compliance. Whatever the answers may be from the viewpoint of any one bank, they do not imply that ripping out and replacing existing core system payments technologies is the answer for SEPA implementation. Renewal of core systems invariably introduces many benefits but typically the cost is significant, and the internal enterprise integration overhead is very high. Bear in mind that all of this is being performed just to achieve new compliance standards in a SEPA market which will deliver a minimal return on those investments. It's not only about direct costs. The operational risk and project effort associated with replacement of each individually related system are very considerable, and most banks have many.

Furthermore, replacing existing hard to change technologies with updated, slightly less rigid, technologies, does not necessarily answer the clear strategic need for extreme processing agility at the edge of the enterprise. This need extends across the entire SEPA financial services community, through 2010 and beyond.

For some years, industry analysts have been advocating the adoption of advanced business process integration technologies based upon a Service Oriented Architecture (SOA). These solutions address the complexities of multi-enterprise business collaboration and data movements between different and remote systems infrastructures. They are the critical technical components for continuing operational agility in the SEPA community.

SOA is a best practice style for creating long-term sustainable business architectures. It enables organisations to rapidly adapt their fixed operational infrastructures to changes in business, technology and legislative environments. Its promise is business agility and process flexibility.

SOA is the answer to the technology need to managing increasing complexity with fewer resources, while the business is increasingly demanding faster response times and lower costs. It is an architectural style that allows for a separation of process logic from the underlying systems, allowing for rapid re-use of business services which are defined with business semantics rather than technology syntaxes. Ultimately, it allows technology to better align resources with business requirements, focusing more on information and less on technology.

This flexibility and agility will be critical to keep up with SEPA's demands, especially where you have a fragmented business community at the edge of the enterprise. The contention therefore is that SOA is the critical foundation for SEPA from a technology viewpoint.

In conclusion, there have been previous market events that presented opportunities for banks and financial institutions to deploy this type of approach to provide long lasting solutions to the continuing challenge of community connectivity. If business sponsors had allowed the budget to accommodate this more sophisticated and strategic approaches earlier, then much of the cost of SEPA implementation might have been absorbed within those earlier more profitable projects. As it is, technology teams have to go forward from where they are and the implementation of further tactical approaches is not the way to go, especially as SEPA will be a continuum rather than a one-off event.

The challenges presented by the changing composition and operations of the continually evolving European financial community can be met only by properly funded and comprehensive technology strategies. It is time to learn the lesson, and get multi-enterprise financial data movement and management into the shape that the future demands.

Appendix – Useful Resources

ECB Links to EU Country Implementation Plans
    http://www.ecb.int/paym/sepa/html/links.en.html
ECB Publications on Payments and Securities
    http://www.ecb.int/pub/pub/paym/html/index.en.html
ECB Update on TARGET2 Developments
    http://www.ecb.int/paym/target/target2/html/index.en.html
EPC Publications
    http://www.europeanpaymentscouncil.eu/knowledge_bank_list.cfm?documents_category=1
Euractiv Summary of the Single Payments Area
    http://www.euractiv.com/en/financial-services/single-payments-area/article-134975
Latest Developments
    http://www.ec.europa.eu/internal_market/payments/framework/index_en.htm
Payment Services Directive, December 2005 – Frequently Asked Questions
    http://www.europa.eu/rapid/pressReleasesAction.do?reference=MEMO/05/461&format=
    HTML&aged=0&language=EN&guiLanguage=en
Payment Services Directive, March 2007– Frequently Asked Questions
    http://www.europa.eu/rapid/pressReleasesAction.do?reference=MEMO/07/152&format=
    HTML&aged=0&language=EN&guiLanguage=en
Regulation 2560/2001 – Frequently Asked Questions
    http://www.europa.eu/rapid/press ReleasesAction.do?reference=IP/02/941&format=HTML&
    aged=0&language=EN&guiLanguage=en

Glossary of Terms

ACH	Automated Clearing House
AML	Anti-Money Laundering
AOS	Additional Optional Services
AP	Accounts Payable
AR	Accounts Receivable
ATM	Automated Teller Machine
BEI	Business Entity Identifier
BIC	Bank Identification Code
CAST	Corporate Action on Standards
CBM	Components Business Model
CDD	Customer Due Diligence
CMF	Credit Mandate Flow
CSSF	Commission de Surveillance du Secteur Financier
DMF	Debtor Mandate Flow
DPO	Days Payable Outstanding
DSO	Days Sales Outstanding
EACT	European Associations of Corporate Treasurers
EAPS	Euro Alliance of Payment Schemes
EBA	Euro Banking Association
EC	European Commission
ECB	European Central Bank
ECON	Economic and Monetary Affairs Committee of the European Parliament
ECU	European Currency Unit
EFTPOS	Electronic Funds Transfer at Point of Sale
EMEA	Europe, Middle-East and Africa
EMV	Europay MasterCard Visa, the chip standard for payment cards
EPC	European Payments Council
EPM	ECB's Payment Mechanism
ERP	Enterprise Resource Planning
ESCB	European System of Central Banks
EU	European Union
Eurosystem	The Central Bank System of the Euro Area

Eurozone	The countries who use the euro as their national currency
FATF	Financial Action Task Force, relates to AML
FSAP	Financial Services Action Plan
HKMA	Hong Kong Monetary Authority
IBAN	International Bank Account Number
IBEI	International Business Entity Identifier
ICP	Interbank Charging Principles
IPR	Intellectual Property Rights
ISO	International Standards Organisation
KYC	Know Your Client
MAS	Monetary Authority of Singapore
MEP	Member of the European Parliament
MiFID	Markets in Financial Instruments Directive (MiFID)
MLD	Money Laundering Directive
MLRO	Money Laundering Reporting Officer
MNC	Multi-National Corporation
NCB	National Central Bank
NNA	National Numbering Agency
NTA	National Treasurers Association
OFAC	Office of Foreign Assets Control, part of the US Department of the Treasury
PE-ACH	Pan-European Automated Clearing House
PE-DD	Pan-European Direct Debit
PEP	Politically Exposed Person
POS	Point of Sale
PSP	Payment Service Provider
PSU	Payment Service User
RDUG	Reference Data User Group
RTGS	Real Time Gross Settlement
SCF	SEPA Cards Framework
SCORE	Standardised Corporate Environment
SCT	SEPA Credit Transfer
SDD	SEPA Direct Debit
SECA	SEPA Euro Cash Area
SEPA	Single European Payment Area
SME	Scheme Management Entity
SME	Small and Medium Enterprises
SOA	Services Oriented Architecture
SSC	Shared Service Centre
SSP	Single Shared Platform
SSS	Securities Settlement System
STEP	Straight Through Euro Processing
STP	Straight Through Processing
SWIFT	Society for Worldwide Interbank Financial Telecommunications
TARGET	Trans-European Automated Real-time Gross settlement Express Transfer
TBG5	International Trade & Business Processes Group Working Group 5 (Finance Domain)

TCO	Total Cost of Ownership
TDES	Triple Data Encryption Standard
TMS	Treasury Management System
TWIST	Transaction Workflow Innovation Standards Team
UCI	Unique Creditor Identifier
UEI	Unique Entity Identifier

Index

Compiled by Indexing Specialists (UK) Ltd